THE JEWISH AMERICANS

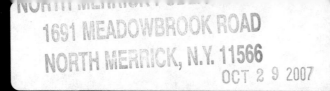

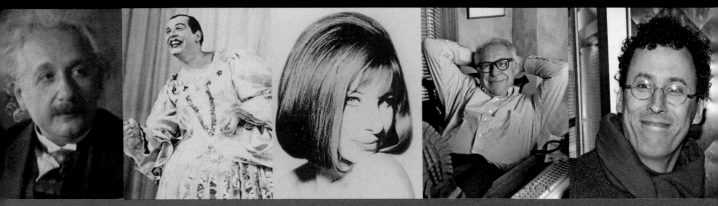

THE JEWISH AMERICANS

THREE CENTURIES OF JEWISH VOICES IN AMERICA

To the memory of my grandparents,

Edith and Aaron Kass
&
Fanny and Abraham Wenger

immigrant Jews who became Jewish Americans

PUBLISHED BY DOUBLEDAY

Published in the United States by Doubleday, an imprint of The Doubleday Broadway Publishing Group,
a division of Random House, Inc., New York.
www.doubleday.com

DOUBLEDAY and the portrayal of an anchor with a dolphin are
registered trademarks of Random House, Inc.

Book design by
Pauline Neuwirth, Neuwirth & Associates, Inc.

Library of Congress Cataloging-in-Publication Data

Wenger, Beth S., 1963–
The Jewish Americans : three centuries of Jewish voices in America /
Beth S. Wenger. — 1st ed.
p. cm.
1. Jews—United States—History. 2. Jews—Cultural assimilation—United States.
3. Social integration—United States. 4. United States—Ethnic relations. I. Title.
E184.35.W42 2007
305.892'4073—dc22
2007025594

ISBN 978-0-385-52139-0

PRINTED IN THE UNITED STATES OF AMERICA

1 3 5 7 9 10 8 6 4 2

First Edition

CONTENTS

✒ PART TWO ✑
A WORLD OF THEIR OWN *(1880–1924)*   87

❧ PART THREE ❧
THE BEST OF TIMES, THE WORST OF TIMES (1924–1945) 197

❧ PART FOUR ❧
HOME (1945–PRESENT) 283

ACKNOWLEDGMENTS

THIS BOOK BRINGS together first-person accounts of several generations of American Jews. Gathering these materials required the efforts of many individuals and it gives me great pleasure to acknowledge the friends, colleagues, and professionals who made this volume possible.

I am fortunate to be part of a community of scholars and I relied often on their expertise and advice. I am grateful for the helpful suggestions of Dianne Ashton, Solomon Breibart, Jocelyn Cohen, Hasia Diner, Karla Goldman, Deborah Dash Moore, Riv-Ellen Prell, Dale Rosengarten, Shuly Rubin Schwartz, Jeffrey Shandler, Daniel Soyer, and Nina Warnke. I owe a special thanks to Susannah Heschel, who allowed me to include excerpts from her father's unpublished writings, and to Paula Hyman, who shared items from her personal archive. Jonathan Sarna graciously allowed me to reprint a document that he translated in this volume.

This book could not have been completed without the knowledgeable assistance of many archivists and librarians. Kevin Proffitt of the American Jewish Archives cheerfully responded to all my inquiries and he and Camille Servizzi fulfilled my every request. Lyn Slome of the American Jewish Historical Society lent her considerable expertise to the project, providing prompt answers to my many questions. Yeshiva University's Shulamith Berger helped me locate key documents and images, as did Arthur Kiron and Seth Jerchower of Penn's Center for Advanced Judaic Studies. I am especially grateful for the special consideration given me by Jesse Aaron Cohen, Fruma Mohrer, and Leo Greenbaum of the YIVO Archives. I also appreciate the assistance of Claire Pingel of the National Museum of American Jewish History, Ellen Kastel of the Jewish Theological Seminary, and Sean Martin of the Western Reserve Historical Society.

This book was written during a year of scholarly leave from the University of Pennsylvania, supported by a fellowship from the American Council of Learned Societies. I am grateful to the ACLS for providing me the time to devote to scholarship.

I was fortunate to receive superb research assistance from Edward Portnoy, whose contributions greatly enriched this volume. Christine Walsh helped to prepare the documents included in the book and her remarkable efficiency allowed me to complete the project in a timely fashion. Mariellen Smith assisted me in securing permissions and I greatly appreciate the skill and knowledge she brought to the project. I relied heavily on the wonderful work of Preeti Mankar, Ceri Fox, and Cheryl van Grunsven of David Grubin Productions, who provided research assistance and garnered permissions for most of the images in the book. Bruce Mundt graciously offered his help at every turn. My thanks also go to Maggie Sliker, who helped secure last-minute information about copyrights and licensing.

This book includes excerpts from some of the interviews that filmmaker David Grubin conducted for *The Jewish Americans* documentary. I thank him for his collaboration and for sharing these with me. I owe a particular debt to the men and women who were willing to contribute their stories and reflections. David Grubin, Jeff Bieber and Jay Sanderson initially brought me into the project and urged me to write this book. My agent, David Black, deserves special thanks for seeing me through this venture, for reasons he knows well.

My editor at Doubleday, Deb Futter, made working on this book a genuine pleasure. I could not have asked for a more available, responsive, or supportive editor. I also greatly appreciate the invaluable assistance of Dianne Choie at Doubleday, who readily responded to my every question and request, no matter how big or small.

As always, I am grateful for the support of my family. The Wengers, Beairds, and Wiatraks participated, in one way or another, as this project unfolded, offering encouragement and advice along the way.

THE JEWISH AMERICANS

THEY CAME TO STAY

❦ ❧

· 1 6 5 4 - 1 8 8 0 ·

WHEN TWENTY-THREE Jews arrived in New Amsterdam (later to become New York) in 1654, they not only found themselves in an unfamiliar New World, but also in a land with no established Jewish community. Coming from European countries where the Jewish community regulated virtually all aspects of religious, social, and economic life, these Jews and those who followed in subsequent years encountered an unprecedented challenge that would characterize the first two centuries of Jewish life in America: How would Jews build a community and culture from the ground up? Even more daunting, how would that Jewish community function when it had virtually no restrictions imposed upon it by the government—and where individual Jews and Jewish institutions had, for the first time, complete freedom to shape Jewish life on their own terms? The encounter with freedom defined the course of American

PART ONE

Jewish history and resulted in the most unique, innovative, and diverse culture that Jews had ever known.

The twenty-three Jews who initiated the opening chapter of Jewish history in the colonies hardly had freedom granted to them immediately. These Jews had fled the island of Recife when the Portuguese seized it from the Dutch. They took refuge aboard the *Sainte Catherine*, which happened to be sailing for New Amsterdam. Governor Peter Stuyvesant, who ruled the Dutch-owned colony, wanted to refuse them admission and requested that his superiors in Holland prohibit Jews from settling in New Amsterdam. Stuyvesant insisted that "the deceitful race," "the hateful enemies and blasphemers of the name of Christ" would only bring harm the new colony.[1] But the Jewish settlers contacted fellow Jews in Amsterdam, who successfully petitioned the Dutch West India Company to overrule Stuyvesant's pleas.

Because Jews had been loyal and economically productive residents of Holland, the Dutch believed they could be the same in the fledgling colony and ruled that Jews would be welcome to live and work in New Amsterdam. This did not mean that Jews received immediate equality or freedom in the New World; they encountered a number of restrictions on their economic and religious activity as well as limitations on office-holding and public service. Over the years, they petitioned and gradually won most rights of trade and commerce. They were allowed to construct a Jewish

Peter Stuyvesant, Director-General of New Netherland, ca. 1660. Attributed to Hendrick Couturier. Oil on wood panel. Negative number 6071.

Collection of The New-York Historical Society

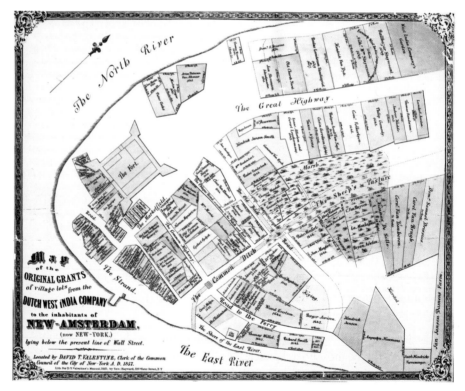

Map of the Original Grants of Village Lots from the Dutch West India Company to the Inhabitants of New Amsterdam, ca. 1640s; located by David T. Valentine and lithographed by George Hayward for Valentine's Manual, 1857. Negative number 54589.

Collection of The New-York Historical Society

cemetery not long after arriving—a pressing need for any new Jewish community and usually the first collective act taken by Jews in each new settlement in colonial America. Jews received the right to worship in private homes relatively quickly, but it took almost thirty years for the community to receive permission to worship publicly, even after the British took over the colony in 1664 and renamed it New York. Jews were not the only group to face such restrictions in colonial America; in fact, many Christian denominations encountered even greater limitations on the practice of their religion, depending on which established church was in control at a given time. There remained many legal obstacles to overcome, but Jews proved willing to press for greater rights, constantly petitioning individual cases and in most cases succeeding in their efforts.

Despite lingering disabilities, Jews lived securely and relatively freely in the New World. There were so few Jews in the colonies that they generally attracted little attention. At the time of the American Revolution, more than a century after the first Jews arrived in New Amsterdam, the Jewish population likely numbered about 2,000 out of a general population of roughly 2.5 million. To lend greater perspective, approximately 242 Jews resided in New York in 1773, constituting the largest Jewish population center at the time.[2] The Sephardim, or Iberian Jews, were the first to settle in the colonies and they

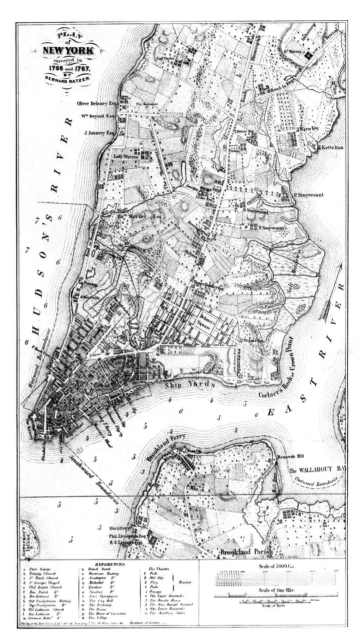

Plan for New York, showing Southern Manhattan and Brooklyn, 1766–67, by Bernard Ratzer; lithograph by Hayward and Lepine. Negative number 56838.

Collection of The New-York Historical Society

remained the elites for more than two generations. All the colonial synagogues practiced Sephardic rite, despite the fact that by 1720, Ashkenazim, Jews from Central and Eastern Europe, made up the majority of the Jewish population, as they would for the duration of American Jewish history.

The first Jews settled largely in port cities along the East Coast in colonies, and later states, with the most liberal policies of toleration. In the young, developing frontier of early America, Jews constructed new lives in an unprecedented environment,

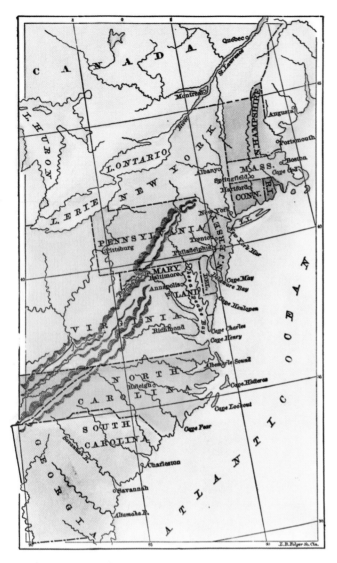

in a country with no legacy of a medieval past and comparatively few restrictions on their individual and communal rights. Those who ventured to this untested terrain spent their first years in America preoccupied with making a living and establishing the rudiments of a Jewish community.

The tiny Jewish settlements of the nascent United States functioned as satellites of the larger, more established Jewish communities in England and Holland. The Atlantic Jewish world of the seventeenth and eighteenth centuries consisted of interconnected, interdependent Jewish communities throughout the New World, with London and Amsterdam as the anchors. For more than a century, early America was simply one of many outposts, along with Jamaica, Barbados, Suriname, and Curaçao; in fact, the American colonies began as the smallest and least developed of the newly emerging communities. Economic ties linked Jewish communities and Jewish families across the ocean and throughout the New World. Indeed, the colonial Jewish economy could be described using family names, such as Lopez, Seixas, Gomez, and Hendricks, whose family connections crossed both sides of the Atlantic Ocean and

Map of the 13 Original American Colonies, undated
Bettmann/CORBIS

New Amsterdam, New Netherland, by Laurens Block, 1650, Watercolor and ink on paper.
Collection of The New-York Historical Society. Accession number 1881.2.

extended up and down the East Coast, fortified by marriages, sibling cooperation, and intricate family ties. Ocean commerce created the nexus of the Jewish economy. Shipping records from the period reveal that Jews depended on trade and cooperation with one another. They traded sugar, furniture, candles, horses, all sorts of meat and fish, barley, rice, and a host of other goods. Some colonial Jews did transport slaves to the New World, though it was hardly a dominant area of trade. While most inhabitants of early America engaged in agrarian pursuits, Jews gravitated toward commerce and used their international connections to build the emerging economy. The unprecedented level of tolerance that Jews found in the New World owed largely to their economic contributions. As one historian has explained, "trade made the colonies and Jews made trade."[3]

Newport, Rhode Island merchant Aaron Lopez (1731–1782).
American Jewish Historical Society, Newton Centre, Massachusetts and New York, New York

Religious observance could be a challenge in early America. By all accounts, many Jews exhibited a certain laxity in keeping the Sabbath and following the Jewish dietary laws (*kashrut*), especially outside their own homes. At the same time, a concerted effort to maintain Jewish practice also existed among the first Jewish generations in America. Life in the New World offered some the first opportunity to live openly as Jews. Aaron Lopez, one of the most successful merchants in Newport, had been born a Catholic to a family living under the Portuguese Inquisition, but once in the colonies reclaimed his Judaism, submitted to circumcision as an adult, and faithfully practiced Judaism throughout his life.[4] The value placed on Jewish observance can be seen in the number of Jews who journeyed across the ocean with cherished ritual objects, such as Shabbat candles and Kiddush cups. In virtually every sizeable community, Jews built a *mikveh* (ritual bath), established the means to obtain kosher meat through a *shochet* (ritual slaughterer), and created synagogues as soon as they had the legal and financial ability to do so.

Observing Jewish law was easier in the larger Jewish communities than in the outlying areas of early America. Writing to her parents in Germany in the early 1700s, Rebecca Samuel lamented the lack of Jewish practice in the small town of Petersburg, Virginia, where she lived. She complained that local Jews kept their businesses open on Saturdays and worshipped without even a Torah scroll on

Seixas Family Circumcision Set.
American Jewish Historical Society, Newton Centre, Massachusetts and New York, New York

Interior of Congregation Jeshuat Israel, now known as the Touro Synagogue, in Newport, Rhode Island.
The Jacob Rader Marcus Center of the American Jewish Archives

Omer Board, ca. 1800, used by Jews in Lancaster, Pennsylvania to count the harvest days between Passover and the Pentecost.
Courtesy of the Center for Advanced Judaic Studies Library, University of Pennsylvania

Rosh Hashanah. "Jewishness is pushed aside here. . . . I crave to see a synagogue to which I can go," Samuel reported, informing her parents that she and her family would soon relocate to the larger Jewish community of Charleston, South Carolina.[5]

In the first century after Jewish arrival, congregations sprang up in the port cities of New York, Newport, Savannah, Philadelphia, and Charleston. When they raised sufficient funds to construct houses of worship, the Jews of these communities built synagogues in the architectural styles of the times; they reflected traditional Jewish custom and design on the inside but contained no outward signs to mark the buildings as Jewish congregations, blending unobtrusively into the American environment. Just as they did in the arena of commerce, Jews relied on mutual support to create and sustain the first synagogues. In 1759, when the Jews of Newport set out to build a synagogue, they turned to the more established congregation in New York "for charitable assistance towards carrying on this work," and the Jewish New Yorkers complied. Some thirty years earlier, Jews from London, Jamaica, Curaçao and Barbados had done the same for New York when it built its first synagogue.[6] Within the Atlantic world, Torah scrolls, religious ornaments, and other necessities were regularly donated and exchanged to fortify fledgling Jewish communities.

No rabbis lived or worked regularly in the United States until 1840, so for almost 200 years, congregations relied entirely on lay leadership. If they had questions about Jewish law, Jews sent them to rabbinic authorities in Europe. Throughout the eighteenth century, synagogues remained the central Jewish institutions in America, and with only one in each community, they operated as monopolies. Synagogues controlled the Jewish cemetery, paid the *shochet* who provided kosher meat, offered rudimentary Jewish education to children, and supervised every Jewish life cycle event from the cradle to the grave. New York's Shearith Israel (Remnant of Israel) congregation initially managed its synagogue affairs according to the European paradigm, exerting supreme control over its members. The congregation exacted fines for all sorts of transgressions, from violating the Sabbath to failing to attend meetings. The synagogue mandated that any Jew who contravened Jewish law would be expelled from the synagogue and excluded from crucial benefits of membership, including burial in the cemetery. Synagogue leaders insisted on the right to tax all Jewish residents in the area, and then to impose penalties on all who failed to pay.[7] Such policies reflected the standard method employed by synagogues in Europe. European governments mandated and recognized an official Jewish community to regulate all Jewish affairs, enabling synagogues to exercise complete authority over Jewish behavior. But in colonial America and later in the United States, the government never sanctioned an official community, so the synagogue could not wield the same authority. In the eighteenth century, when communities remained under the control of only one synagogue, congregations still retained a degree of power over individual Jews, at least over any who wanted the privileges and services controlled by the congregation. Yet Shearith Israel's increasingly harsh regulations reveal a tenor of anxiety and a loss of power over New York Jews, indicating that attempts to regulate Jewish behavior in America were not succeeding. The European model of Jewish communal life would not survive in a nation where participation in the Jewish community was entirely voluntary.

America's open society presented both opportunities and challenges for Jewish communal life and for individual Jews. The small number of Jews in early America and the environment of tolerance meant that Jews and non-Jews interacted on a regular basis. Portraits commissioned by Jews in this period suggest that they had abandoned any sort of distinctive dress. Men shaved their beards, and married Jewish women no longer covered their hair. Their letters reveal that they maintained friendships with non-Jews and participated with them in social and cultural activities. With

First synagogue building constructed by Congregation Shearith Israel on Mill Street, now known as South William Street, in New York City.

Photograph by JoAnn Savio. Courtesy of Congregation Shearith Israel, New York

New York merchant Jacob Franks (1688–1769), ca. 1735. Attributed to Gerardus Duyckinck. Oil on canvas.

Courtesy of Crystal Bridges Museum of American Art

Portrait traditionally identified as Phila Franks (1722–1811), daughter of Abigail and Jacob Franks of New York, ca. 1735. (Some recent scholarship suggests that the portrait might be of Richa Franks.) Attributed to Gerardus Duyckinck. Oil on canvas.

Courtesy of Crystal Bridges Museum of American Art

Best known for her poem "The New Colossus," inscribed on the pedestal of the Statue of Liberty, Emma Lazarus (1849–1887) was only eighteen years old when she wrote this reflection on Newport's Touro synagogue, the oldest existent Jewish house of worship in the United States.

IN THE JEWISH SYNAGOGUE AT NEWPORT
Emma Lazarus

Here, where the noises of the busy town,
The ocean's plunge and roar can enter not,
We stand and gaze around with tearful awe,
And muse upon the consecrated spot.

No signs of life are here: The very prayers
Inscribed around are in a language dead;
The light of the "perpetual lamp" is spent
That an undying radiance was to shed.

What prayers were in this temple offered up,
Wrung from sad hearts that knew no joy on earth,
By these lone exiles of a thousand years,
From the fair sunrise land that gave them birth!

How as we gaze, in this new world of light,
Upon this relic of the days of old,
The present vanishes, and tropic bloom
And Eastern towns and temples we behold.

Again we see the patriarch with his flocks,
The purple seas, the hot blue sky o'erhead,
The slaves of Egypt,—omens, mysteries,—
Dark fleeing hosts by flaming angels led.

A wondrous light upon a sky-kissed mount,
A man who reads Jehovah's written law,
'Midst blinding glory and effulgence rare,
Unto a people prone with reverent awe.

The pride of luxury's barbaric pomp,
In the rich court of royal Solomon—
Alas! we wake: one scene alone remains,—
The exiles by the streams of Babylon.

Our softened voices send us back again
But mournful echoes through the empty hall;
Our footsteps have a strange unnatural sound,
And with unwonted gentleness they fall.

The weary ones, the sad, the suffering,
All found their comfort in the holy place,
And children's gladness and men's gratitude
Took voice and mingled in the chant of praise.

The funeral and the marriage, now, alas!
We know not which is sadder to recall;
For youth and happiness have followed age,
And green grass lieth gently over all.

And still[1] *the sacred shrine is holy yet,*
With its lone floors where reverent feet once trod.
Take off your shoes as by the burning bush,
Before the mystery of death and God.

July 27, 1867.

—————

[1] In the first writing of this poem, this line began with the word "Nathless." However, Lazarus herself later changed the line to begin "And still."

Emma Lazarus, *Admetus and Other Poems*. New York: Hurd and Houghton, 1871.

few barriers to limit social contact and a scarcity of eligible marriage partners, Jewish intermarriage rates remained relatively high through the years of the early republic, reaching perhaps 10 to 15 percent.[8] Some Jews sought Jewish marriage partners in Europe; some remained unmarried, but a significant minority found non-Jewish partners. In 1742, when Phila Franks, daughter of successful New York merchant couple Abigail and Jacob Franks, secretly married Oliver DeLancey, son of a prominent non-Jewish family, her mother was grief-stricken. A devout Jew, scrupulous in her observance, Abigail Franks had often written to her son, reminding him to be meticulous in his Jewish practice, and she simply could not abide her daughter's intermarriage. Upon learning the news, she refused to leave her home and vowed never to see her daughter again. "I am determined," she wrote to her son, "I never will see nor lett none of the family goe near her."[9] While Abigail Franks remained devastated by her daughter's choice, the fact that Phila Franks and other Jews of the period married outside their faith demonstrates the unprecedented level of acceptance that Jews experienced in early America.

While Jews worked to maintain Jewish identity and formulate new models of Jewish community, they also endeavored to become full participants in the new society taking shape around them. In colonial America, naturalization and voting rights were granted to Jews in piecemeal fashion, varying from colony to colony and improving gradually over time. The American Revolution provided the first opportunity for Jews to stake a broader claim in what would become the United States. Though Jews fought on both sides of the conflict, most supported the cause of independence. As merchants, Jews had reason to resist Britain's restrictive economic policies and to feel some allegiance to the revolutionary impulse. Some Jewish men fought in the Revolutionary War. Colonel Isaac Franks and Major Benjamin Nones served alongside George Washington; twenty or thirty Jewish men from Charleston battled the British during the siege of the city. Even those who did not fight demonstrated commitment to the Revolution in other ways. As a show of support for the cause, the Jews of New York and Rhode Island left their homes en masse when the British occupied their cities.

Colonel Isaac Franks who served in the Revolutionary War. Painted by Gilbert Stuart, 1802. Oil on canvas.

Pennsylvania Academy of the Fine Arts, Philadelphia. Bequest of Henry C. Carey. Accession number: 1892.6.86.

As part of America's Bicentennial celebration, the United States Postal Service issued this commemorative stamp honoring Haym Salomon as a "financial hero."

Haym Salomon, the Philadelphia broker later celebrated in exaggerated terms as "the financier of the Revolution," secured loans that propped up the faltering finances of the Revolutionary government and provided for the needs of the troops.[10]

The signing of the Constitution, painted by Howard C. Cristy III.
Library of Congress, Prints and Photographs Division

Being part of the Revolution, in whatever capacity, gave Jews an ability to assert a founding role in the new nation and make a case for greater rights in the emerging American society. Six years after the Revolution, a group of Philadelphia Jews lobbied Pennsylvania representatives to eliminate the state's constitutional requirement for officeholders to swear allegiance on both the Old and New Testaments. In making the case, they cited Jewish service in the war and also pointed out that many immigrant groups would settle elsewhere if such a stipulation remained.[11] Similarly, when the Constitutional Convention convened in Philadelphia in 1787, Jonas Phillips of the city's Mikveh Israel (Hope of Israel) congregation implored the assembly to guarantee religious equality in the new nation. He urged the representatives to remove any religious tests for public oaths, reminding them that, "Jews have been true and faithful whigs, & during the late Contest with England they have

The U.S. Constitution was later translated into Yiddish in an effort to teach citizenship to new Jewish immigrants. New York: Sarasohn and Sons, 1892.
Library of Congress, Hebraic Section

been foremost in aiding and assisting the states with their lives & fortunes."[12] As participants in the creation of the nation, Jews appeared increasingly willing to declare their belonging in the Republic and entitlement to equality. When Benjamin Nones found himself the subject of anti-democratic attack, he cited his service during the Revolution, and defended himself as both "a Jew" and "a Republican," pointing out in great detail "the difference between [the Jew's] situation in this land of freedom" and the experience of Jews in Europe.[13] As America's Jews staked their claim to inclusion, they understood that they inhabited a nation where Jews might achieve a level of equality unmatched anywhere else in the world.

At the parade to celebrate the ratification of the Constitution in 1788, the leader of Philadelphia's congregation walked arm-in-arm with members of the Christian clergy. The city even provided a special kosher table so that Jewish paradegoers could join in the festivities.[14] Such symbolic moments testified to the ideal of religious equality in the United States. Jews wanted to ensure that those principles would translate into American practice. In 1790, as President George

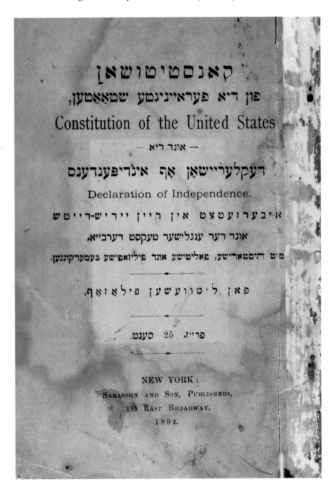

קאנסטיטושאן

פון די פעראייניגטע שטאַאטען,

Constitution of the United States

— אונד די —

דעקלעריישאן אף אינדיפענדענס

Declaration of Independence.

איבערזעטצט אין רײן ייריש-דײטש

אונד דער ענגלישער טעקסט דערבייא.

מיט היסטאָרישע, פּאָליטישע אונד פילזאָפישע בעמערקונגען.

פֿאָן ל. טורעשען פֿילזאָף.

פרייז, 25 סענט.

NEW YORK:
SARASOHN AND SON, PUBLISHERS,
185 EAST BROADWAY,
1892.

Exterior of Newport's Touro Synagogue.

The Jacob Rader Marcus Center of the American Jewish Archives

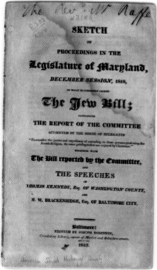

Maryland's "Jew Bill" extended to Jews rights once reserved only for Christians. First introduced in 1818, the bill was passed in 1826.

American Jewish Historical Society, Newton Centre, Massachusetts and New York, New York

Washington toured the country and negotiated how to balance minority rights in the new nation, Newport's Jewish congregation joined other groups in congratulating the new president. "Deprived as we have hitherto been of the invaluable rights of free citizens," the Jews of Newport wrote to Washington, expressing gratitude for "the blessings of civil and religious liberty." Washington replied to the congregation, emphasizing that the United States government gave "to bigotry no sanction, to persecution no assistance," repeating verbatim the words they had written to him, words that Jews regarded for generations as a sacred charter of their rights in America.[15] The Constitution guaranteed Jewish rights on a federal level, but some states continued to bar Jews from holding office. Throughout the 1790s, most states abolished such restrictions. Maryland was a notable exception, maintaining laws that required a Christian oath until 1826 when the so-called "Jew Bill" finally passed after eight years of protracted debate. Not until the ratification of the Fourteenth Amendment did the entire nation eliminate all qualifications for public office.

During the early 1800s, the number of Jews living in America increased dramatically. From a Jewish population of about 2,500 in 1800, the community doubled by 1830, and in the next thirty years grew to approximately 200,000. Thousands of Jews from Central Europe chose to seek better lives in the United States, as changes in the European economy and restrictions on Jewish occupations

and settlement made it increasingly difficult for Jews to survive. Often referred to as "German" Jews, these Jewish immigrants actually came from several regions in Central Europe, including Bavaria, Bohemia, Moravia, Posen, and Silesia. Most were poor or lower middle class and in the early years, the majority were young, unmarried men who came alone; many later brought family members over, initiating a process of chain migration that emptied many European towns and fortified the American Jewish community.

The new Jewish immigrants altered not only the population but also the geography of American Jewry. Like the thousands of non-Jewish immigrants who also arrived in the United States in this period, Jews settled throughout the country. American Jewish life had previously been confined primarily to the East Coast, but the new immigrants settled throughout the Midwest and even as far as California. Small Jewish communities emerged in Saint Louis, Cincinnati, Milwaukee, Sioux City, San Francisco, and dozens of other cities. The majority of young Jewish men who settled these cities began as peddlers, an occupation that required little capital and filled an economic niche in a nation expanding westward and in need of commercial goods. Peddling provided the means to earn a living, but it was also a harsh and often lonely existence for Jewish immigrants who felt isolated in an unfamiliar country. In 1842,

MY SPECULATION IN CHINA WARE. (8)

Caricature of a Jewish peddler depicted with a hooked nose in the frontispiece of "My Speculation in China Ware," by T. S. Arthur, Trials and Confessions of an American Housekeeper. *Philadelphia: Lippincott, Grambo & Co., 1853.*

Courtesy, The Winterthur Library: Printed Book and Periodical Collection

Advertisement for Levi Strauss & Co., San Francisco, California.
American Judaica Collection of Arnold and Deanne Kaplan

Abraham Kohn, who had left Bavaria for America, addressed an entry in his diary to the "misguided fools" who might wish to join him: "You have left your friends and acquaintances, your relatives and your parents, your home and your fatherland, your language and your customs, your faith and your religion—only to sell your wares in the wild places of America, in isolated farmhouses and tiny hamlets."[16] Like many peddlers, Kohn struggled immediately after arriving in America, but just two years later, he was a successful clothing manufacturer in Chicago.

Peddling generally led to more stable retail ventures, allowing Jews to settle down, marry (sometimes returning to Europe to find partners), bring over other family members, and create the foundation for Jewish communities across the United States. Peddlers frequently made the transition to store ownership and often to manufacturing, bringing valuable commercial enterprises to the new communities springing up from coast to coast. Levi Strauss, a Bavarian immigrant who had come to the United States in 1847, moved to San Francisco in the 1850s, intending to sell goods to the "forty-niners" who sought their fortunes in the California Gold Rush. After starting out in merchandising, Strauss began selling pants made out of heavy canvas material to miners who needed the tough, durable garments. Not all Jews shared his degree of success, but many built thriving businesses, playing a vital economic role in America's growing cities. Some Jews ventured out beyond cities as pioneers on America's frontiers, settling in New Mexico, Arizona, and the Great Plains. In the 1870s, Anna and Isidor Solomon, immigrants from Poland, made their way to a remote corner of the Arizona territory and turned a small store into a successful family business in what became a thriving town known as Solomonville.[17] As Jews built businesses and communities across the country, they were part of a changing and expanding America.

Judaism in America also changed dramatically in the nineteenth century, as synagogues multiplied and became more diverse. Even in the first cities settled by Jews in early America, monopolistic synagogues gave way to multiple congregations. Just as their Christian neighbors supported a variety of churches and denominations, Jews with dissenting opinions or

Anna and Isidor Solomon.
Courtesy of New Mexico State University Library, Archives and Special Collections

preferences left existing synagogues to establish congregations of their own. Philadelphia became the first city with a second synagogue in 1802, with the founding of Rodeph Shalom (Pursuit of Peace). New York followed in 1825, and as in Philadelphia, the Ashkenazic Jews who established the second synagogue expressed a desire to worship "in accordance with the rites and customs of the . . . German and Polish Jews."[18] More than Ashkenazic custom motivated a group of young Jews in Charleston to secede from the existing synagogue and create the Reformed Society of Israelites in 1824. Calling for a shorter service, a sermon, and prayers in the vernacular, members of the new society insisted that the service should be understood by the congregation and be conducted in an "impressive and dignified" manner, arguing that such changes were "essential to the rising generation."[19] This pattern defined the growth of American synagogues, as every sizable Jewish community witnessed the creation of multiple congregations, motivated by the customs of different groups of Jews as well as the desire for change and reform.

The development of an organized Reform movement began only in the second half of the nineteenth century. Before this time, synagogues changed to suit the needs of a Jewish population adapting to the American environment, but they were led by laypeople without the time or desire to form an organized movement. In fact, designations such as "Reform" and "Orthodox" had little meaning during this period, since distinct movements had not yet crystallized. Some of the first rabbis who migrated to the United States in the 1840s and 1850s had been introduced to the nascent Reform movement in Europe, but others simply saw the trends already taking shape in American Judaism and harnessed the energy. Beginning in the 1850s, a series of rabbinical conferences occurred in the United States, though with few tangible results. Rabbis, like other Americans, put forward their positions in the open marketplace of ideas,

Congregation Rodeph Shalom, Philadelphia, Pennsylvania.

Interior of Kahal Kadosh Beth Elohim, Charleston, South Carolina, painted by Solomon N. Carvalho from memory, shortly after a fire destroyed the sanctuary in 1838. Oil on canvas.

Interior of Cincinnati's Plum Street Temple (K. K. Bene Jeshurun), dedicated in 1866.

The Jacob Rader Marcus Center of the American Jewish Archives

publishing newspapers and new prayer books that reflected the range of beliefs and practices. David Einhorn, rabbi in Baltimore, was a radical reformer who called for the abolition of all practices not compatible with modernity, including the dietary laws and restrictions for the Sabbath. At the same time, Isaac Leeser of Philadelphia attempted to maintain traditional Judaism in the face of growing reforms, instituting aesthetic changes in synagogue practice, but retaining fealty to rabbinic law.

It was Isaac Mayer Wise, arriving from Bohemia in 1846, who emerged as the principal architect of the Reform movement. After leaving his first post in Albany, New York, Wise accepted a position as rabbi of Cincinnati's Bene Jeshurun (Sons of Righteousness) congregation in 1854 and made the city the center of American Reform Judaism. By the 1870s, Wise had organized the central institutions of the American Reform movement, including the first successful seminary to train American rabbis and the Union of American Hebrew Congregations, an umbrella organization for the country's synagogues. He also published *Minhag Amerika* (American Rite), which became the most widely used prayer book in the United States, as well as two newspapers, one in German and one in English. Hardly a rigorous ideologue, Wise embraced the need to create Americanized expressions of Judaism and to organize American Jews in

The Israelite (later The American Israelite), a weekly Jewish newspaper edited by Isaac Mayer Wise, 1854.

order to preserve Judaism in the United States. Despite the many differences among the reformers in these years, all expressed the need to alter Jewish practice in order to ensure the survival of Judaism in America. By the late nineteenth century, virtually every synagogue maintained some connection with the loose coalition of the emerging Reform movement. By 1880, only 12 of the approximately 200 congregations in America had *not* affiliated with Union of American Hebrew Congregations.[20]

Like other Americans, Jews found their religious, social, and economic lives disrupted by the Civil War. This war demonstrated emphatically that Jews shared no single political outlook, as they fought on both sides of the conflict and expressed differing views about the institution of slavery. In a highly influential sermon, Rabbi Morris Raphall of New York argued that the Bible sanctioned slaveholding, though he sided with the Union during the war. At the same time, Rabbi David Einhorn sharply denounced the practice of slavery, prompting an attack from a secessionist mob that forced him to flee his Baltimore home. Approximately 8,000–10,000 Jews served in the military during the Civil War; since the majority of America's Jews lived in the North and West when war broke out, most fought for the Union. In both the Confederacy and the Union, Jews on the home front actively supported war relief efforts. Women, in particular, participated as volunteers—sewing uniforms, providing medical assistance, and caring for the needy. One Jewish soldier fighting for the Union reported that, "As a general rule, the Jews do not care to make their religion a matter of notoriety," but he also revealed that it was "quite common for Jewish soldiers belonging to the same company, to meet together for worship on Sabbath."[21] Judah Benjamin, the first professing Jew to serve in the U.S. Senate, rose to great prominence in the Confederacy, first as attorney general, then as secretary of war, and finally as secretary of state. Although Benjamin abandoned Jewish practice entirely, he was often the subject of anti-Semitic attacks by Northerners and also by Southerners, especially as the fate of the Confederacy began to decline.

The most dramatic anti-Semitic incident of the Civil War occurred in 1862, when General Ulysses S. Grant issued his infamous Order No. 11 that accused Jews "as a class" of war profiteering and called for the expulsion of Jews from parts of Mississippi, Kentucky, and Tennessee. Vigorous protests from Jews, including a delegation that met with President

Dr. Jacob Da Silva Solis-Cohen, a surgeon in the Union army, ca. 1862.

The Jacob Rader Marcus Center of the American Jewish Archives

Louis Merz, who enlisted in the West Point Guards, Company D, 4th Regiment, Georgia Volunteer Infantry in the Army of Northern Virginia, was killed in the battle of Antietam in 1862.

Cuba Archives of The Breman Museum

Revocation of General Grant's General Order No. 11.

The Jacob Rader Marcus Center of the American Jewish Archives

Judah P. Benjamin served as Secretary of War and later as Secretary of State for the Confederacy.

Library of Congress, Prints and Photographs Division

Lincoln, led the president to command the revocation of the order. Although the incident deeply distressed American Jews, stirring fears about wholesale expulsions and restrictions once imposed against Jews in Europe, their ability to have the order rescinded through political lobbying reassured them that their hopes in America had not been misplaced.[22]

In the years following the Civil War, American Jewry reached its stride, as Jewish businesses expanded and religious and secular Jewish institutions multiplied. In this era of growing confidence and economic success, Jews built scores of new synagogues across the country. Far from the earlier unobtrusive buildings that concealed the synagogues functioning inside, these large houses of worship proudly announced the presence of Jews and Judaism in America. A few, such as Cincinnati's Plum Street Temple and New York's Temple Emanu-El, were elaborate, palatial structures, unprecedented in American Jewish communities. By this time, synagogues had ceased to be the sole institutions of American Jewish life. In 1843, a group of Jewish men founded B'nai B'rith (Sons of the Covenant) as the country's first Jewish fraternal order. In the following decades, Young Men's

Exterior of Cincinnati's Plum Street Temple. Its Moorish architecture, harkening back to the Golden Age of Spain in Jewish history, reflected Isaac Mayer Wise's optimism for the future of American Jewry.

The Jacob Rader Marcus Center of the American Jewish Archives

Hebrew Associations (YMHAs) along with a host of literary societies, lodges, and charitable organizations broadened the canvas of American Jewish culture. In 1859, representatives of twenty-four congregations created the Board of Delegates of American Israelites, the first organization designed to advocate for Jewish interests at home and abroad. By the second half of the nineteenth century, Jews had built the foundations for social, cultural, political, and religious life in America.

By the 1860s and 1870s, most American Jews had become comfortably middle class, in an era when the American middle class was just beginning to take shape. Jews had been fortunate to enter retail and manufacturing trades at a moment when the American economy was about to expand rapidly in those areas. Unlike immigrants who pursued agriculture, Jews had become peddlers because they had little capital and few other easily transferable skills. Peddling led to retail ventures at the very time that demand for commercial goods increased dramatically. The invention of the sewing machine at mid-century also aided a segment of the Jewish population in entering clothing manufacture, suiting the needs of Americans who began to purchase ready-made clothing. For most Jews, the journey was one of modest economic achievement, though a few individuals experienced odysseys of remarkable success. Adam Gimbel arrived from Bavaria in the 1830s, began as a peddler, later opened a small business in Indiana, and ultimately pioneered a family department store chain extending across multiple cities in the United States. Joseph Spiegel, whose brother Marcus rose to the rank of colonel in the Union army and lost his life in battle, opened a home furnishings store in Chicago after he concluded his service in the Civil War.

New York's elaborate Temple Emanu-El, 1868.
Library of Congress, Prints and Photographs Division

Employees posing outside S. Lazarus Sons & Co., Columbus, Ohio, ca. 1885-1886. Created by German-Jewish immigrants, this store provided a foundation for what became a successful chain of Federated Department Stores.
Courtesy of Ohio Historical Society

Cover of the Spiegel Catalogue No.110: Spiegel, May, Stern Co., Home Lovers Bargain Book, 1920.

Chicago Public Library, Special Collections and Preservation Division

In 1905, he and his partners expanded to the mail-order business, building a lucrative national company and delivering Spiegel catalogues and merchandise to America's households. The career of Lazarus Straus, a Bavarian immigrant, began with a small store in Talbotton, Georgia and expanded to a crockery business together with his sons in New York. Before the turn of the century, Isidor and Nathan Straus had purchased R. H. Macy and Company, transforming it into one of the nation's preeminent department stores. Similar stories characterized the experiences of the Bloomingdale, Altman, Filene, and Bamberger families, just to name a few. A considerably smaller number of Jews established careers in the banking industry, though names such as Kuhn, Loeb, Goldman, and Sachs have become part of the American landscape, representing the ideal of Jewish success. For most Jews, America offered more modest opportunities in the form of family businesses, retail, and manufacturing. Nonetheless they experienced remarkable economic mobility in only one or two generations.

Joseph Seligman, the embodiment of the Jewish rags-to-riches story, discovered that despite economic success, barriers to Jews continued to exist in nineteenth-century America. Seligman had come to the United States in 1837 and his brothers followed shortly thereafter. Beginning as a peddler, Joseph and his brothers built clothing stores in several cities. From merchandising they transitioned to manufacturing, and the business grew rapidly, aided by a contract to produce uniforms during the Civil War. Notes of credit from the government as payment helped the family make the transition to the bond market, eventually becoming one of the most successful banking houses in America. Despite his wealth and status, when Joseph Seligman arrived in the upscale community of Saratoga Springs, New York, in the summer of 1877, the Grand Union Hotel refused to offer him accommodations because he was Jewish. This act of exclusion became a defining moment for American Jews who viewed it as evidence that no matter their accomplishments, they would never attain complete acceptance. The late nineteenth century witnessed a backlash against many immigrant groups, as Protestant elites feared that "foreigners" had overtaken the nation and its culture. Social anti-Semitism continued to persist in the United States, even as Jews enjoyed an unprecedented level of equality and acceptance in America.[23]

Nathan Straus, co-owner of Macy's Department Store.

Library of Congress, Prints and Photographs Division

Cartoon from Puck *magazine, June 1877, depicting Joseph Seligman's exclusion from the Grand Union Hotel in Saratoga, New York.*

Library of Congress, Prints and Photographs Division

By 1880, the portrait of American Jewry revealed a flourishing community, complete with religious and social institutions and supporting a highly acculturated, economically stable population. Despite a rising tide of nativism, Jews remained comfortable as citizens and businesspeople, secure in exercising their faith and building their communities. Most American Jewish congregations affiliated with the growing Reform movement, though "reform" meant different things in different places. Traditional synagogues remained a part of most communities as well, fortified by a slow trickle of East European immigrants beginning to arrive in the United States in the 1870s. By the 1880s, that trickle would become a steady stream; and over the following forty years, the millions of East European Jews arriving on American shores would dwarf the approximately 250,000 Jews living in the country in 1880. At the close of the 1870s, the profile of American Jewry was confident, secure, and middle class; Jews functioned as equal members of their communities and full participants in American life. In the two centuries since the first Jews arrived on the shores of New Amsterdam, uncertain about what the New World would bring, Jews had found a home in America that offered unprecedented equality along with freedom to construct Jewish community and culture on their own terms.

"A Hint to the Hebrews." Puck *magazine, 1881.*

American Jewish Historical Society, Newton Centre, Massachusetts and New York, New York

1. Peter Stuyvesant to the Directors of the Amsterdam Chamber of the Dutch West India Company in Samuel Oppenheim, "The Early History of the Jews in New York, 1654–1664," *Publications of the American Jewish Historical Society* 18 (1909), pp. 4–5.

2. Jewish population data is difficult to calculate precisely. Jacob R. Marcus, *To Count a People: American Jewish Population Data, 1585–1984* (Lanham, Md.: University Press of America, 1990); Ira Rosenwaike, "An Estimate and Analysis of the Jewish Population of the United States in 1790," *Publications of the American Jewish Historical Society* 50: 1 (September 1960), p. 31; see also Jonathan D. Sarna, *American Judaism: A History* (New Haven: Yale University Press, 2004) p. 375.

3. Hasia R. Diner, *The Jews of the United States, 1654–2000* (Berkeley: University of California Press, 2004) p. 22.

4. Ibid., p. 16; Morris U. Schappes, *A Documentary History of the Jews in the United States, 1654–1875* (New York: Citadel Press, 1950), p. 58.

5. Rebecca Samuel to Parents, ca. 1792, Henry Joseph Collection of Gratz papers, American Jewish Archives. Reprinted in Jacob R. Marcus, *The Jew in the American World: A Source Book* (Detroit: Wayne State University Press, 1996), pp. 142–143.

6. Request of Newport Jews to New York's Shearith Israel synagogue, in Marcus, *The Jew in the American World: A Source Book*, pp. 85, 84.

7. "The Earliest Extant Minute Books of the Spanish and Portuguese Congregation Shearith Israel in New York, 1728–1786," *Publications of the American Jewish Historical Society* 21 (1913), pp. 36–37, 51–53, 74–75.

8. Malcolm Stern, "The Function of Genealogy in American Jewish History," in *Essays in American Jewish History to Commemorate the Tenth Anniversary of the Founding of the American Jewish Archives under the Direction of Jacob Rader Marcus* (Cincinnati: American Jewish Archives, 1958), pp. 83–86.

9. Leo Hershkowitz and Isidore S. Meyer, eds., *The Lee Max Friedman Collection of American Jewish Colonial Correspondence: Letters of the Franks Family (1733–1748)* (Waltham, Mass.: American Jewish Historical Society, 1968), pp. 116–122.

10. Samuel Rezneck, *Unrecognized Patriots: The Jews in the American Revolution* (Westport, Conn.: Greenwood, 1975), pp. 23–24, 46–49.

11. Extract from the Journal of the Council of Censors, Philadelphia, December 23, 1783, in Schappes, *A Documentary History*, pp. 63–66.

12. Jonas Phillips to the Federal Constitutional Convention, September 7, 1787, in Henry Friedenwald. "A Letter of Jonas Phillips to the Federal Convention, *American Jewish Historical Society Publications* 2 (1894) pp. 108–110.

13. Benjamin Nones, *Philadelphia Aurora*, August 13, 1800.

14. "The Federal Parade of 1788," *American Jewish Archives* 7 (January 1955), pp. 65–67.

15. Abraham Lewis, "Correspondence Between Washington and Jewish Citizens," *Proceedings of the American Jewish Historical Society* 3 (1895), pp. 90–92.

16. Abraham Kohn, "A Jewish Peddler's Diary" (translated from the German by Abram Vossen Goodman), *American Jewish Archives*, vol. 3 (1951), pp. 96–106.

17. Anna Solomon, Autobiography, Typescript, 1904–1913 American Jewish Archives, Cincinnati, Ohio.

18. Israel Goldstein, *A Century of Judaism in New York: B'nai Jeshurun, 1825–1925* (New York, Congregation B'nai Jeshurun, 1930), pp. 55–56.

19. L. C. Moise, *Biography of Isaac Harby with an Account of the Reformed Society of Israelites of Charleston, S. C., 1824–1833* (Columbia, S.C.: R. L. Bryan Co., 1931), pp. 72–73.

20. Diner, *The Jews of the United States*, pp. 119–122; Sarna, *American Judaism*, pp. 91–99.

21. "Sketches from the Seat of War," by "a Jewish Soldier," with the Army of the Potomac in Virginia, February 1862. Reprinted in Schappes, *A Documentary History,* pp. 466, 467–68.

22. Bertram W. Korn, *American Jewry and the Civil War* (New York: Atheneum, 1970).

23. Naomi W. Cohen, *Encounter with Emancipation: The German Jews in the United States, 1830–1914* (Philadelphia: Jewish Publication Society of America, 1984), pp. 17–31, 249–51.

♪ 1 ♪

A PLEA FOR JEWISH RIGHTS IN THE NEW NATION

• JONAS PHILLIPS •

IN THE summer of 1787, the Federal Convention assembled behind closed doors in the city of Philadelphia to draft the Constitution of the United States. Jonas Phillips, a German-Jewish merchant living in the city, sent a letter to the assembly, urging the framers to make sure the new nation granted equal rights to all its citizens. Phillips reminded the members of the convention that Philadelphia's Jews could not participate fully in civic life because the state constitution required office-holders to take an oath proclaiming faith in the New Testament.

The members of the Constitutional Convention likely paid little heed to Phillips's letter, though the document they drafted ultimately reflected his concerns. The United States Constitution did not address Jews directly, nor did it discuss religion at any length. But by prohibiting any religious test for public office and focusing on the rights of the individual, the Constitution set the stage for Jews to enjoy political equality in the United States. The Bill of Rights further cemented the principle of religious freedom and allowed Judaism to flourish on American soil. After the adoption of the federal Constitution, several states continued to restrict Jewish rights; all of them ultimately passed legislation eliminating religious qualifications that had once kept Jews and other minority religious groups from participating equally in civic affairs.

In the letter below, Jonas Phillips boldly argues for Jewish rights in the United States, making particular reference to Jewish service and loyalty in the battle for the nation's independence. At the conclusion of his letter, Phillips also proudly lists the date on the Jewish calendar alongside the date on the secular calendar.

Sires

With leave and submission I address myself To those in whom there is wisdom and understanding and knowledge, they are the honourable personages appointed and Made overseers of a part of the terrestrial globe of the Earth, Namely the 13 united states of america in Convention Assembled, the Lord preserve them amen—

I the subscriber being one of the people called Jews of the City of Philadelphia, a people scattered & dispersed among all nations do behold with Concern that among the Laws in the Constitution of Pennsylvania, there is a Clause Sect 10 to viz—I do believe in one God the Creatur and governor of the universe and Rewarder of the good & the punisher of the wicked—and I do acknowledge the Scriptures of the old & New testament to be given by divine inspiration—to swear & believe that the new testament was given by divine inspiration is absolutely against the Religious principle of a Jew, and is against his Conscience to take any such oath—By the above law a Jew is deprived of holding any publick office or place of Government which is a Contridictory to the bill of Right Sect 2 viz

Portrait of Jonas Phillips (1736–1803) by artist Charles Willson Peale.

American Jewish Historical Society, Newton Centre, Massachusetts and New York, New York

That all men have a natural & unalienable Right to worship almighty God according to the dictates of their own Conscience and understanding & that no man ought or of Right can be Compelled to attend any Religious Worship or Creed or support any place of worship or Maintain any minister contrary to or against his own free will and Consent, nor can any man who acknowledges the being of a God be Justly deprived or abridged of any Civil Right as a Citizen on account of his Religious sentiments or peculiar mode of Religious Worship, and that no authority can or ought to be vested in or assumed by any power whatever that shall in any case interfere or in any manner Controul the Right of Conscience in the free Exercise of Religious Worship—

It is well known among all the Citizens of the 13 united states that the Jews have been true and faithful whigs, & during the late Contest with England they have been foremost in aiding and assisting the states with their lifes & fortunes, they have supported the cause, have bravely fought and bled for liberty which they can not Enjoy—

Therefore if the honourable Convention shall in their Wisdom think fit and alter the said oath & leave out the words to viz—and I do acknowledge the scripture of the new testament to be given by divine inspiration, then the Israelites will think themself happy to live under a government where all Religious societys are on an Equal footing—I solicit this favour for myself my children & posterity, & for the benefit of all the Israelites through the 13 united states of America.

My prayers is unto the Lord. May the people of this states Rise up as a great & young lion, May they prevail against their Enemys, may the degrees of honour of his Excellency the president of the Convention George Washington, be Exhalted & Raise up. May Everyone speak of his glorious Exploits.

May God prolong his days among us in this land of Liberty—May he lead the armies against his Enemys as he has done hereuntofore. May God Extend peace unto the united states—May they get up to the highest Prosperitys— May God Extend peace to them & their seed after them so long as the sun & moon Endureth—and May the almighty God of our father Abraham Isaac &

Jacob indue this Noble Assembly with wisdom Judgment & unanimity in their Counsells & may they have the satisfaction to see that their present toil & labour for the wellfair of the united states may be approved of Through all the world & particular by the united, states of america, is the ardent prayer of Sires

Your Most devoted obed. Servant

JONAS PHILLIPS

PHILADELPHIA 24th *Ellul* 5547 or *Sepr* 7th 1787.

Jonas Phillips to the Federal Constitutional Convention, September 7, 1787, in Henry Friedenwald. "A Letter of Jonas Phillips to the Federal Convention," *American Jewish Historical Society Publications* 2 (1894), pp. 108–110.

❧ 2 ❧

"TO BIGOTRY NO SANCTION"

• CORRESPONDENCE BETWEEN
GEORGE WASHINGTON AND THE JEWS
OF NEWPORT, RHODE ISLAND •

AFTER THE inauguration of President George Washington, the congregations of Savannah, Charleston, Richmond, Philadelphia, New York, and Newport sent letters of congratulation to the new President, praising his leadership and commitment to religious toleration. The correspondence between George Washington and Newport's Jewish community contained the resounding promise from Washington that the United States would give "to bigotry no sanction, to persecution no assistance."

In fact, it was Newport's Jews who first composed the infamous phrase, "to bigotry no sanction . . ." in their letter welcoming the President when he arrived in the city during his grand tour of New England in the summer of 1790; Washington repeated those words verbatim in his reply. Washington had delivered similar assurances to many minority groups in America, as he calculated how best to balance group rights in the new nation. For American Jews, Washington's words became a sacred founding charter of their rights as citizens in the United States. His commitment to the principle of toleration encapsulated Jewish expectations for America. The words "to bigotry no sanction, to persecution no assistance" took on a virtual sanctity among American Jews who regarded the phrase as a guarantee of their rights to live equally and freely as Jews in the United States.

Address of the Newport Congregation to the President of the United States of America

Sir:—Permit the children of the stock of Abraham to approach you with the most cordial affection and esteem for your person and merit, and to join with our fellow-citizens in welcoming you to Newport.

With pleasure we reflect on those days of difficulty and danger when the God of Israel, who delivered David from the peril of the sword, shielded your head in the day of battle; and we rejoice to think that the same spirit which rested in the bosom of the greatly beloved Daniel, enabling him to preside over the provinces of the Babylonian Empire, rests and ever will rest upon you, enabling you to discharge the arduous duties of the Chief Magistrate of these States.

Deprived as we hitherto have been of the invaluable rights of free citizens, we now—with a deep sense of gratitude to the Almighty Disposer of all events—behold a government erected by the majesty of the people—a government which to bigotry gives no sanction, to persecution no assistance, but generously affording to all liberty of conscience and immunities of citizenship, deeming every one of whatever nation, tongue or language, equal parts of the great governmental machine.

This so ample and extensive Federal Union, whose base is philanthropy, mutual confidence and public virtue, we cannot but acknowledge to be the work of the great God who rules in the armies of the heavens and among the inhabitants of the earth, doing whatever seemeth to Him good.

For all the blessings of civil and religious liberty which we enjoy under an equal and benign administration, we desire to send up our thanks to the Ancient of days, the great Preserver of men, beseeching Him that the angels who conducted our forefathers through the wilderness into the promised land may graciously conduct you through all the difficulties and dangers of this mortal life; and when, like Joshua, full of days and full of honors, you are gathered to your fathers, may you be admitted into the heavenly paradise to partake of the water of life and the tree of immortality.

Done and signed by order of the Hebrew Congregation in Newport, Rhode Island.

MOSES SEIXAS, *Warden.*
NEWPORT, August 17, 1790.

George Washington to Moses Seixas, Letterbook copy in the hand of Washington's secretary, 1790.
George Washington Papers, Library of Congress, Manuscript Division.

Washington's Reply to the Hebrew Congregation in Newport, Rhode Island

Gentlemen:—While I received with much satisfaction your address replete with expressions of esteem, I rejoice in the opportunity of assuring you that I shall always retain grateful remembrance of the cordial welcome I experienced on my visit to Newport from all classes of citizens.

The reflection on the days of difficulty and danger which are past is rendered the more sweet from a consciousness that they are succeeded by days of uncommon prosperity and security.

If we have wisdom to make the best use of the advantages with which we are now favored, we cannot fail, under the just administration of a good government, to become a great and happy people.

The citizens of the United States of America have a right to applaud themselves for having given to mankind examples of an enlarged and liberal policy—a policy worthy of imitation. All possess alike liberty of conscience and immunities of citizenship.

It is now no more that toleration is spoken of as if it were the indulgence of one class of people that another enjoyed the exercise of their inherent natural rights, for, happily, the Government of the United States, which gives to bigotry no sanction, to persecution no assistance, requires only that they who live under its protection should demean themselves as good citizens in giving it on all occasions their effectual support.

It would be inconsistent with the frankness of my character not to avow that I am pleased with your favorable opinion of my administration and fervent wishes for my felicity.

May the children of the stock of Abraham who dwell in this land continue to merit and enjoy the good will of the other inhabitants—while every one shall sit in safety under his own vine and fig tree and there shall be none to make him afraid.

May the father of all mercies scatter light, and not darkness, upon our paths, and make us all in our several vocations useful here, and in His own due time and way everlastingly happy.

G. WASHINGTON

Publications of the American Jewish Historical Society 3 (1895), pp. 90–92.

❧ 3 ❧

A MOTHER BEMOANS HER DAUGHTER'S MARRIAGE

· ABIGAIL FRANKS ·

ABIGAIL FRANKS was born in colonial New York, shortly after her parents Moses and Rachel Levy migrated from London. In 1712, Abigail married Jacob Franks, who became one of New York's most successful merchants and president (*parnass*) of the city's Shearith Israel congregation. Abigail and Jacob Franks had nine children, six of whom survived infancy, and raised them in an observant, highly acculturated household.

Franks was an avid letter-writer and she provides a glimpse into the world of colonial Jewry. A highly educated woman, especially for her time, she regularly quoted the classics in her letters. The Franks were in many respects an exceptional family. At a time when women generally received little formal education, the Franks took great care to educate their daughters as well as their sons in both Jewish and secular subjects, providing instruction in several languages, including Hebrew. The Franks socialized with some of New York's elite Protestant families, but remained deeply committed to Jewish life, maintaining a strictly kosher home and regularly attending synagogue.

While Abigail Franks remained scrupulous in her religious practices, she could not control the lack of suitable marriage partners available to her children within colonial America's tiny Jewish population. She once wrote that she feared her daughters might have to live "like nuns." Nevertheless, Franks held high standards for her children and when one potential Jewish suitor arrived, she rejected him as a "stupid wretch." Given her high expectations and devotion to Judaism, Franks was devastated when she learned that in 1742, her daughter Phila had eloped with Oliver Delancey, son of a prominent Christian family. She refused to speak to her daughter ever again or to allow the couple in her home.

Abigail Franks's correspondence with her son Naphtali (whom she addresses as "Heartsey") reveals the pain she experienced over her daughter's intermarriage. There is no evidence that mother and daughter ever reconciled.

Dear Heartsey:

My wishes for your felicity are as great as the joy I have to hear you are happily married. May the smiles of Providence waite allways on y[ou]r inclinations and your dear [wife] Phila's whome I salute with tender affections, pray[in]g kind Heaven to be propitious to your wishes in makeing her a happy mother. I shall think the time teadious untill I shall have that happy information, for I don't expect to hear it by the return of these ships, and therefore must injoyn your care in writting by the first oppertunity (after the birth or wathever it shall please God to bless you with) either by via Carrolina barbadoz, or any other.

I am now retired from town and would from my self (if it were possable to

Abigail Levy Franks (1696–1756), ca. 1735. Attributed to Gerardus Duyckinck. Oil on canvas.

Portrait of Franks Children with Lamb, ca 1735. Attributed to Gerardus Duyckinck. Oil on canvas.

have some piece of mind) from the severe affliction I am under on the conduct of that unhappy girle [your sister Phila]. Good God wath a shock it was when they acquainted me she had left the house and had bin married six months. I can hardly hold my pen whilst I am writting it. Itts wath I never could have imagined, especialy affter wath I heard her soe often say, that noe consideration in life should ever induce her to disoblige such good parents.

I had heard the report of her goeing to be married to Oliver Delancey, but as such reports had offten bin off either off your sisters [Phila and Richa], I gave noe heed to it further than a generall caution of her conduct wich has allways bin unblemish[e]d, and is soe still in the eye of the Christians whoe allow she had disobliged us but has in noe way bin dishonorable, being married to a man of worth and charector.

My spirits was for some time soe depresst that it was a pain to speak or see any one. I have over come it soe far as not to make my concern soe conspicuous but I shall never have that serenity nor peace within I have soe happyly had hittherto. My house has bin my prisson ever since. I had not heart enough to goe near the street door. Its a pain to me to think off goeing again to town, and if your father's buissness would premit him to live out of it I never would goe near it again. I wish it was in my power to leave this part of the world. I would come away in the first man of war that went to London.

Oliver has sent many times to beg leave to see me, but I never would tho' now he sent word that he will come here [to Flatbush]. I dread seeing him and how to avoid I know noe way, neither if he comes can I use him rudly. I may make him some reproaches but I know my self soe well that I shall at least be civill, tho' I never will give him leave to come to my house in town, and as for his wife, I am determined I never will see nor lett none of the family goe near her.

He intends to write to you and my brother Isaac [Levy] to endeavour a reconciliation. I would have you answer his letter, if you don't hers, for I must be soe ingenious [as] to conffess nature is very strong and it would give me a great concern if she should live unhappy, tho' its a concern she does not meritt.

Your affectionate mother,
Abigaill Franks

Leo Hershkowitz and Isidore S. Meyer, eds., *The Lee Max Friedman Collection of American Jewish Colonial Correspondence: Letters of the Franks Family (1733–1748)*, (Waltham, Mass.: American Jewish Historical Society, 1968), pp. 116–120, 122. Printed with permission of the American Jewish Historical Society, New York, New York and Newton Centre, Massachusetts.

✣ 4 ✣

THE CHALLENGE OF
JEWISH OBSERVANCE
IN COLONIAL AMERICA

• REBECCA SAMUEL •

FOR COLONIAL Jews, early America was a frontier, lacking the basic institutions and services required for Jewish life. In larger cities, Jews were able to create congregations and provide for the needs of the Jewish community, but those who ventured out to less-populated areas found Jewish life considerably more difficult. A wide range of religious practices prevailed within the colonial Jewish community. Some Jews retained strict adherence to Jewish law, taking pains to keep kosher and observe Shabbat. Others exhibited a high degree of laxity in Jewish observance, either by preference or because their circumstances made rigorous devotion to Judaism extremely difficult.

Rebecca Samuel and her husband Hyman made their home in Petersburg, Virginia in the early 1790s. Having started a family, Rebecca became increasingly distressed about the dismal state of Jewish life in the small community. In letters written to her parents, who were living in Hamburg, Germany, Rebecca describes her loneliness and sense of isolation as a Jew. She laments the religious laxity among the few Jews who lived in Petersburg, noting the difficulty of obtaining kosher meat and of observing the Sabbath and Jewish holidays. Because she and her husband found the state of Jewish life in Petersburg so deplorable, they made the decision to relocate to Charleston, South Carolina, one of the most substantial Jewish communities during the colonial era.

Petersburg, ca.1792

Dear Parents:

I hope my letter will ease your mind. You can now be reassured and send me one of the family to Charleston, South Carolina. This is the place to which, with God's help, we will go after Passover. The whole reason why we are leaving this place is because of [its lack of] *Yehudishkeit* [Jewishness].

Dear Parents, I know quite well you will not want me to bring up my children like Gentiles. Here they cannot become anything else. Jewishness is pushed aside here. There are here [in Petersburg] ten or twelve Jews, and they are not worthy of being called Jews. We have a *shohet* [slaughterer of animals and poultry] here who goes to market and buys *terefah* [nonkosher] meat and then brings it home. On Rosh Ha-Shanah and on Yom Kippur the people worshipped here without one sefer torah [pentateuchal scroll] and not one of them wore the tallit [a large prayer shawl worn in the synagogue] or the *arba kanfot* [the small set of fringe worn on the body], except Hyman and my

Gomez family Etrog holder, ca. 18th century. This silver mustard pot was transformed into an etrog *(citron) holder and used during the Jewish fall harvest holiday of* Sukkot.

Sammy's godfather. The latter is an old man of sixty, a man from Holland. He has been in America for thirty years already; for twenty years he was in Charleston, and he has been living here for four years. He does not want to remain here any longer and will go with us to Charleston. In that place there is a blessed community of three hundred Jews.

You can believe me that I crave to see a synagogue to which I can go. The way we live now is no life at all. We do not know what the Sabbath and the holidays are. On the Sabbath all the Jewish shops are open; and they do business on that day as they do throughout the whole week. But ours we do not allow to open. With us there is still some Sabbath. You must believe me that in our house we all live as Jews as much as we can.

As for the Gentiles [?], we have nothing to complain about. For the sake of a livelihood we do not have to leave here. Nor do we have to leave because of debts. I believe ever since Hyman has grown up that he has not had it so good. You cannot know what a wonderful country this is for the common man. One can live here peacefully. Hyman made a clock that goes very accurately, just like the one in the Buchenstrasse in Hamburg. Now you can imagine what honors Hyman has been getting here. In all Virginia there is no clock [like this one], and Virginia is the greatest province in the whole of America, and America is the largest section of the world. Now you know what sort of a country this is. It is not too long since Virginia was discovered. It is a young country. And it is amazing to see the business they do in this little Petersburg. At times as many as a thousand hogsheads of tobacco arrive at one time, and each hogshead contains 1,000 and sometimes 1,200 pounds of tobacco. The tobacco is shipped from here to the whole world.

When Judah [my brother?] comes here, he can become a watchmaker and a goldsmith, if he so desires. Here it is not like Germany where a watchmaker is not permitted to sell silverware. [The contrary is true in this country.] They do not know otherwise here. They expect a watchmaker to be a silversmith here. Hyman has more to do in making silverware than with watchmaking. He has a journeyman, a silversmith, a very good artisan, and he, Hyman, takes

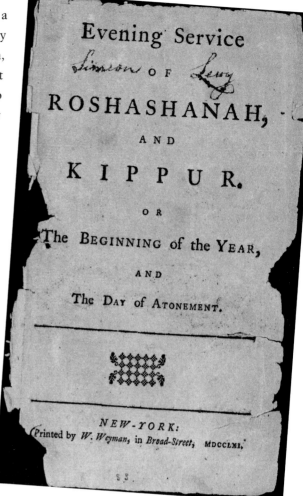

First High Holiday prayer book printed in America, 1761.
American Jewish Historical Society, Newton Centre, Massachusetts and New York, New York

care of the watches. This work is well paid here, but in Charleston, it pays even better.

All the people who hear that we are leaving give us their blessings. They say that it is sinful that such blessed children should be brought up here in Petersburg. My children cannot learn anything here, nothing Jewish, nothing of general culture. My Schoene [my daughter], God bless her, is already three years old; I think it is time that she should learn something, and she has a good head to learn. I have taught her the bedtime prayers and grace after meals in just two lessons. I believe that no one among the Jews here can do as well as she. And my Sammy [born in 1790], God bless him, is already beginning to talk.

I could write more. However, I do not have any more paper.

I remain, your devoted daughter and servant, Rebecca, the wife of Hayyim, the son of Samuel the Levite, I send my family, my . . . [mother-in-law?] and all my friends and good friends, my regards.

Rachel Lazarus, "Orthodox Rachel Lazarus Seeks a More Jewish Community, 1792 (?)" Reprinted from Jacob Rader Marcus, *The Jew in the American World: A Source Book* (Detroit: Wayne State University Press, 1996), pp. 142–143, ©1996 with the permission of Wayne State University Press.

JEWISH SELF-DEFENSE IN POST-REVOLUTIONARY AMERICA

· BENJAMIN NONES ·

IN THE years after the Revolution, Jews enjoyed expanding rights and freedoms. Yet, instances of anti-Semitism did occur, sometimes emerging in the course of political debates in the fledgling nation. Benjamin Nones, a Philadelphia Jew, had served as a soldier in the Revolutionary War, but found himself the subject of attack several years later. In the wake of American independence, a debate raged between the Federalists who supported Alexander Hamilton and the Democratic Republicans who endorsed Thomas Jefferson's vision for the United States. Anti-Semitic rhetoric often appeared in Federalist critiques of the Jeffersonians.

In 1800, the *Gazette of the United States and Daily Advertiser*, a Federalist newspaper, printed a defamatory letter that assailed Benjamin Nones for his Jewish heritage, his political beliefs, and his financial struggles at the time. Nones responded vigorously, acknowledging his financial woes and declaring ardent support for the Republican Party, noting that republics, unlike monarchies, supported Jewish rights. He emphasized his service to the country during the war and proudly defended his Jewish faith, identifying Judaism as the religion upon which Christianity was founded. When the Federalist *Gazette* refused to publish his response, Nones sent it to the city's Republican newspaper, the *Philadelphia Aurora*, which printed his passionate letter.

Sir,

I HOPE, if you take the liberty of inserting calumnies against individuals, for the amusement of your readers, you will at least have so much regard to justice, as to permit the injured through the same channel that conveyed the slander, to appeal to the public in self-defence.—I expect of you therefore, to insert this reply to your ironical reporter of the proceedings at the meeting of the republican citizens of Philadelphia, contained in your gazette of the fifth instant; so far as I am concerned in that statement.—I am no enemy Mr. Wayne[1] to wit; nor do I think the political parties have much right to complain, if they enable the public to laugh at each others expence, provided it be managed with the same degree of ingenuity, and some attention to truth and candour. But your reporter of the proceedings at that meeting is as destitute of truth and candour, as he is of ingenuity, and I think, I can shew, that the want of prudence of this Mr. Marplot, in his slander upon me, is equally glaring with his want of wit, his want of veracity, his want of decency, and his want of humanity.

I am accused of being a *Jew;* of being a *Republican;* and of being *Poor.*

I *am* a Jew. I glory in belonging to that persuasion, which even its opponents, whether Christian, or Mahomedan, allow to be of divine origin—of that persuasion on which christianity itself was originally founded, and must ultimately rest—which has preserved its faith secure and undefiled, for near

[1] Caleb F. Wayne, printer of the *Gazette.*

three thousand years—whose votaries have never murdered each other in religious wars, or cherished the theological hatred so general, so unextinguishable among those who revile them. A persuasion, whose, patient followers, have endured for ages the pious cruelties of Pagans, and of the christians, and persevered in the unoffending practice of their rites and ceremonies, amidst poverties and privations—amidst pains, penalties, confiscations, banishments, tortures, and deaths, beyond the example of any other sect, which the page of history has hitherto recorded.

Benjamin Nones (1757–1826).
The Jacob Rader Marcus Center of the American Jewish Archives

To be of such a persuasion, is to me no disgrace; though I well understand the inhuman language of bigotted contempt, in which your reporter by attempting to make me ridiculous, as a Jew, has made himself detestable, whatever religious persuasion may be dishonored by his adherence.

But I am a Jew. I am so—and so were Abraham, and Isaac, and Moses and the prophets, and so too were Christ and his apostles, I feel no disgrace in ranking with such society, however, it may be subject to the illiberal buffoonery of such men as your correspondents.

I am a *Republican*! Thank God, I have not been so heedless, and so ignorant of what has passed, and is now passing in the political world. I have not been so proud or so prejudiced as to renounce the cause for which I have *fought,* as an American throughout the whole of the revolutionary war, in the militia of Charleston, and in Polafkey's legion,[2] I fought in almost every action which took place in Carolina, and in the disastrous affair of Savannah, shared the hardships of that sanguinary day, and for three and twenty years I felt no disposition to change my political, any more than my religious principles.— And which in spite of the witling scribblers of aristocracy, I shall hold sacred until death as not to feel the ardour of republicanism.—Your correspondent, Mr. Wayne cannot have known what it is to serve his country from principle in time of danger and difficulties, the expence of his health and his peace, of his pocket and his person, as I have done; or he would not be as he is, a pert reviler of those who have done—as I do not suspect you Mr. Wayne, of being the author of the attack on me, I shall not enquire what share you or your relations had in establishing the liberties of your country. On religious grounds I am a republican. Kingly, government was first conceded to the foolish complaints of the Jewish people, as a punishment and a curse; and so it was to them

---

[2] Brigadier General Casimir Pulaski's Legion. Nones fought with Pulaski at the Siege of Savannah in the fall of 1779.

until their dispersion, and so it has been to every nation, who have been as fool-ishly tempted to submit to it. Great Britain has a king, and her enemies need not wish her the sword, the pestilence, and the famine.

In the history of the Jews, are contained the earliest warnings against kingly government, as any one may know who has read the fable of Abimelick, or the exhortations of Samuel. But I do not recommend them to your reporter, Mr. Wayne. To him the language of truth and soberness would be unintelligible.

I am a Jew, and if for no other reason, for that reason am I a republican. Among the pious priesthood of church establishments, we are compassionately ranked with Turks, Infidels and Heretics. In the *monarchies* of Europe, we are hunted from society—stigmatized as unworthy of common civility, thrust out as it were from the converse of men; objects of mockery and insult to froward children, the butts of vulgar wit, and low buffoonery, such as your corre-spondent Mr. Wayne is not ashamed to set us an example of. Among the nations of Europe we are inhabitants every where—but Citizens no where *unless in Republics*. Here, in France, and in the Batavian Republic alone, we are treated as men and as brethren. In republics we have *rights*, in monarchies we live but to experience *wrongs*. And why? Because we and our forefathers have *not* sacrificed our principles to interest, or earned an exemption from pain and poverty, by the direliction of our religious duties, no wonder we are objects of derision to those, who have no principles, moral or religious, to guide their conduct.

How then can a Jew but be a Republican? in America particularly. Unfeel-ing & ungrateful would he be, if he were callous to the glorious and benevo-lent cause of the difference between his situation in this land of freedom, and among the proud and privileged law givers of Europe.

But I am *poor*, I am so, my family also is large, but soberly and decently brought up. They have not been taught to revile a christian, because his reli-gion is not *so old* as theirs. They have not been taught to mock even at the errors of good intention, and conscientious belief.

I hope they will always leave this to men as unlike themselves, as I hope I am to your scurrilous correspondent.

I know that to purse proud aristocracy poverty is a crime, but it may some-times be accompanied with honesty even in a Jew. I was a bankrupt some years ago. I obtained my certificate and I was discharged from my debts. Having been more successful afterwards, I called my creditors together, and eight years after-wards unsolicited I discharged all my old debts, I offered interest which was refused by my creditors, and they gave me under their hands without any solic-itations of mine, as a testimonial of the fact (to use their own language) as a tribute due to my honor and honesty. This testimonial was signed by Messrs. J. Ball, W. Wister, George Meade, J. Philips, C. G. Paleske, J. Bispham, J. Cohen, Robert Smith, J. H. Leuffer, A. Kuhn, John Stille, S. Pleasants, M. Woodhouse, Thomas Harrison, M. Boraef, E. Laskey, and Thomas Allibone, &c.

I was discharged by the insolvent act, true, because having the amount of my debts owing to me from the French Republic, the differences between France and America have prevented the recovery of what was due to me, in time to discharge what was due to my creditors. Hitherto it has been the fault of the political situation of the two countries, that my creditors are not paid; when peace shall enable me to receive what I am entitled to it will be my fault if they are not fully paid.

This is a long defence Mr. Wayne, but you have called it forth, and therefore, I hope you at least will not object to it. The Public will now judge who is the proper object of ridicule and contempt, your facetious reporter, or

Your Humble Servant,

BENJAMIN NONES

Philadelphia Aurora, August 13, 1800.

~ 6 ~

A REFUGE FOR JEWS
IN UPSTATE NEW YORK

• MORDECAI NOAH •

IN THE early nineteenth century, Mordecai Noah, a journalist, playwright, politician, and diplomat, was one of the most prominent Jews in the United States. Born in Philadelphia, he held several political appointments in New York. In 1813, President James Madison appointed him as consul to the Kingdom of Tunis, the highest position held by a Jew in the United States at the time. However, his brief appointment was terminated by Secretary of State James Monroe who explained that, " At the time of your appointment, as Consul to Tunis, it was not known that the religion which you profess would form an obstacle to the exercise of your Consular functions."

Despite his outrage at the dismal and the collective blow struck against the Jews of America, Mordecai Noah went on to conceive one of the most ambitious, if unrealistic, utopian solutions to the problems of world Jewry. At a time when the United States needed immigrants to build the nation and when many Jews sought a place where they could enjoy greater freedoms, Noah envisioned "A City of Refuge for the Jews" in upstate New York. In 1825, Noah staged an elaborate spectacle to dedicate the site of a proposed Jewish settlement on Grand Island in the Niagara River. He named the planned colony "Ararat," after the mountain where Noah's Ark landed after the flood in the Book of Genesis.

With great pageantry, Mordecai Noah dedicated the future site of Ararat, parading in a silk robe, surrounded by dignitaries, and issuing a proclamation detailing the proposed asylum for the Jews. Although a cornerstone was all that ever came of the grand scheme, Noah's vision for a Jewish colony in the United States reflected the hope he placed in the nation's ability to offer a haven for Jews. The notion of providing some place of refuge for Jews was not unprecedented and would meet with greater popularity in later Zionist campaigns. While Mordecai Noah's proposal was far-fetched and widely ridiculed, generations of Jewish immigrants would find less fanciful and more practical expressions of faith in America's potential to offer Jews a better future.

Proclamation to the Jews

WHEREAS, it has pleased Almighty God to manifest to his chosen people the approach of that period, when, in fulfillment of the promises made to the race of Jacob, and as a reward for their pious constancy and triumphant fidelity, they are to be gathered from the four quarters of the globe, and to resume their rank and character among the governments of the earth;

Mordecai Manuel Noah (1785–1851).
American Jewish Historical Society, Newton Centre,
Massachusetts and New York, New York

AND WHEREAS, the peace which now prevails among civilized nations, the progress of learning throughout the world, and the general spirit of liberality and toleration which exists together with other changes favorable to light and to liberty, mark in an especial manner the approach of that time, when "peace on earth and good will to man" are to prevail with a benign and extended influence, and the ancient people of God, the first to proclaim His unity and omnipotence, are to be restored to their inheritance, and enjoy the rights of a sovereign independent people;

Therefore, I, Mordecai Manuel Noah, citizen of the United States of America, late Consul of said States to the City and Kingdom of Tunis, High Sheriff of New York, Counselor at Law, and by the grace of God, Governor and Judge of Israel, have issued this my Proclamation, announcing to the Jews throughout the world, that an asylum is prepared and hereby offered to them, where they can enjoy that peace, comfort and happiness which have been denied them through the intolerance and misgovernment of former ages; an asylum in a free and powerful country, where ample protection is secured to their persons, their property and religious rights; an asylum in a country remarkable for its vast resources, the richness of its soil, and the salubrity of its climate; where industry is encouraged, education promoted, and good faith rewarded; "a land of milk and honey," where Israel may repose in peace, under his "vine and fig tree," and where our people may so familiarize themselves with the science of government and the lights of learning and civilization, as may qualify them for that great and final restoration to their ancient heritage, which the times so powerfully indicate.

The asylum referred to is in the State of New York, the greatest State in the American confederacy. New York contains forty-three thousand, two hundred and fourteen square miles, divided into fifty-five counties, and having six thousand and eighty-seven post-towns and cities, containing one million, five hundred thousand inhabitants, together with six million acres of cultivated land, improvements in agriculture and manufactures, in trade and commerce, which include a valuation of three hundred millions of dollars of taxable property; one hundred and fifty thousand militia, armed and equipped; a constitution founded upon an equality of rights, having no test-oaths, and recognizing no religious distinctions, and seven thousand free schools and colleges, affording the blessings of education to four hundred thousand children. Such is the great and increasing State to which the emigration of the Jews is directed.

The desired spot in the State of New York, to which I hereby invite my beloved people throughout the world, in common with those of every religious denomination, is called Grand Island, and on which I shall lay the foundation of a City of Refuge, to be called Ararat.

Grand Island in the Niagara river is bounded by Ontario on the north, and Erie on the south, and within a few miles of each of those great commercial lakes. The island is nearly twelve miles in length, and varying from three to seven miles in breadth, and contains upwards of seventeen thousand acres of remarkably rich and fertile land. Lake Erie is about two hundred and seventy miles in length, and borders on the States of New York, Pennsylvania and Ohio; and westwardly, by the possessions of our friends and neighbors, the British subjects of Upper Canada. This splendid lake unites itself by means of navigable rivers, with Lakes St. Clair, Huron, Michigan and Superior, embracing a lake shore of nearly three thousand miles; and by short canals those vast sheets of water will be connected with the Illinois and Mississippi rivers, thereby establishing a great and valuable internal trade to New Orleans and the Gulf of Mexico. Lake Ontario, on the north, is one hundred and ninety miles in length, and empties into the St. Lawrence, which, passing through the Province of Lower Canada, carries the commerce of Quebec and Montreal to the Atlantic Ocean.

Thus fortified to the right and left by the extensive commercial resources of the Great Lakes and their tributary streams, within four miles of the sublime Falls of Niagara, affording the greatest water-power in the world for manufacturing purposes,—directly opposite the mouth of the Grand Canal of three hundred and sixty miles inland navigation to the Hudson river and city of New York,—having the fur trade of Upper Canada to the west, and also of the great territories towards the Rocky Mountains and the Pacific Ocean; likewise the trade of the Western States of America,—Grand Island may be considered as surrounded by every commercial, manufacturing and agricultural advantage, and from its location is pre-eminently calculated to become, in time, the greatest trading and commercial depot in the new and better world. To men of worth and industry it has every substantial attraction; the capitalist will be enabled to enjoy his resources with undoubted profit, and the merchant cannot fail to reap the reward of enterprise in a great and growing republic; but to the industrious mechanic, manufacturer and agriculturist it holds forth great and improving advantages.

Broadside depicting Mordecai Noah being attacked by Elijah J. Roberts, a former business associate, on the steps of a theater.

Library of Congress, Prints and Photographs Division

Deprived, as our people have been for centuries of a right in the soil, they will learn, with peculiar satisfaction, that here they can till the soil, reap the harvest, and raise the flocks which are unquestionably their own; and, in the full and unmolested enjoyment of their religious rights, and of every civil immunity, together with peace and plenty, they can lift up their voice in gratitude to Him who sustained our fathers in the wilderness, and brought us in triumph out of the land of Egypt; who assigned to us the safe-keeping of his oracles, who proclaimed us his people, and who has ever walked before us like a "cloud by day and a pillar of fire by night."

In His name do I revive, renew and re-establish the government of the Jewish Nation, under the auspices and protection of the constitution and laws of the United States of America; confirming and perpetuating all our rights and privileges,—our name, our rank, and our power among the nations of the earth,—as they existed and were recognized under the government of the Judges. And I hereby enjoin it upon all our pious and venerable Rabbis, our Presidents and Elders of Synagogues, Chiefs of Colleges and brethren in authority throughout the world, to circulate and make known this, my Proclamation, and give to it full publicity, credence and effect.

Mordecai Noah, *American Jewish Historical Society Publications* 8 (1900), pp. 106–110.

7

CHANGING JUDAISM IN AMERICA

• THE REFORMED SOCIETY
OF ISRAELITES •

YEARS BEFORE any rabbi came to America or an organized Reform movement took shape in this country, ordinary Jews began to make changes in the practice of Judaism. In 1824, a group of young Jewish men in Charleston, South Carolina, petitioned the city's only synagogue, Congregation Beth Elohim, requesting changes in worship practices. Their demands included shorter services, prayer in the vernacular, and weekly sermons delivered in English, among other modest reforms. When the congregation denied the petition, a group of forty-seven men, led by prominent essayist and playwright Isaac Harby, broke away from the existing synagogue and founded the Reformed Society of Israelites for Promoting True Principles of Judaism According to Its Purity and Spirit.

The young men who seceded to form their own society believed that without significant changes, the future of Judaism in America was in danger, threatened by both widespread apathy and the conversion efforts of Christian missionaries. As Jews grew increasingly acculturated and spoke English, the reformers wanted the synagogue to suit the needs and desires of the next generation of American Jews. The group did not succeed in building a new congregation in Charleston. But in the late 1830s, many members returned to Beth Elohim, where they succeeded in instituting most of the reforms initially proposed.

In 1826, members of the Reformed Society of Israelites issued this public appeal for funds to support their efforts, outlining the key aims of their society.

NEARLY TWO YEARS have now elapsed since a large and respectable meeting of Israelites was held in this city, for the purpose of endeavoring to effect some changes, and eradicating many acknowledged errors in the mode of worship at

Exterior of Charleston's Congregation Beth Elohim.

American Jewish Historical Society, Newton Centre, Massachusetts and New York, New York

present observed in the Synagogue. For the attainment of these objects a Society was soon after organized called "The Reformed Society of Israelites," which has since been incorporated by the Legislature. The ends proposed to be attained were chiefly these:

First: To introduce such a change in the mode of worship, that a considerable portion of the prayers be said in the English language, so that by being *understood*, they would be attended with that religious instruction in our particular faith, essential to the rising generation, and so generally neglected; and which, by promoting pious and elevated feelings, would also render the service solemn, impressive, and dignified—such as should belong to all our addresses to the Divine power.

Secondly: To discontinue the observance of such ceremonies as partake strongly of bigotry; as owe their origin only to *Rabbinical* institutions; as are not embraced in the *moral* laws of Moses; and in many instances are contrary to their spirit, to their beauty and sublimity and to that elevated piety and virtue which so highly distinguish them.

Thirdly: To abolish the use of such portions of the Hebrew prayers as are superfluous and consist of mere *repetitions*, and to select such of them as are sufficient and appropriate to the occasion.

Fourthly: To follow the portions of the *Pentateuch* which are to be said in the original Hebrew, with an English Discourse, in which the principles of the Jewish faith,

and the force and beauty of the moral law, may be expounded to the rising generation, so that they, *and all others*, may know how to cherish and venerate those sublime truths which emanated from the Almighty Father, and which are acknowledged as the first, and most hallowed principles of all religion.

Such were, with a few minor alterations, the principal objects that led to the institution of "The Reformed Society of Israelites" in the City of Charleston. This explanation we deem due to those whose assistance may be extended towards erecting this new temple to the service of the Almighty. It is an appeal to all who are influenced by tolerant and unprejudiced feelings, and who can properly appreciate the conduct of those who are actuated in their wish for the above changes, by a

Interior of Congregation Beth Elohim, Charleston, South Carolina. Print rendered from a drawing by Solomon N. Carvalho.

desire to disencumber their religion of what disfigures instead of ornamenting it, and by the religious instruction which distinguishes the present age. It appeals to no sectarian spirit, as it directs itself solely to the bosoms of those that respond to the pure and uncontaminated feelings of an enlightened piety. Exclusive principles belong, more or less, to all sects, but the virtue of Benevolence may belong to all of every sect. Impressed with these sentiments, we therefore make our application general, and to such are influenced by the spirit of true religion, and by a manly and discriminating feeling of what is really good and ennobling in human charity.

Donations will be thankfully received, and all communications noticed by either of the subscribers.

AARON PHILLIPS, President,
MICHAEL LAZARUS, Vice-President,
ISAAC MORDECAI, Treasurer,
D. N. CARVALHO,
ISAAC N. CARDOZO,
E. P. COHEN,
ABRAHAM MOÏSE,
ISAAC HARBY,

COMMITTEE.

Charleston, Sept. 1, 1826.

Barnett A. Elzas, *The Reformed Society of Israelites of Charleston, S.C.* (New York: Bloch Publishing Company, 1916), pp. 23–25.

8

DIARY OF A JEWISH PEDDLER

• ABRAHAM KOHN •

IN THE mid-nineteenth century, more than 200,000 Jewish immigrants made the journey from Central Europe to the United States. They left German-speaking lands in search of greater economic opportunity, hoping to build new lives in America. These Jewish immigrants encountered a Jewish community not yet fully established, and a rapidly expanding nation on the cusp of the commercial age. Most Jews who came to the United States in the mid-1800s were unmarried men; many would eventually establish small retail stores or enter the emerging industry of clothing manufacture. But a majority of these young Jewish men began as peddlers, struggling to make a living during their first years in America.

Abraham Kohn was twenty-three years old in 1842 when he left Bavaria for the United States. Within only two years, he would settle in Chicago, open his own retail business, and help to establish the city's first synagogue. He later became active in local politics. But his early months as a peddler in New England testify to the hardships encountered by this generation of Jewish immigrants. In his diary, Kohn writes powerfully about his despair and loneliness, his discomfort with American culture, and the conflict he experienced over being unable to observe the Sabbath as he traveled. As Abraham Kohn journeyed from town to town as a peddler, he expressed frequent regret about having made the decision to immigrate to an unfamiliar country. To read his diary is to appreciate the doubts and struggles endured by Jewish immigrants and their genuine uncertainty about what life in America might bring.

ON THE EVE of the New Year I found myself with a new career before me. What kind of career? "I don't know"—the American's customary reply to every difficult question. . . .

THE JEW PEDLER.

I was in New York, trying in vain to find a job as clerk in a store. But business was too slow, and I had to do as all the others; with a bundle on my back I had to go out into the country, peddling various articles. This, then, is the vaunted luck of the immigrants from Bavaria! O misguided fools, led astray by avarice and cupidity! You have left your friends and acquaintances, your relatives and your parents, your home and your fatherland, your language and your customs, your faith and your religion—only to sell your wares in the wild places of America, in isolated farmhouses and tiny hamlets. . . .

ONLY RARELY DO you succeed, and then only in the smallest way. Is this fate worth the losses you have suffered, the dangers you have met

Caricature of a Jewish Peddler from Hutchings' California Holiday Pictorial, Christmas, *1857 and* New Year, *1858.*
Courtesy of the California History Room, California State Library, Sacramento, California.

on land and sea? Is this an equal exchange for the parents and kinsmen you have given up? Is this the celebrated freedom of America's soil? Is it liberty of thought and action, when, in order to do business in a single state, one has to buy a license for a hundred dollars? When one must profane the holy Sabbath, observing Sunday instead? In such matters are life and thought more or less confined than in the fatherland? True, one does [not] hear the name "Jew," but only because one does not utter it. Can a man, in fact, be said to be "living" as he plods through the vast, remote country, uncertain even as to which farmer will provide him shelter for the coming night?

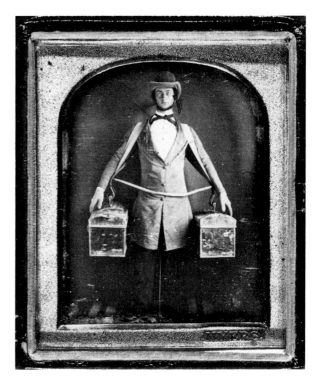

Portrait of a peddler carrying his wares, ca. 1850s.
Library of Congress, Prints and Photographs Division

IN SUCH AN existence the single man gets along far better than the father of a family. Such fools as are married not only suffer themselves, but bring suffering to their women. How must an educated woman feel when, after a brief stay at home, her supporter and shelterer leaves with his pack on his back, not knowing where he will find lodging on the next night or the night after? On how many winter evenings must such a woman sit forlornly with her children at the fireplace, like a widow, wondering where this night finds the head of her family, which homestead in the forest of Ohio will offer him a poor night's shelter? O, that I had never seen this land, but had remained in Germany, apprenticed to a humble country craftsman! Though oppressed by taxes and discriminated against as a Jew, I should still be happier than in the great capital of America, free from royal taxes and every man's religious equal though I am! . . .

TODAY, SUNDAY, OCTOBER 16th, we are here in North Bridgewater, and I am not so downcast as I was two weeks ago. The devil has settled 20,000 shoemakers here, who do not have a cent of money. Suppose, after all, I were a soldier in Bavaria; that would have been a bad lot. I will accept three years in America instead. But I could not stand it any longer.

   As far as the language is concerned, I am getting along pretty well. But I don't like to be alone. The Americans are funny people. Although they sit together by the dozen in taverns, they turn their backs to each other, and no one talks to anybody else. Is this supposed to be the custom of a republic? I don't like it. Is this supposed to be the fashion of the nineteenth century? I don't like it either. . . .

• • •

ON WEDNESDAY, NOVEMBER 9th, Moses and I went to Holden, where we stayed until Sunday with Mr. How. On Monday, we went on, arriving on Tuesday at Rutland. In the morning our packs seemed very heavy, and we had to rest every half-mile. In the afternoon a buggy was offered to us and, thank Heaven, it was within our means. We took off our bundles and anticipated thriving business. Wednesday we proceeded to Barre by horse and carriage, and on Thursday went to Worcerster to meet Juda. Here we stayed together until Friday, November 25th, when we left for West Boylston, staying for the night at Mr. Stuart's, two miles from Sterling. We stayed on Saturday night and over Sunday at the home of Mr. Blaube where I met the most beautiful girl I have ever seen. Her name is Helena Brown and she is from Boston. But despite this girl, I do not yet like America as well as I might wish. But if Heaven causes us to prosper we may yet be entirely satisfied.

Last Thursday was Thanksgiving Day, a general holiday, fixed by the governor for the inhabitants of Massachusetts. Yet it seems to be merely a formal observance, coldly carried through with nothing genuine about it. To the American one day is like another, and even Sunday, their only holiday, is a mere form. They often go to church here, but only to show the neighbor's wife a new veil or dress.

Winter has come. . . . We were at Sterling and Leominster on Monday, November 28th, and we went from there to Lunenburg.

Not far from here we were forced to stop on Wednesday because of the heavy snow. We sought to spend the night with a cooper, a Mr. Spaulding, but his wife did not wish to take us in. She was afraid of strangers, she might not sleep well; we should go our way. And outside there raged the worst blizzard I have ever seen. O God, I thought, is this the land of liberty and hospitality and tolerance? Why have I been led here? After we had talked to this woman for half an hour, after repeatedly pointing out that to turn us forth into the blizzard would be sinful, we were allowed to stay. She became friendlier, indeed, after a few hours, and at night she even joined us in singing. But how often I remembered during that evening how my poor mother treated strangers at all times. Every poor man, every traveler who entered the house, was welcomed hospitably and given the best at our table. Her motto, even for strangers, was, "Who throws stones at me shall be, in turn, pelted by me with bread." Now her own children beg for shelter in a foreign land.

Abraham Kohn, "A Jewish Peddler's Diary" (translated from the German by Abram Vossen Goodman), *American Jewish Archives* 3 (1951), pp. 96, 98, 100, 102. Printed with permission of David Schulhoff.

9

WOMEN'S ROLE IN JEWISH EDUCATION

• REBECCA GRATZ •

BORN IN 1781 to a wealthy merchant family, Rebecca Gratz was one of the most prominent members of the Philadelphia community. Raised in a family with strong commitments to Jewish life and community, Gratz, like other elite Jews of the period, also interacted regularly with non-Jewish members of Philadelphia society.

Rebecca Gratz never married and devoted her life to educational and charitable pursuits. She participated in the social and benevolent activities undertaken by the city's women's organizations and brought the same passion to work within the Jewish community. In 1819, she helped to establish the Female Hebrew Benevolent Society, an organization that aided the Jewish poor in Philadelphia. In later years, Gratz became especially concerned about the state of Jewish education and initiated the creation of a Sunday school for Jewish children modeled on the Christian Sunday schools that flourished throughout the United States. She worried about the potential for young Jews to be swayed by Christian missionaries, and also wanted future generations of American Jews to gain a solid understanding of their own tradition.

In the passage below, Gratz urges members of the Female Hebrew Benevolent Society to support a Jewish Sunday School and refers to a teacher in the city willing to collaborate in the effort. This was certainly Isaac Leeser, the *hazan* (cantor) at Congregation Mikveh Israel who created many of the materials used in the school. In 1838, the Hebrew Sunday School opened its doors, with Gratz as superintendent.

In later years, she worked with Jewish women in other cities, advising them how to organize Jewish schools of their own. Rebecca Gratz's pioneering efforts set the stage for Jewish women's primary role in educating Jewish children. In fact, by the late nineteenth century, most American Jewish children who received formal religious training did so in Sunday schools run by female teachers.

⁓

Ladies,

The season has again arrived when we are assembled to renew our efforts for the relief of those who need aid from their fellow sojourners in this world of many wants and many sufferings—and while we feebly put forth a diminished strength to relieve the cravings of nature we would suggest the wish that our abilities might be directed to *that most pressing need*—the mental impoverishment of those who are rising to take their places among the thousands of Israel scattered throughout the families of the earth. In a little while the remnant of those who first plead for the female poor of this congregation will have passed away and perhaps the sweetest memorial raised to their names will be the record that they laid the corner stone to this institution—It is not too much to hope—too much to expect from the daughters of a noble race that they will be foremost in the work of Charity—provided their young hearts are impressed with its sacred duties. Let us then plead unweariedly for the means of "training them in the way they should go"—we have now a Teacher desirous of opening his store of useful knowledge for the improvement of a rising generation—his opportunities for study in the original language of scripture gives him advantages few here possess—and there unto many of the difficulties complained of among us may be attributed.

Rebecca Gratz (1781–1869) spearheaded the founding of the first independent Jewish women's charitable society and the Hebrew Sunday School in Philadelphia.

American Jewish Historical Society, Newton Centre, Massachusetts and New York, New York

The want of education shuts the door of advancement in private or public stations—which an Israelite might obtain in this country, and the consummation of our highest obligation may even be the wiping off of that stigma which rebellion and disobedience have unleashed upon the nation—may be accomplished when enlightened Jews mingle with the inhabitants of the land respecting their own laws and practicing the virtues required of the chosen people of God. Such as must prepare the way for that "prophet like unto Moses" unto whom the gathering of the people shall be. We need look for no greater miracle than the changed heart that an enlightened faith—piety, self-respect, and charity will engender to make our wilderness bloom—and a light shine on the mountains of ruin—but this is far in advance of our present purpose. The grain must be sown before the harvest can be reaped and if we are only employed in the humble occupation of preparing the soil for future seasons of prosperity—our labor will not be lost to that All-seeing Eye that searches out the smallest grain of good and quickeneth it to an allotted end. Let us then still strive to assist and reform, give freely of our means—and ask a blessing on the mite bestowed. The treasurer's account will inform you of the amount of funds and their expenditure and for the information of those who aid us from other cities we note that there is but one rule of distribution—for the stranger and the wayfarer—and those born at home. Therefore we invite—we solicit every female of the congregation to take an interest in this society—the smallest aid will be gratefully received whether in money or in moneys worth that can be converted into use for the poor and of those who have nothing else to give—we ask good will, good wishes, and good words to cheer and cherish the spirit of charity in which the Female Hebrew Benevolent Society greets and claims kindred with every daughter of Israel.

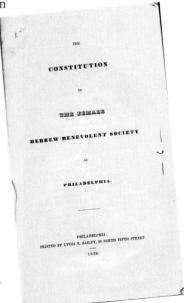

Constitution of Philadelphia's Female Hebrew Benevolent Society.

American Jewish Historical Society, Newton Centre, Massachusetts and New York, New York

Rebecca Gratz, Female Hebrew Benevolent Society Annual Report, 1835, American Philosophical Society, Philadelphia, Pennsylvania, P, Box 17. Printed with permission of the American Philosophical Society.

Isaac Leeser (1806–1868), the hazan of Philadelphia's Congregation Mikveh Israel, designed this catechism as a text for use in Rebecca Gratz's Sunday school.

CATECHISM FOR JEWISH CHILDREN (1839)

CHAPTER II
The Mosaic Religion in Particular

1. **What religion do you profess?**

   I believe in the Mosaic Religion, which was revealed by the Lord; and I esteem the same as the true, pure, and unmixed word of God.

2. **Are you firmly convinced of the truth of this belief?**

   I am firmly and completely convinced of the truth thereof, for the following reason: because the Mosaic Religion is based upon that celebrated revelation which God imparted in the immediate presence of a whole people, amidst extraordinary signs and wonders.

3. **What is the peculiar distinguishing feature of the Mosaic Religion?**

   It teaches that there is but one God, and that He is incorporeal and indivisible; that is to say, that there exists no other being who has power to create any thing, or to destroy the least of those things which God has made. That this God does not possess a material figure like all those things which we can perceive by our senses, which are called corporeal or bodily substances; and that lastly, He cannot by any means be divided into different parts, being always the same, and not liable to change.

4. **Whence is the name "Mosaic Religion" derived?**

   From moses, the son of Amram, of the tribe of Levi, through whom God communicated his law to the people of Israel. So also teaches the Bible:

"Remember ye the law of Moses my servant, to whom I commanded on Horeb statutes and judgments for all Israel." Malachi iii. 22.

5. Was not the Deity known and worshipped already before Moses?

Yes; for the patriarchs, and even before them Enoch and Noah, acknowledged the Lord God, and worshipped Him.

"Enoch walked with God, and was no more here; for God had taken him away. Genesis v.24.

"Noah was a righteous, upright man in his generation: Noah walked with God." Ibid. vi.9.

6. Who were the Patriarchs?

The original fathers of the Israelitish people, now called the Jews: these were Abraham, Isaac, and Jacob or Israel.

"And He (God) spoke, I am the God of thy fathers, the God of Abraham, the God of Isaac, and the God of Jacob." Exodus iii. 6.

CATECHISM

FOR

YOUNGER CHILDREN.

DESIGNED AS A

FAMILIAR EXPOSITION

OF THE

JEWISH RELIGION.

" Which ye shall command your children, to observe to do all the words of this law."
DEUT. XXXII. 46.

BY ISAAC LEESER.

PHILADELPHIA:
PRINTED FOR THE AUTHOR, BY ADAM WALDIE.
5599.
1839

Isaac Leeser's catechism for children became a tool to provide Jewish children with basic knowledge of Judaism at a time when formal Jewish education was in its infancy in the United States. Isaac Leeser, Catechism for Younger Children *Philadelphia, 1839.*

Courtesy of the Center for Advanced Judaic Studies Library, University of Pennsylvania

Isaac Leeser, *Catechism for Jewish Children: Designed as a Religious Manual for House and School* 4th edition (Philadelphia: stereotyped for the author by L. Johnson & Co., 5629 [1869]), pp. 6–7.

~~ 10 ~~

THE ARCHITECT OF
REFORM JUDAISM

• I S A A C   M A Y E R   W I S E •

ISAAC MAYER Wise arrived in the United States from Bavaria in 1846. He first took a pulpit in Albany, New York, where he instituted some minor changes in ritual and established a mixed synagogue choir. After disputes with more traditional members of the community, Wise moved to Cincinnati's Congregation Bene Jeshurun, often called the Plum Street Temple, and transformed the city into the center of the Reform movement in the nineteenth century.

Not a rigorous ideologue, Wise advocated a moderate version of Reform Judaism and aimed to create a unified American Jewish community. In 1857, he published *Minhag Amerika*, a prayer book designed to create a common liturgy for Jews across the country. In order to broadcast his vision for American Judaism, Wise edited two Jewish weekly newspapers—the *Israelite* in English and *Die Deborah* in German. He involved himself in every major Jewish issue of his time, traveling the country and spreading his message of a Judaism suited to the American environment. In 1873, Wise spearheaded the creation of the Union of American Hebrew Congregations, an umbrella organization of American synagogues. Two years later, he served as president of the newly created Hebrew Union College, the first successful institution to train American rabbis.

Wise believed passionately that Judaism could flourish in America's liberal society. Although his vision of bringing together all American Jews in a single unified movement did not ultimately succeed, given the diversity of beliefs and practices that took hold in later generations, his tireless efforts created the foundations for Reform Judaism in the United States. In this excerpt from his memoirs, Wise recounts his determination to Americanize the practice of Judaism.

THE CENTURY-LONG oppression has demoralized the German and Polish Jew, and robbed him of his self-respect. He has no self-respect, no pride left. The hep! hep! times[1] still weigh him down; he bows and scrapes, he crawls and cringes. The Jew respects not the fellowman in another Jew, because he lacks the consciousness of manhood in himself. He parodies and imitates, because he has lost himself. After diagnosing the evil, I set myself to seeking a remedy.

The Jew must be Americanized, I said to myself, for every German book, every German word reminds him of the old disgrace. If he continues under German influences as they are now in this country, he must become either a bigot or an atheist, a satellite or a tyrant. He will never be aroused to self-consciousness or to independent thought. The Jew must become an American, in order to gain the proud self-consciousness of the free-born man. From that hour I began to Americanize with

Isaac Mayer Wise (1819–1900) decisively shaped the development of Reform Judaism in America, building its key institutions, and publishing a widely used prayer book as well as two national newspapers.

[1] A pejorative rallying cry against Jews, used commonly in Germany. The anti-Jewish riots that broke out in Germany in the summer of 1819 were known as the Hep! Hep! Riots.

all my might, and was as enthusiastic for this as I was for reform. Since then, as a matter of course, the German element here, as well as in Germany, has completely changed, although Judeophobia and uncouthness have survived in many; but at that time it appeared to me that there was but one remedy that would prove effective for my co-religionists, and that was to Americanize them thoroughly. We must be not only American citizens, but become Americans through and through outside of the synagogue. This was my cry then and many years thereafter. This, too, increased the hatred of my opponents considerably.

"But, if I succeed in Americanizing my co-religionists, will not Judaism disappear in Americanism," I asked myself, "even as the native Jewish element has approached the different sects so closely in various localities? This must be counteracted by a better knowledge of Jewish history and Jewish sources." My conviction was that a Jewish patriotism, a pride in being a Jew, must be aroused; for this it was that the Jew had lost in the ages of oppression.

The all-important question now forced itself—how? The means to Americanize were easy to find and apply; the means to Judaize were, however, not so apparent: I could not preach my ideas to the whole world, nor could I create an Americanizing-Judaizing literature singlehanded. After lengthy reflection I arrived at the following conclusions:

1. To emphasize strongly the historical mission of Israel in all my speeches and writings, in order to arouse a consecrated self-consciousness.

2. To bring before the public the bright side of the Jewish character, and to leave it to the enemy to exploit our faults; thus to arouse a feeling of self-respect.

3. To popularize by spoken and written words as much Jewish learning as I might possess, in order to inculcate in others respect for Jewish literature.

4. To familiarize the reading public with the brilliant periods of Jewish history in fictional form, in order to appeal by this means to the growing youth so as to awaken in them Jewish patriotism, for there could be no doubt that they would Americanize themselves.

After I had reached the determination how to go to work, I proceeded to do so at once. I had resolved firmly to pay no attention to what my opponents said or wrote. My resolution was to succeed or succumb. I determined that I must bring about a radical reform of character among the public, if there was to be any improvement.

Isaac M. Wise, *Reminiscences*, translated and edited by David Philipson (Cincinnati: Leo Wise and Company, 1901), pp. 331–333.

11

A JEWISH COLONEL
IN THE CIVIL WAR

• MARCUS SPIEGEL •

JUST OVER a decade after arriving in the United States, Marcus Speigel was commanding a Union regiment in the Civil War. Born in a German village in 1829, Spiegel left for America in 1849. Beginning as a peddler, he eventually opened a small store in Ohio. Spiegel volunteered for duty in the Union army in 1861. His distinguished service allowed him to rise from the rank of first lieutenant to the rank of lieutenant colonel, commanding the 120th Ohio Volunteer Infantry within a year.

During his years in the military, Spiegel wrote regularly to his wife Caroline. Caroline was born a Quaker and the couple wed in a civil ceremony in 1853, but Caroline immediately began studying Judaism after their marriage and chose to convert. The family remained deeply committed to Jewish life. His letters reveal profound love for and devotion to his wife and children and his commitment to fight for the Union cause. Colonel Spiegel died in combat in 1864 when the transport *City Belle* was ambushed on the Red River, but his correspondence with his wife has survived. In this letter, Spiegel urges Caroline to support his decision to serve in the military and expresses a sense of duty to his adopted country. Marcus Spiegel's brother Joseph, mentioned in this letter, served as the sutler in the same military company and the two brothers often spoke of opening a store together after the war. Joseph Spiegel, who was captured in the ambush, went on to establish a dry goods store in Chicago and later built the business into the highly successful Spiegel Catalogue Company.

⟿

Camp near Hampton Va
Aug. 29, 1862

My dear beloved and good wife!

To day we received the first mail for quite a while and you may be sure it brought me "bliss" when I tell you two sweet letters from you, one from New York and three from my boys who have gone to the different Hospitals, among which is one from Henry Biegle from New York who says he is getting along finely. Your good letters seem to me attempting to conceal a great deal of trouble, anxiety, and care which you apparently have and are trying to conceal. This must not be, my good Wife; you must not put yourself to any unnecessary trouble or care. You speak of a very hard letter you wrote me on a certain Sunday which I have not yet received, nor does it make any difference; I shall not think hard of you for it. I think it would have been worth $500 at least had I left Brother Joseph in New York. Yet I do not feel sorry for it or anything I [have] done as I have never yet done anything dishonorable and, as for many mistakes in my former life, I mean to offer amends in the future if God will only spare my life; only try and feel easy and happy. If you want me to get along well you must be cheerful; if you want me to be a good Soldier you must rejoice in my little successes as they come; if you want me to take care of myself you must show me in your letters that you are as happy and lively as you well can be; then and then only am I myself. Such knowledge will stimulate me to be friendly and condescending to my inferiors, courteous and polite to my superiors, just, equitable and pleasant to all and mindful to duty, and I am sure success will crown my efforts; honor and glory for us and our beloved offspring will await us. I am now fixed in this institution in a fair way and in my estimation no man can ever be respected or respect himself when his country needs the services of almost every able bodied man she has. I do not see how I can honorably get out of it now, when in fact everything is going as well as I could possibly wish, when everybody loves, honors and respects me. Yet I do intend to come home this Fall in November on a visit and if anything should transpire so as to be transferred or promoted I may be home sooner. Be easy, be happy, be my own dear Wife, loved and worshiped by your true husband who is making a reputation for you, the children and himself, that we may all feel proud of, while in the discharge of the noblest of callings, "serving his Country. " . . .

Ever your true and loving husband
Marcus

Colonel Marcus M. Spiegel in uniform.

Whitestone Photo. The Jacob Rader Marcus Center of the American Jewish Archives

Advertisement for Spiegel, May, Stern Company, Chicago, Illinois
After a 1903 merger with another company, Joseph Spiegel's home furnishings store became Spiegel, May, Stern and Co. It later developed into a highly successful mail-order business.

Frank L. Byrne and Jean Powers Soman, eds. *Your True Marcus: The Civil War Letters of a Jewish Colonel* (Kent, Ohio: Kent State University Press, 1985), pp. 158–159, 160. Copyright 1994 by Jean Powers Soman a/k/a Jean P. Soman. *Your True Marcus: The Civil War Letters of a Jewish Colonel* was reprinted as: Jean Powers Soman and Frank L. Byrne, eds., *A Jewish Colonel in the Civil War: Marcus M. Spiegel of the Ohio Volunteers* (Lincoln, Nebraska & London, England: University of Nebraska Press, 1995).

❧ 12 ☙

A UNION SOLDIER'S PASSOVER SEDER

• J. A. JOEL •

THE CIVIL War divided the allegiances of American Jews, as Jewish soldiers wore the uniforms of both the blue and the gray. Since the majority of Jews lived in the North and West when war broke out, most of the approximately 8,000–10,000 Jewish soldiers fought for the Union. While serving in the army, Jews sometimes experienced incidents of anti-Semitism, but they also expressed strong allegiance to their respective causes and often found significant support from fellow soldiers.

A law passed in 1862 removed the requirement for military chaplains to be members of Christian denominations and stipulated only that they should represent "some religious denomination," allowing Jewish chaplains to serve in the military for the first time. Even so, Jewish observance could be a challenge during wartime. Accounts from soldiers indicate that many Jews remained unconcerned with Jewish practice, as they had been at home, but others attempted to maintain some Jewish rituals. Soldiers were far more likely to make the effort to observe the major Jewish holidays, such as Rosh Hashanah, Yom Kippur, and Passover.

After the war concluded, one Jewish soldier offered this account of how the Jewish soldiers of his regiment attempted to conduct a Passover seder while stationed in West Virginia. Although they could not secure all of the items required for the traditional ritual meal, the soldiers improvised and managed to carry out a meaningful and enjoyable Passover seder.

⁓

THE APPROACHING FEAST of Passover reminds me of an incident which transpired in 1862, and which as an index of the times, no doubt, will prove interesting to a number of your readers. In the commencement of the war of 1861, I enlisted from Cleveland, Ohio, in the Union cause, to sustain intact the Government of the United States, and became attached to the 23rd Regiment, one of the first sent from the "Buckeye State." Our destination was West Virginia,—a portion of the wildest and most mountainous region of that State, well adapted for the guerrillas who infested that part, and caused such trouble to our pickets all through the war. After an arduous march of several hundred miles through Clarksburgh, Weston, Sommerville, and several other places of less note, which have become famous during the war, we encountered on the 10th of September, 1861, at Carnifax Ferry, the forces under the rebel Gen. Floyd. After this, we were ordered to take up our position at the foot of Sewell Mountain, and we remained there until we marched to the village of Fayette, to take it, and to establish there our Winter-quarters, having again routed Gen. Floyd and his forces. While lying there, our camp duties

Jews found themselves on both sides of the Civil War. Here, Jewish Union soldiers are pictured visiting their Southern relatives in Georgia, ca. 1865.
Cuba Archives of The Breman Museum

Confederate Soldier Leon Fischel.
Courtesy of the
Goldring/Woldenberg Institute of
Southern Jewish Life

were not of an arduous character, and being apprised of the approaching Feast of Passover, twenty of my comrades and co-religionists belonging to the Regiment, united in a request to our commanding officer for relief from duty, in order that we might keep the holydays, which he readily acceded to. The first point was gained, and, as the Paymaster had lately visited the Regiment, he had left us plenty of greenbacks. Our next business was to find some suitable person to proceed to Cincinnati, Ohio, to buy *Matzos.* Our sutler being a co-religionist and going home to that city, readily undertook to send them. We were anxiously awaiting to receive our *Matzos,* and about the middle of the morning of the eve of Passover a supply train arrived in camp, and to our delight seven barrels of *Matzos.* On opening them, we were surprised and pleased to find that our thoughtful sutler had enclosed two *Hagedahs* and prayer-books. We were now able to keep the *seder* nights, if we could only obtain the other requisites for that occasion. We held a consultation and decided to send parties to forage in the country while a party stayed to build a log hut for the services. About the middle of the afternoon the foragers arrived, having been quite successful. We obtained two kegs of cider, a lamb, several chickens and some eggs. Horse radish or parsley we could not obtain, but in lieu we found a weed, whose bitterness, I apprehend, exceeded anything our forefathers "enjoyed." We were still in a great quandary; we were like the man who drew the elephant in the lottery. We had the lamb, but did not know what part was to represent it at the table; but Yankee ingenuity prevailed, and it was decided to cook the whole and put it on the table, then we could dine off it, and be sure we had the right part. The necessaries for the *choroutzes* we could not obtain, so we got a brick which, rather hard to digest, reminded us, by looking at it, for what purpose it was intended.

At dark we had all prepared, and were ready to commence the service. There being no *hazan* present, I was selected to read the services, which I commenced by asking the blessing of the Almighty on the food before us, and to preserve our lives from danger. The ceremonies were passing off very nicely, until we arrived at the part where the bitter herb was to be taken. We all had a large portion of the herb ready to eat at the moment I said the blessing; each eat his portion, when horrors! what a scene ensued in our little congregation, it is impossible for my pen to describe. The herb was very bitter and very fiery like Cayenne pepper, and excited our thirst to such a degree, that we forgot the law authorizing us to drink only four cups, and the consequence was we drank up all the cider. Those that drank the more freely became excited, and one thought he was Moses, another Aaron, and one had the audacity to call himself a Pharaoh. The consequence was a skirmish, with nobody hurt, only Moses, Aaron and Pharaoh, had to be carried to the camp, and there left in the arms of Morpheus. This slight incident did not take away our appetite, and, after doing justice to our lamb, chickens and eggs, we resumed the second portion of the service without anything occurring worthy of note.

There, in the wild woods of West Virginia, away from home and friends, we consecrated and offered up to the ever-loving God of Israel our prayers and sacrifice. I doubt whether the spirits of our forefathers, had they been looking down on us, standing there with our arms by our side ready for an attack, faithful to our God and our cause, would have imagined themselves amongst mortals, enacting this commemoration of the scene that transpired in Egypt.

Since then a number of my comrades have fallen in battle defending the flag, they have volunteered to protect with their lives. I have myself received a number of wounds all but mortal, but there is no occasion in my life that gives me more pleasure and satisfaction than when I remember the celebration of Passover of 1862.

The Jewish Messenger, March 30, 1866, p. 2.

RESPONSE TO GENERAL GRANT'S ORDER NO. 11

· ISAAC LEESER ·

IN 1862, in the middle of the Civil War, General Ulysses S. Grant issued Order No. 11, a decree that officially expelled all Jews from the area of his military command, which included portions of Mississippi, Kentucky, and Tennessee. He banished Jews "as a class," charging them with illicit trade practices. After meeting with a delegation of Jews protesting the order, President Abraham Lincoln rescinded it, but the affair left lingering outrage within the Jewish community.

Among those protesting most vigorously was Isaac Leeser, the longtime *hazan* and leader of Philadelphia's Mikveh Israel Congregation. Leeser arrived in the United States from Westphalia in 1824 and became one of the nation's foremost Jewish spokesmen and religious leaders. A traditionalist who modified some religious practices for the American environment, Leeser regularly disagreed with the reform efforts of his contemporary Isaac Mayer Wise. He produced a remarkable number of published works, including some of America's first Jewish prayer books and textbooks as well as the first Jewish translation of the Bible into English. Leeser's list of publications also included the monthly journal the *Occident*, which disseminated his ideas to a national Jewish audience.

In the *Occident*, Isaac Leeser published for his national readership the text of a letter he sent to Philadelphia's local newspaper, the *Public Ledger,* in the wake of Grant's Order No. 11. Written after Lincoln overturned the order, Leeser's letter condemns the United States Congress, particularly the Republican leaders who blocked a Democratic motion to censure Grant and declare the order tyrannical and cruel.

Are Israelites Slaves?

Messrs. Editors:—Your New York correspondent of this morning states that the Jews of that city are indignant at the strange proceedings in the House of Representatives yesterday in laying Mr. Pendleton's[1] resolution condemnatory of General Grant's outrage against Israelites on the table. It is no wonder that such a transaction should make the blood boil in the veins of the most phlegmatic. Has it come to this, that a *crime* like that of the just named commander, vested with the limited authority conferred on him by the President, who can remove him at pleasure shall be passed by in silence, while those whom he has aggrieved have no chance of redress, not even

Portrait of Isaac Leeser (1806–1868), the foremost traditionalist Jewish leader of the nineteenth century.
Courtesy of the Center for Advanced Judaic Studies Library, University of Pennsylvania

[1] In this letter, Lesser refers to Democratic Senator Powell of Kentucky and Democratic Congressman Pendleton from Ohio who advocated the motion to censure General Grant for the order.

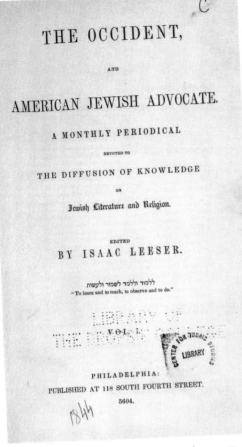

First issue of the monthly Jewish periodical The Occident, *1844.*

that of making themselves heard through the mouth of such congressmen as are willing to take their part?

It would be unnatural if Israelites should rest quiet under such infliction, which is analogous to the expulsions and persecutions they have had had to endure under princes and ecclesiastics elsewhere. But is it not strange, marvelous, that congressmen, who have sworn to support the constitution, do not see that no greater violation of its provisions was ever manifested than in the procedure of General Grant? Is personal liberty merely to be held at the pleasure of a military official? Or, at best, under the kind revocation of the order of banishment by the President, to whom free citizens of the republic have appealed not to drive them from their homes?

Will not the enlightened and the brave patriots and friends of liberty, of all creeds, unite with us Israelites to put down incipient tyranny, which sooner or later will seek, unless checked, a wider field than is afforded by the small numbers of our race in the Union? Think, Messrs. Editors, what an outcry would have been raised had a similar measure been pursued toward any Christian denomination; and still, "is Israel a slave or a bondman born in the house" of a master? All thanks to Messrs. Powell and Pendleton!—and we will not honor them the less that their voice of inquiry was stifled by the louder vociferations of an unthinking majority.

The Occident (February, 1863), pp. 490–491.

~ 14 ~

PIONEER OF THE AMERICAN WEST

• ANNA FREUDENTHAL SOLOMON •

ANNA FREUDENTHAL Solomon, born and married in Poland, migrated to the United States with her husband Isidor and settled first in Pennsylvania. In 1876, after some unsuccessful business ventures in the East, the couple, together with their three children, decided to take a chance on the opportunities of America's expanding western frontier. After a long journey, the family arrived in Las Cruces, New Mexico, where Anna's brothers had already settled and established merchandising businessess. From there, Anna and Isidor ventured out to the remote eastern corner of the Arizona territory known then as Pueblo Viejo to build a business of their own.

The Solomons began by delivering charcoal to a mining company, then created a local store and later a small hotel in the area. Like many women, Anna shared responsibility for running the family business while she raised her children. The Solomon family became pioneers of the fledgling community in the desert, a town that was nothing but mud when they arrived. By 1879, the small community merited a post office, housed in the family store, and the city's name officially became Solomonville, reflecting the couple's founding role in building the community. Four years later, the town became a county seat, greatly boosting business and population, and the Solomons expanded their businesses to supplying credit to local farmers and ranchers as well as selling property in the area. In her memoirs, Anna Solomon recalls her journey from Poland to the American West and her family's early days of pioneering.

WHEN ABOUT TWO years old my parents told me that I was in a trance about a half an hour. I woke up out of this for a life full of experience. My dear parents had just lost a child, a brother of mine who died from the cholera. I recovered from the cholera and grew very strong and hardy. My parents were not in very good circumstances, but worked themselves up, got to do well, did a very good business in a very small Polish town adjoining the Russian border. My parents were liked and respected by everybody. Everybody came to my father for advice. But things had to take a big change for us. My poor mother was a great deal sick. There was no school in the town where we lived. . . . [M]y dear mother was anxious to move to a city where we would have the opportunity of an education. My father finally made up his mind to sell out his business, which he did, to a cousin of mine, Solomon Lesinsky.

We moved to Krushwitz where my father rented a house and started a new business. This was a very sad move for us. Everything went wrong. My parents lost everything they possessed in one year. We left Krushwitz for a very small town, with a very few goods, then I was already nine years old. In one year I had learned how to read and write in Krushwitz. I then already helped my parents in the store, but things did not change. It came from bad to worse. Within one year again, we moved to another place, thinking times would change with us, but they did not. Meantime we were a family of seven children. . . .

THERE WAS SOME money sent us from America from my uncles and cousins, and also a request that my father should go to New Mexico, but the idea for a man who has a wife and seven small children to leave them to themselves was dreadful. My poor mother felt very bad about it, but I was at that time fourteen years old. I encouraged father to go. I was too young to realize the danger of being exposed to a lot of German Soldiers and German and Russian peasants, also the Polish smugglers, who smuggled foods from Germany to Russia. We had at that time a little grocery store, also a boarding house. My dear father finally left for New Mexico. Oh, how blessed was the hour when we received our first letter telling us of his safe arrival in New York, then in New Mexico.

My father was successful in business. Of course, he had to undergo a great many privations. New Mexico was a very wild country to live in in those days, especially during the [Indian] war, in the year 1868. Meantime, my dear mother and myself were struggling along taking care of our little business and the smaller children. . . .

Anna Solomon, undated.
Courtesy of Ann Ramenofsky

WE CONTINUED OUR dry goods business but since we had to borrow money and pay big interest on it, it was a hard struggle to keep it up. My brother Phoebus who at thirteen years of age came to New York, and whom my Uncle Julius Freudenthal sent to school, and after a year or so sent to New Mexico, worked for the firm of Freudenthal and Lesinsky's, and earned the first year by very hard work and privation, $700.00, and sent same home to our parents. After this our live [*sic*] was somewhat happier as my brother Phoebus sent all his earnings home so that enabled us to live comfortable.

My second brother Morris went to New Mexico while my youngest brother Wolff studied medicine. My two sisters, Henriette and Frieda, went to school. My husband, Isidor Solomon, came on a visit to his home, his parents living in Krushwitz. Our parents on both sides were old friends. We got acquainted and were married two months after our engagement. My brother Phoebus sent to my parents $2,000.00. They gave my husband $1,000.00 and the other was used up for wedding and trousseau. The first time I saw my father cry was when I was getting ready to leave home.

The wedding was celebrated in a Park Hotel. It was beautiful. My dear mother looked so happy. I never will forget the happy smile on her dear face, but the parting was very sad. When she told me good bye I knew that I will never see her again although my husband promised to send me home after six years, but circumstances with us at the period of six years, that it was impossible for me to go to Europe. . . .

MY SICK BROTHER died after I was married. My eldest sister Henriette was married five years after me. My husband was established in business in Towanda. We

lived in Towanda four years, where my three oldest children were born. My eldest son, Charles was born in Towanda, my eldest daughter Eva in Mnechung. We lived in Mnechung one year, then we returned to Towanda where my second daughter Rose was born. The four years I lived in Towanda I was the most homesick person on earth. It was lucky I had my children to take my time up. In the year of '76, we got married in '72, in the year of '76 business was getting very dull and my husband sold his business to his partner, that is, his part. My father wrote to my husband not to open a business in the east, but go to New Mexico. We decided to do so. . . .

WE SOLD EVERYTHING we possessed except [our] three children, Charles, who was three years old; Eva was two years, and my youngest daughter Rose three months old, and started on our journey for New Mexico. We had a very hard trip even on the railroad, traveling with those three babies was bad enough, but when we reached La Junta, the end of the railroad in those days, and had to travel by stage, packed in like sardines, traveling day and night for six dayes [*sic*] only stopped to change horses and get something to eat, like chili con carne and frijoles. I forgot, we stopped over in Santa Fe three days, then we started for Las Cruces, New Mexico, where we had our two brothers, Phoebus and Morris, working. At that time my Uncle Julius Freudenthal and Lesinskys, our cousins. When we got there I was tired out to death. My brother and the Lesinskys were very nice to us. I lived in the house of Charles Lesinsky for two weeks, then we went looking for a house. We found one, the best one in town, but I could not help having tears come into my eyes when I saw the mud floors and mud walls, but after a few days I had the house looking very nice and comfortable. . . .

I LIVED AT Las Cruces with the children four months while my husband was looking around for some business location. He finally found a place, and this is the place where we are living now for thirty years. It was very hard for us to go to a country and a place as this was in those days. There was only four Mexican shanties in the whole place, besides our own shanty which my husband rented for $25.00 per month. After we lived here a short time we bought the place and adjoining ranch, and we had the place laid out in lots several years after that, and had the court house build on several of the lots.

I am far ahead of my story. When we were going to leave Las Cruces we bought a two-seated wagon called a buckboard, and a pair of horses. Into this we put a tent, some bedding, our cooking utensils, our provisions, our clothes and our children, and ourselves. We also brought a Mexican clerk along, but he came horseback. It took us several days and nights to get here, but, oh, how often I was frightened thinking that I saw Indians. I did not expect to get here alive with our children. Just before we reached this place we heard a dreadful noise that Indians make when they are on the warpath. It was a beautiful moonlit night. I remembered as if it was last night. When we were almost home the Mexican told us it was a Coyote, as the Indians make the same peculiar noise when on the warpath, as a coyote have.

We arrived here about 12 o'clock at night in August. We slept on the mud floor. [Next] morning my husband [woke] me up to show me some Indians that were here on passes from San Carlos Reservation. I never had seen an Indian before. . . .

AFTER LIVING THERE about three months our ox wagons, with goods from Las Cruces, arrived. What a happy day that was, as until then we had no bed to sleep in, no stove to cook on, no table to eat off, no flour to bake bread. I baked bread out of corn meal for three months, in a dutch oven, cooked our meals outdoors like campers do, but I did not mind all that as I could sell goods and the future commenced to look brighter. Still we had some very dark and sad times. I could not get anyone to help me with my three babies. The worst of all was the washing. I was never used to doing washing. After I had done my second one I took sick with chills and fever. My baby, Rose also took sick. My husband sent for the doctor to Fort Grant, but the Mexican came back after three days and said he could not get the doctor to come. Meantime I commenced to feel a little better and felt like eating something, so we bought a chicken and a Mexican woman cooked it for me, but when I found out what she left in it, I could not eat it.

Chills and fever were dreadful in our place. There were pools of green water standing all over the place. The new land started to be worked, that all helped the sick along. My baby was sick and I had chills and fever for two years, but that did not hinder us from doing a good deal of business. We had a contract to deliver charcoal to the Clifton Mining Company, who belonged then to my uncle J. Freudenthal and my cousins, Charles and Henry Lesinsky. This started our business, and also started the valley. [We] employed a great many people cutting the mesquite wood, making charcoal, and shipping some to Clifton by ox teams. This took a great deal of hard work, to oversee and manage it. We could not get any decent person or persons to help us. My husband attended the outdoors work while I attended the store and the housework. We also started building; at first a bedroom, then a store. I felt like the Queen of England when that store was finished. We kept on building right around the old home. We kept a carpenter building for eight years. . . .

THIS IS THE New Year. The last year has been an exciting year for us. It was also a new starting point in our lives. Harry had got hurt and my husband had to take charge of his business. Harry finally went to New York, stayed with my brother Wolff for a while and then went to work. The town where Harry's store was burned down and we lost a good deal. The children then decided that we should live in California. Here I am living at present.

Anna Solomon, Autobiography, Typescript, 1904–1913, American Jewish Archives, Cincinnati, Ohio. pp. 2, 2–3, 4, 5–6, 6–7, 11. Printed with permission of The Jacob Rader Marcus Center of the American Jewish Archives.

FROM IMMIGRANT TO DEPARTMENT STORE OWNER

• ISIDOR STRAUS •

BORN IN 1845 in the Bavarian town of Otterberg, Isidor Straus came to the United States in 1854. Along with his mother and three siblings, Isidor joined his father Lazarus Straus, who had immigrated some years earlier and started out as a peddler before establishing a small business in Talbotton, Georgia. Following the Civil War, the family relocated to New York, where Lazarus Straus and his sons established a merchandising firm. The brothers Nathan and Isidor Straus parlayed that enterprise into a crockery business, selling china and glassware at Macy's Department Store in the 1870s. By 1888, they had become partners in R. H. Macy and Company, finally assuming ownership of the firm in 1894.

Isidor Straus served briefly as a Democrat in the U.S. House of Representatives in the 1890s and later devoted himself to philanthropic activities. He and his wife Ida died tragically, victims of the sinking of the *Titanic* in 1912. In his memoirs,

Isidor Straus recounts his family's journey to America and their early business ventures.

Isidor Straus, co-owner of Macy's Department Store.

American Jewish Historical Society, Newton Centre, Massachusetts and New York, New York

MY FATHER, WHO was active in the revolution of 1848, finding life burdensome after the collapse of the movement, long contemplated emigrating, but his ties were so many that he found it most difficult to tear himself away, and not until the spring of 1852 could he bring himself to take this decisive step. I believe he landed at Philadelphia and there met a number of former acquaintances who had preceded him to this country, some of whom were established in business in different parts of the country. He was advised to go south to make a start in business, and I believe Ogelthorpe, Georgia, proved to be his destination. There he met some acquaintances from the old country through whom he made a connection with two brothers, Kaufman, who were the owners of a peddler's wagon which circulated with an assortment of dry goods, Yankee notions and the like through several adjoining countries. In those comparatively primitive days, when that state was yet sparsely settled and the rural parts, through the existence of slavery segregated on the large plantations a population equal to, and often greater than, the number the nearest villages contained, the itinerant merchant filled a want, and hence his vocation was looked upon with much favor by the people and he was treated by the owners of the plantations, which he usually visited at regular periods, with a spirit of equality that is difficult to appreciate at the present day. . . .

MY MOTHER WITH her children (Isidor, Hermine, Nathan and Oscar) left Otterberg August 24th, 1854, on her journey to join my father. We were accompanied to Havre only by my mother's youngest brother, Jacob (a half-brother). Our grandfather accompanied us from Otterberg—he on horseback and the rest of us, as narrated before, together with a nursemaid, in a carriage, to Kaiserslautern, where we took the railroad train to Ferbach, which at that time was the French frontier town, and there we remained one night. In those days, I assume, this was considered a long enough journey for a mother with little children to take in a single day.

On the following morning we left for Paris, where we remained until August 29th, when we started for Havre, where we took the steamer "St. Louis," on her maiden trip, for New York. We arrived in New York on September 12th. Before the steamer had fastened to the dock my mother recognized my father impatiently pacing up and down, and I clearly recall the lengthened minutes, which seemed like hours, that elapsed between his first recognition and the time when we could be embraced in his arms. . . .

OUR BUSINESS [IN New York] was opened and the first sale recorded on June 1st, 1866. It was an order left with us by one Meyer Becker, who had a successful country store in Indiana (I think the town was Plymouth). He was the son of a man who had been employed in some capacity by my father in Otterberg, and the man himself had enjoyed some sort of kindness at my mother's hands also in the old country. So he prided himself on becoming our first customer, and for this end left his order to be executed as soon as we opened for business. . . .

IT MUST HAVE been about this time [in 1869], that Nathan extended his territory to the western states, or possibly a year previous. We had grown to such proportions as to have engaged an outside salesman. It was in 1871, after the great Chicago conflagration, that Nathan opened a selling office in Chicago and made occasional trips in the contiguous territory. He saw no future in continuing to depend on traveling to develop the business, as most of it would fall away the moment he would stop going after it. The Chicago sample room was continued about a year, but not with encouraging success, and as Nathan was growing tired of traveling, more particularly as he could see no permanent good or promising future in it, he looked around for ways to make good the loss which his ceasing to do so would entail. It was in this search that he made connection with R. H. Macy & Co., which at first consisted only in selling them a few casks of china, but soon resulted in our opening a department devoted to a full line of crockery, china, bric-a-brac and glassware. This occurred in March 1874, in a basement about 25 × 100, but the department developed so rapidly that additional space was soon added, until it developed into one of the most important departments in the house. . . . [W]e became members of the firm of R. H. Macy & Co., on January 1st, 1888.

Sheet music, "The Titanic's Disaster," ("Khorban Titanic"), 1919, commemorating the deaths of Isidor and Ida Straus aboard the Titanic *in 1912.*

From the Archives of the YIVO Institute for Jewish Research

Isidor Straus, Autobiographical Notes, 1911, MS 8850, Jewish Theological Seminary of America, New York, pp. 3, 9–10, 42, 44, 45. Printed with permission of The Library of the Jewish Theological Seminary of America.

SUCCESS AND EXCLUSION

• JOSEPH SELIGMAN •

IN 1837, at the age of eighteen, Joseph Seligman came to the United States from Bavaria. Like many other immigrant Jews of the era, he began as a peddler. As he accumulated some savings, Seligman financed the immigration of his brothers and began a journey that led from peddling to retail to banking. The Seligman brothers established retail stores—first in Pennsylvania, and later extending throughout the South and from New York to California. During the Civil War, the Seligmans expanded their business, aided by a government contract to produce military uniforms. They also transitioned to banking, supporting the Union cause by selling bonds abroad. While achieving exceptional financial success—for Jews or for other Americans of his generation—Joseph Seligman also maintained close relationships with Presidents Lincoln and Grant. Grant offered him the position of Secretary of the Treasury in his administration, a post that Seligman declined.

Because he had attained such prominence, it came as a great shock to the Jewish community when Joseph Seligman and his family were denied accommodations at the Grand Union Hotel in Saratoga, New York, in 1877. Judge Henry Hilton, who managed the hotel for A. T. Stewart Company, a national dry goods firm, had instituted a policy banning all Jews from the establishment. The incident, which demonstrated the persistence of Jewish social exclusion in America, caused a national sensation and resulted in headlines around the country.

After being summarily dismissed from the Grand Union Hotel—where he had previously received accommodations—Joseph Seligman wrote a formal letter of protest to Judge Hilton and instructed his brother to publish it. A copy of Seligman's letter appeared in the *Chicago Daily Tribune* in June of 1877.

Dear Judge:

My family have for many years patronized the Union Hotel at Saratoga, but were informed yesterday by your managers that orders from headquarters are to exclude all Jewish families from a list of guests this season, alleging as the reason that there existed a prejudice among Americans against the people of that persuasion which had injured the Union to that extent at last, that headquarters proposed to "roast them out," namely, tell them all, without exception, that all rooms except the garrett chambers were occupied. Now permit me, dear Judge, in your own interest, and in the interest of Mr. Stewart's valuable estate, the lion's share of which you seem to have acquired, to say you are adding too many serious mistakes which you have committed since you inherited that estate by refusing admittance to the Union Hotel to a large class of people irrespective of their respectability, wealth, and proper bearing, merely to ponder to a vulgar prejudice under the mistaken notion that by so doing you will fill the house with other

Joseph Seligman, an immigrant who began as a peddler and founded one of the country's most successful banking firms.
The Jacob Rader Marcus Center of the American Jewish Archives

Stereoscopic view of the Grand Union Hotel, Saratoga, New York.

nationalities. You will find yourself mistaken. You are no judge of the American character. The civilized world is beginning to be more tolerant in matters of faith, or creed, or birth than you believe or would have them. They despise intolerance, low cunning, and vulgarity, and will not patronize a man who seeks to make money by pandering to the prejudices of the vulgar. I regret that you are running the Union at a loss. I regret you are making no headway in your wholesale departments in New York and in Chicago, and that even the Ninth Street retail store, so popular and prosperous under the management of the late Mr. Stewart, has lost its best patrons. A little reflection must show to you that the serious falling off in your business is not due to the patronage of any one nationality, but to want of the patronage of all, and that you, dear Judge, are not big enough to keep a hotel nor broad enough in your business views to run a dry-goods store. You have tried competition with experienced and popular houses in the manufacture of carpets, of woolens, of silks, and of scores of articles of minor importance, and you have succeeded in none, and you never will and I would respectfully volunteer an advice, for which I charge you nothing, although you once charged me $10,000 for advice which was worth nothing, that if you want to save the rest of the once valuable estate of Mr. Stewart, you should advertise a large auction, and sell your merchandise and your hotels to the highest bidder; and, no matter at what sacrifice you get rid of them, you will come off better than by holding onto things which you cannot intelligently manage.

Trusting you will avail yourself of this friendly and disinterested advice, I remain, yours very truly.

Joseph Seligman.

Chicago Tribune, June 20, 1877, p. 5.

A WORLD OF THEIR OWN

❦ ❦

• 1 8 8 0 - 1 9 2 4 •

"'AMERICA' HAD been in everybody's mouth," recalled Mary Antin, an East European immigrant who came to the United States as a child in 1894.[1] In the days before her family made the decision to leave Russia, she reported that her hometown was buzzing with talk about the possibilities awaiting Jews in America. Antin's family joined the exodus of 2.5 million Jews who left Eastern Europe for the United States between 1880 and 1924. During this extraordinary epoch in Jewish history, one third of East European Jews moved to the West, and the overwhelming majority migrated to America. In 1880, America housed 3 percent of the world's Jewish population, but by 1920, almost a quarter of world Jewry resided in the United States. Although East European Jews had been trickling into America throughout the 1800s, the mass migration that bracketed the turn of the twentieth century transformed the demographic and cultural character of the American Jewish

PART TWO

Refugees in Russia, ca. 1912.
Library of Congress, Prints and
Photographs Division

*Immigrants traveling in steerage
arriving in the United States.*
Photographer: Alfred Stieglitz,
Library of Congress, Prints and
Photographs Division

community. The new immigrants outnumbered the approximately 250,000 Jews living in the United States in 1880, and soon wove new textures into the fabric of American Jewish life.[2]

Popular historical accounts often cite the pogroms that erupted in 1881 as the spark that ignited the mass migration of East European Jews. However, the factors that prompted Jews to leave were far more complex. A population explosion combined with a deteriorating economy debilitated the Jewish community, resulting in widespread poverty and decreased opportunities to earn a living. Jews, who worked largely as middlemen and traders, found the demand for their services drastically reduced in the latter part of the nineteenth century. A new network of railroads brought goods to Russian cities, displacing Jewish merchants, while the emancipation of the Russian serfs created competition, resentment, and further weakened the general economy. To make matters worse, the East European Jewish population quadrupled in size between 1800 and 1890, making it increasingly difficult for Jews to sustain their own families and communities. The pogroms that broke out in 1881 after the assassination of Tsar Alexander II only exacerbated an already precarious situation. The attacks were followed by a series of restrictive legislations known as the May Laws that squeezed Jews out of many occupations and into already crowded cities and towns. Sporadic violence recurred throughout the Russian Empire in subsequent years and continued for decades to come. The 1903 Kishinev pogrom was particularly devastating, sparking outcries around the world, including protests from Jews across the United States. The pogroms heightened the sense of anxiety and vulnerability among Jews, but emigration occurred at equal

Emma Lazarus wrote this poem as a donation to an auction of art and literary work for the Bartholdi Pedestal Fund, an effort to raise funds for the construction of the pedestal for the Statue of Liberty. In 1903, the text of the poem was mounted on the Statue and has since become a symbol of America's identity as a nation of immigrants.

Emma Lazarus (1849–1887), American Jewish poet.

American Jewish Historical Society, Newton Centre, Massachusetts and New York, New York

THE NEW COLOSSUS
Emma Lazarus

Not like the brazen giant of Greek fame,
With conquering limbs astride from land to land;
Here at our sea-washed, sunset gates shall stand
A mighty woman with a torch, whose flame
Is the imprisoned lightning, and her name
Mother of Exiles. From her beacon-hand
Glows world-wide welcome; her mild eyes command
The air-bridged harbor that twin cities frame.
"Keep, ancient lands, your storied pomp!" cries she
With silent lips. "Give me your tired, your poor,
Your huddled masses yearning to breathe free,
The wretched refuse of your teeming shore.
Send these, the homeless, tempest-tost to me,
I lift my lamp beside the golden door!"

Emma Lazarus's handwritten poem, "The New Colossus."
The poem was placed on the Statue of Liberty in 1903.

American Jewish Historical Society, Newton Centre, Massachusetts and New York, New York

Emma Lazarus, *The Poems of Emma Lazarus*, vol.1 (Boston and New York: Houghton, Mifflin and Company, 1889), pp. 202–203.

Immigrants at Ellis Island.
Library of Congress, Prints and Photographs Division

Jewish women receiving medical exams at Ellis Island.
Courtesy of National Park Service: Statue of Liberty National Monument

pace from areas where no anti-Jewish violence erupted. East European Jews certainly looked forward to the security offered in the United States, but like earlier immigrants, most came less for refuge than for opportunity.[3]

Once they had made the decision to leave, Jews, like other immigrants to America, faced a difficult journey. By the 1890s, the steamship made the voyage safer and somewhat faster than earlier in the century, but most poor immigrants endured the trip in steerage class, traveling in belowdeck compartments of the ship. They suffered through seasickness and miserable sanitary conditions, spending two to three weeks in iron bunks before reaching American shores.[4] Most arrived in New York's port, first at Castle Garden, and after 1892, at Ellis Island. They faced a daunting welcome to the United States. Abraham Cahan, who later became editor of the socialist *Jewish Daily Forward*, compared immigrant reception at Castle Garden to the experience of "recruits at a Russian summons for military service."[5] Jewish immigrants regularly referred to Ellis Island as *Trernindzl* or "Isle of Tears." After they disembarked, the newcomers endured an array of medical tests and interrogation about their political affiliations, employment prospects, and other sources of family and financial support. Shortly after the stream of new immigrants began arriving, Jews already in the United States mobilized to help guide their fellow Jews through the American bureaucracy. Most notably, the Hebrew Immigrant Aid Society (HIAS), organized by East European Jews who had only recently arrived in America, sent representatives to Ellis Island and other major ports to negotiate with authorities who might try to detain or deport Jewish immigrants. HIAS workers distributed information in Yiddish to the newcomers and advised them how to navigate the system. *The Jewish Immigrant,* a bilingual HIAS publication, circulated widely in Eastern Europe, preparing

Students at an Americanization class sponsored by the Hebrew Immigrant Aid Society (HIAS).

From the Archives of the YIVO Institute for Jewish Research

דער אידישער
אימיגראנט
DER YIDDISHER IMMIGRANT
(THE JEWISH IMMIGRANT) — Weekly Publication

The Jewish Immigrant, published by HIAS, offered information and advice to Jewish immigrants.

From the Archives of the YIVO Institute for Jewish Research

Jewish immigrants for what to expect when they arrived. The National Council of Jewish Women, founded in 1893 by middle class women from the earlier Central European migration, also sent delegates to the docks to assist young Jewish women, preventing them from falling into the hands of pimps and white slave traders who preyed on immigrant women traveling alone.[6]

The so-called "uptown" Jews, those from Central Europe who arrived in the mid-nineteenth century, received the new immigrants with some ambivalence, but also with considerable aid and advocacy. Having arrived primarily as peddlers in the mid-1800s, these Jews had attained a degree of social and economic success by the turn of the century. Many worried that the millions of poor, Yiddish-speaking immigrants pouring into the United States would threaten their newly won status and security. In fact, an anti-immigrant backlash swept through the nation beginning in the 1890s, as a constellation of nativists, restrictionists, and agrarian radicals began to fear that foreign elements were destroying America's social order. Their anti-Semitic stereotypes reflected both resentment of new Jewish wealth and depictions of immigrants as swarthy, parasitic, and physically and culturally inferior. Within this climate, leaders of the Jewish community initially argued that immigration ought to be limited and controlled. But deteriorating conditions in Eastern Europe soon softened such opposition and American Jews became advocates of open immigration. Members of the established Jewish community assumed responsibility for the welfare and adjustment of fellow Jews, creating a

The National Council of Jewish Women was a leader in providing aid to Jewish immigrants.

American Jewish Historical Society, Newton Centre, Massachusetts and New York, New York

This cartoon, titled "Their New Jerusalem," depicts Jews fleeing persecution and establishing dominance in New York.
Judge *magazine, 1892*

Cartoon, "The New Transatlantic Hebrew Line-For the Exclusive Use of "The Persecuted." Puck *magazine, January 1881.*
Library of Congress, Prints and Photographs Division

THE "NEW TRANS-ATLANTIC HEBREW LINE"

FOR THE EXCLUSIVE USE OF "THE PERSECUTED."

host of relief societies, educational associations, and settlement houses to ease the transition. Institutions such as Lillian Wald's Henry Street settlement on New York's Lower East Side not only offered medical care and pioneered the notion of public health nursing, but also instructed immigrants about everything from personal hygiene to the arts. The assistance provided to newcomers by philanthropists and social workers was often delivered with a patronizing tone, as reformers endeavored "to exercise a civilizing and elevating influence upon the immigrants."[7] Indeed, a healthy dose of antipathy and resentment characterized the relationship between "uptown" and "downtown" Jews in these years, but their interaction reflected a sense of mutual responsibility and sparked a burst of institutional and cultural energy that sustained the Jewish community for years to come.

For all the help they received from their co-religionists, the newcomers built their own culture, complete with a network of social, cultural, and religious institutions all their own. Unlike other immigrant groups (and in contrast to the previous wave of Jewish migrants), East European Jews came as families, with a greater proportion of women and children than other ethnic groups. Moreover, these Jews came to stay. More than 30 percent of other immigrant groups eventually returned to their homelands, but less than 8 percent of Jews chose to go back to Eastern Europe. Intending from the outset to remain in the United States, Jews came ready to establish a lasting community in America.[8]

New York was the point of entry for most Jewish immigrants and for an overwhelming number, also the final destination. One third of America's Jews lived in

Girls on the roof of the Jewish Training School in Chicago, ca. 1911.
Courtesy of Chicago Jewish Archives, Spertus Institute of Jewish Studies

Henry Street Settlement, ca. 1910.
Courtesy of Henry Street Settlement

New York in 1880. By 1920, that number had risen to 45 percent. Other large cities also housed substantial Jewish populations, with Chicago and Philadelphia the next largest communities, but not nearly approaching New York's density of Jewish population. (In the 1920s, Chicago was home to about 8 percent and Philadelphia almost 7 percent of the nation's Jews.) Although a small number of Jews ventured into rural locales and a few took a chance on the handful of experimental Jewish agricultural colonies, Jewish immigrants settled primarily in urban centers. Up and down the Eastern seaboard from Boston to Baltimore and extending to Detroit, Cleveland, and even to Atlanta and Los Angeles, Jews created eth-

nic enclaves in America's cities. At the turn of the century, Chicago's Maxwell Street, Boston's North End, and South Philadelphia hummed with the sounds of Yiddish being spoken on the streets. Within these urban spaces, immigrants built a thriving Jewish culture, as they went about the business of becoming Americans.[9]

A street scene on New York's Lower East Side.
Library of Congress, Prints and Photographs Division

Levy's Brothers Clothing House, Louisville, Kentucky, ca. 1909.
Newton Owen Postcard Collection, University of Louisville Archives, Louisville, Kentucky

Orchard Street on New York's Lower East Side, looking south from Hester Street, 1898.
Museum of the City of New York, The Byron Collection, 93.1.1.18293

Every major city had its Jewish neighborhood, but none could compare to New York's Lower East Side. In 1892, 75 percent of New York Jews lived on the Lower East Side, a number that fell to 50 percent in 1903 and to 25 percent by 1916. For many immigrants, the Lower East Side was a first stop before moving elsewhere, but the continuing stream of newcomers constantly repopulated the neighborhood during the height of the immigrant era. The sheer density of Jewish population in the district during its heyday made it a dynamic center of Jewish culture, even as its poverty and over-

crowding created miserable living conditions. In the 1890s, one journalist observed that, "nowhere in the world are so many people crowded together in a square mile." With more than 100 blocks that contained 750 people per acre and almost 40 with 1,000 per acre, only the cities of Bombay and Calcutta exceeded the overcrowding of the Lower East Side. Immigrant families crowded into tiny tenement apartments, often taking in additional boarders to help with the rent. Dumbbell tenements, so named because of their shape, contained four apartments on each floor, two on each side, separated by a narrow corridor with water closets for residents to share. A magazine article in 1888 described New York tenements as "great prison-like structures of brick, with narrow doors and windows, cramped passages, and steep rickety stairs." Because their buildings allowed virtually no air circulation, residents often slept on the fire escapes during the summer.[10]

Interior view of a New York City tenement apartment. "Box Street-Dark Bedroom." Photo: Tenement House Department, February 6, 1911.
Museum of the City of New York, Gift of Tenement House Department, 31.93.21

The streets of the Lower East Side testified to the diverse and vibrant culture squeezed into a handful of city blocks. Tenement houses, pushcart peddlers, garment workers shops, storefront synagogues, and all forms of recreation stood side by side in the cramped district. A visitor to the Lower East Side in its heyday would see workers walking home from the factories, intellectuals arguing over politics in local cafés, and residents headed out for an evening at the Yiddish theater. On every block, children played in the streets and young adults enjoyed the urban pleasures of dance halls, arcades, and nickelodeons. A complex society, the Lower East Side also had its seedier elements. In the Red Light district centered on Allen Street, Jewish prostitutes did a lucrative business. Like other poor urban neighborhoods, the East Side contained its share of criminals, who operated gambling rings, extorted local merchants for protection, and controlled prostitution. In later years, a few Jewish criminals, such as Arnold Rothstein and Meyer Lansky, moved beyond the Lower East Side to lead some of America's most notorious underworld syndicates.[11]

Most immigrant Jews came to America intent on adapting to their new environment. The first act often undertaken by "greenhorns"—newly arrived immigrants—was to outfit themselves in American-style clothes, have their photographs taken, and send the pictures to relatives back home as a sign of their transformation. The quest to become American could also be seen in the numbers of Jews learning English and attending night classes; by 1906

Selling coats on the streets of the Lower East Side.
Library of Congress, Prints and Photographs Division

A class for immigrants at New York's Educational Alliance.
From the Archives of the YIVO Institute for Jewish Research

A new immigrant posing for a photograph, circa 1897.
Museum of the City of New York, The Byron Collection, 93.1.1.14589

Borden's Milk Company New Year's Greeting, 1921.

Advertisement for Waterman's Fountain Pen. The Big Stick [Der Groyser Kundes], *March 31, 1911.*

Courtesy of the National Museum of American Jewish History, Philadelphia

Jews made up the majority of students enrolled in New York's evening schools. Many immigrants mastered only a rudimentary English, but they sent their children to the public schools in overwhelming numbers. Although many families needed their children's income to survive and education was not the key to mobility until the next generation, most Jewish children did obtain at least an elementary education during the immigrant era. With an education derived both from the schools and from the streets, the children of immigrants quickly outpaced their parents in understanding how to navigate their way in America.[12] Immigrant Jews and especially their children often grew to be Americans by becoming consumers, adopting the latest trends in fashion and buying new kinds of food and merchandise marketed by American advertisers. Companies selling everything from Borden's Milk to Crisco to Planters Peanut Oil quickly recognized the receptivity of the Jewish buying public and filled Jewish newspapers with advertisements in Yiddish. Immigrant Jews even became the most prolific purchasers of pianos, enticed by regular advertisements in the Yiddish press that offered installment plans for pennies a day.[13] Even while they struggled for economic security, most immigrant Jews aspired to mainstream American values and lifestyles.

Not all adjustments to America proved seamless. Immigration was an enormously disruptive experience, forcing both men and women to assume new roles. Families generally depended on contributions from all members to sustain the household economy. Since both sons and daughters worked for wages, immigrant parents lost a degree of control over their children, who became attuned to the rhythms of American culture. Many immigrant families took in boarders, cared for by wives, which sometimes strained marital relationships. The sheer difficulty of making a living weighed heavily on families as they negotiated slack seasons in the garment industry and periodic unemployment. The most compelling evidence of family disruption was the high incidence of desertion within the immigrant Jewish community. Husbands who preceded their wives to America sometimes looked upon their spouses as un-Americanized greenhorns and abandoned them after they arrived. In other cases, men simply succumbed to the pressures of supporting a family. The problem became so serious that in 1911, the Jewish community created the National Desertion Bureau, an organization that worked to track down deserters. The Yiddish newspaper, the *Jewish Daily Forward*, published the photographs of these men in a regular column under the banner

"Gallery of Missing Husbands." Of course, desertion was not the normative experience for Jewish immigrants. Most endured family pressures and some rough transitions, but they lived within Jewish neighborhoods and communities that cushioned their adjustment to the New World.[14]

The Lower East Side was never the Old World transplanted. The social, cultural, and economic life in the neighborhood reflected an immigrant population adapting to the American environment, not looking to recreate the European *shtetl*. The most abundant organization on the Lower East Side was the *landsmanshaft* or hometown society. Groups of Jews from the same European hometown joined together to provide mutual aid, insurance, sick and death benefits, loans, and all sorts of services for members. Many *landsmanshaftn* also sponsored small synagogues or *shuln* that dotted the Lower East Side. A striking 3,000 *landsmanshaft* societies existed in New York, with more than 400,000 members, winning the allegiance of more Jews than any other organization. At first glance, these grassroots societies might appear to be nostalgic associations that harkened back to Europe. *Landsmanshaftn* did indeed provide a sense of security for immigrants in an unfamiliar country, and newcomers often contacted their *landsleit* as soon as they set foot on American

The Jewish Daily Forward *published photographs of men who had deserted their families in its "Gallery of Missing Husbands" column.*
Jewish Daily Forward, March 27, 1924

Members of the Lebedover landsmanshaft, ca 1920s.
From the Archives of the YIVO Institute for Jewish Research

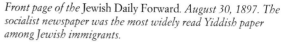

soil. Members also maintained strong connections with their hometowns, regularly sending funds back to Europe in times of need. But while they offered comfort and a bond to home, *landsmanshaftn* functioned primarily to help immigrants construct new lives in America. Providing for all the practical needs of immigrants, *landsmanshaftn* served as anchors that grounded and sustained Jews, allowing them to move forward in the United States.[15]

The Yiddish press also emerged as a medium that expressed and fortified immigrant Jewish culture while helping Jews adapt to American society. At the height of the immigrant era, more than 150 Yiddish newspapers, periodicals, and other publications made their way into circulation. The Orthodox had their papers, as did anarchists, communists, socialists, and all brands of secularists. In these papers, immigrant Jews kept abreast of both national and international events. Most newspapers also serialized literary works, everything from pieces by prominent Yiddish authors to translations of classics such as *Don Quixote.* The *Jewish Daily Forward*, a socialist paper with a relatively moderate political and social outlook, began publication in 1897 and grew into the most popular Yiddish daily, reaching a circulation of 200,000 copies per day. In the *Forward*, readers learned about political struggles at home and abroad while they read articles about American practices and absorbed copious advertisements for American products. Abraham Cahan, the paper's foresighted editor, understood that immigrants could be educated about America through the medium of Yiddish. His newspaper, written in simple, accessible language, taught immigrants about American foods, habits, and manners. An article on the fundamentals of baseball deciphered the American pastime for newcomers, including a diagram of the Polo Grounds to help clarify the "craziness." The *Bintel Brief* (Bundle of Letters), one of its most popular features, was an advice column that answered the questions of readers on topics ranging from family disputes to romance to religious and political dilemmas.[16]

The Yiddish theater, unmatched in its popularity as an entertainment medium within the immigrant Jewish world, served as another crucial mediator between immigrant Jews and their adopted homeland. With tickets that ranged from a quarter to a dollar, the Yiddish theater attracted patrons who earned even the most meager wages.

Abraham Cahan, socialist and editor of the Jewish Daily Forward.

© Brown Brothers, Sterling, PA

The Yiddish theater was also a social institution: Jewish organizations often bought tickets en masse and sold them as fundraising events. Several major cities sponsored Yiddish productions, but New York's Lower East Side remained the vital hub of the American Yiddish theater world. When the neighborhood was at its peak, more than 1,000 performances occurred each year, attracting a collective annual audience that reached two million. Unlike the refined productions of the American stage, Yiddish theater was loud, visceral, and often emotionally cathartic, expressing the shared fears and aspirations of the immigrant community. The leading playwrights and performers of the era—Jacob Gordin, Jacob Adler, and Boris and Bessie Thomashefsky—headlined successful theater troupes that brought the works of Shakespeare and Ibsen to a Yiddish-speaking audience and performed the dramas of immigrant life on stage. The performances of the classics were liberally adapted with

a healthy dose of flamboyance and melodrama; Jacob Gordin's *Der Yidisher Kenig Lir* (*The Jewish King Lear*) replaced the central character of the king with a traditional rabbi grappling with the rebellion of his daughters. Other productions represented and parodied daily immigrant struggles, sometimes to convey pain and emotion and other times to elicit laughter. In later years, many of the devices and rhythms of the Yiddish theater made their way into mainstream American humor and comedic performances.[17]

The diversions of the streets and the stage gave immigrant Jews a brief respite from the harsh conditions that encompassed much of their lives. Jews, like other poor immigrants, remained preoccupied with the daily challenges of earning a living. A large percentage of Jews worked in the garment trade, which made up the backbone

A street peddler on the Lower East Side

Picture Collection, The Branch Libraries, The New York Public Library, Astor, Lenox and Tilden Foundations

*Advertisement for United Hat Stores. The Big Stick
[Der Groyser Kundes], February 17, 1911.*

Courtesy of the National Museum of American Jewish History,
Philadelphia

*Men sewing garments in a Lower East Side sweatshop.
Photo: Lewis Hine, circa 1911.*

Museum of the City of New York, The Jacob A. Riis Collection,
90.13.3.122

*Moe Levy's Men's Wear Shop [Retail], Walker &
Baxter Streets, 1911.*

Museum of the City of New York, The Byron Collection

of the immigrant Jewish economy in major cities such as New York, Philadelphia, and Chicago. To be sure, Jews engaged in a host of other economic pursuits. Like an earlier generation of Jewish immigrants, many became peddlers, but rather than traveling the country, most took their limited capital and became pushcart peddlers in urban centers. In a familiar pattern, Jews often moved from pushcarts to small businesses, such as candy stores, bakeries, dry goods stores, and service establishments. Immigrant Jews also participated in cigar manufacturing, tanning, and other craft and artisan work. Still, it was the needle trades that held particular sway over Jews during the immigrant generation. By the turn of the century, Jewish immigrants increasingly came from industrialized cities in Eastern Europe; a far greater proportion of Jews arrived as skilled and semiskilled workers than any other group. Jews also entered the United States precisely at the moment when the garment industry was reaching its stride. Decades earlier, a previous generation of Jewish immigrants had established a secure foothold in the clothing industry, spurred on by the invention of the sewing machine and the need for mass-produced uniforms during the Civil War. By the time the new immigrants made the journey to America, Central European Jews largely controlled the clothing manufacturing businesses that employed the new arrivals. As early as 1890, German Jews owned more than 90 percent of garment factories on the Lower East Side. Before the century came to a close, three-quarters of workers in the garment industry were Jewish.[18]

In the needle trades, immigrants endured crowded, filthy conditions and labored long hours during peak cycles of production, often as many as seventy hours per week, followed by periodic unemployment during slack seasons. The garment industry relied upon the exploitation of workers, and it blurred the boundaries between work and home. The "task" system, widely used in this period, involved layers of contractors and subcontractors. The contractor, usually an immigrant who had been in America for some time, bought uncut cloth from a manufacturer and agreed to deliver a certain number of garments on a given date for a set price. Contractors could then manage the production themselves or subcontract the work to others on whatever terms they chose. "Normally there was not enough work to

Family members share the labor of making garters in their tenement apartment.

Women sewing garments in a sweatshop.

go around," recalled one Jewish immigrant, "so each of the tailors would bid rock-bottom in order to get the work at all."[19] This system bred the creation of hundreds of sweatshops, located in tenement apartments and makeshift shops, sometimes involving entire families who toiled long hours with little ventilation in the poorest sanitary conditions. Men and women worked together in this enterprise, though on different tasks and with a considerable disparity in pay. Men predominated in the better-paying work as cutters and pressers and in the manufacture of suits and coats, while women concentrated in sewing dresses and shirtwaists.[20]

For Jewish immigrants, work was a family affair, requiring collective contributions from all members. The meager wages earned by Jewish men simply were not sufficient to allow them to be the sole breadwinners. As a rule, married Jewish women did not work for wages, but they contributed vitally to the household economy by caring for boarders, working in family-run businesses, and scrupulously managing the family budget. Indeed, married Jewish women demonstrated their economic clout in 1902 when they organized a massive boycott of kosher meat shops throughout New York in order to bring prices down. In Jewish families, both sons and daughters actively participated in the labor force. Decisions about work versus education generally rested on a combination of birth order and gender. Sons usually received preference for schooling when there were younger siblings, especially daughters, old enough to bring in some income. Nonetheless, Jewish daughters might have the opportunity for greater education if they were among the younger children in the family. Jewish families commonly sent their unmarried daughters to work in the factories, where they absorbed the influences of American culture. Many became swept up in the strike movement.[21]

Front cover, Der Idisher Froyen Zshurnal (The Jewish Women's Home Journal), *August 1922.*
Library of Congress, Hebraic Section

Known as the "poet laureate of labor," Morris Rosenfeld (1862–1923) gave voice to the struggles of Jewish workers through his Yiddish poetry.

Morris Rosenfeld, ca. 1910.
Steven Weiss Collection

My Little Boy
[Mein Yingele]
Morris Rosenfeld

I have a little boy, a fine little fellow is he!
When I see him, it appears to me the whole
world is mine.

Only rarely, rarely I see him, my pretty little son,
when he is awake; I find him always asleep, I see
him only at night.

My work drives me out early and brings me
home late; oh, my flesh is a stranger to me!
oh, strange to me the glances of my child!

I come home in anguish and shrouded in darkness—
my pale wife tells me how nicely the child
plays,

How sweetly he talks, how brightly he asks: "O
Mother, good mother, when will my good, good
papa come and bring me a penny?

I hear it, and I hasten: it must be, yes, it shall
be! The father's love flames up: my child must
see me!

I stand by his cradle, and see and listen, and
hush! A dream moves his lips: "Oh, where is,
where is papa?

I kiss the little blue eyes, they open: "O child!"
They see me, they see me, and soon close up
again.

"Here stands your papa, darling! Here is a
penny for you!" A dream moves the little lips:
"Oh, where is, where is papa?

I stand in pain and anguish, and bitterness, and
I think: "when you awake some day, my child,
you will find me no more!"...

Morris Rosenfeld, with prose translation, glossary, and introduction by Leo Wiener, *Songs from the Ghetto* (Boston: Copeland and Day, 1898), pp. 11, 13.

Executive Board of Local 25 of the International Ladies Garment Workers Union, 1912. Clara Lemlich (top row, third from left), Morris Hillquit (lower standing row, second from right), and Benjamin Schlessinger (front row, second from left).

Courtesy of UNITE HERE Archives, Kheel Center, Cornell University

Women marching to City Hall during the 1909 Shirtwaistmakers Strike.

Courtesy of UNITE HERE Archives, Kheel Center, Cornell University

The Jewish labor movement, which reached its apex in the years preceding the First World War, had roots in the class status of immigrants and the particular dynamics of Jewish political culture. A small cadre of Jews arrived in America with strong ideological commitments, having actively participated in the burgeoning socialist movement in Eastern Europe. A much larger group of Jewish immigrants shared a diffuse leftist sensibility that, when combined with poor working conditions, ignited the Jewish labor movement in America. The earliest Jewish unions—the United Hebrew Trades and the Workmen's Circle—began organizing Jewish workers almost immediately after their arrival, fortified by the *Jewish Daily Forward*'s constant coverage of labor issues. In 1909, a period of massive strikes began when 20,000 shirtwaist workers, mostly young Jewish women along with Italian coworkers, walked out to protest poor pay and working conditions. Clara Lemlich, whose passionate words at a union meeting inspired the general strike, was one of thousands of young, single Jewish women who endured weeks on the picket lines as well as arrests and beatings by police. Just a year later, more than 60,000 mostly male workers in the cloakmakers union walked off the job. The cloakmakers ultimately resolved their strike through arbitration, reaching a settlement agreement negotiated by future Supreme Court Justice Louis Brandeis and other "uptown" Jews eager to put an end to the specter of Jewish manufactures and Jewish workers battling each other on the streets. The settlement, known as the Protocol of Peace, earned some concessions from management—including a fifty-hour workweek—a significant improvement at the time. More strikes by tailors, furriers, and

Workers demonstrate during the 1910 Cloakmakers Strike.

Courtesy of UNITE HERE Archives, Kheel Center, Cornell University other workers followed in subsequent years, spreading through cities from Baltimore to Philadelphia to Chicago.[22]

The emotional catalyst of the Jewish labor movement occurred in 1911, when a fire on the upper floors of the Triangle Shirtwaist Factory killed more than 140 female workers. The tragedy came to symbolize the abuses of owners—who had illegally locked the doors of the factory, in part to prevent workers from organizing. Witnesses recalled the horror of watching young women jumping from the windows and falling to their deaths on the pavement. News of the fire spread across the nation and even to Eastern Europe. The Yiddish press graphically reported the harrowing event, covering the mass funerals of the victims and the angry protest meetings that followed. The tragedy fueled the labor movement and also fed the spirit of socialist politics that captured much of the immigrant Jewish world. Jewish socialism in these years possessed a unique quality, reflecting both campaigns for economic justice and the particular Jewish tradition of *tikkun olam*, repair or improvement of the world. Jewish activists, although avowed secularists, often quoted from the prophets in their speeches. When Clara Lemlich called workers to strike in 1909, the audience seconded the motion by paraphrasing a verse from the Psalms, vowing,

Doctors examine victims of the Triangle Shirtwaist Fire, 1911.

Courtesy of UNITE HERE Archives, Kheel Center, Cornell University

Horrified onlookers watch as firefighters attempt to extinguish the fire at the Triangle Factory, 1911.

Courtesy of UNITE HERE Archives, Kheel Center, Cornell University

"If I turn traitor to the cause, I now pledge, may this hand wither from the arm I raise!"[23] For Jewish immigrants, as Irving Howe has explained, socialism "was not merely politics or an idea, it was an encompassing culture, a style of perceiving and judging through which to structure their lives."[24] In New York, Jewish voters elected socialist candidate Meyer London to Congress three times. Jewish leftists such as Morris Hillquit and David Dubinsky became leading figures in American labor. Jewish socialism ultimately brought Jewish cultural and economic concerns to the forefront of local and national politics and gave immigrant Jews a voice in America.[25]

Another Jewish political movement emerged more tentatively on the American scene, as Zionism made gradual inroads into the immigrant Jewish community. In Eastern Europe, Zionism thrived alongside socialism and other redemptive political movements, but Jews in the United States generally placed their hopes in the promise of America—where Zionist ideologies did not carry the same urgency. By the close of the nineteenth century, the Reform movement had categorically rejected both the hope for return to Palestine and the definition of Jews as a nation. Although a few of the most prominent early leaders of Zionism were Reform Jews, they were the exceptions. East European immigrants embraced the notion of Jewish national

Louis Dembitz Brandeis, leader of the American Zionist movement.

American Jewish Historical Society, Newton Centre, Massachusetts and New York, New York

identity and made up the rank and file of the Zionist movement, but many more supported Jewish socialism than endorsed a Zionist platform. The campaign to establish a sovereign Jewish commonwealth in Palestine sparked little enthusiasm among American Jews. However, as conditions deteriorated in Eastern Europe, support for Palestine as a haven for East European Jews gained greater currency. The British Balfour Declaration in 1917 and the worsening plight of European Jews gradually bolstered the movement, but in these years, Zionism attracted a limited constituency among American Jews.[26]

Against this backdrop, Louis Brandeis emerged as the unlikely leader of the American Zionist movement. Born in Kentucky and educated at Harvard, Brandeis had little connection to his own Jewish identity before his "conversion" to Zionism in his mid-fifties. His contact with fellow Jews while arbitrating the 1910 labor strike, his deep commitment to Progressivism, and his ongoing education about the movement gradually led him to passionate advocacy of Zionism. When Brandeis embraced Zionism, he legitimized the movement, assuaging the fears of those Jews who worried about charges of dual loyalty. Most American Jews, determined to proclaim supreme devotion to the United States, carefully avoided any appearance of divided allegiance to their adopted homeland, particularly in an era of frequent attacks on "hyphenated-Americans." In his championing of Zionism, Brandeis pointedly refuted such accusations, boldly asserting that not only was Zionism consistent with American patriotism, but also that, "loyalty to America demands . . . that each Jew become a Zionist."[27] Brandeis argued that fealty to cultural and ethnic traditions made all minority groups better citizens and enhanced the quality of American society. His leadership brought respectability to Zionism and, equally important, created a philanthropic base that fortified the fledgling movement. Louis Brandeis, like subsequent leaders of American Zionism, understood that most American Jews had no intention of leaving the United States for Palestine. He espoused a version of Zionism that required personal conviction and charitable support, but not relocation. Eschewing the complex matrix of ideologies that swirled through the Zionist movement in Europe, Brandeis articulated a brand of Zionism ideally suited to American sensibilities.[28] In a similar vein, at the same time that Brandeis took charge of the Zionist Organization of America, Henrietta Szold built an even more popular American Zionist group—Hadassah. Founded in 1912, Hadassah pioneered medical care in Palestine and brought Jewish women together in the United States. Avoiding divisive ideological struggles, Hadassah attracted Jewish women of diverse ages and backgrounds, growing into one the largest women's organizations in the country.[29] In these ways, Zionism established a foothold in American Jewish culture, promising refuge for Jews in Europe and reinforcing Jewish identity in the United States.

An organizational and institutional explosion took hold in American Jewish life during the first decades of the twentieth century. During these years, Jews established an enduring foundation that shaped Jewish communal life for years to come. At the turn of the century, Federations of Jewish Charities emerged for the first time to coordinate the efforts of the dozens of communal agencies already dispensing aid to needy Jews. In 1906, following waves of pogroms in Europe, some of America's most prominent Jewish leaders, including Louis Marshall and Jacob Schiff, gathered to form the American Jewish Committee (AJC), an agency to speak for Jewish defense interests worldwide. A few years later, the AJC was challenged by the American Jewish Congress, an organization promoting a more democratically based Jewish leadership and advocating strong support of Zionism, particularly in the midst of the devastation occurring within European Jewish communities during World War I. The ravages of war also sparked the creation of the

Henrietta Szold, founder of Hadassah, ca. 1928.
Courtesy of Hadassah, The Women's Zionist Organization of America, Inc.

Sketch of Leo Frank on the witness stand during his trial, from The Atlanta Constitution, *August 19, 1913.*

Cuba Archives of The Breman Museum

American Jewish Joint Distribution Committee to orchestrate American Jewish relief efforts abroad. As American Jews assumed responsibility to care for the needs of world Jewry, pivotal events at home sometimes motivated Jews to organize. In 1913, when Jewish pencil factory owner Leo Frank was falsely accused and sentenced to death for the murder of a young female employee in Atlanta, Georgia, members of B'nai B'rith created the Anti-Defamation League (ADL) to combat anti-Jewish stereotypes and fight racism. Prominent Jewish lawyers also assisted in Frank's legal defense, but they could not prevent the tragic events in Atlanta. In the most brutal episode of anti-Jewish violence in America, Leo Frank was abducted from jail by an angry mob and lynched. The event shook the Jewish community to its core, but the institution-building continued unabated. American Jews organized to protect their own interests, defend and assist their brethren abroad, and constructed a varied and complex Jewish community in the United States.[30]

The character of Judaism in America grew to reflect the increasing diversity and wide-ranging practices of the millions of Jews who called the United States home. When large numbers of East European immigrants began arriving in the 1880s, the majority of American Jews belonged to synagogues affiliated with the Reform movement, although almost every community also maintained a traditional congregation. Even before the mass migration of East European Jews, America's open society bred a range of religious behaviors not defined by organized movements. In the United States, individual Jews crafted Judaism as they saw fit. The same pattern applied to East European Jewish immigrants who, although often portrayed as strictly devout before coming to America, actually embraced a range of secular and religious outlooks. Some were avowed secularists, though most lived in communities defined to some degree by the rhythms of traditional practice, even if they did not cling ideologically to such beliefs. The popular notion that Jewish immigrants possessed an intense piety that they immediately shed when they set foot on American soil belies the complexity of their beliefs and practices, both before and after they came to the United States. As a general rule, those Jews most fervently attached to retaining a traditionally observant lifestyle were the least likely to leave Europe. Indeed, some European rabbis warned immigrants of the spiritual pitfalls awaiting in America. Between 60 to 80 percent of immigrant Jews in the United States maintained no synagogue affiliation whatsoever. Only a small minority strictly observed the Sabbath,

A Sukkah built for the celebration of the Jewish fall harvest holiday outside of a New York City tenement apartment, 1897.

Courtesy of the Granger Collection, New York

though many more occasionally attended services, especially on High Holidays when rented halls were often converted into synagogues to accommodate worshippers. In the idiosyncratic pattern of American Jewish observance, many Jews continued to purchase kosher meat, even if they did not keep strictly kosher, and selectively to celebrate major Jewish holidays and life cycle events. [31]

When immigrants did seek out worship services, they found traditional styles most comfortable and familiar, but Orthodoxy as a movement remained diffuse and poorly organized in this period. East European Jewish immigrants did overturn the Reform majority in America. By 1910, 90 percent of the approximately 2,000 synagogues in the United States identified as Orthodox. Still, the numbers were deceptive, since most of these synagogues were actually tiny *landsleit* congregations, many lacking even a permanent building. Attempts to bring structure to traditional Judaism met with dismal failure. New York Jews brought Rabbi Jacob Joseph from Vilna to the United States to assume the position of chief rabbi, but he commanded no authority in America; in fact, a number of other communities soon hired their own "chief" rabbis with similar futile results. Deeply committed Orthodox Jews, although small in number, continued to provide their children at least a basic education in Jewish texts and a few attended *yeshivot*, talmudic academies, that began to spring up in select communities. By the turn of the century, a sufficient number

Dr. Bernard Revel and other leaders of the Rabbi Isaac Elchanan Theological Seminary (RIETS) standing on the steps of the Lower East Side building as they transfer Torah scrolls to the new Washington Heights campus, 1929.

Courtesy of Yeshiva University Archives

of Orthodox rabbis had come to the United States to allow for the founding of the Rabbi Isaac Elchanan Theological Seminary (RIETS), designed to deliver rigorous talmudic training on American soil, comparable to the level of instruction offered in Europe. Contingents of Orthodox rabbis also began to organize nationally: the *Agudath ha-Rabbanim* (United Orthodox Rabbis) represented the right-wing of the movement, while the Orthodox Union advocated a more inclusive approach. These organizations worked to bring order to the chaotic and often corrupt kosher meat industry, and to sustain a traditional front within American Jewry.[32]

Although Orthodoxy made limited inroads in this period, Reform Judaism would not prove a viable option for East European immigrants either. By the 1880s, the Reform movement had begun to drift farther away from traditional customs. In 1883, when Jewish leaders gathered to celebrate the first graduation of rabbis from the Hebrew Union College in Cincinnati, the dinner menu contained milk and meat served together and also included shellfish. Later dubbed the *trefa* (unkosher) banquet, the incident came to symbolize the growing rift between factions in American Judaism.[33] Just two years later, the Reform movement issued a statement of principles known as the Pittsburgh Platform that formally cast off all practices "not adapted to the views and habits of modern civilization." Reform leaders rejected adherence to dietary laws, denied any definition of Jews as a nation, and vowed to maintain only practices that elevated the human spirit.[34] Such positions rendered Reform Judaism foreign to most immigrants and elicited growing disapproval from more moderate religious leaders. In 1886, just a year after the release of the Pittsburgh Platform, a group of traditional rabbis joined forces to establish the Jewish Theological Seminary of America in New York, establishing the foundation for Conservative Judaism. Its leaders embraced full participation in American society but rejected the deviations from Jewish law promulgated by the Reform movement. After struggling through its early years, the Seminary ironically gained the backing of leading Reform Jews, such as Jacob Schiff and Louis Marshall, who recognized that immigrants would not be drawn to the Reform movement and saw the potential of creating an Americanized form of Judaism that would appeal to the newcomers. In 1902, Solomon

The menu of the Reform movement's "trefa banquet" reveals the serving of nonkosher foods and the mixing of meat and milk, violating Jewish dietary laws.

The Jacob Rader Marcus Center of the American Jewish Archives

Schechter, a renowned scholar and rabbi from Cambridge University, arrived to assume leadership of the new Seminary. Under his guidance, the Conservative movement retained complete fealty to Jewish law while embracing secular education and American culture. Immigrant Jews did not immediately flock to the new movement, but Conservative Judaism put down strong roots in turn-of-the-century America that flourished in the next generation.[35]

A visitor to the United States in the 1920s would have encountered a highly complex and multifaceted Jewish community, far larger and more diverse than could have been imagined in 1880. The millions of Jews who called the United States home in the twenties resided primarily in cities. Most were skilled workers and small merchants.

Students in the library of the Jewish Theological Seminary.
American Jewish Historical Society, Newton Centre, Massachusetts and New York, New York

Some were becoming white collar employees, and a significant minority had established leading positions in businesses and the professions. American Jewish women and men had created a matrix of organizations, an expanding menu of cultural and political expressions, and new varieties of Judaism. The almost forty-five year surge of Jewish immigration sparked a breathless pace of innovation at home and new assertions of American Jewish leadership abroad.

The 1920s also witnessed the virtual closing of America's doors. Movements for immigration restriction had begun almost at the moment when Europeans first began arriving in the United States. But the restrictionists prevailed in the twenties, enacting a series of legislations that slowed immigration to a trickle. The National Origins Act of 1924 mandated a strict quota system that allowed immigrants from Northern and Western Europe to enter in larger numbers while severely restricting those from Southern and Eastern Europe. For Jews, the results were devastating: In 1921, approximately 119,000 Jewish immigrants arrived in America; by 1925, that number plummeted to just over 10,000.[36] The 1920s brought an end to almost half a century of mass Jewish immigration and marked the conclusion of the most rapid period of growth and creativity in American Jewish history.

"The Immigrant—Is he an acquisition or a detriment?" Cartoon from Judge *magazine, September 1903, Gillam, Sackett & Wilhelms Litho. & Ptg. Co., New York.*
Library of Congress, Prints and Photographs Division

1. Mary Antin, *From Plotzk to Boston* (Boston: W. B. Clarke, 1899), p. 11. In the first edition of Antin's memoir, the publisher mistakenly confused her town of Polotzk in Russia with the city of Plotzk in Poland. Antin allowed the title of the book to remain, but corrected the error in the preface to the second edition.

2. Gerald Sorin, *A Time for Building: The Third Migration, 1880–1920* (Baltimore: Johns Hopkins University Press, 1992), p.12.

3. Kuznets, "Immigration of Russian Jews to the United States: Background and Structure," *Perspectives in American History* 9 (1975), pp. 35–124; John D. Klier and Shlomo Lambroza, *Pogroms: Anti-Jewish Violence in Modern Russian History* (New York: Cambridge University Press, 1992).

4. By the 1900s, technology had improved the comfort of the voyage somewhat and reduced the duration of the journey to approximately six to ten days. Pamela Nadell, "The Journey to America by Steam: The Jews of Eastern Europe in Transition," *American Jewish History* 71:2 (December, 1981): 269–84.

5. Abraham Cahan, *The Education of Abraham Cahan*, trans. Leon Stein, Abraham P. Conan, Lynn Davison from *Bleter fun mein leben*, (Philadelphia: Jewish Publication Society of America, 1969), p. 217.

6. Sorin, *A Time for Building*, pp. 46–50; Faith Rogow, *Gone to Another Meeting: The National Council of Jewish Women, 1893–1993* (Tuscaloosa: University of Alabama Press, 1993), pp. 137–38.

7. Moses Rischin, *The Promised City: New York's Jews, 1870–1914* (Cambridge, Mass.: Harvard University Press, 1962), p. 103.

8. Kuznets, "Immigration of Russian Jews to the United States: Background and Structure," pp. 94–100; Jonathan D. Sarna, "The Myth of No Return: Jewish Return Migration to Eastern Europe, 1881–1914," *American Jewish History* 71 (December, 1981), pp. 256–68.

9. Sorin, *A Time for Building*, pp. 136–37.

10. Rischin, *The Promised City*, pp. 76–94; Sorin, *A Time for Building*, pp. 70–71; Deborah Dwork, "Health Conditions of Immigrant Jews on the Lower East Side of New York: 1880–1914," *Medical History* 25 (1981), pp. 1–18.

11. Rischin, *The Promised City*, pp. 90–91; Jenna W. Joselit, *Our Gang: Jewish Crime and the New York Jewish Community, 1900–1940* (Bloomington: Indiana University Press, 1983).

12. Andrew R. Heinze, *Adapting to Abundance: Jewish Immigrants, Mass Consumption, and the Search for American Identity* (New York: Columbia University Press, 1990), pp. 89–90; Stephan F. Brumberg, *Going to America, Going to School: The Jewish Immigrant Public School Encounter in Turn-of-the-Century New York City* (New York: Praeger, 1986).

13 Heinze, *Adapting to Abundance*, pp. 89–104, 159, 133–44.

14. Reena Sigman Friedman. "Send Me My Husband Who Is in New York City': Husband Desertion in the American Jewish Immigrant Community, 1900–1926," *Jewish Social Studies* 44:1 (Winter, 1982), pp. 1–18; Ari Lloyd Fridkis, "Desertion in the American Jewish Immigrant Family: The Work of the National Desertion Bureau in Cooperation with the Industrial Removal Office," *American Jewish History* 71 (December, 1981), pp. 285–99.

15. Daniel Soyer, *Jewish Immigrant Associations and American Identity in New York, 1880–1939* (Cambridge, Mass.: Harvard University Press, 1997).

16. Mordecai Soltes, *The Yiddish Press: An Americanizing Agency* (New York: Arno Press, 1969); Rischin, *The Promised City*, pp. 119, 127; *Jewish Daily Forward*, August 27, 1909, p. 4.

17. Rischin, *The Promised City*, pp. 133–37; Faina Burko, "The American Yiddish Theater and Its Audience Before World War I," in David Berger, *The Legacy of Jewish Migration: 1881 and Its Impact* (Brooklyn: Brooklyn College Press, 1983), pp. 85–96.

18. Sorin, *A Time for Building*, pp. 74–76; Dwork, "Health Conditions of Immigrant Jews on the Lower East Side of New York."

19. Abraham Bisno, cited in Susan A. Glenn, *Daughters of the Shtetl: Life and Labor in the Immigrant Generation* (Ithaca N.Y.: Cornell University Press, 1990), p. 94.

20. Ibid., pp. 94–96, 112–22; Dwork, "Health Conditions of Immigrant Jews on the Lower East Side of New York."

21. Paula E. Hyman, "Culture and Gender: Women in the Immigrant Jewish Community," in Berger, *The Legacy of Jewish Migration*, pp. 157–68.

22. Glenn, *Daughters of the Shtetl*, pp.167–91; Sorin, *A Time for Building*, pp. 109–35.

23. Irving Howe, *World of Our Fathers* (New York: Simon & Schuster, 1976), p. 299.

24. Irving Howe, *A Margin of Hope: An Intellectual Autobiography* (New York: Harcourt Brace Jovanovich, 1982), p. 9.

25. Sorin, *A Time for Building*, pp. 129–35.

26. Naomi Cohen, *American Jews and the Zionist Idea* (New York: KTAV, 1975).

27. Louis D. Brandeis, "The Jewish Problem, How to Solve It," in *Brandeis on Zionism: A Collection of Addresses and Statements by Louis D. Brandeis* (Washington, D.C.: Zionist Organization of America, 1942), p. 29.

28. Sarah Schmidt, "The Zionist Conversion of Louis D. Brandeis," *Jewish Social Studies* 37 (January, 1975), pp. 18–34.

29. Joan Dash, *Summoned to Jerusalem: The Life of Henrietta Szold* (New York: Harper and Row, 1979).

30. Naomi W. Cohen, *Not Free to Desist: The American Jewish Committee, 1906–1966* (Philadelphia: Jewish Publication Society of America, 1972); Leonard Dinnerstein, *The Leo Frank Case* (New York: Columbia University Press, 1968).

31. Jonathan D. Sarna, *American Judaism: A History* (New Haven, CT.: Yale University Press, 2004), pp. 154–63.

32. Ibid., pp. 182–84, 191–93; Sorin, *A Time for Building*, pp. 175–78.

33. Sarna, *American Judaism,* pp. 144–45.

34. Text of Pittsburgh Platform reprinted in Michael A. Meyer, *Response to Modernity: A History of the Reform Movement in Judaism* (New York: Oxford University Press, 1988), pp. 387–88.

35. Sarna, *American Judaism*, pp. 184–91.

36. L. Hirsch, "Jewish Migrations During the Last Hundred Years," *The Jewish People: Past and Present* (New York: Central Yiddish Culture Organization, 1946), vol. 1, p. 409; John Higham, *Strangers in the Land: Patterns of American Nativism, 1860–1925* (New York: Atheneum, 1963).

1

THE JOURNEY TO AMERICA

• ALEXANDER HARKAVY •

BORN IN Russia in 1863, Alexander Harkavy was a prolific linguist and writer, an immigrant who became an advocate for other Jewish immigrants to America. Best known as the compiler of a comprehensive Yiddish-English-Hebrew dictionary, Harkavy also worked as representative of the Hebrew Immigrant Aid Society (HIAS) during the peak years of immigration. At Ellis Island, he and other HIAS officials helped newcomers navigate the system and represented their interests with the authorities. When HIAS began distributing *The Jewish Immigrant*, a bilingual publication circulated widely in Eastern Europe, Harkavy contributed a column that explained immigration policies and advised immigrants about what to expect when they arrived. Harkavy wrote a number of Yiddish-language guides to American culture designed for immigrants, including a popular letter-writing guide that sold thousands of copies.

As a youth, Alexander Harkavy studied in Vilna, where he became swept up in the Haskalah—the Jewish Enlightenment. In 1882, he set out with a group of idealistic young Jews who traveled to America, intending to establish a farming collective. Realizing quickly that farming did not suit him, Harkavy made his life and career in the city where he provided valuable assistance to immigrants and became a pioneering scholar of Yiddish language. This selection from Harkavy's memoirs describes his own immigrant voyage to the United States.

THE YEARS 1881–1882 were trying days for the Jews of Russia owing to the horrors which broke out against them in the southern districts. Many of our brethren in Russia left at that time for America. In Southern Russia, groups of enlightened Jews, products of the new generation, organized to go and settle in America as farmers. In the spring of 1882 such a movement of group organization also began among the enlightened Jewish youth of Vilna. When this news reached me I joined up. According to the regulations of my group every member was obligated to prepare seventy rubles for travel expenses. My relative having no opposition to my desire to travel to America, she agreed to give me the money out of the legacy left by my father, of blessed memory, over which she had control. . . .

Alexander Harkavy, gifted linguist who also worked for the Hebrew Immigrant Aid Society (HIAS).
From the Archives of the YIVO Institute for Jewish Research

THE DAY SET for our departure from Vilna arrived, and we were ready to go. At ten in the morning every member of our group was supposed to gather by the railway. When the moment came to separate from Vilna, love for my native land welled up within me, and I lamented to myself my decision to set out for America. But everything was set; there was no turning back. Brokenhearted, I parted from my relatives who owned the press and from the auditors in the office of accounting, and I made my way to the railway where members of the group had gathered.

Our first destination was a small city in Lithuania near the Prussian border. We arrived there after noon, and turned in at a hotel outside the city. There we found a Jew engaged in border crossing [smuggling]. We contracted with him to cross us into Prussia at a price of three rubles a head. Toward evening the man brought a large wagon which took us as far as the border district. There we got off the wagon, and the man left us alone. He went off to bargain on our behalf with one of the district's residents. No sooner did he leave than we began to fear for our lives. We were terrified that army borderguards would see and catch us. After an hour, our border crosser returned with a Christian man and both quietly ordered us to come along. Trembling mightily we followed them. They led as into Prussia. The border area was filled with wells of water and slime, and we grew impatient at our pace. Finally, after wandering about for half an hour, we came to the city of Eydtkuhnen in Prussia. The shore time had seemed to us like an eternity. When told by the men that we were no longer in Russia, our joy knew no bounds.

We arrived in Eydtkuhnen after midnight and made straight for the hotel. There we feasted on bread and ale; we were happy and in high spirits. We were pleased both to have safely succeeded in crossing the border of our cruel native land, and to have placed the soles of our feet down on the soil of Germany—which excelled in higher education and in a legal system designed to benefit its citizens. After having eaten, we lay down to rest from the ardors of our journey. We slept very well indeed. . .

We remained in Eydtkuhnen for twenty-four hours, and then traveled on to Hamburg. We remained in this port city for two days. At that time there was in Hamburg a Jewish committee to support Russian emigrants who came there by the thousands on their way to America. We turned to this committee with the request that it purchase for us tickets on an English boat at the special rate offered charitable societies. The committee filled our request, and in this way we saved the treasury of our group some money.

From Hamburg, we traveled over the North Sea to the city of Hartlepool in England, and from there via train to the port city of Liverpool. There we were to wait until the Am Olam[1] from Kiev arrived so that we might go down to the ship along with them. Four days later the group arrived. Great joy filled our hearts when we learned that our allied group had made it. In high spirits we rushed to greet them. After a meeting between the leaders of our two groups, the creation of a legal union was announced: Henceforward, we were like brothers of a single society. The Kiev group with which we had joined had seventy members, men and women. Most were young intellectual men, dreamers just like we were. Among its members was the late poet, David Edelstadt,[2] then about eighteen years old. Our two groups met up with one another on the

---

[1] *Am Olam*, literally "eternal people," was the name of a Jewish organization founded in Odessan in 1881. The organization encouraged Jews to settle in the United States and create agrarian communities, guided by socialist principles.

[2] David Edelstadt (1866–1892), a prominent Yiddish poet and anarchist whose work portrayed the plight of workers and promoted radical causes.

Students in an Americanization class pose on the steps of the HIAS building in New York.
From the Archives of the YIVO Institute for Jewish Research

afternoon of May 15th. That very day, the ship *British Prince* stood at the harbor ready to accept passengers for America. It was destined to take us as well. Just an hour after our union we went down to the ship together. That evening the *British Prince* hoisted anchor, and began to transport us to our ultimate destination: the new world.

The boat *British Prince* was like a city floating on water, so great was the number of its passengers. All its passengers were Russian immigrants; all, save members of our group; were travelling to America as individuals, seeking to improve their position by their own brains and brawn: this one through handiwork, that one through peddling. Members of our group saw themselves as superior to this multitude. "The other passengers are not like us," said we to ourselves, "we are not merely going to America for simple comfort, we are idealists, eager to prove to the world that Jews can work the land!" In our imagination, we already saw ourselves as landowning farmers dwelling on our plots in the western part of the country. So certain were we that our aims in the new world would be achieved that even on the boat we began to debate which kind of community institutions we would build, which books we would introduce into our library, whether or not we would build a synagogue and so forth (with regard to the synagogue, most of the views were negative). We danced and sang overcome with joyous expectations of what America held in store for us. In spite of seasickness, storms, and tempests which visited us on our journey, we were happy and lighthearted. All the days of our Atlantic voyage were filled with joy.

. . .

ON MAY 30TH, fifteen days after our boat set sail from Liverpool, we arrived safely at the North American shoreline and disembarked onto dry land. Our boat stood at the port of Philadelphia in the state of Pennsylvania. Our destination, however, was New York where the Hebrew Emigrant Aid Society was centered, and the next day we were taken there by railroad. Upon our arrival we were brought to a place then known as Castle Garden where we rested from the wearisome journey. Our leader, the head of the Kiev group, went to the administrative office of H.E.A.S. on State Street to inform them of our arrival, and to ask them what they planned to do for us.

Between the time that our group was founded and the time of our arrival large numbers of our brethern had emigrated from Russia and come to New York. So great were their numbers that the shore officers had found it necessary to erect large wooden shacks around Castle Garden to provide them with cover and a place to sleep. The Castle Garden Plaza was filled from one end to the other with immigrants. On the adjoining streets,—State Street, Greenwich Street, and even at the top of Broadway—women sat on the ground, babies in hand, for want of a home. Owing to the flood of Russian immigrants, the aid society was short of means and couldn't undertake great projects on their behalf. All it could do was arrange that the mass of people be provided with bread until such time as the incoming flood would diminish and they could do somewhat more for their benefit.

The officers of the Society received our leader politely, but informed him that in the existing circumstances they could do not a thing for our group. They continued to say, however, that since we had come to America trusting in the Society, they would agree to provide us at the first opportunity with food and lodging. After a short while our leader returned to our camp and told us everything that the Society's officers had said. Our spirits sank. "No more hope of working the land! Our dreams have come to naught! Alas that we have reached such a state!" After a time, however, we calmed down a bit and our spirits improved. When we saw what troubles faced the rest of our brethren wandering about outside, we made peace with our lot and were grateful for the Society's promise to feed us for the time being.

Alexander Harkavy, *Prakim Mechayai* [Chapters From My Life] trans. Jonathan D. Sarna, *American Jewish Archives* 33:1 (April, 1981) pp. 35, 37–40. Printed with permission of Jonathan D. Sarna.

2

GOING WEST

• RACHEL CALOF •

IN 1894, at the age of eighteen, Rachel Bella Kahn left Russia for the United States for an arranged marriage to Abraham Calof. Arriving in New York, Rachel met Abraham and the two journeyed across the country to join his family on its homesteads in North Dakota. The Calofs made their home in Devils Lake, North Dakota, where they raised nine children. In her memoir, written in the 1930s, Rachel Calof describes the hardships of pioneer life—the harsh winters, financial struggles, and lack of privacy. For Calof, the lack of privacy was the most difficult burden of homesteading, as her extended family crowded together in meager accommodations. Rachel Calof offers this account of her wedding to Abraham in Devils Lake and describes their primitive living conditions.

WINTER WAS VERY near now. Abraham had earned his seventy-five dollars. This was the money which hopefully would buy sufficient fuel and food to carry three families (nine people) through the winter. It looked like it might just be done. Prices were reasonable. Flour sold for ninety cents per one-hundred-pound sack.

The roof on our shack was now built and on the basis of this security Abraham and I set our wedding date for November 8, 1894. . . .

THE LAW PROVIDED that a homestead claim could be filed as late as five years from the time a homesteader settled on the land, but I had only the six weeks before my marriage in which to file my claim. Married women whose husbands owned or were claiming land were denied homestead claim rights but single women had the same rights as men. Abraham's land would be in his name but mine would be in my maiden name. . . .

Rachel Bella Kahn around the time of her engagement to Abraham Calof.
Courtesy of David Calof and Roberta Myers

FINALLY THE DAY came. The wedding, my friends, was a knockout. Since Abraham's niece, Doba, had the largest home with two rooms, she offered her palace for the occasion.

My soon to be in-laws, spreading their usual cheer and good will, insisted that the bride and groom had to fast until the ceremony was completed. I was instructed to say my prayers with tears and to implore my dead parents, or at least my departed mother, to attend my wedding. This whole business brought me much distress and, even more, the realization of the family's influence over every aspect of my life, my wedding ceremony included.

My bridal gown, which I had made myself, was of yellow, blue, and white stripes. Abraham's suit hung so low in the back that it might have passed for what is today called "tails."

Those in attendance were Abraham's family, his nieces, Doba and Sarah, and their husbands and their two children. Also present were two families who were about ten miles distant from us. Our wedding gifts were a red felt tablecloth with green flowers, two chickens, and from Charlie and Faga two short women's undershirts. A delayed gift of some little chicks was also promised for next spring by one of the nieces.

The wedding feast was cooking in the kitchen and as the day was coming to a close the wedding was close at hand. The Jewish man certified to perform the ceremony was a member of one of the Jewish families in North Dakota. My fiancé had to work for him for two days hauling hay in payment of his fee.

All brides remember their wedding ceremony and mine was truly memorable. I was seated in a chair. Abraham was given a flour sack which he was instructed to place over my face. Well, at least one could cry in private under the cover.

Being effectively blinded, I was now led to the *huppah* (the wedding canopy) by Doba and her husband. The *huppah* was built of a shawl tied to four sticks. The music was provided by the singing of the women while the men beat time on tin pans.

Following the ceremony the table was set and we sat down to a truly magnificent banquet which consisted of beans, rice with raisins, chicken soup, and roast chicken. The flour sack had been replaced by a handkerchief bound over my eyes. I wanted to remove it to at least be present at my own marriage, but my mother-in-law was quick to forbid it. I did not want to create a scene at my own wedding and so I submitted to these primitive customs. Later, I was to learn that the women present considered me impudent to have made such a suggestion.

The festivities over, bride and groom started home, and in short order, even before my wedding day was over, I was cruelly thrust back into the reality of my life. I learned that the Calof men had decided prior to my marriage that Abe and I must share our home with others for the entire coming winter. What horror. Had any bride ever been more grossly betrayed on her wedding day? This decision resulted from the belief, I was told, that the fuel supply would not be adequate to heat all three shacks through the coming winter and, therefore, Abe's father, mother, and brother Moses would double up with us for the coming months.

In an instant the happiness of my marriage turned to bitterness. The knowledge that I was to spend my honeymoon in a tiny space shared with three strangers was more than I could bear. I hoped that death would take me now, that I would not reach home alive. But my fervent wish was not granted, and it was life, not death, with which I had to cope. . . .

AT THIS TIME the in-laws had a flock of twelve chickens and Abe and I also had twelve. There was no outside coop for the poultry, but if there had been we would have lost the flock in short order because the temperature would soon be going to forty or more degrees below zero and the chickens would have frozen to death. We needed to keep them alive in hopes of having their eggs as well as their meat later on. Each family was to keep its chickens under its bed and the ends and sides were closed off to form a cage. Also there was a calf which had to be accommodated inside. It occupied the remaining corner opposite Moses's sleeping space.

This is how five human beings and twenty-five animals faced the beginning of the savage winter of the plains in a twelve-by-fourteen-foot shack. This is how we lived and suffered. The chickens were generous with their perfumes and we withstood this, but the stench of the calf tethered in the corner was well-nigh intolerable.

I MUST CONFESS that the one hardship which was always unacceptable to me through the formative years was the lack of privacy.

Rachel Calof, *Rachel Calof's Story: Jewish Homesteader on the Northern Plains*. Translated from the Yiddish by Jacob Calof and Molly Shaw. Volume editor, J. Sanford Rikoon. (Bloomington: Indiana University Press, 1995), pp. 34, 35, 37–39, 39–40, 90. Copyright © 1995 by Indiana University Press.

✣ 3 ✣

LANDSMANSHAFTN

• JEWISH HOMETOWN SOCIETIES •

LANDSMANSHAFTN, JEWISH hometown societies, were the most ubiquitous organizations in the immigrant Jewish world. These mutual aid societies, comprised of Jewish immigrants who hailed from the same East European hometown, provided a safety net for newcomers. They offered loans, sick and death benefits, insurance, medical care, and a host of other services to immigrants working to build new lives in America. Hundreds of thousands of Jews joined *landsmanshaft* associations, where they found the comfort of interacting with fellow Jews who shared their background and history. At the same time, these organizations also helped immigrants adapt to life in the United States, assisting them materially and teaching them about American culture. Borrowing from American fraternal lodges, most associations adopted elaborate rituals and regalia, held elections, and conducted business according to strict rules of order, inculcating the values of the democratic process.

In this retrospective account composed in the 1930s, William Bakst recalls the mood and the proceedings of his society, comprised of Jews from the Belorussian town of Oshmyany. Bakst describes the sense of community that the association provided and also details the formal rituals and regalia that were a regular part of the proceedings.

FORTY YEARS HAVE past since I've been involved in the Oshmener scene and I've forgotten the names of a lot of the initial founders who were there at the birth of the "society," and it's difficult for me to relive those moments when we were still young and did a lot of stupid things that young people do.

This won't be at all interesting for current members of the "Oshmener Society," who won't be able to grasp what the "Society" meant to us. For the younger generation, the Oshmener Society is a fine society with a wealthy bank account, a large membership that takes pride in the good name they have in society. But forty-five years ago, the Society was, for us, a holy occupation. We built a nest for ourselves to warm our sick, depressed souls. It was a badly needed place in which we newcomers from Oshmene could drive away sadness and depression. A warm corner where we could spend time with people who were born and raised in the same town.

Akh! How miserable we were then! And how sad it was for us! Our hearts were torn by longing for the Old Country; the atmosphere in the new land was not so friendly for newcomers. We sought to lean on one another, to nestle together in a place where we could have a good cry, something that made it easier on us.

The "Oshmener Society" was borne out of those very moments. Within the society's small membership, we found the friendship, the love and the warmth that a young person cannot live without. A society meeting on Saturday night, every two weeks, was like a much anticipated holiday for which one prepared for as if it was the dearest and most loved thing. The meeting hall was the place where we would get together and tell our stories of suffering and anguish as miserable newcomers in America.

The society created homey relationships: those who were born and raised on Zastshenik Street, behind the bathhouse, became equal to those who were brought up on Zupraner Street and who went to the Technical College; the boys of tailors and shoemakers were just as important in the society as the silk-clad Hasidic youth. The

Members of the Wyszkower landsmanshaft.
From the Archives of the YIVO Institute for Jewish Research

Oshmener Society was a melting pot that cooked us into different and better people. The happiest years for us were the Society's early ones. And none of our current old folks and former young ones will ever forget them.

I Fear the "Regalia." Truth be told, I wasn't one of the first members of the society. When it was first founded, I didn't even have the 50 cent entrance fee and when I was nominated for membership a year later, the president was Brother Joe Hurevitch. In Oshmene, I knew him as Gershke Yekl the Bonehead's kid. When they brought me to a particular meeting to admit me as a new member, the inside guard brought me to the president so he could give me the oath that I would, God forbid, never divulge the Society's secrets and that I would be true to the tasks of the Society, I looked at Gershke Yekl's kid, who was wearing a red sash across his chest and, pounding three times on the table with a gavel, which made everyone stand at attention, I became so frightened that I forgot what they told me to say. Mainly, it was the "regalia" the president wore that scared me. For me, the newcomer, right out of yeshiva and never having seen such a meeting, that red sash over his chest gave me the impression that this was a kind of high level Russian official who pounds his hammer and everyone stands at attention. That simply freaked me out. . . .

There was a tradition that when a member got married, all members would attend the ceremony, marching in together with one member giving a speech and presenting a gift in the name of the Society. I was the main speaker at all weddings. I have the Oshmener Society to thank: for that is where I learned public speaking and I haven't stopped for 44 years . . .

I could write a whole book with stories of the Society's early years. In total, I only belonged to the Society for five years. But into those five years, I put 45 years of work, activity and energy. . . . As I write these lines, I am already an old man of 67 and a lot of water has gone under the bridge from those times about which we know nothing. When I look back on my youth and think of the foolish things in which we were interested, I have to laugh because they seem so dumb, so childish that it makes me wonder how we could have been so foolish. But, still, we long for that time. There is a longing for the misery in which we found ourselves and there is a longing for the joy that would envelope us when we were together. Now, when we are surrounded by our big families, with children, with daughters and sons in-law, with grandchildren, would we want to meet at the corner of Pike and Henry Streets, next to Cohen and Zilverstein's soda water stand and get angry and upset over those foolish things if we could show up now? Seems to me that we'd have to be younger and healthier.

And to the newer, more recent members who have joined in the last few years, Oshmener and non-Oshmener, I would like to say: hold the inheritance we are giving you dearly and be aware that the people put their entire souls into the Oshmener Society in which you take such pride. They bankrupted themselves and denied themselves opportunities they had in America, all in the interests of the Society.

William Baskt, "Ikh bin an oshmener fun oshmene!" in Isaac Rontch, ed., *The Jewish Landsman-schaften of New York* [*Di idishe landsmanshaftn fun Nyu York*] (New York: I. L. Peretz Yiddish Writers' Union, 1938), pp.168–170.

~9 4 ~

MAKING IT IN AMERICA

• JACOB SHOLTZ •

BORN IN Lithuania, Jacob Sholtz came to the United States with his family in 1904. In order to avoid military service and to improve the lives of his children, Sholtz was one of millions of ordinary Jews who made the choice to leave for America. Like many other immigrants, Sholtz had moments of doubt about his decision. In the early years, he thought frequently about returning to Russia.

In 1942, YIVO (established as the Yiddish Scientific Institute in Vilna in the 1920s before relocating to New York) held a contest for the best autobiography by a Jewish immigrant on the theme "Why I Left the Old Country and What I Have Accomplished in America." Sholtz submitted this entry to the contest, describing his decision to come to America and detailing his early business ventures. In this selection, Sholtz also recounts a pivotal turning point when he met a member of his hometown at a *landsmanshaft* meeting. Somehow, the man who Sholtz knew as poor and uneducated in Europe had become a great success in the United States. The encounter buoyed Sholtz's hopes for the possibilities of life in America.

⁓

I GOT THE idea to send the children and their mother to America and I would remain at my job and send them money so they could live there. There they could grow up, go to school and become proper Americans. I was really keen on the idea until the war [between Russia and] Japan broke out. I was expecting to be conscripted at any time, but my heart wouldn't permit it—to go to war for the enemy, not against it! I already had enough money for expenses and before they called me up I still had the right to request a passport. It was said and done. My family and I left the Old Country for a new home—America. At first I was very depressed, worried about making a living and about my newness (greenness) in both the language and the country. This really upset me. Many times I thought about going back. Naturally, I looked for something to do. I tried everything—nothing worked out. I tried other things—I couldn't do it. I could only think about going back. Something happened though—an amazing thing that strongly affected me and made me forget the idea about going back. This is what happened. During those few months of wandering about, a man from my town in the Old Country brought me into a society. So there I was, sitting in a meeting, when a member, a refined-looking man, got up and spoke very intelligently and logically regarding an issue in an excellent Yiddish (my kind of Yiddish). I asked who he was. When they told me, I nearly flipped, and my thoughts of going back totally disappeared. What happened? Here I must tell a bit of past history. The speaker at the meeting who made such a strong impression on me was someone from my town I knew from childhood, from the same street, from the same synagogue. As children, we kept far away from each other. He was very poor and had an awful, even ugly, look to him. He was dirty, raggedy and didn't go to *heder* or any other school. It was a question if he even knew how to pray, even though he held his prayer book open. I forgot about him completely until this encounter at the meeting.

It really changed my thinking. This poor little kid! Here he became a fine, intelligent businessman with a fine family and nice children. How dirty he was there! How clean he became here! He was so ugly back there! How nice and respectable he is here. My ears rang with the words exactly as if he would have said them, "Do not scorn me because I am swarthy," and, of course, David's verse: "The stone forsaken by the builder has become the cornerstone."

How did all of this happen? The changes that occurred from there to here. I decided immediately to stop thinking about going back. Here, in America, this free land with all its equal opportunities for all, is my home. I shook off the last bit of dust from the Old Country and went right into school to learn English and then right out to look for work. I bought a candy store far uptown in Washington Heights on 166th Street. This business went, as they say, accordingly, not bad, but was very difficult since I didn't know the business. I didn't know enough English and it also wasn't in a Jewish neighborhood. Business was just fair until I got the idea to bring a printing press into the store. I found a worker and brought in all the necessities: a press, type, a cutting machine, etc. . . .

The printing business didn't pay off immediately, which depressed me, so I had to sell the store (for half the money) and I was left with just the printing. The worker quit, so I hired another—one good, one bad and it worked out.

A customer came in to get his order—business cards. The worker didn't show up that day. The customer didn't want to hear about it: he wanted his order. It was Sunday, so what could be done? I told myself, let's try to do it. It took me a long time—until late at night. I nearly broke my hands and the machine, but I got the job done. The customer showed up early Monday morning. He took a look at the cards,

Cartoon, "Welcome to All." Uncle Sam welcomes immigrants carrying their belongings into a structure marked "U.S. Ark of Refuge." Lithograph by Joseph Keppler. Puck *magazine, April 1880.*

he thanked me and he paid—and he added, "excellent." That gave me the courage to learn the trade and, little by little, I began to work late into the night. One night a man—an English man—came in. He said he was a printer and worked downtown but lives here on my block. He was curious to meet me, so he sat down and we started talking. A new customer came in to get business cards and needs them immediately. My regular worker had left a while ago. I could do it myself, with a lot of difficulty—and slowly. I ask if he can wait until tomorrow, but he says no and complains that he can get it faster downtown. I sit there, embarrassed. But now, my guest, the printer, gets up and asks if I'll let him do the job. He took off his coat and started working. He finished the job in less than a half an hour. I offer to pay him, but he wouldn't take it. He'd prefer to do it as a favor. He began to come in every evening and did a lot of good work. I didn't want to take advantage of him and said he should get paid by the hour. He made up his own wage. And, actually, it was very cheap. And he'd come in to work for nearly three hours almost every evening. We became such good friends that we became partners in a new project: a weekly paper with a bit of local news and advertisements for businesses. It went quite well and after about eight months we decided to expand. We brought in a bigger machine and more type and we continued to do well and did bigger jobs every week. . . .

Jacob Sholtz, Autobiography #5, American Jewish Autobiographies Collection, RG 102, pp. 7–13, YIVO Institute for Jewish Research, New York. Printed with permission of Jerrold Sholtz.

✤ 5 ✤

VOICE OF THE IMMIGRANT JEWISH COMMUNITY

• ABRAHAM CAHAN •

ABRAHAM CAHAN, a journalist, novelist, and dedicated socialist, arrived in the United States in 1882 and quickly became the leading voice of the Jewish working class. Part of a cadre of young radicals and intellectuals in Eastern Europe, Cahan remained committed to socialism, but adapted his leftist sensibilities to the American environment.

He rose to prominence as an author with the publication of *Yekl: A Tale of the New York Ghetto*, *The Imported Bridegroom and Other Stories*, and *The Rise of David Levinsky*. Cahan's fiction always reflected his abiding concern with economic and social issues and his preoccupation with the tensions inherent in succeeding in America. *The Rise of David Levinsky*, his sweeping tale of the journey of a poor immigrant who becomes a prosperous cloak manufacturer, explores the conflicts and sacrifices that accompanied American success.

While he was writing novels and short stories, Cahan regularly contributed articles to leading magazines and newspapers. In the 1890s, he was one of the founders of the Yiddish-language *Jewish Daily Forward*, serving as its editor after 1902. At its height, the *Forward* circulated to a half million readers. The newspaper became a crucial voice of the labor and socialist movements, while at the same time publishing serialized works of fiction and advice columns. Even as it brought together the Yiddish-speaking community, the *Forward* taught Jewish immigrants about American culture, with regular features that addressed issues of adjustment to the United States. With its simple, straightforward style, the *Jewish Daily Forward* represented the concerns and aspirations of a generation of immigrant Jews.

A pioneering force in American Jewish culture, Cahan gave expression to the experience of immigrant Jews, articulating and producing a distinctly American brand of Jewish socialism, journalism, and fiction. In this passage from his memoirs, Abraham Cahan recalls his early radical beliefs and the ways that they began to change upon his arrival in America.

⌐

THE JEWISH SECTION of the city was itself a center of great variety. There were Russian and Polish Jews, German-American Jews called Yahudim, many of them from Posen, which was the Polish part of Germany. There were Jews from Germany itself. And there were American-born Jews. During my first years in the United States a few Yahudim were still living in the neighborhood of East Broadway. But most of the richer Posen and German Jews had already moved uptown.

About two years after my arrival, the Young Men's Hebrew Association, with headquarters uptown, opened a branch on East Broadway. American-born boys from German-Jewish families joined.

A Yahudi is an impossibility today in the Jewish section. But in those years they owned almost all the small stores and many of the larger ones on Grand Street. With the arrival of the first immigrants from Russia, they began to move further uptown. Actually it was not our coming that caused them to go. When one becomes rich one moves uptown. So it goes even today. Fiftieth Street was far uptown.

Before my arrival not many Jews emigrated from Russia to America. The exceptions were Jews from Kalisz and Suwalki, near the German border. They were the core of the Jewish population on the East Side. Almost all the peddlers and the customer peddlers, as well as the storekeepers on East Broadway and on Canal Street who sold them the clothes, the cloth, the furniture and the jewelry that they peddled, were from the province of Suwalki. Many of the thirty to forty thousand Jewish workers in the city, including a large group of Jews from western Poland, were employed in tailoring men's clothing. The women's cloak trade was small, having only recently been started in the United States. Formerly, better cloaks were imported from Germany. Most women wore shawls.

Abraham Cahan at approximately twenty-three years old.
From the Archives of the YIVO Institute for Jewish Research

The first cloak shops were established by the Yahudim, who were not themselves tailors but who hired as their cutters, operators and pressers the Jews coming over from Poland and Lithuania.

There were very few intellectuals among the earlier immigrant Jews from Russia and Austria. The newcomers from Suwalki included some Talmudic Jews. These aristocrats of the East Side could frequently be heard arguing a passage from the Talmud in the peddler stores on East Broadway. . . .

WITH THE COMING of the new immigrants one began to hear Russian spoken on the streets of the East Side. Once, a woman passing by as a friend and I were conversing in Russian on East Broadway, turned on us with disgust and spat out: "Tfu! The nerve, actually talking Russian! Wasn't it bad enough that you had to hear that dirty language in Russia?"

Even the uneducated immigrants could speak Russian, although they preferred Yiddish. But the intellectual minority spoke only Russian among themselves. This was a new thing in New York and it was because we were the first Russian-Jewish intellectuals in the United States.

We had brought something more than just this new way of conversing. In our hearts we also brought our love for enlightened Russian culture. We had transported from Russia the banner of idealism, scarred and bloodstained in the Russian revolutionary movement.

We could feel the resistance of the old-fashioned Suwalki Jews to the spirit of our new movement. They considered us to be atheists and lunatics; we intellectuals thought of them as ignorant, primitive people.

We were a small minority. Most of our own fellow immigrants shared the suspicions felt by the Suwalki Jews. The Jewish masses in the old country knew little about socialism. Socialist ideas were fenced in by a wall of guns and gallows, by censorship and the fear of the police. The formation of the Jewish Workers' Bund in Vilna was still fifteen years off.[1] A mere handful of Jewish workers in Vilna had grasped the meaning of socialism—and almost all of this handful had come to America.

After my arrival it took me just three days to realize that the establishment of commune colonies was not really my dream. I was not fascinated by village life, by the prospect of laboring on the soil. On the contrary, I felt strongly drawn to the life of the city. My heart beat to its rhythms, and as the heart feels so thinks the head. . . .

IN MY ARGUMENTS with followers of the commune idea I cited all the previous attempts in the United States to establish commune farms and noted that only the Quakers had succeeded.

I told my friends, sometimes in heated arguments, that they were wasting their time and their energy on an impossible dream. I counted myself out of the group for I had begun to feel around me the seething life of a great American city. Formerly I had only read about capitalism. Now it surrounded me on all sides. . . .

I felt America's freedom every minute. I breathed freer than I had ever breathed before. But all the time I was saying to myself, "All of this is a capitalist prison." And the confusion in my brain was compounded by the fact that in the first few months in America I worked like a slave at my first jobs.

From Russia, where distribution of socialist literature was a secret task evoking the tenor of Siberian exile, I had brought the notion that to be dedicated to the cause required the underground performance of such prohibited tasks. Therefore I planned to print socialist propaganda leaflets, to post myself in the street in front of the shops and factories and to distribute them to the workers. This had the taste of underground conspiracy, although there was no risk in doing it here.

I longed to persuade myself that by distributing such socialist leaflets I would be

---

[1] The General Jewish Workers Union of Poland and Russia, "the Bund," was founded in Vilna in 1897. The Bund supported the socialist revolution, addressing the particular needs of Russian Jews while also participating in the struggle of workers throughout Russia.

leading the life of a Russian revolutionary in the United States. The word "leaflet" had a sacred sound. It was "forbidden fruit" even though it was not forbidden. In years to come, hundreds of others, for the same reason, experienced the same illusion. And because there was no secret socialist movement in the United States, they looked upon the native movement with contempt.

What kind of socialism could it be without conspiracy? What good was the fruit if it wasn't forbidden? The power of deeply rooted beliefs is greater than the power of logic and common sense. Socialism itself teaches that the special circumstances of each time and each place must be taken into account in formulating tactics. But the romantic stimulation of danger is powerful. If all is permissible and danger is absent, socialism becomes diluted and revolutionary heroism becomes impossible.

Abraham Cahan, *The Education of Abraham Cahan* trans. Leon Stein, Abraham P. Conan, Lynn Davison from *Bleter fun mein leben* (Philadelphia: The Jewish Publication Society of America, 1969), pp. 223-224, 225-226, 227, 228-229. Reprinted from *The Education of Abraham Cahan*, © 1969 by Leon Stein, published by The Jewish Publication Society, with the permission of the publisher.

ల 6 ల

ADVICE FOR JEWISH IMMIGRANTS

• THE BINTEL BRIEF •

THE BINTEL Brief (bundle of letters) was one of the *Jewish Daily Forward*'s most popular features. The daily column, which began running in the paper in 1906, consisted of letters from readers asking for advice, with responses offered by the editors. In "Dear Abby" fashion, Jewish immigrants wrote with all varieties of problems and concerns, including love, marriage, divorce, work, politics, religion, and generational conflicts. Although the *Forward*'s staff edited the letters liberally (and perhaps even invented letters from time to time), the column reflected the prevailing issues of immigrant Jewish life in America. Abraham Cahan, the *Forward*'s editor, answered the letters himself in the early years, later aided by his staff. The responses reflected the overall spirit of the newspaper, committed to leftist politics but always evenhanded and rarely imposing strict ideologies on its readers.

The three letters below address topics of education, love, and work—recurring themes in the Bintel Brief.

—⌣—

I

September 1, 1910

Esteemed Editor of Forverts!

Although I read Yiddish quite well, I cannot write Yiddish well. I am therefore forced to write this letter in English. My question is as follows:

I am currently 18 years old and work as a bookkeeper and stenographer. My parents are old fashioned, religious people. After I finished public school at the age of 15, I had to go to work in order to help my parents. They did everything in their powers and sent me to a business school, which I completed in a short time and have, since then, worked in my current position.

Because my parents are themselves unaware, they have no idea as to my intellectual needs and desires. Outside of the public libraries, I have no one and nowhere to turn. I used to spend many hours there reading and used to bring books home, too. I never sat for a minute with nothing to do. I read many, many books. But I feel that I may have left out some of the most important ones. I would therefore very much appreciate your help in my quest for knowledge and education, which I was not able to get at school.

I can tell you which books I have read. I've read everything by Hawthorne, Elliot, Dickens, Walter Scott, Madame Worde, S. Brudia and others. I have also read Sinkevitshes and Tolstoy. I love poetry and I have read Shakespeare, Thomas Moore, Byron, Longfellow, Whittier and others.

I now ask you, worthy editor, tell me, what other good books are there for me to read. I know there are many good writers, but I also know that there are many books that are not worth reading. I don't really know what to do. I go home and sit for hours without reading and I think to myself: am I the only one in this situation, or are there others like me?

Thanking you in advance and awaiting your response, I remain your faithful reader,

A. R.
Philadelphia

Abraham Cahan at work, ca. 1937.
Library of Congress, Prints and
Photographs Division

Editor's Response:

In "fiction," we suggest you read all the work of Jack London, William Dean Howells, Upton Sinclair. From the older material: Edgar Allan Poe. The work of these writers is sufficient for years of reading for a working person.

However, we feel it is a tragedy that the reading public mainly nourishes itself *only* on fiction. This is exactly the same as if you ate only candy.

It is true, that [it is difficult] for a young woman whose intellectual needs aren't used to anything other than candy-fiction to nourish herself with something that offers science and knowledge. Especially for a young woman who works all day and who can only read during her off hours and while riding in [trolley] cars, when her spirit is weak and tired.

There is, however, enough to read at an intermediate level between fiction and scientific works. There is travel literature, light, natural science books, historical works and others. Books on all of these subjects are available in the libraries and are worthwhile to read. And there are lots of them, practically without end. Little by little, by reading these materials, one can get used to reading more difficult scientific works.

II

September 13, 1910

Esteemed Mr. Editor of the Forverts!

It's been a while already that I've thought about writing you and pouring out my despairing heart. But I've held everything inside, hoping that it will turn out okay. Now, though, I see that I must come to you for an answer. The story is, briefly, as follows:

I am a boy, 22 years old, four years in the country. I am in business and I make a living. I was raised in Russia in a small shtetl by wealthy parents who didn't want for anything. There I made the acquaintance of a young, beautiful and intelligent young woman. She was older than I. Her husband was in America. As a friend, I used to visit her frequently. We would spend time together and she would show me the letters her husband sent her. Little by little, we became close friends and I began to feel that I couldn't survive without her. If I didn't see her for just one day, I couldn't handle it—I couldn't eat and I couldn't sleep. Quite simply, I began to worship her. Shortly thereafter, her husband sent her a ticket to America. Then my suffering began. My heart began to break. During her last two months, I would visit her every day and, with pain in my heart, look at her and wait for her to part from me. I wept bitter tears day and night, like a small child. I found no solace whatsoever. The closer the day of her departure came, the more horrible my suffering became. The last two days before she left I was nearly out of my head from the pain. I noticed that she was also suffering and that she didn't want to go, but she had to. After she left, I yearned for her every day. I felt my suffering was a waste of time, since I couldn't go on without her. But I soon received a letter from her. She wrote that she missed me and longed for me. I immediately decided to go to America. I didn't really need to go to America: we had everything we needed in our home. My parents really did not want me to go. But I began to beg them and eventually they gave me money and I went.

In America, I went straight to her and her husband. They welcomed me nicely and treated me well. But I didn't have the heart to live with them. I couldn't watch how she sat with him at the table, ate with him, spoke with him. I moved in with a landsman, but I would visit them every day. Her husband treated me very well and I became his best friend. Naturally, he doesn't know that my coming to America was because of her. I speak with her a lot about that. She complains to me that she doesn't live happily with her husband, but that she has no choice—she has to live with him because she married him and had a child with him, but she doesn't love him and never loved him. She married him, she said, because her mother wanted wealthy in-laws. And you can see that they are not a good match. She is pretty, smart, and full of life and he is the opposite of her. He doesn't understand her at all and only loves her for her beautiful body. She doesn't love him, so how can she be happy?

I find myself in a tragic situation. I don't know what to do. Without her, my life is senseless—a wasted life. When I visit her, I take pity on her husband: I don't want to break up a family—that would be a tragedy. But not to visit her—that's a pity for me and maybe for her, too. This is why it's so hard for me. Practically impossible. She is alone in the house every evening (her husband works late). I come and spend time with her, the only solace and joy I have in my life.

Worthy editor, I need some advice in order to prevent a scandal. I'm a friend of her husband and don't want to cause him any pain or suffering. I also don't want to cause her any pain and I am sure, because she tells me, that

The "Bintel Brief" column in the Jewish Daily Forward, *July 5, 1918.*

she is suffering more than I am. I hope you can give me the right advice. I thank you in advance.

Your faithful reader, The Unhappy, Kh.N.

Editor's Response:

What kind of proper advice does he expect from us other than he should tear himself away from this woman and not disturb a family?

He should disabuse himself of the notion that he takes pity on her and that she cannot live happily with her husband. Everyone who is in love with someone else's wife says that. It's comfortable to convince oneself of it. He should not be the judge of their family life. If he will stop playing mind games with her, she will probably be able to live a happy life with her husband and father of her child.

That is generally the only thing that [it] is our duty to say about these kinds of situations.

III

October 10, 1910

Worthy Forverts Editor!

As a faithful reader of your worthy newspaper I request your advice in the following situation.

Two years ago, my mother, my sister, and I came over from Russia. My sister and I received a good education in Russia.

When we arrived here, I was 14 years old and my sister was 13. Being too young to work, my mother sent us to school and was able to take care of us through her hard work. After two years of school, both my sister and I finished with the highest marks. We both want to continue and study in high school, but it's not possible for the both of us. Our mother is too weak to work and support us. She therefore came up with a plan for us—that one will go to high school and the other will work in a shop and help earn money.

Our mother would like to please both of us and said that we have to decide amongst ourselves who will be the one to go to school and who will be the one to work. My sister says that because she is younger, she should be the one to go to school. But I am only one year older and it seems terrible to me that I will have to be a shopgirl forever.

So, Worthy Editor, it has been left to us to ask you for advice as to what we should do. We are depending on you and we ask that you answer as quickly as possible because time is passing quickly. Speaking for the both of us, I remain, attentively,

Sadie K—n

Editor's Response:

It is heartbreaking that due to a meager piece of bread one must give up her studies at such a young age and become a sweatshop slave. If this is the unfortunate situation, the simple and most just way, naturally, is that the older one should go to work. Does the fact that she is only one year older change the situation? Without that extra year both of their fates would be exactly the same, but one year is enough that the weight of fate falls on her side.

She shouldn't lose her courage. Many working girls, even older than she, manage to get an education. She should use all of her free time to study and to go to evening school.

Jewish Daily Forward, September 10, 1910, p. 5; September 13, 1910, p. 5; October 10, 1910, p. 6.

~ 7 ~

AN IMMIGRANT JEWISH GIRL
FROM POLAND

· SADIE FROWNE ·

AFTER SADIE'S Frowne's father died, she and her mother struggled to support themselves in Poland. With the help of relatives already in the United States, the two were able to afford steerage passage and make the journey to America. Sadie Frowne was thirteen years old when she and her mother arrived in New York to build a new life.

Frowne faced challenges beyond those encountered by most Jewish immigrants. Her mother died shortly after their arrival, and Frowne supported herself at a young age. Nevertheless, her account reflects the experiences of many young Jewish women who labored in the factories. Frowne joined other mostly Jewish and Italian women who earned a living doing piecework in the sweatshops. There they received lower wages than men, faced harsh treatment from bosses, and endured occasional harassment from male co-workers. Although she was not a fervent activist, Frowne recounts her participation in the garment workers strikes and recognizes the benefits of union activity. She also explains her careful budgeting strategies and her efforts to obtain an education at night.

Frowne's education about America took place not only through school and work, but also through popular culture. Like many young Jewish immigrant women, she saved money to buy fashionable clothes and took full advantage of the "cheap amusements" offered in New York's parks, theaters, and dance halls. A strikingly upbeat and optimistic person, Frowne pursued a romantic relationship, but clearly strived for independence and self-sufficiency.

Sadie Frowne told her story to a journalist who published it in the newspaper *The Independent* in 1902. A few years later, her account appeared in a collection titled, *The Life Stories of Undistinguished Americans as Told by Themselves.*

⌐◝

WHEN I WAS a little more than ten years of age my father died. He was a good man and a steady worker, and we never knew what it was to be hungry while he lived. After he died troubles began, for the rent of our shop was about $6 a month and then there were food and clothes to provide. We needed little, it is true, but even soup, black bread and onions we could not always get.

We struggled along till I was nearly thirteen years of age and quite handy at housework and shop keeping, so far as I could learn them there. But we fell behind in the rent and mother kept thinking more and more that we should have to leave Poland and go across the sea to America where we heard it was much easier to make money. Mother wrote to Aunt Fanny, who lived in New York, and told her how hard it was to live in Poland, and Aunt Fanny advised her to come and bring me. I was out at service at this time and mother thought she would leave me—as I had a good place—and come to this country alone, sending for me afterward. But Aunt Fanny would not hear of this. She said we should both come at once, and she went around among our relatives in New York and took up a subscription for our passage.

We came by steerage on a steamship in a very dark place that smelt dreadfully. There were hundreds of other people packed in with us, men, women and children, and almost all of them were sick. It took us twelve days to cross the sea, and we thought we should die, but at last the voyage was over, and we came up and saw the beautiful bay and the big woman with the spikes on her head and the lamp that is lighted at night in her hand (Goddess of Liberty).

Aunt Fanny and her husband met us at the gate of this country and were very good to us, and soon I had a place to live out (domestic servant), while my mother got work in a factory making white goods.

I was only a little over thirteen years of age and a greenhorn, so I received $9 a month and board and lodging, which I thought was doing well. Mother, who, as I have said, was very clever, made $9 a week on white goods, which means all sorts of underclothing, and is high class work.

But mother had a very gay disposition. She liked to go around and see everything, and friends took her about New York at night and she caught a bad cold and coughed and coughed. She really had hasty consumption but she didn't know it, and I didn't know it, and she tried to keep on working, but it was no use. She had not the strength. Two doctors attended her, but they could do nothing, and at last she died and I was left alone. I had saved money while out at service, but mother's sickness and funeral swept it all away and now I had to begin all over again.

Aunt Fanny had always been anxious for me to get an education, as I did not know how to read or write, and she thought that was wrong. Schools are different in Poland from what they are in this country, and I was always too busy to learn to read and write. So when mother died I thought I would try to learn a trade and then I could go to school at night and learn to speak the English language well.

So I went to work in Allen Street (Manhattan) in what they call a sweatshop, making skirts by machine. I was new at the work and the foreman scolded me a great deal.

"Now, then," he would say, "this place is not for you to be looking around in. Attend to your work. That is what you have to do."

I did not know at first that you must not look around and talk, and I made many mistakes with the sewing, so that I was often called a "stupid animal." But I made $4 a week by working six days in the week. For there are two Sabbaths here—our own Sabbath, that comes on a Saturday, and the Christian Sabbath that comes on Sunday. It is against our law to work on our own Sabbath so we work on their Sabbath.

In Poland I and my father and mother used to go to the synagogue on the Sabbath but here the women don't go to the synagogue much, though the men do. They are shut up working hard all the week long and when the Sabbath comes they like to sleep long in bed and afterward they must go out where they can breathe the air. The rabbis are strict here, but not so strict as in the old country.

I lived at this time with a girl named Ella, who worked in the same factory and made $5 a week. We had the room all to ourselves, paying $1.50 a week for it, and doing light housekeeping. It was in Allen street and the window looked out of the back, which was good, because there was an elevated railroad in front, and in summer time a great deal of dust and dirt came in at the front windows. We were on the fourth story and could see all that was going on in the back rooms of the houses behind us, and early in the morning the sun used to come in our window.

We did our cooking on an oil stove, and lived well, as this list of our expenses for one week will show:

Ella and Sadie for Food (One Week)

Tea	$0.06
Cocoa	10
Bread and rolls	40
Canned vegetables	20
Potatoes	10
Milk	21
Fruit	20
Butter	15
Meat	60
Fish	15
Laundry	25
Total	*$2.42*
Add rent	1.50
Grand total	*$3.92*

Of course, we could have lived cheaper, but we are both fond of good things and felt that we could afford them.

We paid 18 cents for a half pound of tea so as to get it good and it lasted us three weeks, because we had cocoa for breakfast. We paid 5 cents for six rolls and 5 cents a loaf for bread, which was the best quality. Oatmeal cost us 10 cents for three and one-half pounds, and we often had it in the morning, or Indian meal porridge in the place of it, costing about the same. Half a dozen eggs cost about 13 cents on an average, and we could get all the meat we wanted for a good hearty meal for 20 cents—two pounds of chops, or a steak, or a bit of veal, or a neck of lamb—something like

Women factory workers pose for a photograph.
From the Archives of the YIVO Institute for Jewish Research

that. Fish included butter fish, porgies, codfish and smelts, averaging about 8 cents a pound.

Some people who buy at the last of the market when the men with the carts want to go home, can get things very cheap, but they are likely to be stale, and we did not often do that with fish, fresh vegetables, fruit, milk or meat. Things that kept well we did buy that way and got good bargains. I got thirty potatoes for 10 cents one time, though generally I could not get more than 15 of them for that amount. Tomatoes, onions and cabbages, too, we bought that way and did well, and we found a factory where we could buy the finest broken crackers for 3 cents a pound, and another place where we got broken candy for 10 cents a pound. Our cooking was done on an oil stove, and the oil for the stove and the lamp cost us 10 cents a week.

It cost me $2 a week to live, and I had a dollar a week to spend on clothing and pleasure, and saved the other dollar. I went to night school but it was hard work learning at first as I did not know much English.

Two years ago I came to Brownsville, where so many of my people are, and where I have friends. I got work in a factory making underskirts—all sorts of cheap underskirts, like cotton and calico for the summer and woolen for the winter, but never the silk, satin or velvet underskirts. I earned $4.50 a week and lived on $2 a week, the same as before. I got a room in the house of some friends who lived near the factory. I pay $1 a week for the room and am allowed to do light housekeeping—that is, cook my meals in it. I get my own breakfast in the morning, just a cup of coffee and a roll, and at noon time I come home to dinner and take a plate of soup and a slice of bread with the lady of the house. My food for a week costs a dollar, just as it did in Allen street, and I have the rest of my money to do as I like with. I am earning $5.50 a week now, and will probably get another increase soon.

It isn't piecework in our factory, but one is paid by the amount of work done just the same. So it is like piecework. All the hands get different amounts, some as low as $3.50 and some of the men as high as $16 a week. The factory is in the third story of a brick building. It is in a room twenty feet long and fourteen broad. There are fourteen machines in it. I and the daughter of the people with whom I live work two of these machines. The other operators are all men, some young and some old.

At first a few of the young men were rude. When they passed me they would touch my hair and talk about my eyes and my red cheeks and make jokes. I cried and said that if they did not stop I would leave the place. The boss said that that should not be, that no one must annoy me. Some of the other men stood up for me, too, especially Henry, who said two or three times that he wanted to fight. Now the men all treat me very nicely. It was just that some of them did not know better, not being educated.

Henry is tall and dark, and he has a small mustache. His eyes are brown and large. He is pale and much educated, having been to school. He knows a great many things and has some money saved—I think nearly $400. He is not going to be in a sweatshop all the time, but will soon be in the real estate business, for a lawyer that knows him well has promised to open an office and pay him to manage it.

Henry has seen me home every night for a long time and makes love to me. He wants me to marry him, but I am not seventeen yet, and I think that is too young. He is only nineteen, so we can wait.

I have been to the fortune teller's three or four times, and she always tells me that though I have had such a lot of trouble I am to be very rich and happy. I believe her because she has told me so many things that have come true. So I will keep on working in the factory for a time. Of course it is hard, but I would have to work hard even if I was married.

I get up at half-past five o'clock every morning and make myself a cup of coffee on the oil stove. I eat a bit of bread and perhaps some fruit and then go to work. Often I get there soon after six o'clock so as to be in good time, though the factory does not open till seven. I have heard that there is a sort of clock that calls you at the very time you want to get up, but I can't believe that because I don't see how the clock would know.

At seven o'clock we all sit down to our machines and the boss brings to each one the pile of work that he or she is to finish during the day, what they call in English their "stint." This pile is put down beside the machine and as soon as a skirt is done it is laid on the other side of the machine. Sometimes the work is not all finished by six o'clock and then the one who is behind must work overtime. Sometimes one is finished ahead of time and gets away at four or five o'clock, but generally we are not done till six o'clock.

The machines go like mad all day, because the faster you work, the more money you get. Sometimes in my haste I get my finger caught and the needle goes right through it. It goes so quick though, that it does not hurt much. I bind the finger up with a piece of cotton and go on working. We all have accidents like that. Where the needle goes through the nail it makes a sore finger, or where it splinters a bone it does much harm. Sometimes a finger has to come off. Generally, though, one can be cured by a salve.

All the time we are working the boss walks about examining the finished garments and making us do them over again, if they are not just right. So we have to be careful as well as swift. But I am getting so good at the work that within a year I will be making $7 a week, and then I can save at least $3.50 a week. I have over $200 saved now.

The machines are all run by foot-power and at the end of the day one feels so weak that there is a great temptation to lie right down and sleep. But you must go out and get air, and have some pleasure. So instead of lying down I go out generally with Henry. Sometimes we go to Coney Island, where there are good dancing places, and sometimes we go to Ulmer Park to picnics. I am very fond of dancing, and, in fact, all sorts of pleasure. I go to the theater quite often, and like those plays that make you cry a great deal "The Two Orphans" is good. Last time I saw it I cried all night because of the hard times that the children had in the play. I am going to see it again when it comes here.

For the last two winters I have been going to night school. I have learned reading, writing and arithmetic. I can read quite well in English now and I look at the newspapers every day. I read English books, too, sometimes. The last one that I read was "A Mad Marriage," by Charlotte Braeme. She's a grand writer and makes things just like real to you. You feel as if you were the poor girl yourself going to get married to a rich duke.

I am going back to night school again this winter. Plenty of my friends go there. Some of the women in my class are more than forty years of age. Like me, they did not have a chance to learn anything in the old country. It is good to have an education; it makes you feel higher. Ignorant people are all low. People say now that I am clever and fine in conversation.

We recently finished a strike in our business. It spread all over and the United Brotherhood of Garment Workers was in it. That takes in the cloakmakers, coatmakers, and all the others. We struck for shorter hours, and after being out four weeks won the fight. We only have to work nine and a half hours a day and we get the same pay as before. So the union does good after all in spite of what some people say against it—that it just takes our money and does nothing.

I pay 25 cents a month to the union, but I do not begrudge that because it is for our benefit. The next strike is going to be for a raise of wages, which we all ought to have. But though I belong to the union I am not a Socialist or an Anarchist. I don't know exactly what those things mean. There is a little expense for charity, too. If any worker is injured or sick we all give money to help.

Some of the women blame me very much because I spend so much money on clothes. They say that instead of a dollar a week I ought not to spend more than twenty-five cents a week on clothes, and that I should save the rest. But a girl must have clothes if she is to go into good society at Ulmer Park or Coney Island or the theater. Those who blame me are the old country people who have old-fashioned notions, but the people who have been here a long time know better. A girl who does not dress well is stuck in a corner, even if she is pretty, and Aunt Fanny says that I do just right to put on plenty of style.

I have many friends and we often have jolly parties. Many of the young men like to talk to me, but I don't go out with any except Henry.

Lately he has been urging me more and more to get married—but I think I'll wait.

The Independent, September 25, 1902; Hamilton Holt ed., *The Life Stories of Undistinguished Americans as Told by Themselves* (New York: J. Pott & Company, 1906), pp. 22–28.

~ 8 ~

JEWISH WOMEN ORGANIZE

• HANNAH G. SOLOMON •

IN 1893, when Hannah Solomon assumed the presidency of the newly founded National Council of Jewish Women, she became part of a trend that brought women to the forefront of Jewish communal life. Jewish women had always been important behind-the-scenes players in synagogues and philanthropic activities, but in the 1890s, the creation of an independent national Jewish women's organization was considered a novel idea.

The National Council of Jewish Women was born during the many proceedings that surrounded the World's Fair in Chicago. During the Exposition, the Parliament of World Religions convened. Under its auspices, Jewish women gathered for a Jewish Women's Congress where delegates discussed the feasibility and goals for a national Jewish women's organization. Hannah Solomon chaired the Jewish Women's Committee at the World's Fair and emerged as a natural choice to serve as president when delegates decided to establish the National Council of Jewish Women (NCJW). Married with three children and a member of Chicago's prestigious Reform Temple Sinai, Solomon had been one of the first Jewish women invited to join the influential Chicago Woman's Club, bringing both leadership and experience to the presidency of the NCJW.

The National Council of Jewish Women dedicated itself to religious, philanthropic, and educational endeavors. Composed of ninety-three members at its founding, by 1896 the NCJW had organized local sections in fifty cities and had attracted a membership of over 4,000 women. By 1925, over 50,000 women had joined its ranks. Most of its members were middle-class Jewish women, primarily of Central European descent. Through the NCJW, they worked to enhance commitment to Judaism within their families and communities. They also provided assistance to East European immigrants, taking particular interest in protecting women from the dangers of white slavery.

A consummate leader and administrator, Solomon made a career out of voluntarism and social reform. In the excerpt below, an interview conducted in 1920, Hannah Solomon reflects back on the challenges facing women during the early days of the NCJW.

THEY USED TO think that the woman who belonged to a club was entirely too radical for polite society, and so most of us contented ourselves with sewing circles and coffee-klatches. We learned to play cards and then we were the equals of men. . . .

I was considered quite radical . . . and the good ladies of Chicago were skeptical indeed about whether I was a fit person for their company. . . .

Hannah Solomon, first president of the National Council of Jewish Women (NCJW).

There are thirty thousand of us now . . . [a]ll working together for the welfare of the nation and of our people. Thirty years ago—we had the time of our lives getting a scant dozen together. The Council of Jewish Women had its inception at the Congress of Religions at the World's Fair in Chicago in 1893. If ever there was a lovely place to be born in—it was Chicago at the time of the World's Fair and there the infant council first reared her head. To Susan B. Anthony[1], the great pioneer of women, belongs the idea of calling together the women of America to participate in the World's Fair and the Parliament of Religions, and to bring forward women's work in every field.

To me was assigned the task of organizing the Jewish women. There was never a more difficult job. First of all we had no way of knowing who the leading Jewish women of the country were. Emma Lazarus[2], Julia Richman[3], and Henrietta Szold[4] were perhaps the only nationally known Jewesses in the country at that time. Some of us had become acquainted at summer resorts or occasional out-of-town visits.

Jewish women's organizations were practically unknown. There were, I think two Temple Sisterhoods then in existence—one in New York and one in Chicago—and the women of the Sisterhoods confined their activities to a small measure of philanthropic work for the poor of the congregation and to securing funds for the interior decoration of the synagogue. Imagine today a women's drive for funds for a new carpet for the Temple Emanu-El of New York or the Sinai Congregation of Chicago!

First of all when we tried to organize, we met with objections from the men. Rabbis and laymen did not want to help us in the beginning, because they were skeptical about separating Jewish women from women of other faiths, and were doubtful of the feasibility of bringing together any large number of Jewish women. It took a year of work to create a committee to assist me in carrying out my plans.

We organized mass meetings throughout the country where women delegates were elected. We corresponded with every prominent rabbi in every city, asking for suggestions, and when the Congress met in 1893, we had a representative gathering of Jewish women. On the last day of the Congress, the late Julia Richman, of New York, presented a resolution calling for the formation of a national Jewish women's

---

[1] Susan B. Anthony (1820–1906), pioneer of the women's rights movement in America, active in campaigns for woman's suffrage, temperance, the abolition of slavery, and a wide range of women's rights.

[2] Emma Lazarus (1849–1887), prominent poet and essayist; author of the poem "New Colossus," inscribed on the Statue of Liberty.

[3] Julia Richman (1855–1912), social reformer and educator, particularly active in Jewish organizations and immigrant aid. Richman served as superintendent of the Lower East Side public school district.

[4] Henrietta Szold (1860–1945), author, editor, devoted Zionist and founder of Hadassah, the Women's Zionist Organization of America.

organization, and every women present at the Congress pledged herself to support any organization that might be formed. Officers were elected and I was chosen president. We set about to formulate a constitution and a tentative plan for organization, and in 1896 our first Triennial Convention was held.

The women of the council had vision and they had a definite plan of work, which looked far ahead of the generation in which they themselves were working. At our first triennial we had two aims; religious work and philanthropy. We hoped to establish Sabbath schools and to extend the study of Jewish literature and history. In philanthropy we wanted to introduce preventive work, making the family rather than the individual the object of our care. By these plans, you can readily understand how limited was our field of endeavor in 1896. Charity and religion—these two were the province of womankind. Women's sphere is in the home, they told us. The last thirty years have been devoted to proof of our boast that women's sphere is the whole wide world, without limit.

So well were these original purposes carried out, that there are thousands of Jewish children in the Sabbath schools of the council all over the country. There have been many successful study circles, and in many cities where the council now exists, they are the only Jewish activity in the community.

But as we grew our work naturally expanded. We began Americanization work long before others thought of the existence of such a need. We had settlement houses, clubs and classes, English classes for foreign mothers and working girls—things which still seem novelties today.

In looking back from 1920, wherein our first national drive for funds for Americanization and women's welfare work is launched, we find that the council was the first organized body to claim a place for Jewish womanhood in the affairs of the country. It has furnished opportunities for women's development and has aided them in developing their talents. It has aided many other national organizations; it has furnished plans of study for small communities and assisted in the formation of Jewish Sabbath schools for girls, in many instances paying for instructors. It has carried on preventive and corrective work for the blind and deaf. Often these activities are carried on by the costs of thousands of dollars. The sections themselves and operated at National Council carries on important aid work with workers at Ellis Island, New York, Baltimore, Philadelphia, Seattle and San Francisco. Recently work was undertaken for Jewish women on farms.

In addition, the council takes an active interest in legislation that is of community and women's welfare. It maintains committees on Purity and the Press, Peace

The National Council of Jewish Women took a particular interest in assisting immigrant Jewish women. As this brochure demonstrates, NCJW members attempted to inculcate middle-class notions of domesticity among East European immigrant women.

American Jewish Historical Society, Newton Centre, Massachusetts and New York, New York

and Arbitration, Social Hygiene, Civic and Communal activities, and during the war it assisted in every national activity—Liberty Loans, Thrift Stamps, Red Cross, National Council of Defense and others.

Even the ambitious pioneers of 1893 did not dream of such a scope of work. They could hardly foresee that during the war, the National Council of Jewish Women would be the only organization permitted to carry on welfare work at Ellis Island. They could scarcely foresee the honored place the council holds in the National Council of Women of the United States, the National Federation of Women's Clubs and the International Council of Women.

But our pioneers [built] well, and so carefully that they may yet recognize in the Council of Jewish Women of today, the foundations which they themselves laid—for the spirit of the work has remained unchanged—even though the work itself has changed with changing times. The ranks of the workers still include many of our old timers.

"American Jewish Women in 1890 and 1920," An Interview with Mrs. Hannah G. Solomon, *The American Hebrew*, April 23, 1920.

A BASEBALL PRIMER FOR JEWISH IMMIGRANTS

UNDER ITS editor Abraham Cahan, *The Jewish Daily Forward* was an Americanizing agency. Although the newspaper devoted significant attention to political issues and the cause of Jewish labor, it also aimed to teach Jewish immigrants about American culture. The pages of the *Forward* were filled with explanations of American customs and habits so that Yiddish readers could learn to become Americans.

In this 1909 article, *Forward* editors attempted to explain the game of baseball to Jewish immigrants. Their convoluted and confusing explication of the game demonstrates just how little the authors understood baseball, as they struggle to convey its rules and to identify the different positions on the field. It is highly unlikely that Jewish immigrants were able to glean any sense of the game from this article. Those who followed the American game of baseball, primarily the children of immigrants, did so in the English-language press and later by listening on the radio. Nevertheless, the *Forward*'s attempt to translate the quintessential American game for Jewish immigrants demonstrates the newspaper's commitment to promoting Jewish adaptation and acculturation in the United States.

⁓

Uptown, on 9th Avenue and 155th Street is the famous field known as the "Polo Grounds." Every afternoon, 20 to 35 thousand people get together there. Entrance costs from 50 cents to a dollar and a half. Thousands of poor boys and older people go without some of their usual needs in order to pay for tickets. Professional teams play baseball there and the tens of thousands of fans who sit in row after row of seats all around the stadium, go nuts with enthusiasm. They jump, they scream, they simply go wild when one of "their" players does well or, they are pained or upset when they don't succeed.

A similar scene takes place every day in another place—in the Washington Heights. And the exact same thing goes on in Brooklyn, in Philadelphia, in Pittsburgh, in Boston, in Baltimore, in St. Louis, in Chicago—in every city in the United States. And the newspapers print the results of these games and describe what happened and tens of millions of people run to read it with gusto. They talk about it and they debate the issues.

And here we're only talking about the "professional games": practically every boy, nearly every youth, and not a few middle-aged men play baseball themselves, belong to baseball clubs, and are huge fans. Every college, every school, every town, nearly every "society," and every factory has it's own baseball "team."

Millions are made from the professional games. In connection to this, there is a special kind of "political" battle between different cities. A good professional player gets eight to ten thousand dollars for one season. Some of them are educated, college-educated people. To us immigrants, this all seems crazy, however, it's worthwhile to understand what kind of craziness

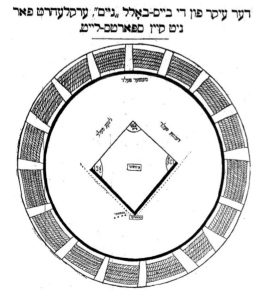

דער עיקר פון די בייס-באָלל "גיים", ערקלעָרדרט פאר ניט קיין ספאָרטס-לייט.

This diagram accompanied the Forward's *article on the fundamentals of baseball. The caption reads, "The Fundamentals of the Base-ball 'Game' Explained for Non Sports Fans." The names of various player positions on the field, the bases, and the three outfield areas are included to help readers understand the game.*
Jewish Daily Forward, August 27, 1909.

it is. If an entire nation is crazy over something, it's not too much to ask to try and understand what it means.

We will therefore explain here what baseball is. But, we won't do it using the professional terminology used by American newspapers to talk about the sport; we must apologize, because we're not even able to use this kind of language. We will explain it in plain, "unprofessional" and "unscientific" Yiddish.

So what are the fundamentals of the game?

Two parties participate in the game. Each party is comprised of nine people (such a party is called a "team"). One party takes the field, and the other plays the role of an enemy; the enemy tries to block the first one and the first one tries to defend itself against them; from now on we will call them, "the defense party" and the "enemy party."

The "defense party" also takes the field and plays. Two of the team players play constantly while the other seven stand on guard at seven different spots. What this guarding entails will be described later. Let us first consider the two active players.

One of them throws the ball to the other, who has to grab it. The first one is called the "pitcher" (thrower) and the second is called the "catcher" (grabber).

Each time, the "catcher" throws the ball back to the "pitcher." The reader may therefore ask, if so, doesn't it happen backwards each time—the catcher becomes a pitcher and the pitcher becomes a catcher? Why should each one be called with a specific name—one pitcher and one catcher?

We will soon see that the way in which the catcher throws the ball back is of no import. The main thing during a game is how the pitcher tries to throw the ball to the catcher. The enemy party, however, seeks to thwart the pitcher. This occurs in the following way:

One of the team's nine members stands between the pitcher and the catcher (quite close to the catcher) with a thick stick ("bat") and, as the ball flies from the pitcher's hand, tries to hit it back with the stick before the catcher catches it.

This enemy player is called "batter." The place where he stands is designated by a number of little stars (****)[on the diagram]. (The other eight players on the enemy team, in the meantime, do not participate. They each wait to be "next.")

Imagine now, that the "batter," meaning the enemy player, finds the thrown ball

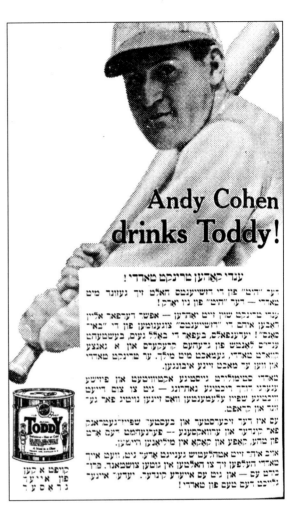

"Andy Cohen Drinks Toddy!"—Toddy, June 14, 1928.

Reprinted with permission. American Jewish Legacy, www.ajlegacy.org, and Shulamith Z. Berger Collection

with his stick and sends it flying. If certain rules, which we will discuss later, aren't broken, this is what can happen with the ball: if one of the "guards" catches the hit ball while it is still in the air, then the opposition of the "batter" is completely destroyed and the batter must leave his place; he is eliminated (he is "out"). He puts down the "bat" and another member of his party takes his place.

The roles of the seven guards of the defense party are also specific: they must try and catch the hit ball in order to destroy the enemy's attempt to hinder them and to get rid of the player doing the obstructing. They stand at various positions because one can never know in which direction the ball will fly. They watch the different trajectories in which the ball might fly, so a guard can be there ready to catch it.

The readers can see the way the seven guards are distributed in our picture.

The official field on which the game is played is a four-sided, four-cornered one. This is in the center of our picture (The two round lines which go around it represent the tens of thousands of seats for the audience. That is how it usually is for the big professional games. It actually looks like a giant circus with a roof only for the audience. The field, with all the players, is under the open sky.)...

"The Fundamentals of the Base-Ball 'Game' Described for Non-Sports Fans," *Jewish Daily Forward*, August 27, 1909, p. 4.

ORGANIZING THE WORKERS

CLARA LEMLICH arrived in the United States as a teenager, having already embraced radical politics while still in the Ukraine. She immediately went to work in a garment factory on the Lower East Side and responded to poor working conditions by devoting herself to the labor movement. She became one of the six men and seven women who founded Local 25 of the International Ladies Garment Worker's Union. In 1909, her passionate speech, calling for an immediate strike in the shirtwaist industry, sparked the "Uprising of the 20,000," a massive strike by women workers.

In addition to labor activism, Lemlich also campaigned for women's suffrage. After she married printing worker Joseph Shavelson and the couple had three children, she continued her activism, helping to organize working-class wives and mothers and lobbying for improved food and housing conditions. In 1929, she launched the United Council of Working Class

Women, which expanded to branches across the country. During the Depression, Lemlich Shavelson organized the first Unemployed Council in Brooklyn and joined the hunger marches in Washington. She was also a charter member of the Emma Lazarus Federation of Jewish Women's Clubs. Lemlich Shavelson became a member of the Communist Party in 1926 and retained a lifelong allegiance to communism. In the 1950s, she participated in the protest marches to save Julius and Ethel Rosenberg. Throughout her life, long after her days as a garment worker, Lemlich Shavelson devoted herself to reform efforts and political activism. In this selection, she looks back on her early days in the sweatshops and Shirtwaistmakers Strike of 1909.

⁓

I PERSONALLY CAME to this [country] in 1903. I knew very little about socialism. I went to work 2 weeks after landing in this country. We worked from sunrise to set 7 days a week. Saturday till 4:30 o'clock. The shops were located in the old delapidat[ed] buildings, in the back of stores. Those who worked on machines had to bring their machines particularly the men. They had to carry the machines on their back both to and from work.

Most of the shops had both a foreman and forelady. The shop we worked had no central heating, no electric power. The shop was heated by [a] coal stove which was in the center of the shop. The ashes were emptied every morning but ashes were taken away once a week. The hissing of the machines, the yelling of the Foreman, made life unbearable. The girls, whether socialist or not (had) many stoppages, and strikes broke out in many shops. However every strike we called was broken by the police and gangsters hired by the bosses. In 1906 some of us girls who were more class conscious called a meeting at 206 East Broadway, where we organized the 1st local of the waist makers. We elected S. Shindler[1] as our first secretary. We named the local Local 25 of the Waist Makers Union.

But since every strike we called was smashed by the bosses, the union decided

---

[1] S. Shindler, a wrapper-maker, was recording secretary of the United Hebrew Trades in 1909. The United Hebrew Trades played an important role in the Shirtwaistmakers Strike.

to call a mass meeting at Cooper Union. The hall was packed. On the platform was Samuel Gompers[2] of the American Federation of Labor, Leonora O'Reilly[3] of the Women's Trade Union League, B. Feigenbaum[4] of the *Jewish Daily Forward*. Each one talked about the terrible conditions of the workers in the shops. But no [one] gave or made any practical or valid solution. Suddenly a young girl in the audience[5] asked for the floor. When she was given the floor she said, "I make a motion that we go out in a general strike." The entire audience rose to its feet. Men threw their hats in the air, women waved their handkerchiefs.

The girl who made the motion was called to the platform. Mr. B. Feigenbaum of the *Jewish Daily Forward*, who was chairman of the meeting, raised the right hand of the girl and made her repeat the famous Jewish oath: "May my right [hand] wither from [my] arm if I betray the cause I now pledge." The following day 20 thousand waist makers, both men and women, came out on strike.

That's why this strike is known in the labor movement [as] the strike of the 20 thousand.

Now as to the question whether the girls were socialist, is hard to tell. All I can tell you [is] that many of us marched in the streets of down town N.Y. with [Alexander] Trach[t]e[n]berg[6] as our leader. Rose Pastor Stokes[7] marched with us. Many of the girls became leaders in the Women's Trade Union League. Some of them joined a political party.

I[n so] far as I am concerned, I am still at it.

Clara Lemlich, labor activist and leader of the Shirtwaistmakers Strike of 1909, ca. 1912.

Courtesy of UNITE HERE Archives, Kheel Center, Cornell University

---

2 Samuel Gompers (1850–1924), longtime president of the American Federation of Labor.

3 Leonora O'Reilly (1870–1927), a union member in the Knights of Labor, was an active member and orator in the Women's Trade Union League. According to historian Morris Schappes, she was not a speaker at the Cooper Union meeting and Lemlich Shavelson might have confused her speaking at another strike meeting.

4 Benjamin Feigenbaum (1860–1923) often used the Bible and Jewish tradition to promote socialist ideals, as in this case when he employed an ancient Jewish oath to endorse a worker's strike.

5 Lemlich Shavelson is describing herself in this account. It was she who delivered the passionate call for a general strike.

6 Alexander Trachtenberg (1884–1966), a charter member of the Communist Party, was a socialist, economist, and educator.

7 Rose Pastor Stokes (1870–1933), a socialist activist, lecturer, and orator, joined the Communist Party in 1919. In 1905, she married wealthy socialist James Graham Phelps Stokes.

Clara Lemlich Shavelson, "Remembering the Waistmakers General Strike, 1909," Morris U. Schappes, ed., *Jewish Currents* (November, 1982), pp. 10–11. Excerpted from *Jewish Currents* magazine (www.jewishcurrents.org).

11

PROTESTING LIVES LOST

• ROSE SCHNEIDERMAN •

IN 1911, more than 140 young immigrant women were killed in a devastating fire in the Triangle Shirtwaist Factory. Trapped in the fire, in part because owners had locked the shop doors, many women jumped to their deaths. The fire occurred in the heart of the Lower East Side and set off waves of grief and anger throughout the immigrant Jewish community. The tragedy came to symbolize the abuses of manufacturers and the exploitation of workers, further galvanizing the Jewish labor movement.

At one of the many rallies that followed the fire, Rose Schneiderman rose to deliver this stirring speech. A Polish immigrant, Schneiderman devoted her life to labor reform and activist causes. An organizer of the International Ladies Garment Workers Union and president of the Women's Trade Union League, Schneiderman also worked on behalf of farm labor and in the campaign for women's suffrage. In later years, President Franklin Roosevelt appointed her to the Labor Advisory Board of the National Recovery Administration.

⁓

I WOULD BE a traitor to these poor burned bodies if I came here to talk good fellowship. We have tried you good people of the public and we have found you wanting. The old Inquisition had its rack and its thumbscrews and its instruments of torture with iron teeth. We know what these things are today; the iron teeth are our necessities, the thumbscrews the high-powered and swift machinery close to which we must work, and the rack is here in the firetrap structures that will destroy us the minute they catch on fire.

This is not the first time girls have been burned alive in the city. Every week I must learn of the untimely death of one of my sister workers. Every year thousands of us are maimed. The life of men and women is so cheap and property is so sacred. There are so many of us for one job it matters little if 143 of us are burned to death.

We have tried you citizens; we are trying you now, and you have a couple of dollars for the sorrowing mothers and brothers and sisters by way of a charity gift. But every time the workers come out in the only way they know to protest against conditions which are unbearable the strong hand of the law is allowed to press down heavily upon us.

Public officials have only words of warning to us— warning that we must be intensely orderly and must be intensely peaceable, and they have the workhouse just back of all their warnings. The strong hand of the law beats us back, when we rise, into the conditions that make life unbearable.

I can't talk fellowship to you who are gathered here.

Mourners picket in the wake of the Triangle Fire, ca. 1911.
Courtesy of UNITE HERE Archives, Kheel Center, Cornell University

Too much blood has been spilled. I know from my experience it is up to the working people to save themselves. The only way they can save themselves is by a strong working class movement.

Rose Schneiderman, quoted in *The Survey*, April 8, 1911, pp. 84–85.

12

POPULAR IDOL OF THE YIDDISH STAGE

• BORIS THOMASHEFSKY •

BORIS THOMASHEFSKY left the Ukraine for New York in 1881 as a young boy, and immediately began working as a cigarette-maker in a Lower East Side sweatshop. At the age of thirteen, he managed to raise funds to bring a group of Yiddish performers from Europe to the United States and took his first role as a young soprano on stage. From the outset, Thomashefsky demonstrated a knack for the business of theater promotion. He pioneered a Yiddish touring company that brought the plays of the renowned Yiddish playwright Avrom Goldfadn to Jewish communities across the United States. While on the road, he met his wife Bessie, and both assumed leading roles on the Yiddish stage.

Thomashefsky emerged as the unrivaled star of *shund*, the Yiddish theater tradition of sensational melodramas complete with musical numbers and often bawdy humor. Despite critics who disdained the lowbrow productions, Thomashefsky's performances gained a mass audience. With his good looks and powerful presence, Thomashefsky attracted a devoted following, especially among female theatergoers. He established a reputation for decadence and for grand performances, playing romantic heroes in a string of popular operettas and melodramas. In later years, when Jacob Adler brought a more serious brand of Yiddish theater to America, Thomashefsky also wanted to prove his ability to carry a dramatic role, and adapted Shakespeare's *Hamlet* for the Yiddish stage. In this selection from his autobiography, first published in serialized form in the Yiddish press, Thomashefsky recounts his decision to play the role of Hamlet. Here, Thomashefsky reveals his rivalry with leading contemporary actors David Kessler and Jacob Adler.

I DECIDED TO direct *Hamlet* in the Thalia Theatre. Naturally, I would play the lead role—*Hamlet*. This was really a daring idea. . . . I should perform in the world famous role of *Hamlet*? I was lucky to have seen great actors play the role of *Hamlet*. As a child, when we lived in Kiev, my father once took me to Savin's Theatre, where I saw a famous Russian actor play in the role of *Hamlet*. Naturally, at the time, I barely understood what was being performed, but the name *Hamlet* had a huge effect on me as a child. I recall that my father told me at the theatre that it was a famous play and that the actor who played the lead was one of the most famous in Russia. . . .

How did it come to pass that *Hamlet* should make it to the Yiddish stage? Competition between the Yiddish theatres was growing day by day. One would try to outdo the other both with the plays and the roles. For example: if Adler put on a play that was well-received by the audience, Kessler[1] would start rummaging about for a play that would overshadow Adler's. At the time, I was looking for a snappy operetta that would do great and make it so Adler and Kessler couldn't compete with my success.

---

[1] David Kessler (1860–1920), one of Thomashefsky's rivals, a prominent actor and manager in early Yiddish theater who sometimes worked with Jacob Adler.

Boris Thomashefsky playing Hamlet, 1901.

The Dorot Jewish Division, The New York Public Library, Astor, Lenox and Tilden Foundations

Adler never performed operettas and Kessler hated them, though he performed them in an earlier period. As a result, I was the only one left in the field of Yiddish operetta. Knowing a bit of music and since I was also a musician, I, myself, wrote the music for the operettas, and the texts were written especially for me by Lateiner[2], and other professors. My operettas were performed in a lavish, opulent way, and that alone was already a guarantee of their success. . . .

Yes, I was the only one that amazed the Jewish public with gold and silver decorations and with electric lights of all colors. As a result, men, women and children ran to the theatre to see Thomashefsky. I was always more successful than my competitors. When Kessler and Adler played together at the Windsor Theatre, my troupe and I were at the Thalia Theatre, which was right across from the Windsor. At the Windsor, they were performing a play by Professor Hurvitz.[3] I can't recall what the play was called, but I remember that Adler and Kessler had the lead roles. But, it was no use—the play was a failure. At the same time, the play I was in had become very successful, and the two great artists, Adler and Kessler, began to think about me, their competitor. In connection to this, they got some help from friends and also from their fan clubs. They refused to allow Thomashefsky to have a big hit while Adler and Kessler had a failure.

So they decided to perform Shakespeare's *Othello*. One of them would play Othello, and the other would play Iago. "That's how we'll give it to Thomashefsky!" Adler and Kessler kept their decision secret and began to translate *Othello* into Yiddish. They assigned the roles and studied the play in secret. The actors in my troupe, as well as other friends, noticed that something was going on in the little world of the Yiddish theatre fan clubs, but nobody knew what, who, or when. All I knew was that Adler and Kessler were getting ready to drop a bomb, and that it would soon explode. Naturally, I really wanted to know what kind of "bomb" it was and, at first, I couldn't figure out what it was.

But in the theatre world, secrets can't be kept for very long, since you have to advertise and let the audience know what you're planning for them. One evening, some of my fans came running to me. They were preoccupied and upset: "You know,

[2] Joseph Lateiner (1852–1935), Yiddish playwright.

[3] Moyshe Ha-Levi Ish Hurwitz (d. 1910), Yiddish playwright.

Mr. Thomashefsky, Adler just announced onstage that he will soon present the world famous, sensational, musical tragedy by William Shakespeare, the greatest work of world literature, *Othello*. He said that he, Adler, would play the role of Othello and that Kessler would play Iago, and that the two would switch roles—one night Adler will play Othello, and Kessler, Iago, and the next night Kessler would play Othello and, Adler, Iago."

The fans also told me that Adler had insulted me on stage, saying that with a play like *Othello*, nobody would be able to follow his act, that you had to be a real actor to perform *Othello*. *Othello* is not "Alexander," the "little crown prince of Jerusalem."[4] Naturally, this really made me resentful of Adler. In our private lives, we were the best of friends, we used to meet every night in the café. We ate, drank and joked together, we told stories. But business is business.

I waited impatiently to finish the last act of the play. When it ended, I went out in front of the curtain and announced to the audience that because our current play is such a success, we can't close it and will continue to perform it, but only on Fridays, Saturdays and Sundays. On Wednesdays, I will soon present William Shakespeare's greatest tragedy, *Hamlet*. I will perform in the role of Hamlet, the Prince of Denmark. The theatre was packed with men, women and girls. The majority of the audience knew as much about Hamlet, the Prince of Denmark, as a religious Jew knows about the taste of bacon. They thought it was some new operetta. My fan club clapped and stomped, with their hands, and their feet and with boards and canes.

At the same time as they rehearsed *Othello* in the Windsor Theatre, we rehearsed *Hamlet* in the Thalia Theatre. Zeifert did the translation of *Hamlet* for me. He gave me the Yiddish translation within twenty-four hours. I hired a director from the Irving Place Theatre (the once famed German theatre), who immediately began preparing our production. He also helped me thoroughly learn the role of Hamlet. He was a good actor and an outstanding director. His name was Walter. He truly put every word in my mouth, showed me the meaning of the most important poses, and explained the ideas that Shakespeare wanted to express in his play. I studied my role day and night. At 7 A.M. when most actors are still sleeping, I was already onstage with Herr Walter studying my role. He showed me every step I had to take, he demonstrated the tone of the words, each passage. He showed me when I could be relaxed and, on the other hand, when I had to be tempestuous, or upset, and so on. . . .

In the Windsor Theatre, they had found out about the "bomb" I dropped. Adler

Boris Thomashefsky performing in the operetta "The Hungarian Singer."

From the Archives of the YIVO Institute for Jewish Research

---

[4] A role previously played by Thomashefsky on the Yiddish stage.

was furious. Such chutzpah! Thomashefsky is playing Hamlet at the same time he's playing Othello!! Every night he gave speeches to his audience about his *Othello*.

It was Adler's nature that he loved starting wars. He also liked to go out and talk to his audience and now he had the perfect occasion. What's this? He, Jacob P. Adler, the king of Yiddish drama is playing Othello and somebody else dares to play Hamlet! He wanted to convince the audience that they should come see his *Othello*, because he and Kessler are justified in presenting such a work, but the other guy, *The Woman of Valor*'s Little Alexander on the other side of the street has no right to perform in a play by Shakespeare! (Adler called me the *Woman of Valor*'s actor because I played in that role with great success years earlier in Lateiner's operetta, *Woman of Valor*).

With God's help, Adler put on *Othello*. It wasn't so great. Neither Adler nor Kessler was a big hit with their performances in "Othello." Most of the audience related to Shakespeare in Yiddish as if it were something alien to them. Meanwhile, I continued rehearsing *Hamlet*. . . .

It was the first time in the history of the Yiddish theatre that Shakespeare's famed tragedy would be produced in Yiddish, and I had the luck to be the first Yiddish actor in its lead role. . . .

The street around the theatre was packed with people. They were pushing each other toward the ticket booth to see me in *Hamlet*. And *Hamlet* was a huge success on the Yiddish stage. But to expect that success to last a long time would have been a mistake. The audience expressed wonder and enthusiasm. But to them, the play was foreign and distant. They were attracted to lighter plays they could relate to. And it was the same thing with Adler and Kessler's *Othello*.

Boris Thomashefsky, *The Story of My Life* [*Mayn lebens-geshikhte*] (New York: Trio Press, 1937), pp. 295–301.

13

THE JEWISH KING LEAR

• JACOB ADLER •

THE YIDDISH theater thrived in the immigrant Jewish world, providing both inexpensive entertainment and a release for the range of emotions experienced by newcomers to the United States. Jacob Adler, known as *Nesher HaGadol*, "The Great Eagle," became one of the brightest stars of the Yiddish stage. Born in Odessa, Adler began acting in Russia and toured through London and the United States before returning permanently to America in 1889. He began performing in the Yiddish theaters on Second Avenue before opening his own company, the Union Theater, on Broadway and Eighth Street.

Adler enjoyed his greatest success after teaming up with the great playwright Jacob Gordin. It was Gordin's *Der Yidisher Kenig Lir* (The Jewish King Lear) that became Adler's signature role and vaulted him to fame. The role fulfilled Adler's desire to bring more serious dramatic roles to the Yiddish theater, a departure from the melodramas that characterized many Yiddish productions. In subsequent years, Adler played the role of Shylock in Shakespeare's *Merchant of Venice* and also brought a Yiddish version of Shylock to the stage.

The entire Adler family participated in the life of the theater; his second wife, Sara, was an accomplished actress and many of his children went on to work in the industry. In these excerpts from his memoirs, Adler describes his pivotal role as the Jewish King Lear and looks back fondly on the audiences of working class Jewish immigrants that flocked to the Yiddish theater in its heyday.

WHEN I ANNOUNCED *The Yiddish King Lear*, the whole cast predicted failure. They swore the play would never "take," that the audience would die of boredom. They begged me not to play an ordinary old Jew in a long coat and a yarmulke. But I stood there steel and iron, all because of a song I remembered in my youth—a song about an old father turned away by his children. Why had that song impressed me so deeply, I asked myself, why had grown men wept every time they heard it? And in spite of the opposition of the cast I put on *The Yiddish King Lear*, which was then and still remains the greatest success of the Yiddish theater. . . .

It was in this era, the New York of the nineties, that we had our first great popular audiences—those lusty, unruly, noisy, madly devoted audiences of a time now past. Looking back from the present to those years I ask myself, where are they now, those "saints of the gallery," those boys and girls who once lived, flourished, made a racket, clapped, stamped, whistled, hooted, wept, and laughed, filling our theater with such fire and such joy? Where now? Where? Withered away, grown old, run out, dwindled, died. Yes, dead as the mastodon, the young "patriot" of those days, his bones buried in the cold depths of earth, and no heirs left to take his place. His high post in the gallery is empty, and the gallery is empty, too, cold and dark with wind blowing between the benches. No wonder it rots away and disappears!

In the Yiddish theater today we see order, decorum, politeness. Respectable people sit, finely dressed, finely fed, those who have forgotten youth. But high in the gallery, holding to the sides of his seat, the young "patriot" sat, and high was his enthusiasm. No two dollars could you ask of him, no dollar fifty. Ten or fifteen cents was all he could pay, and if we needed extras, we put him on the stage in a long coat and a crepe hair beard, and afterward he went up the gallery and saw the rest of the five-act play for nothing.

The poor boy, by day a baster for a tailor, an errand boy on Orchard or Rivington Street, was by night the king, the soul of our theater. Without binoculars he saw the stage better than any critic. And no lady infatuated with a matinee idol ever followed more breathlessly every move and turn of her idol, every transition, every rise and fall of his voice, every gesture, every cadence!

When we were good, how broad and proud his happiness, his triumph. He was more than an onlooker. He *believed* what he saw on the stage, gave himself to it, lived it with his whole heart, his whole soul. And we, the actors, felt his love like a great wave from the gallery to the stage. And because of that oneness, that warmth, we knew we had conquered, knew the audience was with us. And we had the courage to go on, to achieve even more, to strive even higher.

Jacob Adler as Shylock in "The Merchant of Venice," 1903.
Museum of the City of New York, The Byron Collection

And if the gallery was silent, the applause lifeless, we knew the play was wrong, a failure, and we must give another. The love of the gallery was our life. We needed it as water is needed by fish, as air is needed by all that breathes.

I recall that once, at the opening of the season, Gordin made a speech that insulted the gallery. *They struck!* They did not laugh at the comic scenes, did not weep when it was sad, and, when it was over, did not even move their hands. How dismal the whole performance after that! How spoiled for everyone the holiday opening of the season! Heavy and sad the curtain came down, and we actors left the theater that night as though we were already buried.

It was in London they first showed themselves, those never-to-be-forgotten boys and girls, deeply committed and ready for battle. Later we had them in New York, in Argentina, wherever we played. But always they came of the poorer classes. It was from these "folk masses" that we drew our strength. They were the soul, the flame, of our theater.

Jacob Adler, *A Life on the Stage: A Memoir by Jacob Adler*, Translated, Edited, and with Commentary by Lulla Adler Rosenfeld (New York: Alfred A. Knopf, 1999), pp. 323, 326–328. From *A Life on the Stage* by Jacob Adler, copyright © 1999 by the Estate of Lulla Rosenfeld. Introduction copyright © 1999 by Ellen Adler. Used by permission of Alfred A. Knopf, a division of Random House, Inc.

14

A LIFE DEVOTED TO ANARCHISM

• EMMA GOLDMAN •

GROWING UP in Lithuania, Emma Goldman witnessed oppression firsthand and began reading the writings of Russian populists and revolutionaries at a young age. She arrived in the United States in 1885, hoping to find a land of freedom, but quickly became disillusioned by the inequality and injustice in America. After witnessing the violence and mass arrests of anarchists following the 1886 bombing and riots in Chicago's Haymarket Square, Goldman dedicated her life to the anarchist cause and made a career of political activism. She fervently embraced the idea that only anarchism could bring about absolute freedom and lent her efforts to campaigns for worker and women's rights, birth control and sexual freedom, free love and free speech, just to name a few.

Goldman quickly gained a national reputation as a radical anarchist, writing and speaking across the country to broadcast her views. In 1906, she founded *Mother Earth*, a magazine that provided a forum for radical causes. She recognized that her Jewish background fueled her political and philosophical outlook, though she considered religion a tool of oppression. She fervently opposed America's entry into World War I and created the No-Conscription League, which declared the draft an affront to liberty. Goldman and her lifelong compatriot Alexander Berkman were charged with conspiracy to obstruct the draft, and Goldman spent two years in a Missouri prison. Upon her release, J. Edgar Hoover (then working in the Justice Department) immediately arrested her again and successfully lobbied the courts to have her citizenship revoked. No longer a citizen, Goldman became eligible for deportation under the 1918 Alien Act, which permitted the expulsion of alien anarchists. Along with hundreds of other foreign-born radicals, Emma Goldman was deported to the Soviet Union in 1919. She spent the rest of her life traveling through Europe, continuing to speak and write, and retaining her firm commitment to anarchism. In this essay, written just six years before her death, Goldman reflects on her life, career, and convictions.

⁓

ON COMING TO America I had the same hopes as have most European immigrants and the same disillusionment, though the latter affected me more keenly and more deeply. The immigrant without money and without connections is not permitted to cherish the comforting illusion that America is a benevolent uncle who assumes a tender and impartial guardianship of nephews and nieces. I soon learned that in a republic there are myriad ways by which the strong, the cunning, the rich can seize power and hold it. I saw the many work for small wages which kept them always on the borderline of want for the few who made huge profits. I saw the courts, the halls of legislation, the press, and the schools—in fact every avenue of education and

Emma Goldman, deported as an anarchist.

protection—effectively used as an instrument for the safe-guarding of a minority, while the masses were denied every right. I found that the politicians knew how to befog every issue, how to control public opinion and manipulate votes to their own advantage and to that of their financial and industrial allies. This was the picture of democracy I soon discovered on my arrival in the United States. Fundamentally there have been few changes since that time. . . .

[M]Y OBJECTION TO authority in whatever form has been derived from a much larger social view, rather than from anything I myself may have suffered from it. Government has, of course, interfered with my full expression, as it has with others. Certainly the powers have not spared me. Raids on my lectures during my thirty-five years' activity in the United States were a common occurrence, followed by innumerable arrests and three convictions to terms of imprisonment. This was followed by the annulment of my citizenship and my deportation. The hand of authority was forever interfering with my life. If I have none the less expressed myself, it was in spite of every curtailment and difficulty put in my path and not because of them. . . .

I THINK MY life and my work have been successful. What is generally regarded as success—acquisition of wealth, the capture of power or social prestige—I consider the most dismal failures. I hold when it is said of a man that he has arrived, it means that he is finished—his development has stopped at that point. I have always striven to remain in a state of flux and continued growth, and not to petrify in a niche of self-satisfaction. If I had my life to live over again, like anyone else, I should wish to alter minor details. But in any of my more important actions and attitudes I would repeat my life as I have lived it. Certainly I should work for Anarchism with the same devotion and confidence in its ultimate triumph.

Emma Goldman, "Was My Life Worth Living?" *Harper's Magazine* (December, 1934), pp. 52, 53, 55, 58. Copyright © 1934 by *Harper's Magazine*. All rights reserved. Reproduced from the December issue by special permission.

ᵓ 15 ᵉ

JEWISH WOMEN ON STRIKE

• THE KOSHER MEAT BOYCOTT OF 1902 •

JEWISH WOMEN'S participation in politics extended beyond labor strikes and union activism. In May 1902, when the price of kosher meat suddenly increased from twelve to eighteen cents a pound, Jewish women on the Lower East Side declared a strike against local butchers. Taking to the streets, these women set up picket lines, broke into shops, and threw the meat out into the streets. They attacked anyone attempting to purchase meat and fought bitterly with police trying to stop them, resulting in dozens of arrests. In a matter of days, the women had forced local butchers to close their stores and the boycotts spread to other neighborhoods within the city.

Unlike the young, unmarried women who led strikes in the garment industry, the Jewish women promoting the meat boycott were wives and mothers who viewed the strike as an extension of their role as housewives. Politics suffused the lives of immigrant Jews, including both women and men and spanning the generations. The kosher meat boycott lasted about three weeks and concluded with a reduction in prices by the meat wholesalers (known as the Meat Trust). The rising cost of food prices reemerged in subsequent years and resulted in further boycotts and mass protests. The *Jewish Daily Forward*, the voice of the Jewish working class, vigorously supported the meat boycott and offered this editorial praising Jewish women for their actions.

THE ENTIRE CITY is talking about the tumult, the uproar in the Jewish Quarter that began after the price of meat started to rise.

The prices for meat not only went up in the Jewish Quarter. The Trusts are also ripping off the small butchers among the gentiles and the masses at large. Not long ago, the gentiles also came to know how sweet it is to be a pauper in this country. As such, they did nothing to protest. Whoever is able, pays the higher prices; whoever cannot, ends up with less meat. They made no outcry about it. No one noticed their anger. They quietly bent their heads to the powers of capitalism, to the powers that create fat meat industry magnates.

The Jews, the Jewish poor, the women of the poor Jewish masses, were the only ones who let their cries be heard, their pain, their anger. The only ones who came out to fight against a bloody, tyrannical gang of thieves were the wives of Jewish men, children of the Jewish people.

There are many things in which we Jews haven't taken pride. There are many things in Jewry that we would be better off without. The behavior of our women over the last few days, their energy, their battle against the wild, Jewish, beast of a Trust, which would rob even the calcified remains at the bottom of the clay pot of the Jewish pauper, this protest movement by the women of the neighborhood is one that no Jew anywhere should be ashamed of. Whether the battle of these women will be won or not, the Jewish

This cartoon from the Jewish Daily Forward *lauds women for their leadership in the kosher meat boycott, with a caption that boldly proclaims, "the power of women."*
Jewish Daily Forward *May 16, 1902*

people will always be able to take pride in them; this neighborhood battle will always serve as an example that brings attention to the hundreds and thousands of years that Jews have had to submit to foreign rulers; it brings attention to generation after generations of Jews which have been oppressed, enslaved and trampled under the feet of all kinds of tyrants and despots; it shows that the Jew still has enough spirit, enough desire for freedom and rights. And when injustice occurs, or if he or others are wronged, he is the first, before all others, to protest, to fight against these injustices, against these evils.

These Jewish women can be proud of themselves, for their energetic protests against the neighborhood meat vampires, and Jewish men can be proud of their women and this protest. But being proud isn't all there is to do, to be proud of oneself will help little in achieving the goal to which we are striving.

The women and men of the neighborhood are currently furious at the wholesale butchers who are making money off of the blood of the poor. They have come out to do battle against the wild, bloodthirsty capitalistic Trust. This is good and just and this is how it should be. But are the women and men ready to do something against this Trust? That is the question that every person must be asking himself.

We believe that the people can easily become upset about the Meat Trust, just like all the other Trusts, which oppress and choke the people, if the people let them. But we do not believe that much can be accomplished through a few days of street protests by women. It is good, it is very good, that the women took it upon themselves to raise their voices against the leeches of the meat industry. No man's voice can produce such an echo like the voice of a woman who screams and cries for her life, for her babies, for the poor shackled slave who works for his suffering, hungry family. That is only half the job. It is only good to awaken, to raise awareness and the conscience of the people, it is good because it will open the eyes of people who sleep and who refuse to see what is happening in the world.

Only when the eyes of the people open up, when all will see the disgrace and tragedy which is everywhere in society, then the work of the angry will be a completely different one. Then all will see that it is not meat that must be doused with kerosene, and not the poor, innocent butchers, but the huge Trusts, the entire capitalist system with its capitalist politics—everything allows the growing and prospering of the vampires, the leeches, the bloodsuckers of the people—that is what must be doused in kerosene and set aflame. And on the mound of ashes of the current system, a society must be built, where all are free and equal.

Jewish Daily Forward, May 16, 1902, p. 4.

16

STANDARD-BEARER OF CONSERVATIVE JUDAISM

• SOLOMON SCHECHTER •

WHEN SOLOMON Schechter arrived in the United States in 1902, he had already established an international reputation as a scholar and was welcomed as a savior for the Conservative movement's struggling Jewish Theological Seminary. Born in Romania in 1847 and raised in a Hasidic household, Schechter studied in Berlin, both at the city's secular university and at the leading center for critical Jewish scholarship. From Berlin, he went to London, where he taught rabbinic literature at Cambridge University. During his years in Cambridge, Schechter discovered and catalogued previously unknown materials from the Cairo Genizah, a depository for discarded Jewish sacred materials, and his findings earned him widespread scholarly acclaim.

In 1902, Schechter accepted an invitation to assume the presidency of New York's Jewish Theological Seminary, which had been established in 1887 but had faltered in its early years. Under Schechter's guidance, the reorganized Seminary strengthened the nascent Conservative movement in America and established a following among immigrants and their children. Schechter brought superior scholarly credentials in both Jewish and secular subjects; he believed firmly in the ability to balance tradition and modernity. Under his leadership, the Jewish Theological Seminary and the Conservative movement flourished, as Schechter stressed adherence to traditional Jewish observance but also emphasized Judaism's ability to develop and change. In the passage below, taken from an address delivered only two years after he arrived in the United States, Schechter underscored the notion that America's open society allowed Jews the freedom to remain faithful to their religious traditions.

THE FIRST SETTLERS in this country were mostly men who had left their native land for conscience sake, despairing of the Old World as given over to the powers of darkness, despotism and unbelief. And I can quite realize how they must have gloried in the idea of being chosen instruments of Providence who were to restore the spiritual equilibrium of the world by the conquest of new spheres of religious influence and their dedication to the worship of Almighty God.

As a Jew coming from the East of Europe, where my people are trodden down, where seats of Jewish learning and Jewish piety are daily destroyed, I am greatly animated by the same feelings and am comforted to see the New World compensating us for our many losses in the Old. . . .

THERE IS NOTHING in American citizenship which is incompatible with our observing the dietary laws, our sanctifying the Sabbath, our fixing a Mezuzah on our doorposts, our refraining from unleavened bread on Passover, or our perpetuating any other law essential to the preservation of Judaism. On the other hand, it is now generally recognized by the leading thinkers that the institutions and observances

Solomon Schechter (1847–1915), chancellor of the Jewish Theological Seminary.

American Jewish Historical Society, Newton Centre, Massachusetts and New York, New York

of religion are part of its nature, a fact that the moribund rationalism of a half century ago failed to realize. In certain parts of Europe every step in our civil and social emancipation demanded from us a corresponding sacrifice of a portion of the glorious heritage bequeathed to us by our fathers. Jews in America, thank God, are no longer haunted by such fears. We live in a commonwealth in which by the blessing of God and the wisdom of the Fathers of the Constitution, each man abiding by its laws, has the inalienable right of living in accordance with the dictates of his own conscience. In this great, glorious and free country we Jews need not sacrifice a single iota of our Torah; and, in the enjoyment of absolute equality with our fellow citizens we can live to carry out those ideals for which our ancestors so often had to die.

Solomon Schechter, "Altar Building in America," in *Seminary Addresses and Other Papers* (New York: Burning Book Press, 1959), pp. 83, 85–86. Printed with permission of The Library of the Jewish Theological Seminary of America.

17

MAKING ZIONISM AN AMERICAN MOVEMENT

• LOUIS D. BRANDEIS •

IN THE opening decades of the twentieth century, the Zionist movement in America had only a small following. East European immigrants comprised the majority of Zionist supporters, while most of the more established Jews considered Zionism incompatible with allegiance to America. Many Jews worried about charges of "dual loyalty," fearing that support for a Jewish homeland in Palestine might suggest the lack of complete devotion to America.

Louis Brandeis, a native-born Jew from Kentucky and Harvard-educated attorney, emerged as the most unlikely advocate of American Zionism. Brandeis had grown up in a highly acculturated family, and demonstrated little connection to the Jewish community until he reached his fifties. In 1910, he negotiated a settlement in New York's cloakmakers strike. While doing so, he met leading members of the Jewish community, many of them Zionists, who piqued his interest in the

Zionist cause. A staunch progressive, Brandeis found in the culture of East European immigrants, and in the Zionist movement in particular, what he believed to be a genuine expression of democratic ideals—ideals that had long been fundamental elements of his own political principles. Brandeis was also profoundly influenced by philosopher Horace Kallen's arguments for cultural pluralism that called for America to be a nation where different ethnic and national cultures could thrive, enriching the quality of American life. Embracing the idea of ethnic pluralism, Brandeis came to advocate Zionism as a movement that would not only benefit Jews, but also improve American society.

A prominent attorney by the time he became the leading spokesmen for American Zionism, Brandeis lent the Zionist movement legitimacy and respectability. He argued fervently that Zionism was no threat to American patriotism—and that, in fact, support for Zionism made Jews better Americans. Brandeis envisioned a Jewish homeland that would both provide a refuge for East European Jews and serve as model of democracy. He insisted that Zionism would benefit America, the world, and the Jewish people.

In this address, delivered in the middle of World War I, Brandeis articulates his own journey toward Zionism, the role of Palestine in fostering Jewish self-respect, and the compatibility of commitment to the Zionist movement and loyalty to America.

⁓

DURING MOST OF my life my contact with Jews and Judaism was slight. I gave little thought to their problems, save in asking myself, from time to time, whether we were showing by our lives due appreciation of the opportunities which this hospitable country affords.

My approach to Zionism was through Americanism. In time, practical experience and observation convinced me that Jews were by reason of their traditions and their character peculiarly fitted for the attainment of American ideals. Gradually it became clear to me that to be good Americans, we must be better Jews, and to be better Jews, we must become Zionists.

To the worldly wise [Zionist] efforts at colonization appeared very foolish. Nature and man presented obstacles in Palestine which appeared insuperable; and the colonists were ill equipped for their task, save in their spirit of devotion and self-sacrifice.

Those who undertake to describe Palestine are apt to speak of it as a miniature California, in its climate, its topography and its agricultural possibilities. Others have compared it with Sicily—long the granary of Rome. . . .

THE BURDEN HAS fallen upon America to maintain, after years of travail, the Zionist movement now so promising. The organization which has hitherto directed the movement has its headquarters in Berlin. The governing committee is composed mainly of citizens of the different nations now at war with one another. Some of the members are Russians, some Germans, some Austrians. The president of the Zionist body is a German. The leading financial institutions, through which the business of the organization is conducted, were formed under British law. The war has scattered these officers under conditions which prevent their cooperating or indeed communicating with one another. This prevents them from directing affairs in Palestine.

The establishment in a neutral country of a provisional committee to take up the work thus became necessary; and such a committee was naturally established in America, the only neutral country which has a large Jewish population, and where more than one-fifth of all the Jews in the world live. The committee so formed has at the outset the task of providing funds necessary for maintaining the Zionist Organization and institutions. Hitherto ninety per cent of all money required for this purpose was raised in Europe. The European Jews are now prevented from contributing practically anything. Upon us falls the obligation and the privilege of providing the needed funds. For this purpose it is necessary to raise at present $100,000 besides the other larger sums which the Jews of America must raise to relieve those made destitute by the war.

When we consider how large and generous has been the contribution of the Irish of America for the cause of home rule, the present demand

Louis D. Brandeis, ca. 1919.

upon the Jews for Zionist purposes seems small indeed. The Jews in America can be relied upon to perform fully their obligation. And indeed there are special reasons why we should be eager to do so. Palestine gives promise of doing for us far more than we can ever be called upon to do for Palestine. For the Jewish renaissance in Palestine will enable us to perform our plain duty to America. It will help us to make toward the attainment of the American ideals of democracy and social justice that large contribution for which religion and life have peculiarly fitted the Jew. . . .

It is the laborious task of inculcating self-respect—a task which can be accomplished only by restoring the ties of the Jew to the noble past of his race, and by making him realize the possibilities of a no less glorious future. Every Irish-American who contributed to advancing home rule was a better man and a better American for the sacrifice involved. Every American Jew who aids in advancing the Jewish settlement of Palestine, though he feel sure that neither he nor his descendants will ever wish to go there, will likewise be a better man, and a better American for doing so.

There is one other consideration to which the Jews of America must give thought. Though the result of this war should be, as we hope, the removal or lessening of the disabilities under which the Jews labor in eastern Europe, nevertheless when peace comes, emigration from the war-stricken countries will certainly proceed in large volume, because of the misery incident to the war's devastations. More than one-half of the Jews of the whole world live in that territory near the western frontier of Russia which has become one of the two vast battlefields of the nations. Is it desirable that America should be practically the only country to which the Jews of eastern Europe may emigrate? Is it not desirable that Palestine should give a special welcome to the emigrant Jews as the Zionists propose?

I am impelled all the more to ask you for your support, both moral and financial, because at this critical juncture we should all stand together, so that when the occasion arises we may be of lasting service to our people. Now is not the time to foreshadow the policy which we should engage upon. But when the nations approach peace, the Jews of America, if united, may be a factor in obtaining for the Jews of other parts of the world something more real than promises of amelioration; something more lasting than philanthropy. This greater undertaking depends upon the readiness with which you rally in every possible way to the cause. Your loyalty to America, your loyalty to Judaism should lead you to support the Zionist cause.

Jacob DeHaas, *Louis D. Brandeis: A Biographical Sketch* (New York: Bloch Publishing Company, 1929), pp. 163, 166–168, 168–170. Reprinted with permission of Bloch Publishing Company.

FOUNDER OF HADASSAH

• HENRIETTA SZOLD •

BEST KNOWN as the founder of Hadassah, the Women's Zionist Organization of America, Henrietta Szold was an accomplished and highly educated woman with a long list of contributions to American Jewish life. Born in Baltimore in 1860, the daughter of a prominent rabbi, Szold received a superior education, learned many languages, and was thoroughly conversant in classical Jewish texts. She worked as a writer, editor, and translator for the Jewish Publication Society, and also studied at the Jewish Theological Seminary. Because of her intellectual gifts, the Seminary allowed her to participate in classes reserved only for men at the time, as long as she promised not to seek rabbinic ordination.

In 1909, Szold traveled to Palestine and began a lifelong commitment to the Zionist cause. After joining a small group of American Jewish women who founded Hadassah in 1912, she became its first president. Hadassah grew into the largest

Jewish women's organization, with a special interest in improving health conditions and medical facilities in Palestine. Beginning in the 1920s, Szold spent much of her life in Palestine, with periodic visits to the United States to aid her family and promote the cause of Zionism in America. She believed passionately that a Jewish homeland in Palestine would provide a solution to worldwide Jewish problems and reinvigorate Jewish culture. Moreover, she insisted that through Hadassah and commitment to Zionism, American Jewish women could build a deeper and more meaningful Jewish life in the United States.

The first excerpt below, a letter written to Augusta Rosenwald, wife of Sears president and philanthropist Julius Rosenwald, describes the situation that Szold observed in Palestine and her hopes for the Zionist movement in America. The second selection shows a more personal side of Henrietta Szold. Her letter to a close friend, a man who offered to recite the Mourner's Kaddish after her father's death (a duty reserved for men in traditional Jewish practice), reveals Szold's strength and independence as a Jewish woman.

Letter To Mrs. Julius Rosenwald, New York, January 17, 1915

Your night letter has come to hand, and you will receive a copy of all recent telegrams that have reached the Provisional Executive Committee for General Zionist Affairs concerning the situation both in Palestine and among the refugees in Jaffa. Most of our information at present concerning Palestine comes from a group of Palestinians who have taken up their abode in Alexandria, in order that they may serve as intermediaries between Palestine and ourselves. If it were not for them, we should lack information about many points, and we should not be able to get money to our people in Jaffa.

I asked them to do so in order to make up for the meagerness of the letters received from our own nurses. I am enclosing the most recent *Bulletin* issued by Hadassah, in which you will see that we received only postcards.

You will notice that though Mr. [Aaron] Aaronsohn[1] advises the nurses to return to the United States, they have made no move to do it as far as we know.

Let me congratulate you and Palestine upon having secured, as you tell me in your telegram, a "splendid response from local organization." I wish there were a way of Hadassah's being kept informed of all you do. I have requested Mrs. Lesser to employ a stenographer at our expense and to dictate to her a full account of what has happened for our benefit. It would be so valuable to us from the point of view of propaganda.

However, the paramount consideration is that you are advancing the cause of Palestine. From my point of view, as I need not tell you, that is the cause of the Jew and, most important of all, of Judaism. In many respects the war catastrophe has left me bewildered and uncertain. In one respect I see more clearly than ever—that is in respect to Zionism. The anomalous situation of the Jew everywhere—the distress, misery, and in part degradation (witness Poland!) of seven millions, more than half, of our race; the bravery of the Jews who are serving in all the armies; the size of the contingent we are contributing to every front—means to me that the Jew and his Judaism must be perpetuated and can be perpetuated only by their repatriation in the land of the fathers.

It is a miracle that, though we Zionists were not hitherto able to bring many to our way of thinking, nevertheless many in these days of stress think with pity of our little sanctuary. They have come to us and said: "Even if we do not see eye to eye with you, we are going to help you save the sanctuary you have established." Perhaps they feel that it will yield sanctuary, refuge, and protection in the days of readjustment soon to dawn, we hope.

If you succeed, in your appeal to the Federation of Temple Sisterhoods, in conveying to the Jewish women of America the need of such a sanctuary for the Jew, the need of a center from which Jewish culture and inspiration will flow, and if you can persuade them to set aside one day of the year as a Palestine Day, on which thoughts and means are to be consecrated to a great Jewish world-organizing purpose, you will have accomplished a result that will bring immediate blessing to those now in distress and in terror of life, and a

---

[1] Aaron Aaronsohn (1876–1919), Zionist leader and agronomist, part of a family of Zionist pioneers in Palestine.

Henrietta Szold at the Greek Hostel in Palestine, ca. 1921.

Courtesy of Hadassah, The Women's Zionist Organization of America, Inc.

blessing for all future times redounding to the benefit not only of those who will make use of their sanctuary rights in Palestine, but also those who like ourselves, remaining in a happy, prosperous country, will be free to draw spiritual nourishment from a center dominated wholly by Jewish traditions and the Jewish ideals of universal peace and universal brotherhood.

If you and they do not follow us Zionists so far, at least they will respond to the appeal for material help—at least they will recognize that for the sake of Jewish dignity and self-respect, even the purely philanthropic work in Palestine, for which so large a part of Jewry has long felt a keen responsibility, may never again be allowed to relapse into a pauperizing chaos. They may refuse to accept the whole Zionist ideal. But the wonderful vitality shown by the Zionist settlement in the Holy Land—the resourcefulness of the colonists, who could supply the cities with grain and food for months, and the usefulness of the Zionist bank in averting panic and the direst distress—they make of me a more confirmed and conscious Zionist than ever. I need not analyze the elements I have enumerated for you. You, who have been in the Holy Land, even if you do not—may I say, not yet?—agree with me, your mind will instinctively understand the leap mine makes in these troublous days to the Zionist conclusion.

Troublous days? I have often wondered during these months how many of us Jews here in America realize that we are living through times comparable only to the destruction of the second Temple and of our commonwealth by the Romans, and exceeding by far the horrors of the exodus from Spain and Portugal, and the abject misery and suffering of the pogrom years 1881, and 1903, and 1905 in Russia.

The Jew speaks of the first *Hurban*[2]—the utter destruction of Solomon's Temple. He speaks of the second *Hurban*, the ruin of the second Temple by Titus. I feel that a future Graetz[3] will speak of this war as the Jews' third *Hurban*.

There is only one hope in my heart—the effective aid being rendered to Palestine by all Jews without difference. In the first *Hurban* the Jews could

---

[2] Hurban, the Hebrew word meaning "destruction," is used to describe the destruction of the first and second Temples in ancient Israel.

[3] Heinrich Graetz (1817–1891), the premier Jewish historian of his generation whose *History of the Jews* served as the standard work in the field.

not protect their sanctuary against the hordes of Nebuchadnezzar. In the second *Hurban* the Roman legions destroyed the Temple, leaving only the western wall, the last vestige of glory, now turned into a place of wailing. There is no third Temple on the hill of Zion to be destroyed in this third *Hurban*; but in Zion, nevertheless, there is a sanctuary, the refuge that has been established by Jewish pioneers, with the sweat, blood, and labor of those who believe. As American Jewesses they cannot possibly reject the centralized organization of Palestine, an endeavor for which Zionism stands first and last.

With cordial wishes for success, and, may I add this only once only, with Zion's greetings. . . .

Letter To Haym Peretz, New York, September 16, 1916

It is impossible for me to find words in which to tell you how deeply I was touched by your offer to act as "Kaddish" for my dear mother. I cannot even thank you—it is something that goes beyond thanks. It is beautiful, what you have offered to do—I shall never forget it.

You will wonder, then, that I cannot accept your offer. Perhaps it would be best for me not to try to explain to you in writing, but to wait until I see you to tell you why it is so. I know well, and appreciate what you say about, the Jewish custom; and Jewish custom is very dear and sacred to me. And yet I cannot ask you to say Kaddish after my mother. The Kaddish means to me that the survivor publicly and markedly manifests his wish and intention to assume the relation to the Jewish community which his parent had, and that so the chain of tradition remains unbroken from generation to generation, each adding its own link. You can do that for the generations of your family, I must do that for the generations of my family.

I believe that the elimination of women from such duties was never intended by our law and custom—women were freed from positive duties when they could not perform them, but not when they could. It was never intended that, if they could perform them, their performance of them should not be considered as valuable and valid as when one of the male sex performed them. And of the Kaddish I feel sure this is particularly true.

My mother had eight daughters and no son; and yet never did I hear a word of regret pass the lips of either my mother or my father that one of us was not a son. When my father died, my mother would not permit others to take her daughters' place in saying the Kaddish, and so I am sure I am acting in her spirit when I am moved to decline your offer. But beautiful your offer remains nevertheless, and, I repeat, I know full well that it is much more in consonance with the generally accepted Jewish tradition than is my or my family's conception. You understand me, don't you?

Marvin Lowenthal, *Henrietta Szold Life and Letters* (Westport, Conn.: Greenwood Press, 1942), pp. 85–88, 92–93. "Letter to Mrs. Julius Rosenwald—New York, January 17, 1915" by Henrietta Szold, "Letter to Haym Peretz—NY, Sept. 16, 1916" by Henrietta Szold, from *Henrietta Szold Life and Letters* by Marvin Lowenthal, copyright 1942 The Viking Press, renewed © 1970 by Harold C. Emer and Harry L. Shapiro, Executors of the Estate. Used by permission of Viking Penguin, a division of Penguin Group (USA) Inc.

PHILANTHROPIST AND COMMUNAL LEADER

• JACOB SCHIFF •

INVOLVED IN virtually every major Jewish issue of his day, Jacob Schiff combined success on Wall Street with energetic commitment to the Jewish community. Born in Frankfurt in 1847, Schiff worked in finance in Germany and the United States before taking a position at the banking firm of Kuhn, Loeb & Company in 1875. Ten years later, Schiff became head of the firm; in that role he aided in the development of many leading American companies. He also helped to expand and consolidate America's railroads and provided loans to the government.

A member of a highly successful circle of Jews that included the Rothschilds and the Warburgs, Jacob Schiff played a pivotal role in both national and international Jewish affairs. An outspoken critic of Russia's persecution of Jews, Schiff helped to fund Japan's war with Russia in the early 1900s, and gave generously to Jewish relief efforts in Eastern Europe. A Reform

Jew, Jacob Schiff supported the Hebrew Union College and was also one of the key founders of the Conservative movement's Jewish Theological Seminary. He was a founder of the American Jewish Committee and a prime supporter of the Henry Street Settlement. Schiff helped sponsor the Galveston Plan, an attempt to admit Jewish immigrants through the port of Galveston, Texas, and resettle them throughout the country in an effort to ease overcrowding in Northeastern cities. Schiff had a great passion for Jewish literature and history, helping to build the Jewish Division of the New York Public Library and supporting both the Jewish Publication Society and the Harvard Semitic Museum. He also gave generously to secular causes, including New York's Montefiore Hospital, the Tuskegee Institute, and the American Red Cross.

In the address below, delivered at the celebration of the 250th anniversary of Jewish settlement in the United States in 1905, Schiff reflects on Jewish progress in America, articulating his faith in the promise of American Jewish life.

WHEN SOME MONTHS since it was decided to celebrate the settlement of Jews in the United States, and in this very city, two hundred and fifty years ago, the people of the Jewish faith throughout the land felt glad and proud, because this beloved country of their adoption had become the great exponent of human liberties and of freedom of conscience, furnishing an example to the world how great and powerful a people can become who give equal opportunity to all, no matter what their origin or their profession of faith may be. . . .

I am grateful for the honor, which has so graciously been bestowed upon me, to preside over this celebration; and before I exercise the great privilege to present to you the honored speakers of the day, I ask to be permitted to give expression in a few words to the feelings which animate us upon this momentous occasion.

When, in 1655, two hundred and fifty years ago, people of our race and faith first set foot upon these shores to become permanent settlers, hardly a century and a half had passed since Columbus had unlocked the gates of this hemisphere to the civilized world. Thus the heritage which the great Genoese presented to mankind was availed of by our own people at so early a period of the development of the New World that we believe we are justified in the claim that this is our country, to a like extent as it has become the country of other early and later comers, in common with whom we have built this great nation, of which, we now form part and parcel.

Look at the record of the wonderful and glorious progress and development of our country, and upon every page will be found the name of the Jew as having rendered meritorious and patriotic service. Not that we claim that the Jewish citizen has at any time done more than his simple duty; but in the attempt, so frequently made, to consider us a foreign element, it is well and proper, upon an occasion like the present, to emphasize the fact that two hundred and fifty years

Jacob Schiff, (1847–1920), prominent Jewish communal leader.

From the Archives of the YIVO Institute for Jewish Research

ago, and ever since, the Jew who has landed on these shores has come to this country to throw his lot with its people, to share their burdens, to benefit by their opportunities, to become an American, in the best meaning of this proud title and all it stands for.

And having said this, we may add that, as Jews, we are ever mindful of the untold blessing which the fact, that the beacon light of human liberty and freedom is kept burning brightly by the people of the United States, brings not only to those of their race whose good fortune it is to be among the dwellers within this blessed land, but even to their brethren in faith in foreign lands, who still suffer under restrictions unworthy of modern civilization. . .

We who *are* Americans pledge ourselves anew, upon this momentous occasion, to our fellow-citizens, from whatever race they may have sprung or whatever faith they may profess, that we shall ever stand ready to be one with them in every endeavor to further augment the greatness of this, our beloved common country, and the respect in which it is held throughout the world.

Jacob Schiff, *The Two Hundred and Fiftieth Anniversary of the Settlement of the Jews in the United States: Addresses delivered at Carnegie Hall, New York, on Thanksgiving Day, 1905* (New York: New York Co-Operative Society, 1906), pp. 8–10.

THE LYNCHING OF LEO FRANK

THE MOST violent eruption of anti-Semitism in American history occurred in Atlanta, Georgia in 1915. Two years earlier, Leo Frank, a native New Yorker and prominent Atlanta citizen, was accused of murdering Mary Phagan, a thirteen-year-old employee in the pencil factory that he owned. Frank, a member of the city's prestigious Reform Temple and president of his B'nai B'rith lodge, found himself the subject of anti-Semitic attacks throughout the course of the trial. Despite shaky evidence, Frank was convicted and sentenced to death. Georgia's governor commuted the sentence to life imprisonment, but an angry mob kidnapped Frank from prison and lynched him. Years later, in 1986, Leo Frank received a posthumous pardon.

Leo Frank's murder was a horrifying exception to Jewish experience in the United States. In America, anti-Semitism rarely turned violent and never gained the sort of political power that took hold in many European nations. Nonetheless, the event shook American Jews to the core. In the wake of the lynching, Jewish groups across the country protested the despicable crime, but the *Jewish Daily Forward* reacted with its particular brand of politically charged outrage and anger. Editors of the Yiddish socialist newspaper attacked the bigotry of the South, called upon officials to bring the murderers to justice, and underscored the hypocrisy of a government that deported anarchists but allowed Leo Frank's killers to remain free.

FRANK IS DEAD.

The tragedy has ended in blood and death. The hand that stalked the disconsolate one for a period of more than two years did not rest until it put an end to his young life.

A heavy hand! A murderous hand!

This was the same hand that dangled him between life and death for months and years. It locked all the doors of justice and allowed only one way out—the electric chair. It followed him even after the clemency he received by way of a criminal's knife. It dragged him out of prison and took out its final, bloody revenge on him. Frank is dead.

Barbaric racial hatred; fanatic, glowing hatred of all things "foreign"; barbaric traditions of former slave owners who don't care about human life; corrupt police, a corrupt administration, a corrupt court. All united to rob a human being of his life.

In no other country in the world could such a thing happen this way. In no other country would anyone understand how Frank's death would be possible.

Frank is dead.

We will not wonder if tomorrow they will have a picnic and play music on the spot where Frank was murdered, or if the crowd will eat and drink and sing and dance or if politicians will give speeches there. It was not that long ago in the same "South," at that same place, where they hanged two Negroes. That is what was done by the wild tribes in Africa, when they would chase a stranger and roast and eat him. That is the way of all wild peoples. The barbarians of the South are no exception.

Leo Frank ca. 1910s.
Cuba Archives of The Breman Museum

*Lynching of Leo Frank,
Marietta, Georgia, 1915.*

Library of Congress, Prints and
Photographs Division

We would like to take note of one thing. If you ask our administration: our president, our Justice Department, our governors, our chiefs of police, they would tell you that American is a civilized country and in a civilized country, anarchy is not permitted. And truly, when the police detect even the slightest sign of anarchist activity, they use all their facilities to chase them and shut them down. Even if there is no real anarchist activity, they're still ready to find a "conspiracy" and act as if they've saved the whole society. Frank's murder is a completely anarchistic conspiracy. It is the most outspoken, well prepared, well executed conspiracy against law and order and against human life. That is the real danger to the existence of society.

Will the police be as swift to find the conspirators in this case? Will they truly sit the murderers down at the defense table? Will they show that murder is murder, that blood letting cannot be tolerated in organized society?

We have the basis on which to doubt. The history of such murders speaks very clearly.

Jewish Daily Forward, August 18, 1915, p. 4.

THE BEST OF TIMES, THE WORST OF TIMES

1924-1945

A CENTRAL paradox defined the two decades between the imposition of strict immigration quotas in 1924 and the conclusion of World War II: Even as Jews became increasingly comfortable as middle class Americans, they had never felt less secure in the United States. The 1920s ushered in a time of upward mobility for immigrants and their children—not an era of fantastic prosperity for most, but a new stability derived from greater job security and economic progress. Better neighborhoods, improved housing conditions, and the opportunity for children to remain in school fueled Jewish optimism in the interwar years. Yet, at the same time, a rising tide of anti-Semitism emerged from different quarters of American society during these years, prompting fears about Jewish security and opportunity in America. Discrimination at home combined with the menace of Nazism abroad unsettled American Jews, even as they experienced success and advancement.

PART THREE

Brooklyn's Pitkin Avenue, ca. 1940s.

Courtesy of Brooklyn Public Library-Brooklyn Collection

The era culminated with the destruction of one-third of world Jewry, leaving America's Jews as the largest surviving community. During these turbulent decades, American Jews experienced both progress and rejection, accomplishment and tragedy, as they navigated through an uncertain and contradictory age.

In a single generation, the economic profile of American Jewry shifted rapidly from working to middle class. In 1900, 60 percent of American Jews worked in blue-collar trades, but thirty years later that number had been cut in half. As one observer noted, the children of immigrants did not follow their parents into the factories but rather "were going into business, office work, or the professions."[1] Another generation would pass before Jews predominated as professionals, but by the 1920s, the profile of American Jewry had been permanently altered. Not all Jews enjoyed the comforts of the middle class in the twenties; some Jews remained in the trades, usually in highly skilled positions. Still, an unmistakable trend had begun, initiating an enduring pattern of white-collar work and middle class status, particularly for the younger generation.

As Jews attained a more secure economic status, they also sought out new neighborhoods. Across the United States, Jews remained urban dwellers, but they abandoned crowded immigrant quarters in favor of emerging middle class districts. In Chicago, this meant that the Jewish population shifted from Maxwell Street to Lawndale and communities to the north. In New York, Jews left the Lower East Side for more desirable districts in Brooklyn and the Bronx. Creating new ethnic enclaves, Jews continued to live together with other Jews in neighborhoods where they built a distinct Jewish culture. Describing her East Bronx childhood, Vivian Gornick recalled that, "The dominating characteristic of the streets on which I grew was Jewishness in all its rich variety."[2] In the new communities they constructed, second generation Jews nurtured a version of Jewish culture suited to their American middle class aspirations.

The second generation, generally considered to span the period from 1920s until World War II, witnessed the coming of age of the children of immigrants and equally important, represented "a cultural generation," defined by the delicate negotiation between an increasingly familiar American culture and the immigrant world that persisted in homes and neighborhoods.[3] Second

Second-generation Jews moved to tree-lined streets and modern apartment buildings like these in the Bronx, 1928.

Milstein Division of United States History, Local History & Genealogy, The New York Public Library, Astor, Lenox and Tilden Foundations

generation Jews stood between these poles, on their way to belonging in America in ways their immigrant parents could not have imagined, but continuing to live in neighborhoods grounded in the rhythms of Jewish culture. The children of immigrants flocked to the public schools, but they usually did so surrounded by Jewish students and teachers, where the lessons learned about America came through the filter of Jewish community. As second generation Jews grew increasingly comfortable as Americans, Jewish culture and community remained intact.

The children of immigrants came of age with great expectations for their futures in America. Author Alfred Kazin vividly remembered the hope that his immigrant parents placed in him: "It was not for myself alone that I was expected to shine, but for them—to redeem the constant anxiety of their existence. I was the first American child, their offering to a strange new God; I was to be the monument of their liberation."[4] By the 1920s and 1930s, most young Jews not only attended elementary and high school, but a significant number had begun to go to college. Although men attended college more frequently than women, both Jewish women and men pursued higher education

in disproportionate numbers. Particularly in large urban centers, Jews filled the seats at public colleges (which remained affordable and accessible to the children of immigrants). At New York's Brooklyn College, Hunter College, and City College, Jews constituted from 80 to 90 percent of the student body. Many of these colleges later became bastions of Jewish youth culture, nurturing political ideologies and movements, particularly during the height of the Great Depression.[5]

Students attending a lecture at New York's City College, 1946.

Courtesy of the Archives of the City College of New York, CUNY

Harvard University, ca. 1910.
Library of Congress, Prints and
Photographs Division

The heavy representation of Jews in colleges, especially their steadily growing presence within leading private universities, led to fears that America's elite campuses might become "too Jewish." During the interwar years, as Jewish students became a greater percentage of the student body, many private universities imposed quotas on Jewish enrollment. Although often not established as official policy, quotas existed in practice in many elite schools between 1920 and 1940, particularly those located in urban areas with significant Jewish populations. In 1922, Harvard University President A. Lawrence Lowell publicly advocated limiting the number of Jewish students, ostensibly as a means to reduce anti-Semitism on campus. By the early 1920s, Jewish students comprised more than 20 percent of the enrollment at Harvard, a number that had tripled from 6 percent in 1908. Harvard's president insisted that, "The anti-Semitic feeling among the students is increasing, and it grows in proportion to the increase in the number of Jews."[6] According to Lowell's logic, controlling the proportion of Jewish students at the university would prevent prejudice and anti-Jewish sentiment. The suggestion provoked outrage both from the Jewish community and the general public, and a university committee ultimately repudiated it. Nonetheless, new admissions policies that involved limiting class size, recruiting from broader areas of the country, and instituting the criterion of "character" resulted in a de facto quota system at Harvard as well as other elite colleges and professional schools throughout the interwar years.[7]

Not only universities but also many businesses and professions barred Jews from employment in the twenties and thirties. Jewish doctors could not work at some hospitals and Jewish attorneys found the doors of the most prestigious law firms closed to them. At a time when "Gentiles Only" advertisements remained legal, many employers, including most public utilities companies, had the right to refuse jobs to Jews. Jews often responded by establishing their own law firms and hospitals and opening businesses that served a primarily Jewish clientele. In effect, Jews created an economic subculture and nurtured an ethnic economy that bolstered their mobility in an era of educational and occupational discrimination. Employment restriction combined with the concentration of Jews in white-collar professions and skilled labor created a distinct Jewish economic profile in these years. In an anti-Semitic climate, as a 1936 *Fortune* magazine article noted, that profile fueled the impression that the Jews were "clannish."[8]

Anti-Semitism emerged from different groups within American society, each targeting Jews as the cause for the political and social problems of the day. As immigrants

THE JEWISH AMERICANS

established themselves within American society, certain nativist groups believed that they were eroding the fundamental social and religious order of the nation. Hate groups expanded in this climate; the Ku Klux Klan grew to a membership of over four million in the mid-1920s. Jews, one of many racial and religious groups under attack, were (paradoxically) labeled both capitalist schemers and seditious revolutionaries. In the wake of the Bolshevik Revolution and given the overrepresentation of Jews in leftist politics, the KKK and other hate groups portrayed Jews as dangerous radicals. At the same time, Jews were also accused of being capitalist conspirators, taking over Wall Street and Hollywood, and destroying the Christian character of the nation. There was little consistency to these ideologies, but together they created an unsettling upsurge in anti-Jewish agitation emanating from distinct corners of American society.

Against this backdrop, Henry Ford emerged as one of the most prolific and determined purveyors of anti-Semitic propaganda. Beginning in 1922, Ford initiated a seven-year campaign designed to defend middle America against a perceived Jewish menace. After purchasing the struggling *Dearborn Independent* in 1919, he built the newspaper's circulation rapidly, even giving away free

Ku Klux Klan rally, Washington, D.C., 1926.
Library of Congress, Prints and Photographs Division

copies to spread his message. Anti-Semitic articles and editorials became a regular feature in the paper, detailing imagined Jewish political threats, assailing Jewish control of the entertainment industry, and probing the ways that Jews had insinuated themselves into the American pastime of baseball. The paper serialized the *Protocols of the Elders of Zion*, the notorious forgery first circulated in Eastern Europe that purported to offer proof of an international Jewish conspiracy. Ford later published the *Protocols*, along with other anti-Semitic writings, in book form as *The International Jew*, a four-volume diatribe that Ford funded generously to ensure wide circulation. The Jewish community responded with a vigorous campaign against Ford. Some Jews encouraged a wholesale boycott of his popular automobiles. Others, led by prominent Jewish attorney Louis Marshall, advocated challenging Ford in a court of law. Marshall spearheaded a libel suit that ultimately forced Henry Ford to issue a public apology to the Jewish community. Although

Henry Ford, ca. 1934.
Library of Congress, Prints and Photographs Division

many Jews suspected that Ford's apology was less than sincere, it nonetheless constituted a signal victory, proving to Jews that in the American legal system, anti-Semitism would not stand.[9]

Anti-Semitism remained an ongoing concern for Jews throughout the interwar years, but not one that impeded their continued engagement with American culture. Jews established a distinct presence in American entertainment, increasingly visible on stage, on screen, and in a variety of other media. During these years, Yiddish culture began to lose its centrality within the Jewish community, especially among the younger generation. The Yiddish theater retained a loyal audience and indeed flourished during the 1920s, as Molly Picon achieved her first stardom on the stage and two majestic Yiddish theaters opened on New York's Second Avenue. A viable Yiddish radio and movie industry also developed, targeting a select audience of immigrant Jews. Yet, while Yiddish culture remained a vital part of the Jewish landscape, a growing number of Jews were turning to mainstream, English-language sources of entertainment. As consumers, producers, and artists, Jews emerged as key participants in the creation of America's new popular culture.[10]

Jews entered the entertainment industry in the same modest way that they pursued other economic endeavors, as small businesspeople and entrepreneurs. Marcus Loew, who came to own a nationwide chain of movie theaters, began as a factory worker; studio mogul Louis B. Mayer was a junk dealer; Samuel Goldwyn made gloves; and the Warner Brothers worked as cobblers and bicycle dealers. For most of these men, the journey to movie production began with the fledgling nickelodeons that predominated on the Lower East Side, providing cheap entertainment in local storefronts. As new technology brought improvements in audio and film quality, movie production became big business, with new theaters opening and a burgeoning industry taking shape. The Jews who began as storefront entrepreneurs found themselves positioned to assume a leading role in the budding motion picture business, first in New York and later in Hollywood. The half-dozen studios run by Jews made an indelible mark on American mass entertainment

Molly Picon stars in "Hello Molly," 1928.
From the Archives of the YIVO Institute for Jewish Research

in the years after World War I. At the same time, the Jewishness of the industry also precipitated anti-Semitic attacks from those convinced that Jews were corrupting the ideals of the American public.[11] For those who believed that Jews constituted a foreign social element that undermined the essential Christian character of American civilization, the ascendancy of Jews in the entertainment industry represented a serious threat.

Even as Jews operated behind the scenes as pioneers of the early movie studios, they also claimed a central role as entertainers. Al Jolson, Sophie Tucker, Fanny Brice, Benny Goodman, Irving Berlin, and George Gershwin were just a few of the many Jewish performers and musicians who burst on the American scene. Some, like Fanny Brice and Sophie Tucker, explicitly brought Jewish inflections to their performances. Irving Berlin wrote music for Jewish performers and the Jewish stage, but he also created enduring classics in which ethnic sensibilities were sublimated to shared American themes. In Berlin's "God Bless America" and "White Christmas," immigrant expectations of America appeared only faintly in the background of songs that expressed national aspirations and ideals.

In a nation composed of immigrants, the themes of ethnic culture and adjustment had a place in mainstream entertainment. The 1927 film *The Jazz Singer*, starring Al Jolson, exemplified the struggle between immigrant religious traditions and the lure of American culture and success. The story is quintessentially Jewish: Jakie Rabinowitz, son of a cantor, rises to great fame as an American entertainer, disappointing his immigrant father who wants him to remain faithful to Judaism and to his legacy as a cantor. The film brings resolution to the conflict, as Jakie pursues his American career but returns to take his dying father's place to chant Kol Nidre on Yom Kippur Eve. *The Jazz Singer* portrays a Jewish story, but one that resonates with broader themes of generational and cultural conflict, appealing to a wide American audience. As entertainers, Jews

Studio mogul Louis B. Mayer.
Library of Congress, Prints and Photographs Division

Fanny Brice, ca. 1910.
Library of Congress, Prints and Photographs Division

Al Jolson, ca. 1940s.
Library of Congress, Prints and Photographs Division

This 1909 song, set in a vaudeville theater, reveals Irving Berlin's roots in the immigrant culture of the Lower East Side. Fanny Brice performed this song using a heavy Yiddish accent in a production of The College Girls. *The song depicts the outrage of Sadie's beau Moses as he watches her dance provocatively on stage.*

Composer Irving Berlin at his piano, 1935.
© Bettmann/CORBIS

THE JEWISH AMERICANS

SADIE SALOME GO HOME!

Words and Music by Irving Berlin and Edgar Leslie

Sadie Cohen left her happy home
To become an actress lady,
On the stage she soon became the rage,
As the only real Salomy baby.
When she came to town, her sweetheart Mose
Brought for her around a pretty rose;
But he got an awful fright
When his Sadie came to sight,
He stood up and yelled with all his might:

(Refrain)
   Don't do that dance, I tell you Sadie,
   That's not a bus'ness for a lady!
   'Most ev'rybody knows
   That I'm your loving Mose,
   Oy, Oy, Oy, Oy,
   Where is your clothes?
   You better go and get your dresses,
   Ev'ryone's got the op'ra glasses.
   Oy! such a sad disgrace
   No one looks in your face;
   Sadie Salome, go home.

From the crowd Moses yelled out loud,
"Who put in your head such notions?
You look sweet but jiggle with your feet.
Who put in your back such funny motions?
As a singer you was always fine!
Sing to me, 'Because the world is mine!'"
Then the crowd began to roar,
Sadie did a new encore,
Mose got mad and yelled at her once more:

Gertrude Berg, as featured in a Life *magazine story, 1949. Photographer: George Karger.*

Getty Images

brought their particular traditions to the larger public and also helped to construct the idioms of American culture.

No Jewish performer translated Jewish ethos to American audiences better than Gertrude Berg, better known to the public as Molly Goldberg. As writer, producer, and star of *The Goldbergs* (originally titled *The Rise of the Goldbergs*), Berg created an enduring portrait of Jewish family life that survived from its debut on radio in 1929 through its television run in the 1950s. Gertrude Berg, who unlike her character Molly Goldberg spoke with no accent, spent her childhood summers in the Catskills where her father managed a hotel. A region that came to be known as the Borscht Belt, the Catskills emerged as a favorite Jewish vacation spot, attracting both middle class Jews who frequented the extravagant Jewish-owned hotels like Grossinger's as well as the working class who inhabited the modest bungalows with their *kuchaleins*, kitchens where vacationers could prepare their own meals. The Catskills gave rise to a unique brand of Jewish humor, song, and entertainment where performers such as Sid Caesar, Eddie Cantor, and Danny Kaye got their starts. Gertrude Berg moved from performing skits in front of Jewish vacationers in the

Catskills to popular fame on radio and television as Jewish matriarch Molly Goldberg. Molly Goldberg became one of America's most popular characters, dispensing wisdom to her middle-class Jewish family in the Bronx, New York. Although Molly spoke with an ethnic accent and the show openly featured the family's Jewish identity and occasional holiday observances, the storylines reflected ordinary experiences and humor that connected with American audiences. The public found in Molly Goldberg "an immigrant keeper of the national dream," while Jewish listeners took pride in hearing their own culture broadcast on American airwaves.[12]

Public moments, when Jews appeared on the national stage, often served to galvanize the community and to define Jews in the eyes of other Americans. In 1934, baseball player Hank Greenberg authored one such symbolic moment as a member of the American League champion Detroit Tigers. With his distinctively Jewish last name, Greenberg inspired communal pride as a prolific major league hitter, perhaps the most famous American Jewish athlete of his day. In 1934, Greenberg chose not to play in a game on Yom Kippur, instead attending services at a Detroit synagogue. Although he had, in fact, participated in a game a few days earlier on Rosh Hashanah when the pennant race still remained

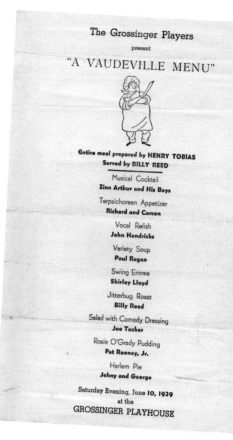

Grossinger's Players "Vaudeville Menu," 1939.
Archives of the Catskills Institute

Hank Greenberg of the Detroit Tigers, ca. 1930s.
National Baseball Hall of Fame Library, Cooperstown, N.Y.

in doubt, Jews nonetheless championed his decision to give priority to his Judaism on the Day of Atonement. At the same time, in a nation that valued religion, most Americans respected his decision to remain faithful to his religious convictions. Greenberg retained little connection to Judaism throughout his life, but claimed his Jewish identity proudly. For American Jews, Hank Greenberg served as a powerful icon—physically strong, playing the quintessential American game, and publicly asserting his Jewish heritage. [14]

American Judaism was changing during the interwar years, responding to the new conditions of American Jewish life. In their new middle class neighborhoods, Jews built scores of new synagogues designed physically and programmatically to reflect their needs and aspirations. The 1920s witnessed an enormous synagogue building boom across the United States, as Jews constructed increasingly large and elaborate edifices. Between 1916 and 1926, the number of American synagogues nearly doubled. Many of these new structures were synagogue centers, complete with social, educational and recreational facilities, all under one roof. The synagogue center, the so-called "shul with a pool," attempted to make the synagogue the focal point of Jewish activity, both sacred and secular, in order to attract Jews for more than worship alone. Drawing Jews to the synagogue became a pressing concern because although the number of synagogues increased dramatically during the interwar years, attendance at worship services did not. In fact, in 1930, only one third of Jewish families affiliated with a synagogue and only a quarter of Jewish children received any Jewish education. Five years

Swimming in the pool at the Brooklyn Jewish Center, ca. 1920s.

Courtesy of the Ratner Center for the Study of Conservative Judaism, Jewish Theological Seminary

later, three-quarters of Jewish youth in New York reported that they had not attended a single religious service in the past year. With the synagogue center, Jews could participate in congregational life, even if it was simply to play sports, enjoy a meal, or participate in a social program. While synagogue centers failed to produce greater devotion to Judaism, as some leaders had hoped they might, they did create a new physical space for the expression of Jewish identity. Second generation Jews may not have possessed a newfound commitment to Jewish observance, but their tremendous investment in synagogue expansion in the 1920s testified to their profound desire to perpetuate Jewish community.[14]

Rabbi Mordecai Kaplan, one of the most influential pioneers in twentieth-century Judaism, popularized the idea of the synagogue center in his writings and in his leadership of the Society for the Advancement of Judaism (SAJ), founded in New York in 1922. Secularly educated at City College and Columbia University and ordained in both a traditional Orthodox setting and at the Conservative Jewish Theological Seminary, Kaplan conceived the movement that later became Reconstructionist Judaism, the

Mordecai M. Kaplan with Alexander Marx and Louis Finkelstein, 1952. Photographer: Gjon Mili.
Getty Images

only branch of Judaism created entirely on American soil. Mordecai Kaplan did not set out to found a new movement; indeed he spent his entire career as a faculty member at the Jewish Theological Seminary, where he had a profound influence on a generation of Conservative rabbis. Finding all of Judaism woefully deficient in its ability to inspire commitment from second generation American Jews, Kaplan advocated the creation of an organic Jewish community in which religion played a role alongside recreation, art, customs, social experiences, and every other aspect in the lives of individual Jews. In his 1934 magnum opus, *Judaism as a Civilization*, Kaplan posited that American Jews inhabited two civilizations—one American and one Jewish—that were entirely compatible, but each required sustenance and development. To cultivate Jewish civilization in America, Kaplan advocated a commitment to language (Hebrew), land and peoplehood (through support of the Zionist movement in Palestine), and the construction of a dynamic culture that embraced every facet of Jewish life. Kaplan's controversial rejection of both a supernatural God and the notion of Jews as the chosen people aroused critics from every branch of Judaism, yet his philosophy aptly diagnosed both the problems in American Judaism and the essential character of Jewish identity in the United States. Reconstructionism did not

Exterior of the spacious Brooklyn Jewish Center, ca. 1920s.

Courtesy of the Ratner Center for the Study of Conservative Judaism, Jewish Theological Seminary.

emerge as a separate movement until the post–World War II era, but Kaplan's program reverberated within the practice of virtually all aspects of American Judaism during the interwar years.[15]

Conservative Judaism was the fastest growing movement during these years, capturing the loyalty of second generation Jews who found its synagogue customs familiar and its practices consistent with middle class American norms. As it grew, the movement differentiated itself from both Reform and Orthodoxy, retaining commitment to Jewish law, unlike the Reform movement, but demonstrating greater flexibility than the Orthodox in many legal interpretations and in instituting the practice of seating women and men together in most synagogues. Although a wide gulf existed between the ideology expressed by the movement's leaders and the actual practices of its adherents, Conservative Judaism overwhelmingly claimed the allegiance of the children of East European immigrants. The movement also encouraged the involvement of women, not yet as equal religious participants, but as essential contributors to building a strong foundation for Conservative Judaism. In 1941, the movement's Women's League published the extremely popular *Jewish Home Beautiful* that combined the aesthetics of middle class domesticity with instructions for preparing Sabbath and holiday

The proper setting for a Passover table, as displayed in The Jewish Home Beautiful, *1941.*

Courtesy of the Women's League for Conservative Judaism

meals, outlining the proper ways to construct a refined American Jewish home.[16]

Some Orthodox Jews also began to advocate greater accommodation to American culture. American Orthodoxy had always been exceptionally diverse, with some groups resisting Americanization as much as possible and others attempting to preserve traditional observance while embracing what America had to offer. Perhaps the clearest articulation of an Americanized Orthodoxy in these years came in the creation of Yeshiva College (later Yeshiva University), dedicated in 1928. Its founder, Bernard Revel, was trained in Talmudic academies as well as secular universities and championed the vision of an Orthodox institution committed to both Jewish learning and the liberal arts and sciences. In blending secular

Opening of the Main Building of the Rabbi Isaac Elchanan Theological Seminary (RIETS) and Yeshiva College, December 1929.
Courtesy of Yeshiva University Archives

Published in 1941 by the Women's League of Conservative Judaism, The Jewish Home Beautiful *instructed Jewish women how to combine middle class domesticity with Jewish tradition.*

Men build our houses, our beautiful
    houses,
And plan every detail with infinite grace.
Choice wood hewed from tall trees and
    stone
    hauled from quarries,
Each girder, each rafter, each beam set
    with care.
Men build our houses, our beautiful
    houses,
But women make these houses—homes.

What is the JEWISH HOME BEAUTIFUL?
Must it be filled with rare antiques, soft
with luxurious carpets, sparkling with crystal and silver? Must the JEWISH HOME
BEAUTIFUL boast every new gadget, every
modern device invented by the ingenuity of
man? What is the JEWISH HOME
BEAUTIFUL?

The JEWISH HOME BEAUTIFUL may be
    mansion or hovel,
On Boulevard, Avenue or slum crowded
    street.

(Continued on next page)

(Continued from previous page)

With woman as priestess to tend to its
   altars,
Each home is a Temple, each hearth is a
   shrine.
While men build our houses and men fill
   our houses,
Women make these houses—homes.

The JEWISH HOME BEAUTIFUL has ever
been praised in song and story. From the
days of Abraham when Sarah's Home
Beautiful, a crude and simple tent in the
desert, was deemed worthy of a visit by
three angels of the Lord, the Jewish woman
has stamped her personality upon her
household. Her home was beautiful with
the beauty of holiness. Her charm and spirituality was reflected in the warmth and
cheer of her fireside.

As in days gone by, so today, the Jewish
woman, rich in memories and traditions of
the past, takes her pattern from the mothers of yesterday and creates new beauty,
new spirituality for the Jewish home of
tomorrow. Every Sabbath is a holy day.
Every festival, every holiday she observes
with symbol and ceremony.

Betty D. Greenberg and Altheas O. Silverman, *The
Jewish Home Beautiful* (New York: The Women's
League of the United Synagogue of America, 1941), p.
41. Reprinted with permission of the Women's League
for Conservative Judaism.

study with traditional Jewish education, Revel aimed to
create a "Torah-true American Jewry," capable of sustaining Orthodoxy within the American environment.[17]
Yeshiva University emerged as a bastion of acculturated
Orthodoxy, training rabbis and professionals and educating women and men who became the backbone of
Americanized Orthodoxy in years to come.

The 1920s brought prosperity to individual Jews and
tremendous growth within Jewish religious and organizational life, but the Great Depression stalled the progress of
American Jews and threatened the viability of their institutions. Because Jews were not heavily represented in heavy
industry and unskilled labor, the hardest hit sectors of the
urban American economy, they fared better than many
other ethnic groups during the Depression. "We were
never really hungry," Irving Howe remembered about his
working class Bronx family, "but almost always anxious."[18]
Despite their comparative good fortune, many Jews lost
jobs and businesses. Raised with high expectations, the children of immigrants encountered bleak job prospects,
regardless of educational attainment. Jewish social service
agencies were taxed beyond their capacities in caring for
the unemployed. The elaborate synagogues built in the
1920s struggled under enormous debts. The setbacks of the
1930s turned out to be temporary, but significant realign-
ments in Jewish life took place during the Depression
years. Young Jews who remained in school when no jobs
could be found saw those decisions rewarded in the post-
World War II era. They married later and began having
fewer children, establishing enduring patterns of Jewish
family life. Jewish politics also shifted dramatically in the
thirties. The economic crisis prompted a resurgence in
radicalism and union activity, but it also marked the beginning of Jewish allegiance to the Democratic Party. Before
the Depression, Jews had voted for candidates across the
political spectrum, but their support for Franklin Roosevelt's program created a lasting marriage between Jews
and the Democrats. The appointment of Jews as prominent
officials within the New Deal Administration and the great

numbers of Jews who found work in the expanded civil service further cemented Jewish commitments to Roosevelt and the new Democratic coalition. Jews became so closely associated with Roosevelt's program that anti-Semitic groups frequently attacked the New Deal as the "Jew Deal."[19]

The 1930s marked the apex of anti-Semitism in the United States, an era when more hate groups mobilized against Jews than any other time in American history. Building throughout the 1920s, anti-Semitism peaked in the turbulent climate of the Great Depression. The economic crisis rekindled notions of Jewish financial manipulation, while Jewish visibility in the New Deal Administration fueled the suspicions of conspiracy theorists. Roosevelt's Secretary of the Treasury Henry Morgenthau Jr., Supreme Court Justice Felix Frankfurter, and financier and adviser Bernard Baruch were among the most frequent targets of attack, representing the alleged agents of the Jewish plot to gain supremacy. While Jews were accused of taking over Washington, a priest in Detroit took to the airwaves to rail against Jewish domination. Father Charles Coughlin's bitter diatribes against Jews in the guise of defending ordinary Americans from the ills of communism, socialism, and dictatorship reached millions of radio listeners, growing increasingly harsh and more popular in the mid-1930s. From across the

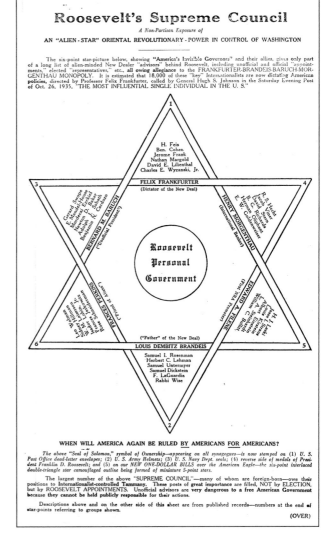

Anti-Semitic poster listing the supposed Jewish conspiracy in the Roosevelt Administration, 1930s.

The Jacob Rader Marcus Center of the American Jewish Archives

Father Charles Coughlin speaking at a 1936 rally in Cleveland, Ohio.

Bettmann/CORBIS

"WHAT EVERY CONGRESSMAN SHOULD KNOW"

Cover of an anti-Semitic pamphlet circulated by William Dudley Pelley, founder of the Silver Legion, an American Nazi organization created in 1933.

American Jewish Historical Society, Newton Centre, Massachusetts and New York, New York

political and ideological spectrum, organizations from the Silver Shirts to the German-American Bund labeled Jews as responsible for the nation's problems. Anti-Semitism in the United States never had the political potency or virulence that it possessed in Europe, but the parades, demonstrations, and widely disseminated publications of hate groups made Jews apprehensive about their status and security in America.

The rise of Nazi party in Germany intensified Jewish fears, supplied some of the rhetoric for anti-Semitic groups in the United States, and preoccupied American Jews during the 1930s. Since their first arrival on American shores, Jews had been deeply engaged with the situation of fellow Jews abroad. As they reacted to European events in the mid-1930s, they had no way to foresee the cataclysmic destruction that would occur just a few years later. Therefore, American Jewish responses must be measured in the context of what Jews knew at the time rather than in hindsight. In fact, American Jews responded immediately to Hitler's ascension to power, though they seldom agreed about the best approach. In 1933, just two months after the Nazi government took control, American Jews held a mass rally in New York's Madison Square Garden. Organized by Reform rabbi and influential communal leader Stephen Wise, the protest was intended to draw attention to the anti-Jewish policies being imposed in Germany. At the same time, many Jewish groups, including the Jewish War Veterans and the American Jewish Congress, called for a boycott of German goods in an attempt to put pressure on the Nazi regime. But not all Jews believed that mass rallies and boycotts were the proper responses; some argued that behind-the-scenes lobbying efforts would be more effective and less likely to elicit accusations of undue Jewish influence. Organizations such as B'nai B'rith and the American Jewish Committee opposed the boycott of German goods, believing that it might lend credence to anti-Semitic claims of Jewish conspiracy and damage the American economy in the middle of the Depression.[20] The American Jewish community was extraordinarily diverse, nurturing a constellation of ideological and political viewpoints, so it is not surprising that Jews held different opinions about how best to respond to the Nazi threat.

In 1933, the American Jewish Congress spearheaded a boycott on German goods to protest the Nazi regime's discriminatory policies.

American Jewish Historical Society, Newton Centre, Massachusetts and New York, New York

Before the United States entered World War II, the attempt to aid European Jews was addressed as a refugee question. Beginning in the 1930s, a series of international conferences focused on finding a haven for Jews looking to leave Europe. However, in the midst of a worldwide economic crisis, no nation, including the United States, expressed a willingness to liberalize immigration quotas. The British government which controlled Palestine during these years, would not allow the territory to be considered as an asylum. A series of committees, proposals, and bills produced only limited results.

Once the United States entered the war, the issue shifted from a refugee issue to a question of rescue, as large-scale emigration from Europe became virtually impossible. President Franklin Roosevelt articulated a policy of "rescue through victory," insisting that winning the war was the primary means to save European Jews. While the American government understandably made military victory the priority after the U.S. entered the war, there were individuals in the State Department who actively worked to thwart efforts to permit European Jews to enter the country. Assistant Secretary of State Breckinridge Long, whose diaries reveal fervent anti-Semitic beliefs, promoted policies that severely restricted the number of Jewish refugees who might have been allowed entry to the United States. In 1943, due largely to the persistent efforts of Secretary of the Treasury Henry Morgenthau, Jr., the obstruction within the State Department became public and was brought to the attention of President Roosevelt. The following year, Roosevelt issued an Executive Order establishing the War Refugee Board, designed to save as many victims of Nazism as possible. By 1944, only limited opportunities existed to rescue European Jews, yet the War Refugee Board succeeded in saving approximately 200,000 Jews, mostly from Hungary, before the Nazis deported the remaining population.[21]

The persecution of Jews in Europe preoccupied American Jews in the 1930s and 1940s. Jewish newspapers and organizations reported events as they unfolded and responded as best they could. America's Jews protested and lobbied as the Nazis instituted discriminatory policies, forced Jews into ghettoes, and engaged in violence

Stamp issued during the boycott on German goods.

Gift of Yehuda Nir in memory of his father, Samuel Grunfeld. Collection of the Museum of Jewish Heritage-A Living Memorial To The Holocaust, New York. Photograph by Peter Goldberg.

Henry Morgenthau, Jr. (1891-1967), Secretary of the Treasury during the Roosevelt Administration, ca. 1945.

Library of Congress, Prints and Photographs Division

and murder. Not until 1942 did Hitler's advisers devise plans for the mass extermination of the entire Jewish population. As the first reports of the massacre of Jews began filtering into the United States in July, 1942, more than 20,000 Jews rallied in protest at Madison Square Garden, joined by Christian clergy and other public officials, calling for action to prevent the total annihilation Europe's Jews. Shock and disbelief gripped the American Jewish community, as all Americans struggled to make sense of the sheer number of killings being reported. The following month, Gerhard Riegner, the World Jewish Congress representative in Geneva, sent a telegram to Rabbi Stephen Wise and other Jewish leaders, providing detailed information about the Nazi extermination plans and documenting the mass killing of Jews taking place in death camps. Wise forwarded the information to the State Department, which requested that he not go public until the details could be corroborated. After waiting for months with no government action, Wise received confirmation of the reports and held a press conference to broadcast the grim facts about the full extent of Nazi atrocities.[22]

From the time that Hitler assumed power through the years of the Holocaust, American Jews engaged in heated debates about the best way to respond to the crisis. During these years, no issue divided the community as much as the Zionist question. Zionism had been gaining support throughout the interwar years and the need for a Jewish homeland appeared more pressing in the face of the Nazi menace. Even the Reform movement, which had previously maintained staunch opposition to Zionist ideas, softened its position in a 1937 statement of principles, endorsing the notion of a Jewish homeland. As the crisis in Europe worsened and Jewish groups discussed how to respond, many Zionists insisted that the establishment of a Jewish state was the only possible solution. From the refugee issue to the best use of

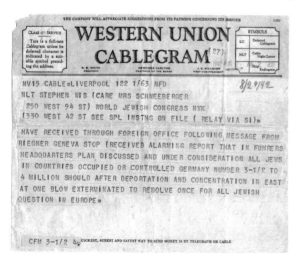

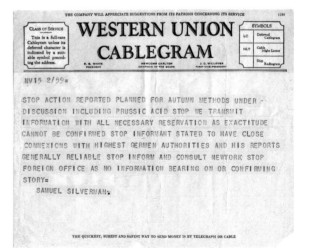

funds, the most ardent Zionist groups insisted that all energies be directed to creating a haven for Jews in Palestine. News of Hitler's extermination plans made the Zionist leadership in America more assertive and in 1942, they gathered at New York's Biltmore Hotel to demand the immediate creation of a sovereign Jewish state. The Holocaust also sparked the more radical wing of the Zionist movement. Peter Bergson, whose real name was Hillel Kook, organized rallies and took out powerful newspaper advertisements with the slogan, "We Shall Never Die." Deeply affected by the campaign, journalist Ben Hecht staged a pageant that adopted the slogan as its title. Hecht enlisted the services of well-known actors such as Edward G. Robinson and Paul Muni, who took the show—and its dramatic message for Jews to fight for their own survival—to several American cities.[23]

Rabbi Stephen Wise speaking at a rally in Madison Square, 1944.

Library of Congress, Prints and Photographs Division

In responding to the Holocaust, American Jews spoke loudly, but not in a unified voice. Those groups that preferred behind-the-scenes negotiations clashed with those who believed that rallies and protests were the most effective means to call attention to the plight of European Jewry. Some Jews wanted to find a haven for Jews anywhere possible; others adamantly insisted that a Jewish homeland in Palestine was the only viable solution. Zionists also battled internally about proper tactics and strategies. Given its size and diversity, the American Jewish community had never expressed a singular outlook on any issue, and the same pattern prevailed during the heated debates over how to rescue European Jews. Moreover, even had American Jews acted in complete solidarity, they could not have altered American policies in an era when the nation was consumed by the Great Depression and the Second World War. By the time the American government and the American Jewish community grasped the full extent of the Nazi plan, there were limited options for rescue.[24]

The Holocaust and World War II permanently altered the Jewish world. More than half a million American Jews served in the armed forces, more than in any other American war. Jewish soldiers, mostly the children of immigrants, not only fought for their country, but many also witnessed firsthand the destruction of European Jewry. In the military, Jews and non-Jews from across the country encountered each other's cultures, religions, and prejudices, sometimes gaining new understandings and often prompting Jews to reevaluate their

Military Passover Seder in the Admiralty Islands, ca. 1944.

Gift of Mildred Shapiro. Collection of the Museum of Jewish Heritage-A Living Memorial To The Holocaust, New York. Photograph by Peter Goldberg

ethnic identities.[25] When the war came to an end, American Jewry was left to grapple with the loss and anguish that accompanied the decimation of European Jewry. The painful close of centuries of vibrant Jewish life in Europe, the place of ancestry for most American Jews, also marked the opening of a new chapter in Jewish history. With Europe in ashes, American Jewry emerged as the largest Jewish community in the world, left to assume the mantle of leadership and the maintenance of Jewish culture in a post-Holocaust world.

NOTES

1. Will Herberg, "The Jewish Labor Movement in the United States, "*American Jewish Yearbook* 53 (1952): 53–54.

2. Vivian Gornick, quoted in Deborah Dash Moore, *At Home in America: Second Generation New York Jews* (New York: Columbia University Press, 1981), p. 63; Irving Cutler, *The Jews of Chicago: From Shtetl to Suburb* (Urbana: University of Illinois Press, 1996), p. 119; Moore, *At Home in America*, pp. 60–87.

3. Moore, *At Home in America*, p. 10.

4. Alfred Kazin, *A Walker in the City* (New York: Harcourt Brace Jovanovich, 1951), pp. 21–22.

5. Leonard Dinnerstein, "Education and the Advancement of American Jews," in Bernard J. Weiss, ed., *American Education and the European Immigrant, 1840–1940* (Urbana: University of Illinois Press, 1982), pp. 44–60; Ruth Jacknow Markowitz, *My Daughter the Teacher: Jewish Teachers in the New York City Schools* (New Brunswick: Rutgers University Press, 1993), p. 21; Beth S. Wenger, *New York Jews and the Great Depression: Uncertain Promise* (New Haven: Yale University Press, 1996), pp. 64–69.

6. Leonard Dinnerstein, *Antisemitism in America* (New York: Oxford University Press, 1994), p. 84; *The Jewish Independent* [Cleveland], June 16, 1922, pp. 1, 9.

7. Henry L. Feingold, *A Time for Searching: Entering the Mainstream, 1920–1945* (Baltimore: Johns Hopkins University Press, 1992), pp. 15–18.

8. Dinnerstein, *Antisemitism in America*, pp. 88–90; Wenger, *New York Jews and the Great Depression*, pp. 23–24; "Jews in America," *Fortune* (February, 1936).

9. Feingold, *A Time for Searching*, pp. 8–13.

10. Hasia R.Diner, *The Jews of the United States, 1654–2000* (Berkeley: University of California Press, 2004), p. 153; J. Hoberman and Jeffrey Shandler, "The Media that 'Speak Your Language': American Yiddish Radio and Film," in Hoberman and Shandler eds., *Entertaining America: Jews, Movies and Broadcasting* (New York: Jewish Museum, under the auspices of the Jewish Theological Seminary of America; Princeton: Princeton University Press, 2003) pp. 104–108.

11. Larry May and Elaine May, "Why Jewish Movie Moguls: An Exploration in American Culture," *American Jewish History* 72 (September, 1982), pp. 6–8; J. Hoberman and Jeffrey Shandler, "Hollywood's Jewish Question," in *Entertaining America*, pp. 47–53.

12. Donald Weber, "Goldberg Variations: The Achievements of Gertrude Berg," in Hoberman and Shandler, eds., *Entertaining America*, pp. 117, 113–123.

13. Hank Greenberg, *Hank Greenberg: The Story of My Life* with Ira Benkow (Chicago: Triumph Books, 2001), pp. 55–59.

14. *Census of Religious Bodies, 1936—Jewish Congregations: Statistics, History, Doctrine and Organization* (Washington, D.C.: United States Government Printing Office, 1940), table 2, p. 2; Wenger, *New York Jews and the Great Depression*, pp. 168, 184; Arthur A. Goren, *The American Jews* (Cambridge, Mass.: Belknap Press of Harvard University Press, 1982), p. 80.

15. Mel Scult, *Judaism Faces the Twentieth Century: A Biography of Mordecai M. Kaplan* (Detroit: Wayne State University Press, 1993).

16. Betty D. Greenberg and Althea O. Silverman, *The Jewish Home Beautiful* (New York: Women's League of the United Synagogue of America, 1941); Jonathan D. Sarna, *American Judaism: A History* (New Haven: Yale University Press, 2004), pp. 237–42.

17. Bernard Revel, "The Yeshiva College" [1926], in Aaron Rothkoff, *Bernard Revel: Builder of American Jewish Orthodoxy* (Philadelphia: Jewish Publication Society, 1972), pp. 260, 255–262.

18. Irving Howe, *A Margin of Hope: An Intellectual Autobiography* (New York: Harcourt Brace Jovanovich, 1982), p. 6.

19. Wenger, *New York Jews and the Great Depression*.

20. Feingold, *A Time for Searching*, pp. 235–37.

21. Henry L. Feingold, *The Politics of Rescue: The Roosevelt Administration and the Holocaust, 1938–1945* (New Brunswick: Rutgers University Press, 1970), esp. pp. 131–37, 244–94.

22. David S. Wyman, *The Abandonment of the Jews: America and the Holocaust, 1941–1945* (New York: Pantheon Books, 1984), pp. 24–26, 42–52.

23. Feingold, *The Politics of Rescue*, pp. 175–76.

24. Ibid., pp. 308–330.

25. Deborah Dash Moore, *GI Jews: How World War II Changed a Generation* (Cambridge, Mass.: Belknap Press, 2004).

LIFELONG SOCIALIST

• IRVING HOWE •

Born in 1920, Irving Howe grew up in a working class Bronx neighborhood during the Great Depression. During the economic crisis, his parents lost the small grocery store that they managed, and Howe witnessed firsthand the political, social and economic upheavals of the 1930s. Drawn to radical politics by the age of fourteen and later an active participant in the lively debates that took place at New York's City College, Howe was initially attracted to Trotskyism but soon became a democratic socialist—an identity and an outlook he maintained throughout his life.

As an intellectual and literary critic, Howe quickly established himself in the New York literary world. In addition to works of criticism, he was also a founding editor of *Dissent* in 1954 and a regular contributor to the *Partisan Review*, *Commentary*, *The New York Review of Books*, and *The New Republic*. Howe transmitted his passion for Yiddish literature and Yiddish culture to a wide American audience, popularizing the works of Isaac Bashevis Singer and authoring the bestselling *World of Our Fathers*, which chronicled the immigrant Jewish community in America.

Howe served as Distinguished Professor of Literature at the City University of New York. In 1982, he penned his autobiography, *A Margin of Hope*. In these selections, he describes the character of the Bronx Jewish neighborhood of his childhood.

THE EAST BRONX, when I lived there as a boy, formed a thick tangle of streets crammed with Jewish immigrants from Eastern Europe, almost all of them poor. We lived in narrow five-story tenements, wall flush against wall, and with slate-colored stoops rising sharply in front. There never was enough space. The buildings, clenched into rows, looked down upon us like sentinels, and the apartments in the buildings were packed with relatives and children, many of them fugitives from unpaid rent. These tenements had first gone up during the early years of the century, and if not quite so grimy as those of the Lower East Side in Manhattan or the Brownsville section of Brooklyn, they were bad enough. The halls on the ground floor leading to the staircase always seemed dark and at night spooky; even in my middle teens, when I was trying to brace myself to visions of political heroism, I would still feel a slight shudder of nerves whenever I started up the staircase. . . .

Irving Howe speaking at a conference in 1975.
From the Archives of the YIVO Institute for Jewish Research

IN THE EARLY thirties—by then I was entering my teens— the East Bronx was still a self-contained little world, lacking the cultural vivacity that had brightened the Lower East Side of Manhattan a decade or two earlier but otherwise, in custom and value, not very different. Yiddish was spoken everywhere. The English of the young, if unmarred by accent, had its own intonation, the stumbling melody of immigrant speech. A mile or two from my building—I did not know it then—there lived a cluster of Yiddish writers who would gather on Sundays near a big rock in Crotona Park, where I would go to play ball or wander around. At the corner newsstands the Yiddish daily, the *Forward*, sold about as well as the *News* and the *Mirror*, the two-cent tabloids with crime stories, pictures, gossip. . . .

TWO OR THREE blocks from where we lived stood the peeling McKinley Square Theatre, in which a company of Yiddish actors, as mediocre as they were poor, tried to keep alive. You had to patronize them once in a while with a thirty-five-cent ticket, said my father, because it was a scandal to see fellow Jews "dying of hunger three times a day." (Blessed Yiddish: no one just dies of hunger, you die three times a day.) The nearest synagogue, in a once baroque structure, was also struggling through the Depression, and as if to acknowledge reduced circumstances my own bar mitzvah took place not there, since that would have cost too much and probably made us feel uncomfortable, but in a whitewashed store-front *shul*, ramshackle and bleak with its scattering of aged Jews. This sort of penniless congregation no longer exists in Jewish neighborhoods, but its equivalents can still be found among the more exotic black denominations. A few blocks past the synagogue, on Wilkins Avenue, stood the loft in which a secular Yiddish school by the Workmen's Circle, a fraternal order more or less socialist in outlook. My father, though hardly pious, would not let me go there because he felt ill at ease with the bluntly secular. It was as if he knew what "the real thing" was in Judaism, even though himself gradually slipping away from it. That loft on Wilkins Avenue turned out to be more important in my life than any synagogue.

An inexperienced eye moving across the East Bronx would have noticed little difference between one part and another. That eye would have been mistaken, for the immigrant world had its intricate latticing of social position. All through the years of the Depression our neighborhood clung to its inner supports of morale, its insistence upon helping its own in ways that were its own—which meant keeping as far as possible from the authority of the state, suspect as both gentile and bourgeois. Many people in the East Bronx would have starved—and perhaps some did a little—rather than go on "relief." The psychology of the *shtetl* householder in Eastern Europe, with his desperate improvisations to appear independent, had an odd way of recurring among these garment workers, some of whom still dreamed of managing their own little businesses, even if no more than a candy store with its shuffle of pennies across the counter. Almost everyone dreaded "charity."

• • •

IN OUR NEIGHBORHOOD many of the women went to work. They would stand long hours at the counters of grocery and candy stores or join their men in the forty-five-minute subway ride to the garment center, a trip that made your bones ache even before starting to work. Even when the women went downtown, the family remained the center of life. Sometimes the family was about all that was left of Jewishness; or, more accurately, all that we had left of Jewishness had come to rest in the family. Jewishness flickered to life on Friday night, with a touch of Sabbath ceremony a few moments before dinner; it came radiantly to life during Passover, when traditional dignities shone through its ritual. Our parents clung to family life as if that was their one certainty: everything else seemed frightening, alien, incomprehensible. Not that they often talked about these things. Speaking openly would have been still more frightening, a shattering of defenses. Only in moments of crisis could that happen—as in those hysterical scenes that broke out when adolescents tried to slip away into lives of their own.

In the worst of times, between 1930 and 1934, there were still hours of happiness, many of them. An infection of hope had seized these Jews, not really for themselves (a possibility their sardonic realism taught them to discount), but hope at once passionate and abstract, fixed equally upon America and their children. Whatever their faith or opinions, they felt that here in America the Jews had at least a chance, and as it turned out they were right. . . .

RADICALISM IN OUR part of the city seemed more than marginal exotica, and in the city as a whole more than an alien import. It had a place and strength of its own. It was still the belief of a minority, but a minority that kept growing. Socialism, for many immigrant Jews, was not merely politics or an idea, it was an encompassing culture, a style of perceiving and judging through which to structure their lives. . . .

IT WAS DIFFERENT in the Jewish neighborhoods. Attitudes of tolerance, feelings that one had to put up with one's cranks, eccentrics, idealists, and extremists, pervaded the Jewish community to an extent that those profiting from them did not always stop to appreciate. The Jewish labor movement had established a tradition of controversy and freedom, so that even when some groups like the Communists willfully violated this tradition, it still exerted an enormous moral power in the immigrant streets. Trotskyist meetings were sometimes broken up, but never spontaneously, only by decision of the Communist Party. Most of the time the Jewish neighborhood was prepared to listen to almost anyone with its characteristic mixture of interest, skepticism, and amusement. Not that these audiences were easily taken in by our grandiose speeches. You might be shouting at the top of your lungs against reformism or Stalin's betrayals, but for the middle-aged garment worker taking a stroll after a hard day at the shop you were just a bright and cocky Jewish boy, a talkative little *pisher*.

Irving Howe, *A Margin of Hope: An Intellectual Autobiography* (New York: Harcourt Brace Jovanovich, 1982) pp. 1–5, 9, 24. Excerpts from *A Margin of Hope: An Intellectual Autobiography*, copyright © 1982 by Irving Howe, reprinted by permission of Harcourt, Inc.

֍ 2 ֍

WRITER AND FEMINIST

• VIVIAN GORNICK •

VIVAIN GORNICK, born in 1935, grew up in a working class Jewish neighborhood in the Bronx, the daughter of immigrant parents who had come to the United States from the Ukraine. Like thousands of other Jewish immigrants, her father Louis labored in the garment industry as a presser in a dress factory, while her mother Bess found work as an office clerk and bookkeeper. In a family of committed socialists, Gornick imbibed the passionate political ideologies that swirled through the Jewish community in the interwar years.

Like many second generation Jews, Vivian Gornick pursued higher education, both at City College and New York University. She became well known as a reporter for the *Village Voice* in the 1970s and was also a regular contributor to the *Nation* and the *New York Times*. A pioneering feminist, Gornick's articles gave voice to the burgeoning women's movement. Her Jewish identity has remained a thread throughout her work, in her critical essays as well as her memoirs, and she has often drawn parallels between the marginality experienced by both Jews and women. Her many published works include *Woman in Sexist Society: Studies in Power and Powerlessness*, *Fierce Attachments: A Memoir*, and *Approaching Eye Level*. In this passage from *The Romance of American Communism*, Gornick recalls the politically charged environment of her working class family and community.

M Y FATHER STOOD upright on the floor of a dress factory on West 35th Street in New York City with a steam iron in his hand for thirty years. My uncles owned the factory. My father was Labor, my uncles were Capital. My father was a Socialist, my uncles were Zionists. Therefore, Labor was Socialism and Capital was Nationalism. These equations were mother's milk to me, absorbed through flesh and bone almost before consciousness. Concomitantly, I knew also—and again, as though osmotically— who in this world were friends, who enemies, who neutrals. Friends were all those who thought like us: working-class socialists, the people whom my parents called "progressives." *All* others were "them"; and "them" were either engaged enemies like my uncles or passive neutrals like some of our neighbors. Years later, the "us" and "them" of my life would become Jews and Gentiles, and still later women and men, but for all of my growing-up years "us" and "them" were socialists and non-socialists; the "politically enlightened" and the politically *un*enlightened; those who were "struggling for a better world" and those who, like moral slugs, moved blind and unresponsive through this vast inequity that was our life under capitalism. Those, in short, who had class consciousness and those *lumpen* or bourgeois who did not.

THIS WORLD OF "us" was, of course, a many-layered one. I was thirteen or fourteen years old before I consciously understood the complex sociology of the progressive planet; understood that at the center of the globe stood those who were full-time organizing members of the Communist Party, at the outermost periphery stood those who were called "sympathizers," and at various points in between stood those who held Communist Party membership cards and those who were called "fellow travelers." In those early childhood years these distinctions did not exist for me; much less did I grasp that within this sociology my parents were merely "fellow travelers." The people who came to our house with the *Daily Worker*[1] or the Yiddish newspaper *Der Freiheit* [2] under their arms, the people at the "affairs" we attended, the people at the *shule* (the Yiddish school I was sent to after my public-school day was over), the people at the rallies we went to and the May Day parades we marched in, the people who belonged to the various "clubs" and were interminably collecting money for the latest cause or defense fund—they were all as one to me; they were simply "our people." On a Saturday morning, the doorbell in our Bronx apartment would ring, my father would open the door, and standing there would be Hymie, a cutter in my father's shop, a small, thin man with gnarled hands and the face of an anxious bulldog. "*Nu*, Louie?" Hymie would say to my father. "Did you see the papers this morning? Did you see—a black year on all of them!—what they're saying about the Soviet Union *this* morning?" "Come in, Hymie, come in," my father would reply. "Have a cup of coffee, we'll discuss it." I did not know that there was a difference between Hymie, who was also only a "fellow traveler," and my cousins David and Selena, who were YCLers,[3] or my uncle Sam, who was always off at "a meeting," or Bennie Grossman from across the street who had suddenly disappeared from the neighborhood ("unavailable" was the word for what Bennie had become, but it would be twenty years before I realized that was the word). It was, to begin with, all one country to me, one world, and the major characteristic of that world as I perceived it was this:

Author Vivian Gornick.
Courtesy of Vivian Gornick

At the wooden table in our kitchen there were always gathered men named Max and Hymie, and women named Masha and Goldie. Their hands were work-blackened, their eyes intelligent and anxious, their voices loud and insistent. They drank tea, ate black bread and herring, and talked "issues." Endlessly, they talked issues. I sat on the kitchen bench beside my father, nestled in the crook of his arm, and I listened, wide-eyed, to the talk. Oh, that talk! That passionate, transforming talk! I understood nothing of what they were saying, but I was excited beyond words by the richness of their rhetoric, the intensity of their arguments, the urgency and longing behind that hot river of words that came ceaselessly pouring out of all of them. Something important was happening here, I always felt, something that had to do

---

[1] *The Daily Worker*, published in New York by the Communist Party, began circulation in 1924.

[2] *Die Freiheit* (Freedom), a newspaper published by the Jewish section of the Communist Party, beginning in 1922.

[3] The Young Communist League.

with understanding things. And "to understand things," I already knew, was the most exciting, the most important thing in life.

It was characteristic of that world that during those hours at the kitchen table with my father and his socialist friends I didn't know we were poor. I didn't know that in those places beyond the streets of my neighborhood we were without power, position, material or social existence. I only knew that tea and black bread were the most delicious food and drink in the world, that political talk filled the room with a terrible excitement and a richness of expectation, that here in the kitchen I felt the same electric thrill I felt when Rouben, my Yiddish teacher, pressed my upper arm between two bony fingers and, his eyes shining behind thick glasses, said to me: "Ideas, dolly, ideas. Without them, life is nothing. With them, life is *everything*."

Sometimes I would slip off the bench and catch my mother somewhere between the stove and the table (she was forever bringing something to the table). I would point to one or another at the table and whisper to her: Who is this one? Who is that one? My mother would reply in Yiddish: "He is a writer. She is a poet. He is a thinker." Oh, I would nod, perfectly satisfied with these identifications, and return to my place on the bench. *He*, of course, drove a bakery truck. *She* was a sewing-machine operator. That other one over there was a plumber, and the one next to him stood pressing dresses all day long beside my father.

But Rouben was right. Ideas were everything. So powerful was the life inside their minds that sitting there, drinking tea and talking issues, these people ceased to be what they objectively were—immigrant Jews, disenfranchised workers—and, indeed, they became thinkers, writers, poets.

Vivian Gornick, *The Romance of American Communism* (New York: Basic Books, 1997), pp 2–5.
Reprinted by permission of Basic Books, a member of Perseus Books Group.

ঌ 3 ঌ

JEWISH QUOTAS AT HARVARD

• AN EXCHANGE BETWEEN ALFRED A. BENESCH AND A. LAWRENCE LOWELL •

IN 1922, Harvard President A. Lawrence Lowell publicly suggested that quotas be imposed to control the numbers of Jews admitted to Harvard College. By the 1920s, the Jewish presence on many elite campuses had begun increasing substantially, causing a backlash among those who feared an incursion into the genteel institutions of American higher education. Lowell proposed quotas as a solution to growing anti-Semitism on campus, insisting that limiting the proportion of Jews admitted would decrease prejudice against Jewish students who attended the university. Although a Harvard committee ultimately rejected President Lowell's proposal, Harvard along with other leading universities did, in fact, institute unofficial quota systems throughout the interwar years. By including application questions about religious preference and family name changes, by making character a condition of admission, and by initiating policies of geographic diversity, many colleges effectively limited the number of Jewish students.

When President Lowell suggested a Jewish quota system, Cleveland attorney and Harvard alumnus Alfred A. Benesch initiated a correspondence with him. After graduating from Harvard, Benesch, the son of Jewish immigrants from Czechoslovakia, had become a prominent lawyer and civic leader in Cleveland as well as chairman of the Cleveland branch of the Anti-Defamation League. Entering politics as a city councilman in 1912, Benesch went on to become Ohio Director of Commerce and President of the Cleveland Board of Education. In his correspondence with Lowell, Benesch protests the proposal to limit the number of Jewish students at Harvard, pointing out its moral and logical deficiencies.

My Dear Dr. Lowell: In common with other Jewish graduates of Harvard, I was astounded at the official statement issued last week with reference to the restriction of enrollment. Even had the statement made no special mention of students of the Jewish race, it would have been objectionable because of the undoubted implication. Containing, as it did, however, particular reference to the Jews, it is tenfold more objectionable because of the direct suggestion made to those who might not otherwise perceive its purpose.

It is utterly impossible for me to comprehend how an institution of learning which has throughout its history received contributions from men of all religious faiths, and which has enjoyed an enviable reputation for non-sectarianism, can even contemplate the adoption of a regulation obviously designed to discriminate against the Jews. The late Jacob H. Schiff for years maintained a deep interest in Harvard and was loyal to Harvard's traditions. Do you think that he would remain silent, were he alive today, in the face of such action on the part of the university authorities?

Felix Warburg and other eminent Jews of New York City and elsewhere were liberal contributors to the Harvard Endowment Fund. Are their feelings not to be considered?

I am a graduate of more than twenty years' standing. I have contributed to the Endowment Fund and am contributing now annually to the Scholarship Fund established by my class, the class of 1900. You would criticise me with poor grace, were I to withhold any further contributions under the existing circumstances.

Shortly after my graduation I wrote an article entitled, "The Jew at Harvard," in which, I think, I successfully combated the notion then prevalent that Harvard was anti-Semitic. I hope that I shall not be under the necessity of writing a similar article with a changed point of view. I hope, too, that the regulation which has unhappily stirred up so much unpleasant publicity for Harvard does not find its origin in the fact that Jewish students, numbering perhaps 10 per cent of the student population at Harvard, are the successful contestants for perhaps 50 per cent of the prizes and scholarships.

Cleveland attorney and Harvard alumnus A. A. Benesch.
Courtesy of The Western Reserve Historical Society, Cleveland, Ohio

Students of the Jewish faith neither demand nor expect any favors at the hands of the university; but they do expect, and have a right to demand, that they be admitted upon equal terms with students of other faiths, and that scholarship and character be the only standards for admission.

I am still hopeful that the newspaper reports are not based entirely upon fact and that I may hear from you soon a true statement of the situation.

Very respectfully yours,
Alfred A. Benesch.

Dear Mr. Benesch: There is no need of cautioning you not to believe all that you see in the newspapers. As a colleague said to me yesterday, there is perhaps no body of men in the United States, mostly Gentiles, with so little anti-Semitic feelings as the instructing staff at Harvard University. But the problem that confronts this country and its educational institutions is a difficult one, and one about which I should very much like to talk with you. It is one that involves the best interests both of the college and of the Jews, for I should feel very badly to think that these did not coincide.

There is, most unfortunately, a rapidly growing anti-Semitic feeling in this country, causing—and no doubt in part caused by—a strong race feeling on the part of the Jews themselves. In many cities of the country Gentile Clubs are excluding Jews altogether, who are forming separate clubs of their own.

A. Lawrence Lowell, President of Harvard University.
Library of Congress, Prints and Photographs Division

Private schools are excluding Jews, I believe, and so, we know, are hotels. All this seems to me fraught with very great evils for the Jews, and very great perils for the community. The question did not originate here, but has been brought over from Europe—especially from those countries where it has existed for centuries.

The question for those of us who deplore such a state of things is how it can be combated, and especially for those of us who are connected with colleges, how it can be combated there—how we can cause the Jews to feel and be regarded as an integral part of the student body. The anti-Semitic feeling among the students is increasing, and it grows in proportion to the increase in the number of Jews.

If their number should become 40 per cent of the student body, the race feeling would become intense. When, on the other hand, the number of Jews was small, the race antagonism was small also. Any such race feeling among the students tends to prevent the personal intimacies on which we must rely to soften anti-Semitic feeling.

If every college in the country would take a limited proportion of Jews, I suspect we should go a long way toward eliminating race feeling among the students, and as these students passed out into the world, eliminating it in the community.

This question is with us. We cannot solve it by forgetting or ignoring it. If we do nothing about the matter the prejudice is likely to increase. Some colleges appear to have met the question by indirect methods, which we do not want to adopt. It cannot be solved except by a co-operation between the college authorities and the Jews themselves. Would not the Jews be willing to help us in finding the steps best adapted for preventing the growth of race feeling among our students, and hence in the world?

The first thing to recognize is that there is a problem—a new problem, which we have never had to face before, but which has come over with the immigration from the Old World. After the nature of that problem is fairly understood, the next question is how to solve it in the interest of the Jews, as well as of every one else.

Very truly yours,
A. Lawrence Lowell

My dear Mr. Lowell: I find myself in complete harmony with some of the statements in your letter of June 9, but in complete disagreement with others.

I hope and believe it is true that the instructing staff of Harvard University is not anti-Semitic at heart. I am apprehensive, however, that the wave of anti-Semitism which has been inundating the country during the last year or more has not left the members of the staff untouched. I am apprehensive, too, that some members of the Harvard alumni have not been inactive in expressing and making felt their anti-Jewish and unsocial proclivities.

Although I agree with you that, unhappily, there is a rapidly growing anti-Semitic feeling in this country, I must take issue with you upon the proposition that this feeling is caused in part by a strong race feeling on the part of the Jews. Is not the strong race feeling on the part of the Jews the result rather than the cause? In other words, has not the strong race feeling been developed as a measure of self-defense?

You throw out the suggestion that "If every college in the country would take a limited proportion of Jews. I suspect that we should go a long way toward eliminating race feeling among the students, and, as the students passed out into the world, eliminating it in the community."

Carrying your suggestion to its logical conclusion would inevitably mean that a complete prohibition against Jewish students in the colleges would solve the problem of anti-Semitism. Moreover, it might lead to the establishment of a distinctively Jewish university, a consummation most sincerely to be deplored.

If it be true—and I have no doubt that it is true—that the anti-Semitic feeling among the students is increasing, should it not be the function of an institution of learning to discourage rather than to encourage such a spirit? If certain members of the student body foster so un-American a spirit, Harvard University, which has always stood for true democracy and liberalism, should be the first to condemn such a spirit, and exert every effort to prevent its growth.

If it is at all possible for you to call a meeting of a group of Jewish graduates, together with the members of the corporation and such other graduates as are interested in this vital problem, such meeting to be called within the next ten days or two weeks, I shall be very glad personally to make the sacrifice of time and money to attend such meeting. I believe, as you do, that a matter of this character can best be discussed by word of mouth.

Respectfully yours,
Alfred A. Benesch

The Jewish Independent [Cleveland], June 16, 1922, pp. 1, 9.

҂9 4 ҈

COMMUNAL LEADER

• LOUIS MARSHALL •

THE SON of immigrant parents, Louis Marshall was born in Syracuse, New York, in 1856 and became one of the most influential Jewish communal leaders of his generation. Graduating from Columbia Law School in 1877, Marshall began a distinguished legal career, first in Syracuse and later in New York City. In New York, he immediately immersed himself in Jewish communal affairs, serving as president of the city's prestigious Temple Emanu-El and on the Board of Directors of the Jewish Theological Seminary. Marshall assumed the presidency of the American Jewish Committee in 1912 and held the position until his death in 1929, becoming involved in every major Jewish issue of his day.

Marshall lobbied forcefully against restrictive immigration policies. When Leo Frank was wrongly accused of murder in 1913, Marshall helped to organize the legal defense and to initiate appeals after his conviction. After World War I, Marshall attended the Paris Peace Conference and helped to formulate the minority rights provisions in the constitutions of the new European states created after the war. Although he was not a Zionist, after the 1917 Balfour Declaration, he supported the idea of Jewish settlement in Palestine and considered it a solution to the crisis of East European Jewry. When Henry Ford began disseminating anti-Semitic propaganda through the publication of *The Dearborn Independent* and *The International Jew*, Marshall undertook a lengthy campaign to silence him. Spearheading legal action against Ford, Marshall ultimately forced him to issue a public apology. The two selections below—a telegram Marshall sent to Ford and a letter to President Calvin Coolidge urging him to stop Ford's propaganda—reveal Marshall's tireless efforts to quash Ford's anti-Semitic campaign.

Telegram to Henry Ford

June 3, 1920
To Henry Ford

In the issues of May twenty-second and twenty-ninth of the Dearborn Independent which is understood to be your property or under your control there have appeared two articles which are disseminating anti-semitism in its most insidious and pernicious form. [Stop] The statements which they contain are palpable fabrications and the insinuations with which they abound are the emanations of hatred and prejudice. [Stop] They constitute a libel upon an entire people who had hoped that at least in America they might be spared the insult the humiliation and the obloquy which these articles are scattering throughout the land and which are echoes from the dark middle ages. [Stop]

Louis Marshall (1856-1929).
The Jacob Rader Marcus Center of the American Jewish Archives

Your agencies are said to be engaged in circulating this mischief breeding sheet. [Stop] On behalf of my brethren I ask you from whom we had believed that justice might be expected whether these offensive articles have your sanction whether further publications of this nature are to be continued and whether you shall remain silent when your failure to disavow them will be regarded as an endorsement of them by the general public. [Stop] Three million of deeply wounded Americans are awaiting your answer.

Letter to President Calvin Coolidge

March 18, 1925
To the President, Calvin Coolidge

The noble words contained in your inaugural address are still ringing in my ears:

"The fundamental precept of liberty is toleration. We cannot permit any inquisition either within or without the law or apply any religious test to the holding of office. The mind of America must be forever free."

This redeclaration of the spirit which permeates our system of government, leads me to bring to your attention a condition the continuance of which it is earnestly hoped by hundreds of thousands of American citizens may be obviated by such action as you may be able to take.

It is well known that for several years past *The Dearborn Independent*, which is the personal organ of Mr. Henry Ford and is described in its title as The Ford International Weekly, he being the President of the corporation which issues this publication and his name appearing upon its editorial page, has been engaged, week to week, in a systematic attack upon the Jews. The articles published abound in monumental falsehoods and malicious inventions, couched in virulent terms and designed to arouse suspicion, hatred and prejudice against those of the Jewish faith. There is no libel, no product of superstition or base concoction, that has ever been aimed at the Jews, that has not been rehashed in the columns of this sheet. Mr. Ford has attacked the Jews singly and collectively. Men who have striven to perform their duties as citizens or in the discharge of their public obligations, have been shamefully maligned. These articles have been reprinted by Mr. Ford in a series of booklets entitled *The International Jew*, and have been spread broadcast throughout the world. They have been translated into various

European languages in those countries by professional anti-Semites for the purpose of provoking enmity against the Jews, to such an extent as frequently to result in concerted attacks upon them, in many cases involving loss of life.

To indicate the methods resorted to for the purpose of carrying on this work of intolerance, I call your attention to a circular letter, a photostatic copy of which is in my possession, issued by the Ford Motor Company to its agents throughout the United States, in which those receiving the circular are admonished that they had not "sent in a single Dearborn subscription" during the year and that they had disregarded the company's "special request to send in" their "estimated monthly subscriptions, so we can remove your name from the nonproducers' list sent to the Home Office each month." The letter then calls attention to the fact that the addressee had "signed a sales agreement to secure 288 subscriptions during 1925." He is told: "You are fully expected to live up to this agreement by sending in enough subscriptions each month to keep you up to or ahead of your monthly estimates until you have reached your yearly quota." He is then informed that there are only two explanations for his "apparent disregard of our letters urging you to secure your estimate," and that the second of the explanations specified may be that the agent had "deliberately neglected Dearborn Sales through lack of any desire or intention to cooperate with the Branch." In an underscored sentence the agent is then informed: "This is a spirit upon the part of a dealer which is very detrimental to the future progress of the Ford organization." In conclusion the Ford Motor Company says: "Your Dearborn activities during March will be sufficient proof as to which of the two possible explanations are correct in your case. We feel sure that the second explanation does not apply to you, therefore, we request that you send into us as many subscriptions as you are able to secure during the first and second ten-day periods, in time for us to receive them on the 26th."

The Ford Motor Company thus seeks to coerce its agents, by means of carefully phrased threats, into becoming distributors of propaganda calculated to poison the public mind against the Jews, indifferent to the consequences, and designed not only to arouse the spirit of intolerance, but to inflict lasting injury upon the entire country, by sowing the evil seeds of racial and religious animosity.

I am confident that it is within your power to abate this iniquity.

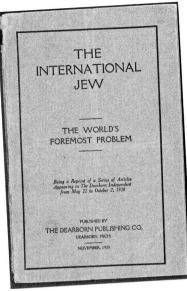

The International Jew, *front cover, 1920.*

Gift of Abe Binderman. Collection of the Museum of Jewish Heritage-A Living Memorial To The Holocaust, New York. Photograph by Peter Goldberg.

Telegram to Ford, Louis Marshall Papers, Collection #359, Box 4, Folder 5; Louis Marshall to Calvin Coolidge, Louis Marshall Papers, Collection #359, Box 1597, Folder "March 1925," American Jewish Archives, Cincinnati, Ohio. Printed with permission of The Jacob Rader Marcus Center of the American Jewish Archives.

FOUNDER OF RECONSTRUCTIONIST JUDAISM

· MORDECAI M. KAPLAN ·

MORDECAI KAPLAN, founder of the only movement within American Judaism created entirely in the United States, was one of the most influential Jewish thinkers in America. Born in Lithuania in 1881, Kaplan immigrated to the United States as a young child and received both traditional Jewish training and a secular education. Ordained at the Conservative movement's Jewish Theological Seminary, he became dean of the JTS Teacher's Institute in 1909, where he spent the rest of his career. In 1922, he founded the Society for the Advancement of Judaism (SAJ), designed as a new kind of congregation that would embrace all kinds of Jews and address the totality of Jewish experience.

Mordecai Kaplan spent much of his life diagnosing the problems of American Judaism and searching for the means to make Jewish life both meaningful and integral within the lives of American Jews. He did not set out to found a separate movement;

indeed, it was his students who initiated the establishment of Reconstructionism as a new branch of Judaism. Kaplan wanted to "reconstruct" all of American Jewish life. He posited that American Jews lived simultaneously in two civilizations, one Jewish and one American. For Kaplan, Judaism could thrive in America only if it became an evolving civilization that encompassed all aspects of Jewish experience, including culture, the arts, social life, and customs, as well as religion. He believed passionately in Zionism as a force that could strengthen the sense of Jewish peoplehood and urged Jews to create organic communities capable of revitalizing Jewish life in America.

Kaplan's ideas elicited significant controversy during his life, because he rejected the notion of Jews as the Chosen People and did not consider belief in a supernatural God a critical element in Judaism. (He argued that God was a "process that makes for salvation.") Members of the faculty at the Conservative seminary where he taught often criticized Kaplan for his willingness to alter traditional prayers and customs that he considered no longer relevant or meaningful. Nonetheless, Kaplan profoundly influenced a generation of Conservative rabbis who found his approach to Judaism ideally suited to the American environment.

Kaplan kept a detailed private journal from 1913 through the late 1970s. The two selections below reveal the germination of his philosophy of Reconstructionist Judaism.

I

Sunday, October 4, 1914

Two weeks ago to-day was the eve of Rosh Hashono. For the first time in eleven years I passed the high holidays without preaching anywhere. This had a very depressing effect upon me. It brought home to me that sense that there was no room for me in the only aspect of Jewish life that I look upon as having a future, namely the religious. I owe it probably to circumstances that I am an observant Jew, though in my beliefs I am a thoroughgoing radical. Otherwise I should have landed in the Reform movement. What is peculiar about my mode of life is that I do not hide my radical views from anyone; I state them freely to superiors, colleagues and students. My radicalism is, however, not of the usual kind, since it only relates to the outward forms of religion not to the fact of religion itself. I often feel particularly embittered because I am not able to give full vent to the enthusiasm for vital religion on account of the shackles which the outward forms and institutions impose upon me. This is the reason I refused the pulpit of the 85th Street Congregation [Kehilath Jeshurun] when it was offered to me last year by a committee of fifteen sent by the congregation to interview me. I have felt all along that Orthodoxy is the bane of Judaism. The only hope for Judaism is in the introduction of radical and sweeping changes to be made from the point of view of Catholic Israel. Still I had not the courage to tell them that I was not Orthodox. . . .

Mordecai M. Kaplan (1881–1983).
The Jacob Rader Marcus Center of the American Jewish Archives

II

Friday, June 15, 1928

Being a Jew presents difficulties never experienced before, first because the social and cultural interests of the Jew are pre-empted and crowded out by the life of civic community of which he is a part; secondly, because even if he can spare the time, energy and resources for the cultivation of his spiritual heritage, he finds that heritage challenged by the general trend of modern ideology. Unfortunately these two causes are seldom thought of as two distinct factors to be reckoned with in our attempt to counteract the difficulty of being and living as a Jew. The tendency to escape Judaism or to find loyalty to it a burden is ascribed to some general deteri-oration in the stamina of the Jew, or to the spirit of the age. It is, therefore, hoped that by appealing to the courage [and] self-respect of the Jew we shall be able to evoke from him the self-sacrifice necessary to live as a Jew. This method of solving the problem of Judaism I believe to be ineffective and futile. The solution depends upon our realizing that the problem is essentially that of restoring the equilibrium between the collective life of the Jew and his environment. The solution will there-fore depend upon the deliberate effort to modify the environment or reckon with it, even more than upon any repentant mood on the part of the Jew. Such an approach is itself novel and calls for a conception of Judaism which would warrant it. In viewing Judaism as a civilization we have such a warrant, for a civilization is necessarily determined by environmental influences. When it is on the wane we must look for the cause to some maladjustment between all those elements that consti-tute the civilization and the conditions that obtain in the environment.

Diaries of Mordecai M. Kaplan, Special Collections, Jewish Theological Seminary of America, Sun-day, October 4, 1914, Volume I, p. 93; Friday, June 15, 1928, Volume IV, p. 20. Printed with permis-sion of The Library of the Jewish Theological Seminary of America.

᷑ 6 ᷒

CRAFTING AN AMERICAN ORTHODOXY

• BERNARD REVEL •

WHEN BERNARD Revel arrived in the United States in 1906, American Orthodoxy was in disarray. Despite the presence of small Orthodox synagogues and *yeshivot* as well as Orthodox rabbinic associations, no organized movement had taken shape on American soil. Born in Kovno, Lithuania, Revel arrived in the United States at the age of twenty-one, already ordained as a rabbi. In the United States, he continued to pursue Jewish scholarship while at the same time studying at secular universities.

In 1915, Revel assumed the presidency of the newly merged Etz Chaim Yeshiva and Rabbi Isaac Elchanan Theological Seminary in New York. In that role, he began to conceive his plan to build a college that would provide students an education in both traditional Jewish sources and secular subjects. For Revel, creating an institution that offered both classical Jewish training and instruction in the liberal arts and sciences was the only way to ensure that Orthodoxy would survive in the American environment. In 1927, the cornerstone was laid for the newly established Yeshiva College and the following year, the institution dedicated its new building on a magnificent campus in the city's Washington Heights neighborhood. In later years, as it expanded to include several schools, Yeshiva University succeeded in training Jewish laypeople, rabbis, and professionals, and bringing Orthodoxy into the American mainstream. In this address, delivered when Yeshiva College was just taking shape, Bernard Revel outlines his vision for the new institution.

NOT MERELY DOES the future of American Jewry depend upon this strengthening in our youth of the bonds of love and understanding of the ideals and eternal truths of Israel, but to a great degree world Jewry is coming to look for its spiritual strength to America. Providence has destined us to play a dominant role in the history of world Jewry and Jewish culture. Many European centres of Jewish learning have suffered greatly from the ravages of the war and the disorganized economic life and spiritual upheaval that have followed it. Russian Jewry, for many centuries the stronghold of Jewish life, learning and idealism, has fallen into temporary confusion and disorganization. The mantle of responsibility is descending upon American Jewry, today the largest single group, as well as the most blessed materially, in the Jewish world. The stream of Jewish learning and idealism from abroad, which has been enriching American Jewish life, is drying up. It is our imperative task to create in this land a Jewish life, inspired and guided by the conceptions and teachings, ideas and ideals, that have ensured the continuity of Israel through all ages and climes, that have been the greatest spiritual force in the history of mankind, and the spirit that guided the minds and inspired the hearts of the Fathers of this Republic. Throughout the ages the historic homes of the Jewish soul, the Yeshivoth, have been the centers of intensive Jewish learning, the reservoirs of intellectual energy and spiritual strength, the conscience

Bernard Revel (1885–1940).
Courtesy of Yeshiva University Archives

of Universal Israel, the instruments for the continued transmission of the divine light of Sinai, to the entire household of Israel. They constitute a glorious chapter in the long history of Israel and, next to the Synagogue, form the most vital institution in the preservation of Judaism. In them the knowledge of and love for the Torah has been cultivated and fostered in the hearts of the Jewish youth. Recognizing that in order to maintain Jewish life and culture in this country as a real and living force, the historic home of the Torah must be transplanted to this land, a small and loyal group of pioneers founded the Yeshiva in America, sanctifying through it the name of the Jewish sage and saint of the last century, Rabbi Isaac Elchanan.[1]

In the whirlpool of modern American life, where antagonistic social and economic forces, where swirling temptations or the mere pressure of the torrent, bear so many of our youth down the gulf of religious and moral disintegration, the Yeshiva stands out as a rock of strength, founded upon the "Torah and the love of God." Situated in the midst of the most crowded section of the world's most tumultuous city, with building equipment most inadequate, in its daily struggle for existence the Yeshiva established itself as the worthy successor of the great Jewish sanctuaries of learning of all the ages, the Yeshivoth. In their spirit, and in loving devotion to the ideals of the Torah which it holds as its standard and guide, the Yeshiva must take a place in American Jewish life commensurate with the responsibilities of American Jewry and the opportunities for the full development of a Jewish life. . . .

THE YESHIVA HAS sent forth many loyal, spiritually endowed, and mentally equipped rabbis throughout the United States and Canada, who live the life of the Torah, and are constructive forces in their communities for good and for God. From the Teachers Institute, the teachers' training department of the Yeshiva, have gone forth many earnest and equipped teachers, to carry the message and the spirit of the Torah to American Jewry. But the Yeshiva does not exist merely for the training of rabbis and of teachers. Important as this task is, and carefully as the responsibilities it involves are accepted in its Teachers Institute and in its Rabbinical Department, the Yeshiva looks beyond these fields of service to the general development of Jewish life and culture, to the evolving of a system of Jewish education that will bring harmony into the life of the American Jewish youth and will develop not only his usefulness as a member of his community, but his Jewish consciousness and his will to live as a Jew and advance the cause of Jewry and Judaism; an education

[1] Rabbi Isaac Elchanan Spektor (1817–1886), Lithuanian-born rabbi and chief rabbinic authority in the city of Kovno. The Rabbi Isaac Elchanan Theological Seminary (RIETS) in New York was named in his memory.

through which the human conscience and the Jewish conscience develop harmoniously into the synthesis of a complete Jewish personality, that indicates the guiding laws of life in accordance with the immortal truths of Judaism in harmonious blending with the best thought of the age and the great humanitarian ideals upon which our blessed country is founded.

Bernard Revel, "The Yeshiva College," pp. 3–4, 5–6, Bernard Revel Papers, Folder 12/2–40, Yeshiva University Archives, New York. Printed with permission of Yeshiva University Archives.

❧ 7 ❧

CREATOR OF *THE GOLDBERGS*

• GERTRUDE BERG •

GERTRUDE BERG portrayed her character Molly Goldberg on radio and television from 1929 until 1956. At the height of its popularity, her series *The Goldbergs* brought the daily lives of a Bronx Jewish family to a wide American audience. Until the early 1950s, the show openly featured the family's Jewish ethnicity as well as the occasional celebration of Jewish holidays. *The Goldbergs* depicted an immigrant family with middle-class sensibilities and delivered a brand of humor that listeners and viewers across the country found familiar, regardless of the ethnicity of the television family. Americans tuned in to hear the matriarch Molly Goldberg dispense her particular brand of Jewish homespun wisdom.

Unlike her character, Gertrude Berg spoke with no Yiddish accent and was a pioneering figure in broadcasting. She modeled many of the characters on her own family members, but adapted patterns of Jewish humor for American audiences.

Berg was writer, producer, and star of *The Goldbergs*, the guiding force in its creative portrayals and commercial decisions. When the series was canceled, Berg went on to star on Broadway. After her death her character was revived in the musical *Molly*. In her 1961 memoir *Molly and Me*, Berg reflected on the creation of the characters that comprised *The Goldbergs*.

WHEN *THE GOLDBERGS* went on the air we went on sustaining. I didn't know the difference between sustaining and commercial and even if I had, I wouldn't have cared. All I knew was that I was on the air, that somebody out there must be listening, and that there wasn't a happier person in the world than me. The problem of what to write about solved itself easily when I decided that what I had was two families—a real one and a radio one. I translated my life with my grandmother, my mother and father, my friends, the people I had heard about, into the Goldbergs and began to relive it on the air.

Molly, when I first began to work with her, was an amalgam of my mother and my grandmother, Czerny. Into that combination I put in a few characteristics of some of the guests at the hotel that I felt Molly should have. Some of the people who stayed at Fleischmanns[1] experimented with the English language and from them Molly developed a manner of speaking that put the horse in the cart and threw an eye into the soup. From my grandfather Mordecai, Molly picked up her formal English. This manner of speech I used only when Molly was in a situation where she thought a little educated talk was needed. In some scripts she spoke to her son Sammy's violin teacher, an educated man, in a self-conscious manner to make up for her own simple beginnings. "Professor," she might say, "Maestro, kind sir, how is the progressing, of my offspring with the three B's, Bach, Beethoven, and Berlin?" or, just asking a policeman directions, Molly finds herself torn between what she knows the police to be in America and what she knew them to be in Europe. With respect tinged with an almost forgotten fear, she says to them,

Gertrude Berg on the cover of Billboard *magazine, 1934.*

Courtesy of Syracuse University Library, Special Collections Research Center, Syracuse, New York

---

1 Gertrude Berg's father ran a small Catskills hotel in Fleischmanns, New York.

Cover of The Rise of the Goldbergs, *which contained stories from the first season of* The Goldbergs *on radio.*
Courtesy of Donald Weber.

"Mr. Policeman, Officer of the law, Your Honor, could you be so kindly if you would to inform me of the location of where is Fourteenth Street?" And when the cop, a word she would never use, tells her she is on Fourteenth Street, Molly's reaction is the relief of many immigrants at not only having found their way but also of not being arrested for asking a simple question. "You are most kind, dear Mr. Officer," she would say, and "very pleased to have made your acquaintance."

Molly's respect for learning came from all the immigrant families I knew in New York City. America, for them, was a land of opportunity and the greatest opportunity they found was the chance to give their children an education. America was full of good and wonderful things and the schools were the best. Everyone I knew wanted his boys and girls to go to college and the parents worked hard to accomplish it. In return, the greatest pleasure they could have was to see their child handed a diploma. Of course there were other pleasures like hearing their boy saying educated words or playing the piano or watching him read a book.

Molly became a person who lived in the world of today but kept many of the values of yesterday. She could change with the times, as did my grandmother and my mother, but she had some basic ideas that she learned long ago and wanted to pass on to her children. Next to the Constitution of the United States, the Ten Commandments came first. Not only were all men created equal, they also had to honor their mother and their father. Abraham, Isaac, and Jacob interchanged easily with Washington, Lincoln, and Jefferson, and the Philistines had nothing on a person who didn't vote.

Molly's husband, Jake, too, was a combination of people and their ideas. He was more like my grandfather Harris, I think, than anyone else. But he had touches of my father Jake's stubbornness and ability to go from one mood to another without reason or explanation. He also had a bit of Lew in him. He was a stickler for being correct in his dealings with everyone and he was too kind to be a good businessman. Not only could Molly and the children take advantage of him, but so could anyone else—if he liked them. If he didn't, it would take a little longer before they could get the better of him.

The children, Sammy and Rosie, were myself, my cousins, my own children, and some parts of all the friends I had grown up with. They also expressed a point of view: that of the first-generation Americans who were trying to make sense out of growing up in one world, America, but coming from another, the European world of their parents. They were being pulled by the new and held back by the old. It was a difficult position even for two nice children. For instance, they felt they had to correct their parents' pronunciation. But European immigrants of that generation did not take kindly to correction from below. Also, authority didn't mean to them what it meant to their elders. They weren't afraid of it. (This was an American tradition that they learned very easily.) Sammy and Rosie were important to *The Goldbergs* because they helped to teach their immigrant parents how to become Americans. At the same time, the parents tried to teach them some of the rich traditions of the Old World, thus combining the best elements of two dissimilar worlds. Or such was my intention anyway.

The first script in what I called *The Rise of the Goldbergs* was taken from a real-life situation. It was the one about Jake working in the dress business and wanting to go into business for himself. He needed some money to rent a loft and some machines. There was some money in his own home that he didn't know about—hidden away in a teapot in the dish closet. Molly had been saving it for a rainy day and when Jake told her what he wanted, she considered that the rainy day had arrived. Down came the teapot and the hundred dollars, which just made the difference. The saved money idea came from my grandmother, who was always putting away a penny here and a penny there for when something would be needed. Jake's desire to be his own boss was that of my grandfather and my father; the details of the situation and the solution came from me.

That was script number one.

Gertrude Berg, *Molly and Me* (New York: McGraw-Hill, 1961), pp. 189–192.

STAR OF YIDDISH THEATER AND FILM

• MOLLY PICON •

FOR MORE than seventy years, Molly Picon delighted audiences with her performances, first in Yiddish theater and film and later on Broadway and in Hollywood movies. Born on New York's Lower East Side in 1898, she spent her early years in Philadelphia. She won her first local theater contest at the age of five. As a young child, she began performing with a Yiddish theater company and after she left high school, Picon joined a traveling vaudeville troupe.

Her long career in the Yiddish theater commenced in earnest after her marriage to Jacob "Yonkel" Kalich. Kalich wrote and directed a string of Yiddish productions with Picon as the star. In the 1920s, Picon gained notoriety with plays such as *Yonkele* (Little Yonkel), *Gypsy Girl*, *Mamale* (Mommy), and *The Circus Girl*. In many of her performances, Picon played young girls dressing or behaving like boys; her waiflike characters and crossing of gender boundaries became her signature style. In the 1920s and 1930s, she starred in several classic Yiddish films, including *Yidl Mitn Fidl* (Yiddle with his Fiddle), filmed in Poland, that told the story of a young girl who dresses as a boy so that she and her father can support themselves as traveling musicians. Picon also reached American audiences, hosting a national radio program sponsored by Maxwell House coffee.

In the 1940s, Picon made her Broadway debut. Decades later she was still performing physical comedy in the 1960s production of *Milk and Honey*. She received an Oscar nomination for her role as an Italian mother in the film version of Neil Simon's *Come Blow Your Horn*. Continuing to work in films in the 1970s, Picon played memorable roles in *Fiddler on the Roof* and *For Pete's Sake* with Barbara Streisand. In 1979, at the age of 81, Molly Picon was still performing, starring in her one-woman show, *Hello Molly*. In this selection from her autobiography, Picon describes her experience in Poland in the 1930s while shooting the film *Yidl Mitn Fidl*.

YONKEL HAD LEFT earlier for Warsaw to work on a script for our first Yiddish musical film, *Yiddel Mit'n Fiddle*. Abe Ellstein, our composer, was with me and he had started writing music to the lyrics of Manger, a gifted Yiddish poet. He and I then left for Poland by train. Riding through Germany was painful, and I hated to look out the windows. I could feel the waves of hatred as we went through the towns, and we arrived in Warsaw heavy-hearted.

Fortunately, once again being with actors, musicians, stagehands, and the Polish director, Pshebilski, shook off the depression we were in, and we began to work on the film. Our producer, Joseph Green, and his wife, Annette, gave parties for us, and we

Molly Picon (1898–1992). Hand-colored photograph from Zipke, *1924.*

American Jewish Historical Society, Newton Centre, Massachusetts and New York, New York

worked twelve hours a day on the script and the songs until we were ready to shoot outdoors in Kazimierz, a shabby, broken-down village, where King Kazimierz (Casimir III) had once reigned with his Jewish queen.

I had never seen such poverty—outdoor plumbing, rickety wooden houses bent into fantastic shapes, and the people unbelievably threadbare. The skeletal children, with their long *payess* (sideburns) and little *yarmulkes* (skullcaps), wore trousers that were in shreds and shoes tied on their feet with rope. My heart went out to every one of them. We gave them coins (they wouldn't accept food—it wasn't kosher), and with the coins they bought grapes and came back to share them with me.

The story of *Yiddel* concerned a girl who had to wear boys' clothes so she could perform on the fiddle with her father, who played a bass. Together they played in all the backyards of Poland.

The whole town was on our heels while we filmed their story. We ordered them around, and they followed us like lambs. When the stagehands and camera men yelled "*Psha krev*" (a Polish cuss word), every time the sun went down, the whole town yelled with them. The filming went on from 6:00 A.M. to 6:00 P.M. every day, and with a *slontze nyeman* (no sun) and a *psha krev*, we made *Yiddel*.

The wedding scene in *Yiddel* took over thirty consecutive hours to film. The food had to be truly kosher, because we hired the Orthodox Jewish men, women and children of Kazimierz to be the guests. As we filmed, they ate, and for the successive shots of the table, the food had to be replenished, over and over again. Our poverty-striken guests couldn't figure out what was happening. They thought they had been invited to a real wedding, and when one woman asked why so much food, we explained to her it wasn't a real wedding, we were just making a film. I don't think she had ever seen a film, but she said, "Why didn't you tell me that before? With so much food, I could have brought my daughter to get married for real. She has a *chassen* (bridegroom), but we have no money for a dowry to make a proper wedding." I have a slight suspicion that Yonkel gave her the

Harry Kalmanowitch, Ay Que Muchacha! (What a Girl!-Oy iz dos a meydl!), *Teatro Excelsior, Buenos Aires, Argentina, 1932.*

American Jewish Historical Society, Newton Centre, Massachusetts and New York, New York

money, because later in the day she smiled at me and said, "Are you lucky to have such a rich husband."

Years later, when Norman Jewison asked me to play the part of Yente in *Fiddler on the Roof*, he told me that when he visited Israel he had gone to see *Yiddel* in a museum there to absorb the atmosphere and character of the *shtetl* in which *Fiddler* was to be filmed. He also said *Yiddel* was fifty years ahead of its time.

9

STUDIO MOGUL

• JACK WARNER •

BORN IN 1892 to immigrant Jewish parents from Poland, Jack Warner was the youngest of the four brothers who made the Warner Brothers Studio a leader in film production in the twentieth century. Beginning their business by distributing and exhibiting films, the brothers expanded to film production in the 1910s and finally opened the Warner Brothers Studio in the 1920s. Their first great success came with the production of *The Jazz Singer* in 1927, a film that brought sound to the big screen and signaled the end of the silent film era. The Warner brothers relied on their immigrant father's advice to ensure that the film authentically portrayed immigrant Jewish family life and the culture of the Lower East Side; they even shot many of the film's scenes in the neighborhood.

In its heyday, the Warner Brothers Studio produced scores of successful Hollywood films and secured the contracts of many of the leading stars of the era, including Errol Flynn,

Humphrey Bogart, Bette Davis, and John Garfield, just to name a few. In his autobiography, Jack Warner describes the studio's first success in producing the *Jazz Singer*.

HOLLYWOOD WAS FULL of good-looking young Jewish singers who could get in by the part, but none of them could put the tears in their voice. As Cantor Rabinowitz pleads in the play [*The Jazz Singer*]: "You must sing it with a sigh, like you are crying out to your God." Wait a minute. What about Al Jolson? His father had been a cantor in Russia, and in Washington, too. And Jolson had the sob in his voice. I hustled around and tracked Jolie down in Denver, where he was playing in *Big Boy* for one of the Shubert companies.

Jack Warner, ca. 1945, Hulton Archive.
Getty Images

I phoned Morrie Saifer, one of our New York executives, who by coincidence was in Denver, too. I told him to grab a taxi, go to the theater, and ask Jolson cold turkey how much he wanted to do *The Jazz Singer*. Saifer called back in an hour and, as we say these days, he was shook up. "Jolson wants a flat seventy-five thousand," he said. "One third down—in cash. The rest at $6,250 a week, until it's paid."

"Get back there and tell him he's got a deal," I said.

Jolson signed the contract, and we dug up the scratch for him. For a good many years—and Jolie himself was the culprit—the story persisted that we paid him with Warner Brothers stock. Even Hedda Hopper sanctified the myth in her first book, and the so-called insiders always believed that Jolson's considerable wealth piled up when our stock soared from $9 to $135 a share. But it was never true, and I can't imagine why Jolie spread that talk unless there was a tax angle involved.

It is ironic, I think, that *The Jazz Singer* qualified as a talking picture only because of a freak accident. Sam was supervising the song recording when Jolson, in a burst of exuberance, cried out; "You ain't heard nothin' yet, folks. Listen to this."

Jolson had often used these words on the Broadway stage as a sort of trademark, and when Sam listened to the phrase on the playback he realized that the singer's speaking voice could have a shattering wallop.

He had Al Cohn write a soliloquy in which Jolson stops singing after the first chorus of "Blue Skies" and talks to his mother, saying: "Did you like that, Mama? I'm

Al Jolson in The Jazz Singer*, 1928.*

glad. I'd rather please you than anybody I know of." The monologue went on for some 250 words, and then Jolson sang another verse of "Blue Skies."

It is intriguing to note that for all these years the Hollywood biographers have mentioned Jolson's ad lib "You ain't heard nothin' yet" as being the bomb that would blast the entertainment world. No one ever denied this romantic legend, but it never happened. The so-called historic phrase was not in the picture. . . .

With Al Jolson actually talking to the audience from the screen—and people were not prepared for that emotional surprise—the critical response was overwhelming. The picture set off a chain reaction, with these early results; Movie theater attendance soared to 95,000,000 a week, almost double the previous total. There had been only a hundred theaters wired for sound, but by the end of 1928 there were more than one thousand. One year after that, four thousand theaters were showing talking pictures, and Western Electric's income from these installations totaled more than $37,000,000.

Jack Warner with Dean Jennings, *My First Hundred Years in Hollywood* (Random House: New York, 1964), pp. 176–177, 180.

10

RED-HOT MAMA

· SOPHIE TUCKER ·

BILLED AS "The Last of the Red Hot Mamas" in the 1930s, Sophie Tucker's career lasted fifty years, spanning vaudeville, musical productions, and later film. Born in 1884 while her mother was en route from Russia to the United States, Tucker grew up performing for the customers at her family's restaurant in Hartford, Connecticut. After an early marriage and divorce, Tucker (who changed her last name from Abuza, a name her family chose after arriving in the United States) made her way to New York and supported herself by singing in local establishments. Always heavy and lacking typical star looks, Tucker broke into vaudeville and like many of her era, spent some time performing in blackface. She abandoned blackface when by a stroke of luck her costume trunks were lost and she was forced to go on stage without it, and it was then that she began to shape her unique style.

Poking fun at her own large figure, she sang songs like

Sophie Tucker—"The Last of the Red Hot Mamas,"
1924.

The Jacob Rader Marcus Center of the American Jewish
Archives

"Nobody Loves a Fat Girl But How a Fat Girl Can Love." Tucker incorporated bawdy, off-color routines into her performances with double entendres and physical comedy that appealed to a wide audience. In music halls throughout the United States and Europe, she achieved fame with renditions of "I Ain't Takin' Orders from No One," and "No Man Is Ever Gonna Worry Me" as well as her signature song, "Some of These Days." In the mid-1920s, she gained great acclaim performing "My Yiddishe Mama," a sentimental ballad immensely popular with Jewish audiences.

As her success grew in the interwar years, Tucker supported several charitable causes, including many Jewish concerns. She also started her own foundation and served as president of the American Federation of Actors. She continued to star on Broadway and in film during the 1930s and '40s and performed until close to her death in 1966. In this passage from her memoirs, Tucker describes how rising anti-Semitism in Europe led to an audience eruption during her performance of "My Yiddishe Mama" in interwar France.

ON FRIDAY NIGHT the house had quite a lot of French Jews. Several notes had been sent back to me, and the managers also told me there were a great many requests for me to sing "My Yiddisha Mama." I was leary of this. I told the managers they would have to leave it to my own judgment as the act went along.

I went out to do my regular program. . . . And after every song someone in the audience would call for "Yiddisha Mama." Immediately the roughnecks would shout "no!"

I was in a hell of a fix and perfectly helpless as the audience fought back and forth—something I had never seen or heard of in any theater.

I finished my routine, singing the chorus of "Some of These Days" in French. I had made up my mind not to sing "My Yiddisha Mama." Then came more shouts and calls for it. . . .

I thought—and it was one of the stupidest blunders I ever made—so many have asked for it, I ought to sing it. I'll explain why I'm singing it. The song itself will touch everybody in the house.

I explained, and then sang the song in English. Everything was all right until I started the first sentence in Yiddish. Then up went "boo!" from all over the house! The boos were answered by a yell from the Jews and cries to be quiet. The others yelled back to the Jews. They didn't want the song.

The noise was so great I couldn't hear my own voice, nor could I hear Teddy at the piano. I thought: in a minute there'll be a riot. Quick as a flash I turned to Teddy and said, "Switch!" Before the audience knew what the hell was happening I was singing, "Happy Days Are Here Again."

My God, I only hoped they were!

Sophie Tucker, 1924.
The Jacob Rader Marcus Center of the American Jewish Archives

Sophie Tucker, *Some of These Days: The Autobiography of Sophie Tucker* (Garden City, New York: Doubleday, Doran and Company, 1945), pp. 257–258.

❧ 11 ❧

JEWISH BASEBALL ICON

• HANK GREENBERG •

HANK GREENBERG was a champion on the baseball field during his career with the Detroit Tigers during the 1930s and 1940s, and an important symbolic figure in American Jewish culture. By far the most well-known and successful Jewish athlete in the United States at the time, a two-time American League Most Valuable Player, Greenberg became a hero to American Jews for more than simply his athletic prowess. In 1934, he chose not to play in a game on Yom Kippur, the Day of Atonement. Although Greenberg had participated in a crucial game on Rosh Hashanah when the pennant race was still in doubt, American Jews considered his choice to observe Yom Kippur rather than play baseball a significant public demonstration of Jewish pride during an especially difficult period for Jews in the United States. Greenberg endured anti-Semitic slurs during his career and recognized the symbolic power of his success for the Jewish community.

Throughout his life, Hank Greenberg exhibited pride in his Jewish heritage, but retained little connection to Judaism or the Jewish community, though he did contribute generously to Jewish causes. He was one of the first prominent baseball players drafted in World War II and returned home from the war to lead the Detroit Tigers to victory in the World Series in 1945. In his memoirs, Greenberg recalled the attention that surrounded his decision not to play on Yom Kippur.

A TRULY EXCITING moment in my Major League career took place on September 10, 1934—Rosh Hashanah, the Jewish New Year. The team was fighting for first place, and I was probably the only batter in the lineup who was not in a slump. But in the Jewish religion, it is traditional that one observe the holiday solemnly, with prayer. One should not engage in work or play. And I wasn't sure what to do. It became a national issue. There was a big question in the press about whether I would play first base for the Tigers that day.

On the front page of that morning's *Detroit Free Press* was a headline in Yiddish, and then over it the English translation, "Happy New Year, Hank." To this day, I am very proud of that. . . .

THE NEWSPAPERS HAD gone to the top rabbi in Detroit and asked him if it would be socially acceptable for me to play on that day. The rabbi was supposed to have looked in the Talmud and he came up with the theory that since it was the start of a new year, and it was supposed to be a happy day, he found that Jews in history had played games on that day, and he felt that it would be perfectly all right for me to play baseball. That momentous decision made it possible for me to stay in the lineup on Rosh Hashanah, and lo and behold I hit two home runs—the second in the ninth inning—and we beat Boston 2–1. . . .

I WAS A hero around town, particularly among the Jewish people, and I was very proud of it.

Hank Greenberg of the Detroit Tigers, ca. 1930s.
National Baseball Hall of Fame Library, Cooperstown, N.Y.

On Yom Kippur, my friends, a family named Allen, took me to shul [synagogue]. We walked in about 10:30 in the morning and the place was jammed. The rabbi was davening [praying]. Right in the middle of everything, everything seemed to stop. The rabbi looked up; he didn't know what was going on. And suddenly everybody was applauding. I was embarrassed; I didn't know what to do. It was a tremendous ovation for a kid who was only twenty-three years old, and in a synagogue, no less!

People remember that I didn't play on Yom Kippur. They remember it as every year, but in fact the situation arose only once, in 1934.

It's a strange thing. When I was playing I used to resent being singled out as a Jewish ballplayer, period. I'm not sure why or when I changed, because I'm still not a particularly religious person. Lately, though, I find myself wanting to be remembered not only as a great ballplayer, but even more as a great *Jewish* ballplayer.

I realize now, more than I used to, how important a part I played in the lives of a generation of Jewish kids who grew up in the thirties.

I guess I was a kind of role model, and strangely enough, I think this may have begun in sports with Babe Ruth, though, of course, much of the interest in me had the special nature of my religion. When Babe emerged as the great homerun hitter, the baseball fans took him to heart and made a hero out of him. While Babe wasn't exemplary off the field, they overlooked it and only talked about his prowess on the field. He was a hero and despite his sexual appetite and drinking too much and eating too much, he also used to go to a lot of hospitals and visit kids who were sick, and the photographers would go with him. He did a lot of good in that respect. From then on, ballplayers were elevated from being just more or less outcasts in society; they were becoming accepted. Even the best hotels were accepting them. The players started to dress a little better and act a little differently and they curbed their manner of speech somewhat.

In a nutshell, the Major League ballplayer became a respectable citizen. And so the ballplayer learned that he had to set an example for young America, for the kids, and do all sorts of things like autographing and making appearances at different places, trying to be a role model. That was expected of ballplayers, since they were getting all this publicity and adulation from the fans.

It was also a somewhat optimistic time economically, and this also helped focus people's attention on baseball. Detroit was just starting to come out of the Depression in

1934. The newspapers used to comment frequently on the emergence of the Detroit Tigers as a pennant-winning team, since it was the first time they had won a pennant in twenty-five years. They claimed that the spirit of Detroit, the enthusiasm of the fans, plus the brightening economic picture all came together to create a very exciting, charged atmosphere in Detroit.

Hank Greenberg with Ira Berkow, *Hank Greenberg: The Story of My Life*, (Chicago: Triumph Books, 1989), pp. 55, 56, 58–59. Reprinted with permission of the publisher.

SPEAKING OF GREENBERG
by Edgar A. Guest

The Irish didn't like it when they heard of Greenberg's fame
For they thought a good first baseman should possess an Irish name;
And the Murphys and Mulrooneys said they never dreamed they'd see
A Jewish boy from Bronxville out where Casey used to be.
In the early days of April not a Dugan tipped his hat
Or prayed to see a "double" when Hank Greenberg came to bat.
In July the Irish wondered where he'd ever learned to play.
"He makes me think of Casey!" Old Man Murphy dared to say;
And with fifty-seven doubles and a score of homers made
The respect they had for Greenberg was being openly displayed.
But on the Jewish New Year when Hank Greenberg came to bat
And made two home runs off Pitcher Rhodes—they cheered like mad
    for that.

Came Yom Kippur—holy fast day world wide over to the Jew—
And Hank Greenberg to his teaching and the old tradition true
Spent the day among his people and he didn't come to play.
Said Murphy to Mulrooney, "We shall lose the game today!
We shall miss him on the infield and shall miss him at the bat,
But he's true to his religion—and I honor him for that!"

BUSINESSMAN AND PHILANTHROPIST

• JULIUS ROSENWALD •

KNOWN AS much for his extraordinary philanthropic ventures as for his business prowess, Julius Rosenwald made Sears, Roebuck & Co. a thriving national company while also supporting a number of Jewish and secular causes, including funding a sweeping project for black education in the South. Born in Springfield, Illinois, in 1862, the son of immigrant Jewish parents, Rosenwald began manufacturing men's clothing in partnership with one of his cousins. Among his customers was Richard Sears, who owned a growing mail order company. When Sears decided to sell a portion of his business in 1895, Julius Rosenwald became part owner, bringing efficient management to sales practices and rapidly multiplying the company's worth. When Sears resigned in 1908, Rosenwald became president of Sears, Roebuck & Co. Rosenwald held the post until 1924, when he transitioned to chairman of the company in order to devote his energies to philanthropic work.

Sears, Roebuck & Co., catalogue cover, 1897-1898.

Julius Rosenwald and his wife Augusta supported a variety of causes and foundations. They gave generously to Jewish institutions and charities, both in Chicago and throughout the world. In the 1920s, Rosenwald funded a project for Jewish colonization in Russia, designed to solve the crisis facing East European Jews by settling them in agricultural colonies. He also contributed funds to aid Jews in Palestine, though he was not a Zionist. Rosenwald never limited his philanthropy to Jewish causes alone. He created 5,000 schools to provide education to African Americans in the rural South, also building thousands of libraries connected to those schools. Rosenwald generously supported the public schools, several colleges and universities, and YMCAs. He also founded Chicago's Museum of Science and Industry.

In this selection from 1925, Julius Rosenwald announces his support for a plan to create Jewish agricultural colonies in Russia. Preferring this program to the notion of resettling Jews in Palestine, Rosenwald reveals his penchant for philanthropic projects designed to create self-sufficiency. While Jewish colonization in Russia ultimately did not prove successful, the plan testifies to the many different solutions offered to ameliorate the plight of East European Jews.

THIS IS A subject that has interested me for many years. I have contended—whether rightly or wrongly—that the only way to help our co-religionists in these benighted lands [Eastern Europe], is to help them where they are.

My experience and what I have been able to find out from the experience of others shows that subsidized immigration, where you have to transport masses of people, is absolutely impractical. . . .

MY UNWILLINGNESS TO join in the Palestine movement was not at all based on my being opposed to Zionism. I am not opposed to Zionism. I have been willing to help any efforts made in Palestine, for years, and have done so, but I have never been a believer in subsidizing immigration to the extent of moving people in masses from one country to another and trying to establish them with funds which, to my mind, is impossible at the present time. I do not believe that it is possible to establish—and then not always successfully—a family in Palestine or in Argentine or anywhere else where land must be bought and the people taken care of until they are self-supporting, for less—and I think on an average it will be more as time goes on—for less than $5,000 a family.

I have thought and thought and thought about this subject, year in and year out, and particularly for the past six or seven months since I have given a greater amount of study to this Russian situation.

I am firmly convinced that the Jews have never had an opportunity to do a real constructive thing, a real constructive piece of work, for their co-religionists, until this time. I have always felt that whatever they did heretofore has been palliative. During the war I was willing to go along and I was willing to give in a large measure for palliative relief.

I am willing no longer to give in any large measure for palliative relief. I believe that the people will always require assistance. This thing is going to continue. There will always be orphans and sick. There will always be poverty, but I believe those

Julius Rosenwald with his wife, Augusta.
Library of Congress, Prints and Photographs Division

things have got to become local duties imposed upon the people who live in a community. We can't hope to provide funds for people all over this world who are poverty stricken. Furthermore I don't believe it is helpful in the long run to make people dependent upon charity. If we can put them in a position to help themselves, I am in heartiest accord with work of that nature. I am very anxious indeed to have this the primary motive in connection with any campaign which might be started in this country. . . .

WHAT I WOULD like to see would be that this agricultural work . . . be made the first feature of our program. . . .

"Julius Rosenwald Pledges $1,000,000 Toward New $15,000,000 Reconstructive Fund," *Jewish Daily Bulletin*, September 15, 1925, p. 3.

❧ 13 ❧

"IS THERE A JEWISH POINT OF VIEW?"

• ALBERT EINSTEIN •

IN THE mid-1930s, at a time when Hitler had already taken power and quotas had sharply curtailed the number of Jewish immigrants able to come to the United States, approximately 150,000 German Jews were permitted to enter the country. Unlike previous groups of immigrants, the German Jews who came to America in the 1930s were generally middle-aged professionals and businesspeople. They settled together in areas such as Manhattan's Washington Heights, a neighborhood that came to be known as the "Fourth Reich."

Among these immigrants were many prominent scientists, writers, and artists who made a notable impact on American life. One of these refugee scholars, Albert Einstein, left an indelible mark on both American and Jewish culture. Born to a highly acculturated Jewish family in Bavaria, Einstein became one of the leading scientists of his generation, winning the Nobel Prize in 1921.

Einstein never embraced the notion of a personal God nor believed in adherence to Jewish law, but he retained a strong sense of Jewish identity and by the 1920s, became an ardent Zionist. He traveled to America in the 1920s to raise funds for Palestine and the Hebrew University, and he delivered the university's inaugural address in 1923.

Einstein fled Germany in 1933, renouncing his German citizenship and settling in the United States, where he accepted a position as Professor of Theoretical Physics at Princeton University. At the 1939 World's Fair in New York, Einstein opened the Jewish Pavilion.

In the selection below, Albert Einstein explains his sense of Jewish identity, defining Judaism not as set of beliefs, ritual behaviors, or commandments, but as an ethical system and moral outlook.

⌐⌐

IN THE PHILOSOPHICAL sense there is, in my opinion, no specifically Jewish point of view. Judaism seems to me to be concerned almost exclusively with the moral attitude in life and to life. I look upon it as the essence of an attitude to life which is incarnate in the Jewish people rather than the essence of the laws laid down in the Torah and interpreted in the Talmud. To me, the Torah and the Talmud are merely the most important evidence of the manner in which the Jewish concept of life held sway in earlier times.

The essence of that conception seems to me to lie in an affirmative attitude to the life of all creation. The life of the individual only has meaning in so far as it aids in making the life of every living thing nobler and more beautiful. Life is sacred, that is to say, it is the supreme value, to which all other values are subordinate. The hallowing of the supra-individual life brings in its train a reverence for everything spiritual—a particularly characteristic feature of the Jewish tradition.

Judaism is not a creed: the Jewish God is simply a negation of superstition, an imaginary result of its elimination. It is also an attempt to base the moral law on fear, a regrettable and discreditable attempt. Yet it seems to me that the strong moral tradition of the Jewish nation has to a large extent shaken itself free from this fear. It is clear also that "serving God" was equated with "serving the living." The best of the Jewish people, especially the Prophets and Jesus, contended tirelessly for this.

Judaism is thus no transcendental religion; it is concerned with life as we live it and as we can, to a certain extent, grasp it, and nothing else. It seems to me, therefore, doubtful whether it can be called a religion in the accepted sense of the word, particularly as no "faith" but the sanctification of life in a supra-personal sense is demanded of the Jew.

But the Jewish tradition also contains something else, something which finds splendid expression in many of the Psalms, namely, a sort of intoxicated joy and amazement at the beauty and grandeur of the world, of which man can form just a faint notion. This joy is the feeling from which true scientific research draws its spiritual sustenance, but which also seems to find expression in the song of birds. To tack this feeling to the idea of God seems mere childish absurdity.

Is what I have described a distinguishing mark of Judaism? Is it to be found anywhere else under another name? In its pure form, it is nowhere to be found, not even in Judaism, where the pure doctrine is obscured by much worship of the letter. Yet

Albert Einstein (1879–1955).
Library of Congress, Prints and Photographs Division

Judaism seems to me one of its purest and most vigorous manifestations. This applies particularly to the fundamental principle of the sanctification of life.

It is characteristic that the animals were expressly included in the command to keep holy the Sabbath day, so strong was the feeling of the ideal solidarity of all living things. The insistence on the solidarity of all human beings finds still stronger expression, and it is no mere chance that the demands of Socialism were for the most part first raised by the Jews.

How strongly developed this sense of the sanctity of life is in the Jewish people is admirably illustrated by a little remark which Walter Rathenau[1] once made to me in conversation: "When a Jew says that he's going hunting to amuse himself, he lies." The Jewish sense of the sanctity of life could not be more simply expressed.

---

[1] Walter Rathenau (1867–1922), a prominent German-Jewish industrialist and politician. Rising to the post of foreign minister of Germany, Rathenau was assassinated by right-wing extremists.

Albert Einstein, "Is There a Jewish Point of View?" *Ideas and Opinions*, [1934] (New York: Crown Publishers, 1954), pp. 185–87. [First Published in *Mein Weltbild* (Amsterdam: Querido Verlag, 1934)]. From *Ideas and Opinions* by Albert Einstein, copyright 1954 and renewed 1982 by Crown Publishers Inc. Used by permission of Crown Publishers, a division of Random House, Inc.

๛ 14 ๛

RABBI AND ACTIVIST

• STEPHEN S. WISE •

BORN IN Budapest in 1872 to a family of rabbis, Stephen Wise came to the United States as a young child. He received private rabbinic ordination in Europe and a secular education at Columbia University. After beginning his rabbinic career as a Reform rabbi in 1900 in Portland, Oregon, Wise returned to New York and founded the Free Synagogue in 1907, a unique institution that reflected his passion for social justice. At the Free Synagogue, there were no fixed dues. Other innovative policies included free seating, freedom of the pulpit, and an opportunity for both women and men to become members and officers.

Stephen Wise became one of America's most influential Jewish leaders. A committed Zionist, he helped to create the American Jewish Congress, an organization that offered a populist, democratic alternative to the non-Zionist American Jewish Committee. Wise served as president of the American

Jewish Congress for more than twenty-five years. In 1922, he established the Jewish Institute of Religion, a new rabbinical seminary that reflected his abiding concern with making Zionism and social justice integral elements within Jewish life. Throughout his life, Wise worked for liberal causes, working on labor issues and actively supporting the NAACP and the ACLU.

When the Nazis came to power, Wise was among the most outspoken communal leaders, calling for a boycott against German goods in 1933. A powerful orator, he delivered some of the most stirring speeches opposing the Nazi regime and calling upon the United States to act forcefully. It was Wise who delivered the devastating news of the Final Solution to the American public. These selections reflect Wise's eloquent rhetorical style and passionate crusade during the trying years of Nazism.

ONE OF THE most tragic moments of my life came in the summer of 1942. We were, of course, in constant touch during the war with both the London and Geneva offices of the World Jewish Congress. On August 1, Dr. Gerhart Riegner, young and able director of our Geneva office, learned that a German industrialist had come to Switzerland in order to communicate the fact that a plan had been discussed in Hitler's headquarters for the extermination of all Jews in Nazi-occupied lands. These Jews, then totaling between three and a half and four millions, were to be deported to concentration camps in Eastern Europe and then exterminated through prussic acid and crematoria in order to liquidate the Jewish problem in Europe with one blow. The report would have seemed fantastic were it not for evidence Riegner had already received that mass deportations from France and Czechoslovakia had already begun. On checking, Riegner discovered that the industrialist, evidently an anti-Nazi, held one of the most vital positions in the German war economy, which gave him access to Hitler's headquarters and all Nazi war plans. Through intermediaries, he conveyed to Riegner the full details of the plan that was to result in the murder of millions of Jews.

Stephen Wise (1874–1949).
Library of Congress, Prints and Photographs Division

Realizing the tremendous significance of his information, Riegner submitted it to the American and British consulates in Geneva, asking that they immediately inform me, as president of the World Jewish Congress, and Sidney Silverman, dynamic Labor member of the British parliament and chairman of the British Section of the congress. I did not receive the contents of Riegner's message until the twenty-eighth of August. I later learned from Riegner that throughout August he had waited desperately for word from London and New York. On August 24, he was finally informed by the American consul in Geneva that the substance of the message to me had been transmitted by the legation in Berne to the State Department and that the latter had indicated telegraphically that it was disinclined to deliver the message in question in view of the apparently unsubstantiated character of the information that formed its main theme. Fortunately, however, Silverman finally received Riegner's message through the British Foreign Office and transmitted its contents to me on August 28. I immediately communicated with Sumner Welles, then undersecretary of state, and then, as always, deeply understanding and sympathetic. Welles asked me not to release the information until an attempt had been made to confirm it.

During September and October, Riegner continued to receive first-hand reports from countries all over Europe that the plan for mass extermination was being rapidly implemented. All these reports he transmitted to the State Department through Leland Harrison, American minister in Berne. In November, four sworn statements reached the State Department through Harrison, fully substantiating Riegner's reports. Mr. Welles telegraphed that I come at once to the State Department. I went, sensing that I might hear the direst tidings and asked my son, James Waterman Wise, then in the service of the World Jewish Congress as its Washington representative for Latin American affairs, to accompany me.

In the office of Mr. Welles, we took our places and I shall never forget the quiet but deeply moving way in which he turned to us and said, every word etching itself into my heart, "Gentlemen, I hold in my hands documents which have come to me from our legation in Berne. I regret to tell you, Dr. Wise, that these confirm and justify your deepest fears." He handed me the original documents from Berne which confirmed our dreadful apprehensions. The documents' red seals suggested the blood of my people pouring forth in rivers. Mr. Welles added, "For reasons you will understand, I cannot give these to the press, but there is no reason why you should not. It might even help if you did."

We hurriedly called a press conference. To those present, I brought the startling and ghastly news that had just been imparted to us, that in addition to the two or three million Jews estimated already to have been slain in the camps and their gas—and even gasless—ovens, the Nazi regime was resolved to annihilate the rest of the Jewish population of Europe. I was free to mention the source of our awful tidings, namely the State Department.

The response was what might have been expected. There was general horror throughout the country, wherever the press dispatches carried, and heartbreak everywhere in American Jewry.

Stephen Wise, *Challenging Years: The Autobiography of Stephen Wise* (New York: G.P. Putnam's Sons, 1949), pp. 247-276. "Death by Bureaucracy," from *Challenging Years* by Stephen Wise, copyright 1949 by G.P. Putnam's Sons, renewed © 1976 by Justine Wise Polier. Used by permission of G.P. Putnam's Sons, a division of Penguin Group (USA) Inc.

ADVOCATE FOR RESCUE

• HENRY MORGENTHAU JR. •

WHILE SERVING as Secretary of the Treasury under President Franklin Roosevelt from 1934 until 1945, Henry Morgenthau Jr. became the driving force for the creation of the War Refugee Board in 1944. After documenting that the State Department had actively blocked efforts to admit those Jewish refugees who could be saved, Morgenthau convinced the President to establish the War Refugee Board, which succeeded in rescuing approximately 200,000 Jews, mostly from Hungary, the last substantial Jewish community remaining in Europe in 1944.

Born in New York in 1891, Morgenthau owned a dairy and apple farm in Dutchess County, New York and worked with the U.S. Farm Administration during World War I. When his friend and Dutchess County neighbor Franklin Roosevelt became Governor of New York, Morgenthau joined his administration as Chairman of the State Agricultural Advisory

Commission and later as State Commissioner of Conservation. After Roosevelt was elected president in 1932, Morgenthau became one of his chief advisors, serving briefly in the Federal Farm Board and Farm Credit Administration before moving to the Treasury Department, where he served until 1945. As Secretary of the Treasury, Morgenthau played a critical role in financing the war effort and drafting the plan for postwar Germany. In the selection below, taken from the opening and closing passages of the report he submitted to the President, Morgenthau reveals his deep distress at the mishandling of the refugee crisis by the State Department and implores the President to take definitive action.

⌒

Personal Report to the President

One of the greatest crimes in history, the slaughter of the Jewish people in Europe, is continuing unabated.

This Government has for a long time maintained that its policy is to work out programs to save those Jews and other persecuted minorities of Europe who could be saved.

You are probably not as familiar as I with the utter failure of certain officials in our State Department, who are charged with actually carrying out this policy, to take any effective action to prevent the extermination of the Jews in German-controlled Europe.

The public record, let alone the facts which have not yet been made public, reveals the gross procrastination of these officials. It is well known that since the time when it became clear that Hitler was determined to carry out a policy of exterminating the Jews in Europe, the State Department officials have failed to take any positive steps reasonably calculated to save any of these people. Although they have used devices such as setting up intergovernmental organizations to survey the whole refugee problem, and calling conferences such as the Bermuda Conference to explore the whole refugee problem, making it appear that positive action could be expected, in fact nothing has been accomplished.

Henry Morgenthau, Jr., with President Franklin D. Roosevelt in a cabinet meeting, ca. 1938.

Library of Congress, Prints and Photographs Division

The best summary of the whole situation is contained in one sentence of a report submitted on December 20, 1943, by the Committee on Foreign Relations of the Senate, recommending the passage of a Resolution (S.R. 203), favoring the appointment of a commission to formulate plans to save the Jews of Europe from extinction by Nazi Germany. The Resolution had been introduced by Senator Guy M. Gillette in behalf of himself and eleven colleagues, Senators Taft, Thomas, Radcliffe, Murray, Johnson, Guffey, Ferguson, Clark, Van Nuys, Downey and Ellender. The Committee stated:

"We have talked; we have sympathized; we have expressed our horror; the time to act is long past due."

Whether one views this failure as being deliberate on the part of those officials handling the matter, or merely due to their incompetence, is not too important from my point of view. However, there is a growing number of responsible people and organizations today who have ceased to view our failure as the product of simple incompetence on the part of those officials in the State Department charged with handling this problem. They see plain Anti-Semitism motivating the actions of these State Department officials and, rightly or wrongly, it will require little more in the way of proof for this suspicion to explode into a nasty scandal. . . .

The facts I have detailed, in this report, Mr. President, came to the Treasury's attention as a part of our routine investigation of the licensing of the financial phases of the proposal of the World Jewish Congress for the evacuation of Jews from France and Rumania. The facts may thus be said to have come to light through accident. How many others of the same character are buried in State Department files is a matter I would have no way of knowing. Judging from the almost complete failure of the State Department to achieve any results, the strong suspicion must be that they are not few.

This much is certain, however. The matter of rescuing the Jews from extermination is a trust too great to remain in the hands of men who are indifferent, callous, and perhaps even hostile. The task is filled with difficulties. Only a fervent will to accomplish, backed by persistent and untiring effort can succeed where time is so precious.

Henry Morgenthau Jr., Personal Report to the President, Diaries, Book 694, pp. 194–195, 201–202.

ೋ 16 ೋ

WITNESS TO HISTORY

• R U T H   G R U B E R •

RUTH GRUBER'S distinguished professional career included a doctorate from the University of Cologne at the age of twenty as well as international travels as a journalist and writer, but it was her pivotal role in the rescue effort of European Jews during the Holocaust that transformed her identity as a Jew. Born in Brooklyn in 1911, the daughter of East European immigrants, Gruber received her education at New York University and the University of Wisconsin before pursuing a doctorate abroad. She launched a career as a journalist, writing for the *New York Times* and other newspapers and traveling throughout Europe, even to the Soviet Arctic.

In 1944, after the creation of the War Refugee Board, Secretary of the Interior Harold Ickes asked Gruber to serve as a special assistant in the effort to rescue European Jews and bring them to the newly established haven created by the government at Fort Ontario in Oswego, New York. Although she served as a government representative, Gruber forged a very personal relationship with the Jewish refugees. She became determined to chronicle their story and bring it to the American public. As she describes below, Gruber's engagement with the rescue effort profoundly altered her own Jewish identity.

⁓

THEY WERE A cross section of Europe's culture, Europe's occupations, Europe's nationalisms. Living with them on the ship made me aware that the most indestructible thing in the world is man. He survives the Gestapo, he survives the Vichy French, the Yugoslav Ustachi, the Poles, and the Ukrainians, who all helped in the slaughter. He survives hunger and wanderings and crippling torture. These people lived because they scratched and tore and hid and bought false identity papers and never believed in their own death.

I realized that every one of them was alive through a miracle. But I began to see something far more profound: that every Jew in the world was alive through a miracle; that since Egypt's Pharaoh, persecutors had tried to do to Jews what Hitler was now trying to do in Europe. Before Hitler, I was an innocent, convinced that someday there would be no more nationalism, no more racism, no more anti-Semitism. Hitler had taught me I was wrong. I became a "Hitler Jew" with three thousand years of history.

Now I realized that even if we were born Jews, there was a moment in our lives when we *became* Jews. On this ship, I was becoming a Jew.

Like some mythical leviathan taking us farther and farther from the furnaces and hell of Hitler's Europe, the ship had become a journey out of darkness and fear, out of despair and death, to hope and

Ruth Gruber escorting refugees into the refurbished Fort Ontario army base in Oswego, New York, 1944. Photographer: Alfred Eisenstaedt.
Getty Images

THE BEST OF TIMES, THE WORST OF TIMES

281

life and light. From this voyage on, I knew, my life would forever be inextricably interlocked with Jews. I felt myself trembling in the Atlantic night, trembling not from the wind but from the revelation. . . .

EVERYTHING IN ME seemed to be focusing on one goal. I wanted the press to capture in a few minutes what had taken me days and nights to question and learn. I wanted the reporters to grasp, instantaneously, years of terror and running; I wanted them to understand, so that they could tell the rest of the country about human courage and heroism and the human will to live.

But there were pitfalls. I had been on both sides of press tables—interviewing as a journalist, interviewed as a government official. Reporters tried to be objective. But who was really objective? The most widely listened-to radio commentator in America was a Detroit priest, Father Coughlin, a vituperative anti-Semite. Would some of the reporters be Coughlinites?

Refugee children at Fort Ontario, Oswego, New York, ca. 1944.
From the Archives of the YIVO Institute for Jewish Research

At Hoboken, soldiers helped the refugees down from the ferries onto the terminal dock of the old Delaware, Lackawanna and Western Railroad. One hundred MPs, in full battle uniform, with several attractive young WACs, lined up at attention. Twelve army ambulances carried off more than a score of the sick and elderly, and several pregnant women, to be put in the army hospital car. The rest of us were marched by the MPs into a blacked-out waiting room, cavernous, empty of passengers.

I stepped out of the line and waited to corral the refugees who were to meet the press. We kept together while the MPs moved the throngs of people to the tracks. Some of the soldiers lifted little children from their tired mothers' arms and carried them. Others picked up hand baggage; the grateful refugees hurried at their side, afraid to lose sight of the few things they had saved.

Ruth Gruber, *Haven: The Dramatic Story of 1,000 World War II Refugees and How They Came to America* (New York: Three Rivers Press, 1983), pp. 113–114, 125–126. From *Haven* by Ruth Gruber, copyright © 1983, 1984, 2000 by Ruth Gruber. Used by permission of Three Rivers Press, a division of Random House, Inc.

HOME

๛ ๛

"FOR THE majority of Jewish young people, things looked bright in the late 1940s and the future even brighter," explained sociologist Peter Rose. "They had made it into American society."[1] For American Jews, the postwar years brought unprecedented acceptance and prosperity. Along with other Americans, Jews participated in the exodus to the suburbs and shared in the increased affluence that followed World War II. Even as they wrestled with grief and horror in the wake of the Holocaust, American Jews understood that they now comprised the world's largest Jewish community and assumed responsibility for its leadership. While American Jews eagerly supported the establishment of a sovereign Jewish state, they also found in Israel a new source of Jewish identity at home. During the postwar years, American Jewish identity took on new dimensions, as Jews participated in the Civil Rights and feminist movements and became increasingly

PART FOUR

In the wake of the Holocaust, America's Jews assumed responsibility for refugees in Europe and Palestine. United Jewish Appeal poster. New York, Fodor, 1945–46.

Courtesy of the HUC Skirball Cultural Center, Museum Collection. Photography by Susan Einstein

visible in popular culture. In an era of resurgent ethnic pride that began in the 1960s, American Jews also more publicly claimed their Jewishness. In the closing decades of the twentieth century, Jews cultivated multiple expressions of what it meant to be Jewish in America, creating a culture unparalleled in its variety, diversity, and options.

When World War II ended, thousands of Jewish soldiers returned home to build new lives. Like other Americans of their generation, Jews reaped the benefits of the G.I. Bill, taking advantage of funding for higher education and low interest home loans. Though most remained close to urban centers, American Jews joined non-Jews in opting for the more spacious accommodations of the new suburban neighborhoods springing up across the country. Not only did postwar Jews move beyond city centers, but they also relocated to new areas of the country. Before the war, over 40 percent of Jews lived in New York City, with the remaining population residing predominantly in large cities in the Northeast and Midwest. But after 1945, the fastest-growing Jewish communities emerged in the Sunbelt, in cities such as Miami and Los Angeles, where the postwar generation enjoyed an array of economic and cultural opportunities. In their new surroundings, Jews continued to cluster in distinct neighborhoods, but none contained the same density of Jewish population as the districts where they had grown up. Jews lived in closer proximity to non-Jews, but barriers to social interaction continued to exist, particularly in the immediate postwar years. One Jewish suburban transplant explained that while relations remained cordial during daily encounters, "Jews and Christians do not meet socially even in suburbia." American Jews eagerly embraced the better housing and increased prosperity of the suburbs, but their first experiences with suburban life also created some anxiety.[2]

Postwar Jews grappled with the question of whether Jewish identity could survive on the suburban frontier. Without the Jewish stores on every corner, the concentrated Jewish population, and the connection to the immigrant generation that characterized their old neighborhoods, some Jews openly wondered about the future of Jewish life in the suburbs. It was the synagogue that emerged as the primary expression of Jewishness in new suburban communities. Between 1945 and 1965, Jews constructed more than 1,000 synagogues across the

Temple Emanuel, Miami Beach, Florida, 1949.
State Archives of Florida

country, the largest synagogue-building boom in American history. While all branches of Judaism experienced some growth, it was the Conservative movement that captured the allegiance of most suburban Jews, becoming the largest Jewish denomination in the immediate postwar years. Synagogue membership, which had always been extraordinarily low, suddenly spiked in the postwar era. By the close of the 1940s, approximately 40 percent of American Jews affiliated with synagogues and that number grew to 60 percent by the late fifties. Although these numbers remained significantly below Catholic and Protestant church memberships, they exceeded by far the affiliation figures for Jews in any previous or subsequent era. Jews joined synagogues in record numbers, but attendance at worship services continued to lag far behind. The synagogue became popular because it represented the central and sometimes the only institution for expressing Jewish identity in the suburbs.

When Congregation Beth Sholom relocated to the Philadelphia suburbs in the 1950s, the renowned architect Frank Lloyd Wright designed its new building. Wright described the structure as a "luminous Mount Sinai."
Courtesy Beth Sholom Congregation

Although they might not have attended regularly, American Jews counted on the synagogue to perpetuate a sense of Jewish connection for themselves and their children. Joining in the national baby boom of the postwar years, young Jewish parents sent their children to Sunday school and Hebrew school at an unprecedented rate. In previous generations, Jewishness was transmitted through neighborhoods, extended families, and informal interactions; only a minority of Jewish children received any formal religious training. But by the late 1950s, an estimated 80 percent of young Jewish children attended religious schools, as parents came to consider Jewish education the chief vehicle for transmitting tradition and ensuring Jewish continuity. Postwar synagogues became increasingly child-centered, focused on Bar Mitzvah and, beginning in the 1950s and more frequently in the 1960s, Bat Mitzvah celebrations, along with recreational and social activities. Family rituals became the most popular Jewish practices, with Passover and Hanukkah the most widely observed Jewish holidays, the latter providing American Jews with a useful alternative to Christmas.[3]

The revival of the synagogue reflected the mood of the nation and the new ways that Jews structured their sense of belonging in America. These were the years that Americans chose to add the phrase "under God" to the Pledge of Allegiance and "In God We Trust"

Bar Mitzvah invitation, ca. 1950s.

Collection of the Museum of Jewish Heritage-A Living Memorial To The Holocaust, New York. Photograph by Peter Goldberg.

to the currency—a Cold War statement of faith in the face of the "godless" communist threat. At a time when religious rhetoric ran high, Judaism seemed to have made it into the tripartite pantheon of American religions, legitimated alongside Protestantism and Catholicism as one of America's faith traditions. Judaism's new status in America could first be discerned in the popular account of the heroic deaths of four military chaplains during World War II. In 1943, Rabbi Alexander Goode was one of four chaplains of various denominations killed during an attack on the SS *Dorchester*. The chaplains, who purportedly went down with their ship linked arm-in-arm, were memorialized in a 1948 U.S. postage stamp that honored "interfaith in action." The concept of the "Judeo-Christian tradition" took shape as a dominant motif in American society during the postwar years. Former Marxist and Jewish intellectual Will Herberg underscored that notion in his bestselling 1955 book, *Protestant-Catholic-Jew*, that asserted the primacy of religious identity above all else in American culture. Jews themselves exhibited no great return to religious faith and continued to express strong ethnic identities, but the embrace of Judaism as a legitimate American religion, on equal footing with Christian denominations, gave Jews a new stature during the first two decades after the war.[4]

Chaplain Alexander Goode, one of the four chaplains killed on the SS Dorchester.

The Jacob Rader Marcus Center of the American Jewish Archives

The decline in anti-Semitism after World War II also enhanced the confidence and sense of well being among American Jews. After the defeat of Nazism, anti-Semitism came to be seen as unpatriotic and un-American. In 1947, two pivotal Hollywood films, *Crossfire* and *Gentleman's Agreement*, directly confronted American anti-Semitism in an attempt to expose the evils of bigotry. *Crossfire* described the murder of a Jewish war hero, named Joseph Samuels, killed by a fellow soldier who harbored anti-Semitic beliefs, including the mistaken impression that Jews shirked military duty. While underscoring Jewish willingness to fight for the country, *Crossfire* emphasized that religious prejudice was an affront to American ideals. In the film, after the soldier is

A Jewish prayer service in the military during World War II, ca. 1940s.

American Jewish Historical Society, Newton Centre, Massachusetts and New York, New York

Scene from the 1947 film Crossfire.

Getty Images

arrested for murder, Samuels's non-Jewish friend and fellow soldier declares, "[W]e don't want people like you in the U.S.A. There's no place for racial discrimination now." *Gentlemen's Agreement*, an Academy Award-winning film based on Laura Hobson's novel, followed a reporter's vicarious experience as an American Jew, as he posed as a Jew in order to research an article about American anti-Semitism. In the course of the film, the reporter and his young son learned firsthand the bigotry that Jews faced, exposing the ignorance and dangers of anti-Semitism.[5]

Hollywood's preoccupation with depicting the evils of anti-Semitism reflected the postwar concern with promoting an image of America as a nation committed to tolerance and equality. Public opinion surveys from the era reveal that most Americans had also taken that message to heart. Beginning in late 1940s, a series of polls demonstrated a sharp decrease in the number of non-Jews who believed that Jews wielded too much power, were unscrupulous in business, or possessed objectionable personal traits. Moreover, anti-Semitic attitudes continued to decline in subsequent decades. In 1948, more than 20 percent of Americans indicated that they did not want Jews as neighbors; by 1959, that number had fallen to only 2 percent. By 1950, many states had already banned employment discrimination, and more sweeping legislation followed in later years. Pressured by government and the courts, universities began to eliminate Jewish quotas and companies abolished discriminatory hiring

Poster for the film Gentleman's Agreement, *1947.*

Library of Congress, Prints and Photographs Division

A United Jewish Appeal campaign for Soviet Jewry, ca. 1970s.
Library of Congress, Prints and Photographs Division

practices. Even the Anti-Defamation League, whose raison d'être was fighting anti-Semitism, conceded that the postwar years were a "golden age" that brought a momentous decline in anti-Semitism.[6]

Even in the midst of the postwar "golden age," while they pursued the new opportunities available in America, Jews remained ever cognizant of the cataclysmic events that had so recently decimated European Jewry. Before the 1960s, the term "Holocaust" was not yet codified as the sole designation used to characterize the destruction of European Jews, but American Jews began memorializing the dead long before they possessed a single term to identify the tragedy. On the local level, in synagogues, in prayer books, and in a host of ceremonies and publications, American Jews remembered the devastating loss of millions of European Jews. In 1947, a stone was laid in Riverside Park for a proposed monument dedicated to the heroes of the Warsaw Ghetto Uprising and the six million who died, though the memorial never came to fruition. Before *Yom HaShoah* (Holocaust Remembrance Day) became widely observed in the United States, Jews commemorated the tragedy on *Tisha B'Av* (the ninth day of the Jewish month of Av), a traditional day of mourning on the Jewish calendar. Falling in the middle of summer, these *Tisha B'Av* remembrances became especially popular at Jewish summer camps where many young Jews first came to appreciate the loss. During these years, thousands of displaced persons, survivors of the Holocaust, settled in the United States; almost 40,000 arrived in 1949 alone. Some refugees had escaped Europe before the war, including a group of prominent artists and scholars such as Albert Einstein. Those who arrived after the Holocaust included some of Europe's most distinguished rabbis and scholars, Jews who would not have chosen to come to America had Europe not been destroyed. Many of the leaders of Hasidic dynasties arrived as survivors and created Hasidic enclaves in the United States that would grow and flourish. Only in later years did a more fully developed Holocaust consciousness emerge as a primary Jewish communal concern, producing scores of museums, books, and films. But even in these early years, American Jews expressed the need to remember the destruction of European Jewry.[7]

Just three years after the conclusion of World War II, rabbis from the Displaced Persons camps in cooperation with the United States Army arranged for the publication of a nineteen-volume edition of the Talmud in Germany in order to meet the needs of Holocaust survivors living in the American Zone. This edition of the Talmud is dedicated to the United States Army. Title page, Talmud Berakhot [The Survivor's Talmud, Vol. 1] Munich-Heidelberg: United States Army, 1948.
Courtesy of the Center for Advanced Judaic Studies Library, University of Pennsylvania

For many American Jews, support for the State of Israel was a natural corollary to remembering the tragedy in Europe. In May of 1948, when Israel declared its independence, American Jews celebrated the event as a triumph; they also raised millions of dollars to support the fledgling nation. There were a few dissenters within the Jewish community. The American Council for Judaism, founded in 1942 by a group of Reform rabbis who opposed any definition of Jews as a nation, continued to object to the idea of a Jewish State. But the organization represented only a tiny fraction of American Jews and its membership quickly dwindled; most Reform Jews rallied around the new state.[8] Israel received enthusiastic and virtually unanimous support within the Jewish community, but the relationship between Israel and America did require some negotiation. American Jews wanted to be absolutely certain that both Israelis and their fellow Americans understood that their primary loyalty as citizens was to the United States. In 1950, a pivotal exchange between Israeli Prime Minister David Ben-Gurion and Jacob Blaustein, president of the American Jewish Committee, established the ground rules for relations between American Jews and Israel. Both leaders stipulated that American Jews maintained political allegiance only to the United States, that Israel would respect the right of Jews in other nations to build their own cultures according to their own needs, and that Israel would recognize that American Jews considered themselves no longer in exile, but fully "at home" in America.[9] For more than a decade after the founding of Israel, American Jews learned how to balance expressions of loyalty to the new state with unwavering commitment to America. Throughout the 1950s, financial support came readily, but Israel was not yet a central focus within American Jewish culture, as it would become in later years.

Jewish war veterans rally to support Jewish immigration to Palestine, ca. 1940s.

Gift of Dr. Marvin Margoshes. Collection of the Museum of Jewish Heritage-A Living Memorial To The Holocaust, New York. Photograph by Peter Goldberg.

In 1948, the Zionist Organization of America issued this stamp which juxtaposes American and Israeli independence.

Courtesy of the National Museum of American Jewish History, Philadelphia

Beginning in the 1960s, Israel emerged as a crucial rallying point and essential building block of American Jewish identity. The first signs came in the remarkable popularity of Leon Uris's best-selling historical novel *Exodus*, published in 1958, that told the story of the creation of the state. Two years later, Otto Preminger adapted the

Based on the 1958 Leon Uris novel, the film Exodus *chronicled the story of the founding of Israel using the motifs of Hollywood and American culture.* Exodus *movie poster. Artist: Saul Bass, 1961.*

Library of Congress, Prints and Photographs Division

story for the screen and cast Paul Newman and Eva Marie Saint in the starring roles. Borrowing from the motifs of American westerns, *Exodus* depicted Jews' attachment to the land and their battle to tame the frontier. The movie was a box office blockbuster, attracting both Jews and non-Jews, and portraying an image of Israel that Americans could embrace.[10]

If *Exodus* set the stage, it was the 1967 Six-Day War that galvanized unprecedented Jewish support for Israel. The attack on Israel underscored the vulnerability of the new nation and even prompted fears of another Holocaust. After the outbreak of fighting, American Jews immediately sprung to action, holding rallies, urging U.S. support, and raising more than $300 million dollars for Israel in 1967 alone. After the victory, Israel became the centerpiece of programming and philanthropy within the Jewish community. Virtually every synagogue gift shop sold Israeli-made items to American Jewish consumers who used them for rituals and decoration within their homes. When Israel faced an attack again in the 1973 Yom Kippur War, a similar drama played out, as American Jews rushed to support the nation both politically and financially. Israel came to play a particular role in American Jewish culture—a canvas on which American Jews painted a portrait of an ideal Jewish society that they could enjoy vicariously, a nation that both ensured Jewish security and bolstered Jewish identity in the United States. In the years following the Yom Kippur War, as settlements emerged on the West Bank and Israel ruled a large Palestinian population, some American Jews began to voice concern about the policies of the Israeli government. The invasion of Lebanon, the Intifada, and the campaign for Palestinian rights gave rise to American Jewish organizations such as the New Jewish Agenda that endorsed the peace movement and a Palestinian state. In recent years, different outlooks toward Israel have created divisions among Jewish groups, but support for Israel and attachment to its culture remain powerful forces within the American Jewish community.[11]

In the 1960s, at the same time that identification with Israel became a dominant motif in American Jewish culture, a more fully developed Holocaust consciousness also began to take shape. The universal lessons of the Holocaust first reached a wide audience, both Jewish and non-Jewish, with the publication of *The Diary of Anne Frank* in the 1950s. A Pulitzer-Prize winning play based on the diary opened to popular acclaim in 1955, followed by an equally successful film adaptation in 1959. Through the story of Anne Frank, Americans learned to identify with persecuted Jews forced into hiding, but

Millie Perkins as Anne Frank in the 1959 film. Photographer: Ralph Crane.

Getty Images

Frank's story ended before the horrors of the Holocaust began and transmitted a core message of faith in humanity's goodness. The capture and subsequent trial of Adolf Eichmann in 1960 brought the full brunt of the murder of six million Jews before the public, as the American media covered the sensational courtroom drama, complete with the emotional testimony of survivors and the image of Eichmann enclosed in a bulletproof glass booth. That same year witnessed the publication of the English translation of Elie Wiesel's *Night*, one of the first accounts by a Holocaust survivor available to a wide readership. During the 1960s, the term "Holocaust" came into popular usage to refer to the destruction of European Jews and the first scholarly accounts of the Nazi extermination were published. By the 1970s, *Yom HaShoah* became regularly observed in America and soon Jewish communities across the country built Holocaust monuments, memorials, and museums. President Jimmy Carter established a federal Holocaust Memorial Council in the late 1970s which ultimately resulted in the opening of the United States Holocaust Memorial Museum in Washington, D.C., in 1993; that same year Stephen Spielberg's film *Schindler's List* won the Oscar for best picture. The outpouring of interest in remembering the Holocaust resulted from the gradual coming to terms with the loss of six millions Jews, the increased number of survivor accounts, and the identity politics that followed the Six-Day War. Although some Jews criticized the preoccupation with the Holocaust at the expense of other Jewish communal concerns, there can be little doubt that remembering the Holocaust came to stand alongside supporting Israel as cornerstones of American Jewish identity in the postwar era.[12]

American viewers watched the 1961 trial of Adolf Eichmann in Jerusalem on television. Here, Eichmann takes notes during the trial, sitting in the bulletproof glass booth designed to protect him from assassination.
Courtesy of United States Holocaust Memorial Museum

A large crowd fills Eisenhower Plaza during the dedication ceremony of the U.S. Holocaust Memorial Museum in Washington, D.C., April 22, 1993.
Courtesy of United States Holocaust Memorial Museum

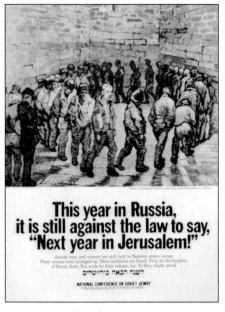

This year in Russia,
it is still against the law to say,
"Next year in Jerusalem!"

Jewish men and women are still held in Russian prison camps.
Their arrests were trumped-up. Their sentences are harsh. Pray for the freedom
of Soviet Jews. But work for their release, too. So they might speak

לשנה הבאה בירושלים

NATIONAL CONFERENCE ON SOVIET JEWRY

Poster, National Conference on Soviet Jewry, ca. 1960s.

Library of Congress, Prints and Photographs Division

FREE THEM NOW

FREEDOM MARCH
FOR SOVIET JEWS
Sunday·May 6·12noon
General Public Assemble at 71st St.& 5th Ave.

Sponsored by the constituent agencies of the
GREATER NEW YORK CONFERENCE
ON SOVIET JEWRY
212-354-1316

Poster, Freedom March for Soviet Jews, Greater New York Conference on Soviet Jewry, 1973.

Library of Congress, Prints and Photographs Division

Heightened consciousness of the Holocaust also helped to spark the campaign for Soviet Jewry in the sixties and seventies. When World War II ended, approximately two million Jews remained in the Soviet Union, subject to the religious persecution and human rights abuses of the government. In the 1960s, Elie Wiesel published *The Jews of Silence* to draw attention to the plight of Soviet Jews; as a Holocaust survivor, he called on American Jews to prevent another potential tragedy. Jewish college students founded the Student Struggle for Soviet Jewry, whose members organized large protest rallies proclaiming the slogan, "Let My People Go." As a growing number of Russian Jews openly challenged the Soviet government and petitioned to leave the country, these "refuseniks" garnered the attention and sympathy of America's Jews. Activists traveled to the Soviet Union to smuggle books and ritual objects to Russian Jews and Bar and Bat Mitzvah celebrations in the United States were "twinned" with those of Jewish children in Russia who did not have the freedom to mark the occasion. American Jews succeeded in bringing attention to the cause and helping thousands of Russian Jews gain admission to the United States. After the fall of the Soviet Union, those numbers grew dramatically and Russian Jews created distinct communities in areas such as "Little Odessa" in Brooklyn's Brighton Beach. The Soviet Jewry movement reflected the growing sophistication of American Jewish lobbying efforts, the lessons learned from the Holocaust, and the changing climate of American politics in a new era of mass protests and demonstrations.[13]

As much as American Jews focused on remembering past tragedy and supporting campaigns abroad, political movements at home played an equally important role in shaping American Jewish identity. Even before the postwar era, Jews had cultivated such a deep commitment to liberalism that advocating liberal causes became an expression of Jewish identity. Preserving equality and social justice in America functioned as a virtual Jewish creed, leading to Jewish overrepresentation in some of the pivotal political movements of the 1960s. Postwar Jews were vocal participants in the campaigns for Civil Rights and women's rights, bringing Jewish values and a liberal agenda to the American political arena.

That is not to say that Jews had put past fears of being labeled political subversives completely behind them. The trial, conviction, and eventual execution of Julius and Ethel Rosenberg in the early 1950s prompted some concern that Jews would be painted as communist sympathizers, a serious threat at the height of the Cold War. While committed Jewish leftists defended the Rosenbergs against the charges, many Jewish leaders supported the guilty verdict and urged Jews to stand firm in the battle against communism. The American Jewish Committee, the Anti-Defamation League, and other Jewish organizations allowed the House un-American Activities Committee to examine their records. The Jewish Welfare Board urged Jewish community centers to ban radical speakers from their buildings. The American Jewish Committee initiated an internal investigation to root out communism in Jewish communal affairs. Some prominent Jewish leaders supported the death sentence imposed on the Rosenbergs, but most, including the leading Yiddish newspapers, argued that although the Rosenbergs had committed serious crimes, the sentence was far too harsh. Fortunately, several polls conducted after the trial and execution revealed no increase in anti-Semitic attitudes or heightened belief that Jews were inclined toward communism, providing valuable reassurance to Jews who worried about the specter of a Jewish couple occupying center-stage in America's most notorious communist episode.[14]

Whatever their apprehensions, American Jews stood at the forefront of the Civil Rights Movement in the 1960s. Since the early twentieth century, Jews had been involved in working for equal rights and had been active supporters of the NAACP and the Urban League. In part as an expression of self-interest, Jews believed that a society that guaranteed freedom to all its members would ensure a secure future for all minority groups, including themselves. Faith in the liberal promise of America combined with an abiding commitment to social justice led Jews to fight for the protections offered by a democratic society and the elimination of all forms of prejudice. While Jews had spoken out against racial discrimination before, the postwar years were the first time that Civil Rights initiatives received top priority on the Jewish communal agenda. On the local and national level, Jewish community relations councils—which had previously focused on combating discrimination against Jews—embraced broader social justice campaigns as a crucial part of their missions. Not only Jewish organizations but also virtually all branches of American Judaism declared their support for the Civil Rights struggle. New York's Orthodox Rabbi Leo Jung hailed the 1954 Supreme Court ruling abolishing segregation in public schools as

Ethel Rosenberg and Julius Rosenberg leaving federal court after being indicted.
Bettmann/CORBIS

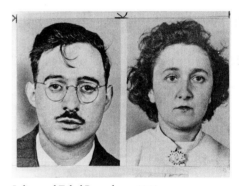

Julius and Ethel Rosenberg, 1950.
Photo of Julius Rosenberg: Hulton-Deutsch Collection/CORBIS
Photo of Ethel Rosenberg: © CORBIS

Rabbi Abraham Joshua Heschel (right), walking with (from left) Ralph Abernathy, Martin Luther King, and Ralph Bunche during a civil rights march from Selma to Montgomery, Alabama, 1965.
Bettmann/CORBIS

A JEWISH CENTER BOMBED IN SOUTH

Jacksonville Negro School Also Hit in Blasts Laid to an 'Underground'

JACKSONVILLE, Fla., April 28 (UP)—A Jewish center and a Negro school were bombed here today. Members of a group called "The Confederate Underground" were said to be responsible for the outbreak, the third such in the South this year.

The bombs, believed made of nitroglycerin, were hurled within a period of three or four minutes at the buildings, which are four miles apart.

One bomb struck the rear of the combination synagogue and community center in an old residential section of the city. The other exploded in the arcade entranceway of the James Weldon Johnson Junior High School.

The police said no one was reported injured. One blast broke the rear windows of the Jewish center, buckled the metal side of a near-by garage and cracked windows in an apartment house. Damage at the school was estimated at $2,000.

Shortly after the blasts, a man telephoned a former newspaper man and said:

"This is The Confederate Underground. We have just blown up a Jewish center of integration. Every segregationist in

The New York Times reports the bombing of a synagogue in Jacksonville, Florida. April 1958.

Andrew Goodman, ca. 1964.

Library of Congress, Prints and Photographs Division

"a red letter day in American history." The Reform movement, long a leader in social action campaigns, put out "A Call to Racial Justice" in 1963, imploring members to work for universal civil rights as part of their responsibilities as Jews. In one of the most iconic photographs of the Civil Rights era, Rabbi Abraham Joshua Heschel of the Jewish Theological Seminary appears walking arm-in-arm with Martin Luther King Jr. and other black activists during a march in Selma, Alabama—an act he described as eliciting "a sense of the Holy."[15] For Jews in the South, the Civil Rights Movement brought particular dangers. Nevertheless a significant number embraced the cause. Many Southern rabbis spoke out in campaigns for desegregation, putting their congregations in peril. A string of synagogue bombings occurred in Southern cities in the late 1950s, including the bombing of the largest and most prosperous Reform temple in Atlanta in 1958.[16]

On a grassroots level, beyond the proclamations of organizations and the activities of prominent leaders, Jewish Americans were heavily represented in the rank and file of the Civil Rights Movement. Jews constituted somewhere between half and three-quarters of those who contributed to Civil Rights organizations, and more than half of the white volunteers who headed South during the Mississippi Freedom Summer in 1964. A disproportionate number of young Jews attending college in the 1960s became members of Students for a Democratic Society and took part in campus protests. Most did not participate as Jews per se, but the imperative for racial justice extended beyond those in the Jewish community who saw their work as part of a Jewish mission. For instance, Andrew Goodman and Michael Schwerner, two Jewish civil rights workers, traveled to Mississippi to join their African American co-worker, native Mississippian James Chaney, during Freedom Summer in 1964. The three young men never returned, eventually found murdered by the Klan. Goodman and Schwerner, though only two of the many men

Federal agents and officers of the Mississippi Highway Patrol examine the charred remains of the station wagon driven by Andrew Goodman, Michael Schwerner, and James Chaney. June 1964.

Bettmann/CORBIS

and women of both races who participated in the struggle, became symbols of the extent of Jewish commitment to the cause.[17]

Jewish interests in social justice converged with the African American struggle for Civil Rights in the 1960s, but the alliance between blacks and Jews had always been tenuous. Jews believed wholeheartedly in the universal goal of equal rights and opportunities, but they may have been naïve in not recognizing the pervasive power of race in American society. The barriers that Jews had overcome in their quest to open the door to the American dream could not be broken down so easily for African Americans within the highly charged racial climate of the United States. As the campaigns for desegregation in the South gave way to race riots in Northern cities, African Americans found that their disadvantaged neighborhoods had scores of businesses owned and operated by Jews. While American Jews saw themselves as partners in the crusade for Civil Rights, the economic chasm and power differential between the two groups belied a true alliance, exposing the disparity between black and white in America.[18]

The bitter teachers' strike that erupted in the Ocean Hill-Brownsville section of Brooklyn in 1968 highlighted the deep fissures beneath the relationship between Jews and African Americans. Ocean Hill-Brownsville had once been a predominantly white working class and lower middle class district, but by the 1960s a growing number of African Americans had moved to the area. While the neighborhood and the school board were overwhelmingly African American, many of the teachers remained Jewish, members of the largely Jewish United Federation of Teachers. In 1968, in an experimental program to institute greater community control over public schools, the school board fired nineteen teachers and administrators, most of them Jewish. The move sparked an almost two month strike that brought to the surface simmering racial tensions and pitted Jews and African Americans against one another. Though the teachers were ultimately reinstated, the damage was done. By the end of the 1960s, as African Americans took greater control of their own struggle and a new Black Power movement emerged, Jews and blacks found their interactions increasingly strained. But even while Jews and African Americans endured recurring racial conflicts and diverging agendas,

"Black vs. Jew: A Tragic Confrontation," Cover story, Time *magazine, January 31, 1969.*
Time-Life Pictures, Getty Images

United Federation of Teachers President Albert Shanker addresses a rally of teachers in support of striking colleagues in Ocean Hill-Brownsville, May 23, 1968.
Robert F. Wagner Labor Archives, New York University. United Federation of Teachers Photographs Collection.

Betty Friedan, president of the National Organization for Women (NOW), lobbying for women's civil rights, 1967.

Library of Congress, Prints and Photographs Division

individual Jews and Jewish communal organizations remained committed to the campaign for civil rights and continued to regard social justice as a Jewish issue.[19]

On the heels of the Civil Rights struggle, the feminist movement emerged to change the lives of Jewish women and men and to alter the character of Judaism and Jewish culture in America. By the 1960s, young Jewish women attended college at a disproportionate rate, so it is not surprising that they also became heavily represented as leaders in the burgeoning feminist movement. The Jewish community had a long history of women activists; in previous generations, women had worked in factories and led labor strikes. But the feminist movement of the 1960s was a departure, focusing on women's self-fulfillment and quest for equality. Jewish women assumed pivotal leadership roles in second wave feminism. (The first wave occurring during the campaign for suffrage earlier in the century.) Andrea Dworkin, Robin Morgan, and Shulamith Firestone were just a few of the prominent Jewish women who joined best-selling author Betty Friedan in asserting a new feminist agenda in America. Best known for her pioneering 1963 treatise, *The Feminine Mystique*, Betty Friedan was a founding member and the first president of the National Organization for Women. During one feminist demonstration, Friedan rose to speak and invoked her Jewish heritage, making reference to the prayer traditionally recited by Jewish men each morning. "Down through the generations in history," Friedan proclaimed, "my ancestors prayed, 'I thank Thee, Lord, I was not created a woman,' and from this day forward I trust that women all over the world will be able to say, 'I thank Thee, Lord, I *was* created a woman.'" The 1960s feminist movement, including many of its Jewish advocates, often disparaged Judaism as a patriarchal religion that perpetuated women's second-class status. In later years, such rhetoric diminished within feminist circles and Friedan herself made an effort to reconnect with her Jewish roots.[20]

Those American Jewish women who espoused feminist convictions and also remained deeply committed to Judaism created a Jewish feminist movement with its own distinct agenda. Jewish feminism's goals, as one scholar explained, were to assert "both Jewish visibility within the feminist movement and feminist consciousness within the U.S. Jewish community."[21] While defending Judaism as more than a patriarchal religion, Jewish feminists also demanded changes in many traditional Jewish practices. They wanted to participate equally in prayer, to be called to the Torah, to serve as witnesses and even rabbis, and to eliminate inequities in Jewish divorce procedures which left women at the mercy of men to grant the divorce. Even before Jewish feminism, women had gradually been gaining greater access to public religious rituals. Mordecai Kaplan first introduced the Bat Mitzvah ceremony for his own daughter in 1922, and by the 1960s and 1970s, it had become a regular practice, particularly in Conservative synagogues. The Conservative movement, which was the largest branch of Judaism in this period, had slowly begun granting women the right to recite the blessings over the Torah. By the 1970s, many synagogues counted women in the *minyan*, the tradition quorum of ten required for prayer. The demands of Jewish feminists, which varied within the different movements of Judaism, were made possible by the small changes that had been occurring gradually over time combined with a more militant style adopted from contemporary feminism.

The Jewish feminist movement brought the question of whether women could serve as rabbis to all branches of Judaism. The Reform movement ordained American Judaism's first female rabbi, Sally Priesand, in 1972. Since they were not bound by restrictions in Jewish law that limited the religious functions that women could perform, Reform leaders admitted women as rabbis with comparatively little debate and with the strong support of key leaders in the movement. Social acceptance of the first generation of female rabbis came more slowly. The Reconstructionist Rabbinical College, which opened its doors in 1968 and became an independent movement in Judaism, admitted women as candidates for the rabbinate from the outset. In Conservative Judaism, the battle over women's ordination involved a decade of protracted, often bitter debate. A group of Jewish feminists who called themselves *Ezrat Nashim* (a Hebrew term that literally means "women's help" and was also the term for the women's section in the ancient Temple and the women's gallery in synagogues) appeared at the annual meeting of Conservative rabbis in 1972 to demand full inclusion in all religious practices, including admission to the rabbinate. After more than a decade of discussion, tabled resolutions, and internal strife, the Conservative movement ordained its first female rabbi, Amy Eilberg, in 1985. Although Orthodoxy's adherence to traditional interpretations of Jewish law prohibits women from functioning as rabbis, the movement has nonetheless grappled with ways to allow its female constituents to assume greater roles in the synagogue. Responding to the demands of contemporary feminism, many Orthodox schools now provide women a sophisticated education in Jewish texts. And some

Sally Priesand being ordained by the Reform movement as America's first woman rabbi. June 1972.

The Jacob Rader Marcus Center of the American Jewish Archives

A women's prayer service during an international conference of the Jewish Orthodox Feminist Alliance (JOFA) ca. 2000.

Reprinted with permission from the Jewish Orthodox Feminist Alliance, Inc.

congregations have permitted women to assume a certain set of public religious roles. Since 1997, the Jewish Orthodox Feminist Alliance has been working to "expand the spiritual, ritual, intellectual and political opportunities for women within the framework of *halakha* [Jewish law]."[22]

Feminism has altered American Judaism far beyond changes in women's roles alone. In its wake, there have been new rituals, including the *Simchat Bat*, the celebration of the birth of daughter, and innovations in the language of prayer, such as gender-neutral ways of referring to God. The egalitarian spirit also sparked the *havurah* (fellowship) movement that began in the 1960s. In a *havurah*, women and men gather together for prayer, innovating the forms and practices of Jewish worship, without a rabbi or any official leader and with all members participating equally. In similar fashion, *The Jewish Catalog*, which first appeared in 1973, advertised itself as "A Do-It-Yourself Kit," that provided creative ways to connect with Judaism and Jewish culture. The countercultural settings of the 1960s produced a new emphasis on spirituality, grassroots leadership, and egalitarianism that has in recent decades become incorporated within mainstream Judaism, reshaping the quality of Jewish culture and community.[23]

While American Judaism experienced innovations, Jews and Jewish culture also appeared in new ways on the broader American stage—in

Cover of The First Jewish Catalog, *1973.*

Reprinted from *The First Jewish Catalog: A Do-It-Yourself Kit* © 1973 by Richard Siegel, Michael Strassfeld, and Sharon Strassfeld, published by The Jewish Publication Society, with the permission of the publisher.

The Detroit Tiger's Hank Greenberg, ca. 1930s.
© Bettmann/CORBIS

sports, entertainment, and mass media. The postwar years began with two very different symbolic Jewish moments. In 1945, baseball player Hank Greenberg, who had already won the adoration of the Jewish community by choosing not to play in a game on Yom Kippur in 1934, returned from service in World War II to hit the game-winning home run that earned the American League pennant for the Detroit Tigers. Already an icon, Greenberg's triumphant home run further cemented his status as "the perfect standard-bearer for the Jews." In the same month that Greenberg projected an ideal image of American manhood, Bess Myerson came to represent the pinnacle of American femininity, winning the crown of Miss America. Myerson, the first Jewish woman to claim the title, was not a member of genteel society, but rather the product of a Yiddish working-class family in the Bronx. She had refused to change her name in order to camouflage her Jewish identity, a move that likely would have made her more popular with American audiences. In publicly embracing her Jewish roots, she, too, garnered the approbation of Jews across the country who saw in her election as Miss America the potential for Jews to be fully accepted in American society. Greenberg and Myerson—both openly Jewish and widely acclaimed figures in mainstream American culture—embodied the collective hopes of a generation of American Jews.[24]

The last third of the twentieth century witnessed an explosion of Jewish characters and ethnicity in American popular culture.

Bess Myerson seated on her throne after being crowned Miss America, 1945.
Bettmann/CORBIS

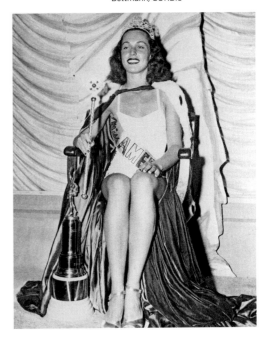

In his cutting edge, provocative comedy (ruled obscene by the courts in the 1960s), Lenny Bruce (1925–1966) used humor to critique the political, religious, and racial issues of mainstream culture. In this selection from his comedy, he muses on the differences between Jews and non-Jews.

JEWISH AND GOYISH

Lenny Bruce

Dig: I'm Jewish. Count Basie's Jewish. Ray Charles is Jewish. Eddie Cantor's *goyish*. B'Nai Brith is *goyish*; Hadassah, Jewish. Marine corps—heavy *goyim*, dangerous. Koolaid is *goyish*. All Drake's Cakes are *goyish*. Pumpernickel is Jewish, and, as you know, white bread is very *goyish*. Instant *potatoes*—*goyish*. Black cherry soda's very Jewish. Macaroons are *very* Jewish—very Jewish cake. Fruit salad is Jewish. Lime jello is *goyish*. Lime soda is very *goyish*. Trailer parks are so *goyish* that Jews won't go near them. Jack Paar Show is very *goyish*. Underwear is definitely *goyish*. Balls are *goyish*. Titties are Jewish. Mouths are Jewish. All Italians are Jewish. Greeks are *goyish*—bad sauce. Eugene O'Neill— Jewish; Dylan Thomas, Jewish. Steve is *goyish*, though. It's the hair. He combs his hair in the boys' room with that soap all the time.

Comedian Lenny Bruce performing, ca. 1950s, Hulton Archive.
Getty Images

The Essential Lenny Bruce, compiled and edited by John Cohen (New York: Bell Publishing, 1970), p. 31. Originally published in 1967 by Ballantine Books. Printed with permission of Douglas Music.

To be sure, in the early days of television, Jewishness made a slow retreat from the American viewing public. The popular series *The Goldbergs* that had begun on radio ended its television run in 1956, by which time the writers had relocated the family to the suburbs and erased much of the ethnic distinctiveness that had once characterized the show. In the 1950s, during television's "Golden Age," Jewish characters abounded, particularly on variety shows. Jack Benny, Red Buttons, Buddy Hackett, and Groucho Marx were just a few of the Jewish comedians who shaped early television. Milton Berle (born Milton Berlinger) became a television sensation on NBC's *Texaco Star Theater*, reaching an estimated 75 percent of the viewing audience, which at the time consisted predominantly of urban Americans, many of them Jews. Although he avoided explicit references to his Jewish identity, "Uncle Miltie's" raucous skits clearly drew from Jewish styles of vaudeville, parody, and "shtick," even including cross-dressing. Once television spread to the American heartland, producers considered Berle's brand of humor too urban and ill-suited to the tastes of middle America, canceling his show in 1956. Airing during approximately the same years, Sid Caesar's *Your Show of Shows*—whose writers comprised a virtual who's who of Jewish comedians, including Carl Reiner, Mel Brooks, Neil Simon, Woody Allen, and Larry Gelbart—was broadcast live every Saturday night in the 1950s. Despite the occasional use of Yiddishisms and a distinctly Jewish brand of humor, the show refrained from overtly marking the comedy as Jewish. Indeed, by the 1960s, even veiled references to Jewishness faded into the background. When Carl Reiner proposed a sitcom based on his experiences as a writer on *Your Show of Shows* with himself in the starring

Milton Berle performing in a dress on NBC's Texaco Star Theater, *ca. 1948.*
Courtesy of Photofest

Writing staff of Sid Caesar's Your Show of Shows, *ca. 1950s. From left, front row: Gary Belkin, Sheldon Keller, Michael Stewart, Mel Brooks; back row: Neil Simon, Mel Tolkin, Larry Gelbart.*
Courtesy of Photofest

Sid Caesar and Imogene Coca performing a comedy routine on Your Show of Shows, *ca. 1954.*

Library of Congress, Prints and Photographs Division

Barbra Streisand, Columbia Record Photo, ca 1960s.

The Jacob Rader Marcus Center of the American Jewish Archives

role, CBS insisted that he replace the lead character with a less ethnic type. Thus was born the *Dick Van Dyke Show*, with Rob Petrie as the head writer and Carl Reiner, who directed, playing the role of Alan Brady.[25]

The ethnic revival in America that followed on the heels of the Civil Rights Movement reinvigorated interest in racial and ethnic heritage and brought Jewish characters back to the media forefront. The new celebration of Jewish ethnicity could be seen in the popularity of nostalgic films such as *Fiddler on the Roof* and those that portrayed postwar Jewish culture, including screen adaptations of the novels *Marjorie Morningstar* and *Goodbye Columbus*. The latter's satiric portrait of Jewish affluence, complete with scathing depictions of indulgently lavish weddings and nose jobs, upset some Jewish critics, but also reflected a sense of ethnic comfort. The Jewish nose itself emerged as a source of caricature and a marker of Jewishness that some wanted to erase. When Barbra Streisand portrayed the popular Jewish entertainer Fanny Brice in the 1968 film *Funny Girl*, her character posed the question "is a nose with deviations a crime against the nation?" (Ironically, the real Fanny Brice chose to have cosmetic surgery on her nose in the 1920s, while Barbra Streisand created a signature style by refraining from doing so.) By the 1970s, as television shows from *The Jeffersons* to *Sanford and Son* highlighted African American families, so, too, Jewish characters such as Rhoda Morgenstern made a return to the small screen. By the 1980s and beyond, explicitly Jewish characters on television ceased to be an anomaly. From the angst-ridden struggles of *Thirtysomething*'s Michael Steadman to the caustic humor of Jerry Seinfeld, Jews appeared nightly on American Television. Though the portraits have varied, Jews have become ubiquitous figures within the increasingly diverse (albeit still selective) representation of religious, racial and ethnic groups within contemporary American popular culture.[26]

One 1970s television series, *Bridget Loves Bernie*, touched a nerve in the American Jewish community through its portrayal of an intermarried couple. A success in the Nielsen ratings when it debuted in 1972, the show lasted just one season, a victim of protests by Jewish groups insisting that the sitcom poked fun at a serious issue. During the 1960s, intermarriage rates began to increase dramatically; in an era when many Jewish communal leaders regarded the trend as a grave threat, they did not want to see the issue become the subject of television comedy. In subsequent decades, as a host of surveys revealed Jewish intermarriage rates approaching 50 percent, the Jewish community became preoccupied with the meaning and long-term consequences of the trend. While some commentators have claimed that intermarriage threatens the very survival of Jews as a people, others point to the tendency for intermarried couples to maintain Jewish identity and raise their children as Jews. Recognizing the reality of mixed marriage in contemporary Jewish culture, many synagogues have incorporated outreach to intermarried couples as a part of standard programming. The Reform movement issued a pivotal 1983 decision on patrilineal descent, allowing the children of Jewish fathers and non-Jewish mothers to be considered Jewish, as long as their parents raise them in the Jewish tradition. Evaluating

First broadcast in 1972, Bridget Loves Bernie's *depiction of an intermarried couple in a situation comedy drew protests from some segments of the Jewish community.*
Courtesy of Photofest

the effects of intermarriage remains an ideological question that divides the Jewish community, though the fact that intermarriage occurs with such regularity testifies to the tremendous acceptance of Jews in American culture as well as to the natural consequence of living in a liberal, open society.[27]

IN THE OPENING years of the twenty-first century, snapshots of American Jewry reveal a community of extraordinary diversity and creativity, a community that defies neat categorization. While a Jewish woman sits on the Supreme Court, a Hasidic rap artist named Matisyahu is winning popular acclaim. A religiously observant Jewish senator from Connecticut earned the Democratic Party's nomination for Vice President of the United States in the year 2000, even as approximately 40,000 American Jews were joining movements committed to secular Judaism.[28] More Jewish children attend Jewish day schools than ever before, many of them having grown up playing Jewish versions of American board games and donning *kippot* (skullcaps) with Sesame Street characters and sports themes. Kosher pizza and sushi restaurants have sprung up in cities across the country, even as most American Jews do not consider keeping kosher part of their Jewish identities. Being Jewish in America cannot be defined in singular terms; it spans a range of expressions from religious to secular, cultural to political, spiritual to culinary, familial to communal, artistic to intellectual, committed to indifferent.

Justice Ruth Bader Ginsburg, 2005.
Photograph by Robin Reid, Collection of the Supreme Court of the United States.

For more than a century after the first Jews arrived in what would become the United States in 1654, American Jewry was little more than a tiny outpost on the edge of the Jewish world. Regarded for much of its history as a nation that could not sustain a viable Jewish community, America has become the largest center of Jewish population, harboring a greater range of options for expressing Jewish identity than anywhere else in the world. The United States has drawn Jewish immigrants from around the globe, each adding to the mosaic of American Jewish life. Freely borrowing and adapting from American culture, Jews have molded inherited Jewish practices into American forms. At the same time, Jews have transported their unique ethnic traditions to the United States, adding to and often shaping the contours of American culture. From the outset, Jews in America had the choice of whether and how to be Jewish. Three hundred and fifty years later, it is that freedom to invent, innovate, and create new expressions of Judaism and Jewish culture that best characterizes Jewish experience in America.

Di Kats der Payats, *Yiddish translation of the classic Dr. Seuss children's book,* The Cat in the Hat. *New York: Twenty-Fourth Street Books, LLC, 2003.*

1. Peter I. Rose, "The Ghetto and Beyond," in Peter I. Rose ed., *The Ghetto and Beyond: Essays on Jewish Life in America* (New York: Random House, 1969), p. 12.

2. Deborah Dash Moore, *To the Golden Cities: Pursuing the American Jewish Dream in Miami and L.A.* (New York: The Free Press, 1994), p. 4; Albert Gordon, *Jews in Suburbia* (Boston: Beacon Press, 1959), p. 170.

3. Jonathan D. Sarna, *American Judaism: A History* (New Haven: Yale University Press, 2004), pp. 277–79, 284–88.

4. Edward S. Shapiro, *A Time for Healing: American Jewry Since World War II* (Baltimore: Johns Hopkins University Press, 1992), p. 17; Will Herberg, *Protestant-Catholic-Jew: An Essay in American Religious Sociology* (Garden City, N.Y.: Doubleday, 1955).

5. Patricia Erens, *The Jew in American Cinema* (Bloomington: Indiana University Press, 1984), pp. 170–80; Lester D. Friedman, *Hollywood's Image of the Jew* (New York: Frederick Ungar, 1982), pp. 125–30.

6. Shapiro, *A Time for Healing*, p. 39; Sarna, *American Judaism*, p. 276.

7. Hasia R. Diner, *The Jews of the United States, 1654–2000* (Berkeley: University of California Press, 2004), pp. 261–65, 284; Sarna, *American Judaism*, pp. 293–306.

8. Thomas A. Kolsky, *Jews Against Zionism: The American Council for Judaism* (Philadelphia: Temple University Press, 1983).

9. *American Jewish Yearbook* 53 (1952), pp. 564–68.

10. Moore, *To The Golden Cities*, pp. 248–60.

11. Shapiro, *A Time for Healing*, pp. 206–212.

12. Judith Doneson, *The Holocaust in American Film* (Philadelphia: Jewish Publication Society, 1987), pp. 57–83; Edward T. Linenthal, *Preserving Memory: The Struggle to Make America's Holocaust Museum* (New York: Viking Press, 1995); Peter Novick, *The Holocaust in American Life* (Boston: Houghton Mifflin, 1999).

13. Elie Wiesel, *The Jews of Silence* (New York: Holt, Rinehart and Winston, 1966); Paul S. Appelbaum, "The Soviet Jewry Movement in the United States," in Michael N. Dobkowski, ed., *Jewish American Voluntary Organizations* (Westport, Conn.: Greenwood Press, 1986), pp. 613–38.

14. Ronald Radosh and Joyce Milton, *The Rosenberg File: A Search for Truth* (New York: Holt, Rinehart, and Winston, 1983); Jeffrey M. Marker, "The Jewish Community and the Case of Julius and Ethel Rosenberg. " *Maryland Historian* 3 (Fall 1972), pp. 106–117; Deborah Dash Moore, "Reconsidering the Rosenbergs: Symbol and Substance in Second-Generation American Jewish Consciousness," *Journal of American Ethnic History* 8 (Fall 1988), pp. 21–37; Shapiro, *A Time for Healing*, pp. 35–37.

15. Stuart Svonkin, *Jews Against Prejudice: American Jews and the Fight for Civil Liberties* (New York: Columbia University Press, 1997); Michael E. Staub, *Torn at the Roots: The Crisis of Jewish Liberalism in Postwar America* (New York: Columbia University Press, 2002), pp. 60–61; Susannah Heschel ed., *Moral Grandeur and Spiritual Audacity: Essays of Abraham Joshua Heschel* (New York: Farrar, Straus & Giroux, 1996), p. xxiii.

16. Janice Rothschild Blumberg, *One Voice: Rabbi Jacob Rothschild and the Troubled South* (Macon, Ga.: Mercer University Press, 1985); Mark K. Bauman and Berkley Kalin, eds., *The Quiet Voices: Southern Rabbis and Black Civil Rights, 1880s to 1990s* (Tuscaloosa: University of Alabama Press, 1997).

17. Jonathan Kaufman, *Broken Alliance: The Turbulent Times Between Blacks and Jews in America* (New York: Charles Scribner's Sons, 1988), pp. 86–88, 19, 15–18.

18. Kaufman, *Broken Alliance*, pp. 267–80; Staub, *Torn at the Roots*, pp. 76–111.

19. Eli Lederhendler, *New York Jews and the Decline of Urban Ethnicity, 1950–1970* (Syracuse: Syracuse University Press, 2001), pp. 175–180; Jerald E. Podair, *The Strike that Changed New York: Blacks, Whites, and the Ocean Hill-Brownsville Crisis* (New Haven: Yale University Press, 2002).

20. Betty Friedan, cited in Joyce Antler, *The Journey Home: Jewish Women and the American Century* (New York: The Free Press, 1997), p. 259.

21. Ellen Umanksy quoted in Sylvia Barack Fishman, "The Impact of Feminism on American Jewish Life," *American Jewish Yearbook* 89 (1989), p. 13.

22. Sarna, *American Judaism*, pp. 287–88, 338–44; for the mission statement of the Jewish Orthodox Feminist Alliance, see www.jofa.org.

23. Riv-Ellen Prell, *Prayer and Community: The Havurah in American Judaism* (Detroit: Wayne State University Press, 1989); Richard Siegel, Michael Strassfeld, and Sharon Strassfeld, *The First Jewish Catalog: A Do-It-Yourself Kit* (Philadelphia: Jewish Publication Society of America, 1973).

24. Hank Greenberg, *Hank Greenberg: The Story of My Life*, with Ira Berkow (Chicago: Triumph Books, 2001), pp. 55–59; Shana Alexander, *When She Was Bad: The Story of Bess, Hortense, Sukhreet & Nancy* (New York: Random House, 1990), pp. 15–31; Shapiro, *A Time for Healing*, pp. 8–15.

25. Joyce Antler, "Not 'Too Jewish' for Prime Time," in *Television's Changing Image of American Jews* (New York: The American Jewish Committee and The Norman Lear Center, 2000), pp. 31–35; J. Hoberman and Jeffrey Shandler, eds., *Entertaining America: Jews, Movies and Broadcasting* (New York: Jewish Museum, under the auspices of the Jewish Theological Seminary of America; Princeton: Princeton University Press, 2003), pp. 144–49.

26. Hoberman and Shandler, *Entertaining America*, pp. 244–56, 154; Shapiro, *A Time for Healing*, p. 256; Antler, "Not 'Too Jewish' for Prime Time," pp. 35–38.

27. Antler, "Not 'Too Jewish' for Prime Time," p. 37; Egon Mayer, *Love and Tradition: Marriage Between Jews and Christians* (New York: Plenum Press, 1985); Sylvia Barack Fishman, *Double or Nothing: Jewish Families and Mixed Marriage* (Hanover: Brandeis University Press, 2004).

28. The newspaper *USA Today* saw fit to cover the phenomenon of secular Judaism. See *USA Today*, September 18, 2003.

A WORLD WAR II SOLDIER
WRITES HOME

• JOSEPH FEIVISH •

FOR THE half million American Jews who participated in World War II, military service was a transformative event. In the military, Jews and non-Jews from across the country encountered one another as never before. For many Jews, the World War II experience redefined their identity as Americans and often deepened their sense of themselves as Jews. Some Jewish soldiers confronted the destruction of European Jewish communities firsthand. Others interpreted their war service as both a duty to their country and a campaign against the Nazis who had murdered their fellow Jews.

Twenty-four-year-old Sergeant Joseph Feivish wrote this letter to his parents while stationed in Italy in 1944. By the time he penned this letter, Nazi atrocities had been largely disclosed, but the full realization of the extent of the destruction was just coming to light. Joseph Feivish, an electrician from New York, was the son of immigrants who had come to

America from Poland in 1913. Feivish had married in 1941 before entering the service and like many other GIs, returned to the United States after the war to start a family; he and his wife had two daughters. He resumed his work as an electrician in New York, joining his father in the family business. In this letter, Joseph Feivish relays the story of his encounter with Jewish survivors in Europe and details the profound effect the meeting had on him.

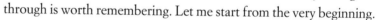

ITALY
Sept., 1944

Dear Folks:

I visited a large city yesterday in which a large number of European Jews sought refuge. These people are fortunate in that they escaped with their lives. Not one family, however, remained untouched. I spoke to numerous refugees, men, women and children. Their plight is over now but what they have gone through is worth remembering. Let me start from the very beginning.

I came into town about nine o'clock in the morning and had until eight o'clock at night to do with as I pleased. I went in with Alfie, who incidentally is Italian and speaks the language 50-50. We roamed around town and saw various sights of historical nature. When we rode into town, I noticed a synagogue and thought it might be a good idea to see what was happening there. I went inside and saw a very respectable Jew walking around, shawl and all. I approached him and asked him in Yiddish if he spoke Yiddish. His reply was a snappy "No Capish." I tried again and still got the same answer. I left slightly disillusioned, but when I got outside I overheard an English soldier speaking Yiddish to a few people. I stuck my two word vocabulary in and the people were overjoyed to see me.

Here I met a very nice woman, I should say about 35 to 40 years old. She had with her two daughters who were the cutest kids you could find. She told me what she went through. Seven years ago, she was forced to leave her home in Poland. For seven long years, she's been roaming from

Sergeant Joseph Feivish during his service in World War II.

Courtesy of Shirley Feivish Caro

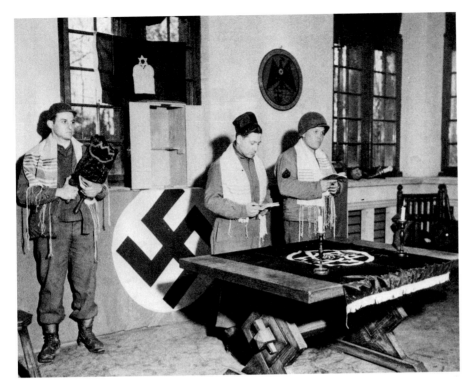

place to place, from country to country in search of freedom. Her husband and only son were killed by the Germans. They were taken as hostages and shot before her very eyes. She related the different times she has seen women and children dragged through the streets like dogs. Taking the men away to labor camps, killing them as hostages and other such barbaric practices are not enough. They have to torture women and children too. This woman had with her a brother-in-law. He is her sister's husband. Now that they are finally free, they are alone and desolate, families broken up and without a home.

Another case is a man I had a long talk with. He too has been without a home for years. He has been in Italy two years and of them 14 months were spent in an Italian prison. Seven months of that time was in solitary confinement. He was on the verge of death. When Mussolini fell, he was freed and he hid until the Allies' arrival. We treated him to a meal in a very nice restaurant and his gratitude was endless. His wife is in Switzerland but he has lost contact with his two children.

We left him a little while after lunch and started to walk along a main street. Here a stranger approached me and asked, "Parlez-vous francais?" After I said yes, he asked if I was Jewish and spoke Yiddish. I was as astonished as he was by the odd meeting. This man is here with his wife and one child. He asked me to try to contact his brother in Chicago to tell him that he is well and alive.

He took me up to his room where his wife and six-year-old daughter were. The kid was like a little doll. Al was talking to her in French while I conversed with the parents. The room was small and dingy. It had a small window with shutters behind them. Seven months these people lived in this room and for 20 days prior to their liberation, none of them left that room for an instant. The shutters were closed tight until the victorious entrance of American soldiers.

That day was like a dream come true for these people. They told no one that they are Jewish for fear of paying the consequences for that alone. This man told me that he was going to declare himself now, with the lady who gave them refuge. Even after he knew he was free, the fear still lingered on his mind. I can't express the joyous expressions on their faces every time I spoke to them. Each word I said meant so much to them.

This day I learned a lot. Not only did I speak more Yiddish than I ever spoke before in a day, but I learned a lot about human nature—good and bad. I learned a lesson that I won't forget.

The day of reckoning will come and those Nazi rats will pay dearly for the misery they have caused. They aren't civilized people as I had previously thought. They are cunning savages. Now, with victory in sight, we must plan for a world in which horror of this type cannot exist. A recurrence of this nature must not overtake the world.

I only hope to come home soon so that we may plan a life with peace and love in a better world.

SGT. JOSEPH FEIVISH

Isaac E. Rontch, *Jewish Youth at War: Letters from American Soldiers* (London: Marstin Press, 1945), pp. 48–50. Reprinted with pride and permission of Shirley Feivish Caro.

COMMENTARY–
A MAGAZINE FOR
POSTWAR JEWRY

• ELLIOT COHEN •

JUST MONTHS after the conclusion of World War II, *Commentary* magazine published its inaugural issue, introducing a new journalistic outlet for a new era in American Jewish history. Sponsored by the American Jewish Committee, *Commentary* was designed as a nonpartisan magazine that would resist parochialism and give voice to a new generation of Jewish intellectual dialogue. The articles in *Commentary* addressed Jewish matters as well as national and international issues. Declaring itself a Jewish magazine, *Commentary* both spoke to an American audience and engaged in broader conversations. In later years, the magazine's perspective shifted to reflect a more conservative outlook. At its founding, *Commentary* brought new energy and creativity to its pages, signaling the intellectual maturity of American Jewry.

Commentary's first editor, Elliot Cohen, was raised in Mobile, Alabama, the son of immigrants who ran a dry cleaning store and nurtured intellectual pursuits. Educated at Yale University, Cohen served in his senior year as president of the Yale chapter of the Menorah Association, a society dedicated to promoting Jewish intellectual concerns on college campuses. After pursuing graduate work in English at Yale, Cohen left to work at the *Menorah Journal*, where he served as managing editor from 1925 until 1931. He assumed editorship of the newly established *Commentary* magazine in 1945, a post he held until his death in 1959. In the first issue of *Commentary*, Cohen outlines the vision that animated the new journal and captures the sense of a new era unfolding for American Jewry.

IT IS TRADITIONAL to begin a new magazine with brave declarations. If we do not, we trust we shall be forgiven.

We begin at a moment heavy with a sense of human destiny. Every school-boy who listens to the radio knows that 1945 marks an epoch in world history. World War II has ended; the United Nations have won the greatest military victory of the ages; yet we stand troubled and hesitant before the glorious era of peace which we have awaited so long, and which now we seem not to know how to deal with.

In war, our country has demonstrated a giant's strength, in production, in cooperation, in planning, in courage. It remains to be seen—and present omens are ambiguous—whether this same giant's strength can be mustered as greatly and as wisely for the arts of peaceful living and the problems of peaceful world governance.

And since August 7, shadowing every moment of our thinking and feeling, there is the fearsome knowledge that through our inventiveness we have unleashed a power that has proved it can end a world war by a single blow, and that only waits to prove that it can—by other well-directed blows—build new, undreamed civilizations, or end the human race. Though ten thousand editorial writers the world over have said it again and again, it is still true: here man faces an ultimate challenge. Here, in its starkest form, we sometimes think, is what the scripture must have meant by the haunting phrase "the knowledge of good and evil."

As Jews, we are of an ancient tradition that, in a very special sense, keeps a vigil with history. We are particularly sensitive to the march of events, perhaps because, as some say ruefully, they have so often marched over us. So, at the least, we share with the rest of humanity the deep unease of breathing air almost visibly clotted with fantastic utopias or unimaginable cataclysms. And, in addition, we suffer our own special questionings, which in all candor, we believe humanity should share with us, possibly for the common good.

As Jews, we live with this fact: 4,750,000 of 6,000,000 Jews of Europe have been murdered. Not killed in battle, not massacred in hot blood, but slaughtered like cattle, subjected to every physical indignity—*processed*. Yes, cruel tyrants did this; they have been hurled down; they will be punished, perhaps. Yes, there were men and women in other lands who raised their voices in protest, who lent helping hands. But we must also record this fact: the voices were not many, the hands were not many. There was a strange passivity the world over in the face of this colossal latter-day massacre of innocents, whether Jews or other "minorities."

Commentary's *first editor Elliot Cohen (1899–1959).*
Courtesy Commentary

And we must face this fact, too: that the kind of thinking and feeling that set loose this nightmare phenomenon still burns high in many countries, and lies latent in all. We have no gauge to measure the potentialities of this great Nazi secret weapon of World War II. But there are many—and they are not guided by personal hurt alone—who believe that here is a force that, in the political and social scene, can wreak destruction comparable to the atomic bomb itself. It was the *ignis fatuus* that lured the German people to their doom. It was the flame of the torch that kindled World War II. To resist it; to learn how to stamp it out; to re-affirm and restore the sense of the sanctity of the human person and the rights of man:—here, too, our world is greatly challenged. How that challenge is to be met is, of course, of particular interest to Jews, but hardly less to all mankind, if there is to be a human future.

At this juncture, in the midst of this turbulence and these whirlwinds, we light our candle, COMMENTARY. Surely here is an act of faith.

It is an act of faith of a kind of which we seem peculiarly capable, we who, after all these centuries, remain, in spite of all temptation, the people of the Book.

We believe in the Word. We believe in study—as a guide to life, for the wisdom it brings to the counsels of men, and for its own sake. We have faith in the intellect, in the visions of visionary men, in the still, small voices of poets, and thinkers, and sages.

COMMENTARY is an act of faith in our possibilities in America. With Europe devastated, there falls upon us here in the United States a far greater share of the responsibility for carrying forward, in a creative way, our common Jewish cultural and spiritual heritage. And, indeed, we have faith that, out of the opportunities of our experience here, there will evolve new patterns of living, new modes of thought, which will harmonize heritage and country into a true sense of at-home-ness in the modern world. Surely, we who have survived catastrophe, can survive freedom, too.

Elliot Cohen, "An Act of Affirmation," *Commentary: A Jewish Review* (November, 1945), pp. 1–2. Reprinted from *Commentary*, November 1945, by permission; all rights reserved.

3

JEWISH MISS AMERICA

• BESS MYERSON •

WHEN BESS Myerson became the first Jewish woman to be crowned Miss America in 1945, she carried with her the collective pride and expectations of the American Jewish community. Born in the Bronx in 1924, Myerson grew up in the leftist Sholom Aleichem Cooperative Houses. The daughter of an immigrant working class family, Myerson was the product of a Jewish neighborhood steeped in radical politics and had spent her childhood attending Yiddish school in the afternoons.

In winning the title of Miss America, Myerson symbolized the ability of American Jews to become fully integrated in American life, although she did experience incidents of anti-Semitism during her participation in the pageant. Myerson earned the adulation of the Jewish community for her staunch refusal to change her name to something that sounded "less Jewish" in order to improve her chances of winning the pageant. After her days as Miss America, Myerson became a regular panelist on game shows such as *I've Got a Secret*, before moving into politics. She served as Commissioner of Consumer Affairs under New York Mayor John Lindsay and directed the mayoral campaign of Ed Koch, later serving as Commissioner of Cultural Affairs in his administration. In 1980, Myerson made an unsuccessful bid for the Senate. In this passage, Myerson recalls the symbolic import that her election as Miss America held within the Jewish community.

IN THOSE WEEKS after the vaudeville tour ended, when I was going out to the bond rallies, speaking at hospitals, performing at meetings, I really thought I was achieving something. At twenty-one I had not yet learned that fame is not the same thing as impact.

Earl Wilson[1] was writing columns about me. Everybody was quoting me. My picture appeared everywhere. I was having what psychiatrists call a "narcissistic high." Loving every minute of the attention and the adulation. Gaining a dangerous confidence in the irresistibility of my charms. Believing what people told me, and worse, believing that *they* believed what they told me.

It was like quicksand to be out there being praised, and I was sinking into it. My father saw that, and he saved me from it.

Right before I left home for the vaudeville tour, he said to me, "Now, Besseleh, don't forget who you are out there."

He was not saying, "Don't forget you're a Myerson." Not my father. He did not have that kind of vanity. He was saying, "Don't forget you're a Jew. Whatever you do will be laid at the feet of your people."

The immediate effect of his warning was to make me all the more afraid of every decision, and all the more docile and dependent with my managers. If I was criticized—as in Wilmington, where some people thought my unglamorous, borrowed fur too

Bess Myerson as Miss America, 1945.
Bettmann/CORBIS

---

[1] Earl Wilson (1907–1987), newspaper columnist, known especially as a Broadway gossip columnist.

dowdy for Miss America—I was filled with anxiety that the local Jews might have been embarrassed by me.

The long-term effect was to protect me against the ravages of my own vanity. To keep my head above the quicksand. To commit my year to something more than my own glory.

At the moment I won, I looked out at the crowd in the Warner Theatre and saw all the Jewish people hugging each other, congratulating each other, as though *they* had won. I wanted to call out to them, "Hey, folks! Look at me! Look at ME! Am I not the victor here?"

My ego trip was shortchanged. On the other hand, I felt thrilled to have made so many strangers so happy. I didn't want to be *their* beauty queen. But if I was— and I surely was—I didn't want to disappoint them.

Bess Myerson posing, 1945.
Library of Congress, Prints and
Photographs Division

4

AMERICA'S RELATIONSHIP TO THE NEW STATE OF ISRAEL

· JACOB BLAUSTEIN ·

IN 1950, just two years after the creation of the State of Israel, Jacob Blaustein, a highly successful businessman, was serving as president of the American Jewish Committee. In that capacity, he traveled to Israel for an historic meeting with Prime Minister David Ben-Gurion. In 1949, Ben-Gurion had called for American Jewish youth to immigrate to Israel, a call that unsettled some members of the American Jewish community. Although American Jews welcomed the establishment of Israel, they wanted assurances that the Israeli government would not interfere in American Jewish affairs or challenge Jewish loyalties to the United States.

During Jacob Blaustein's visit to Israel, Ben-Gurion thanked American Jews for their support of the new nation and reiterated that immigration to Israel was entirely a matter of choice. In his response, printed below, Blaustein underscored that American Jews considered the United States their home and the object of their political loyalty as citizens. His comments reflect the negotiation of Jewish commitments and identities following the establishment of Israel.

⸺

I AM VERY happy, Mr. Prime Minister, to have come here at your invitation and to have discussed with you and other leaders of Israel the various important problems of mutual interest.

This is the second time I have been here since the State of Israel was created. A year and a half ago my colleagues and I, of the American Jewish Committee, saw evidence of the valor that had been displayed, and felt the hopes and aspirations that had inspired the people to win a war against terrific odds. This time, I have witnessed the great achievements that have taken place in the interval and have discussed the plans which point the road upon which the present-day Israel intends to travel.

I find that tremendous progress has been made under your great leadership; but also, as you well know, tremendous problems loom ahead. The nation is confronted with gigantic tasks of reconstruction and rehabilitation, and with large economic and other problems, as is to be expected in so young a state.

I am sure that with your rare combination of idealism and realism, you will continue to tackle these matters vigorously; and that with your usual energy, resourcefulness and common sense, you will be able to overcome them.

Travelling over the country and visiting both old and newly established settlements, it has been a thrill to observe how you are conquering the desert of the Negev and the rocks of Galilee and are thus displaying the same pioneering spirit that opened up the great West and my own country. It has been satisfying to see right on the scene, how well and to what good advantage you are utilizing the support from the American Jewish community. I am sure, too, that the American tractors and other machinery and equipment acquired through the loan granted by the Export-Import Bank will further contribute to the technological development of your country.

But more than that, what you are doing and creating in this corner of the Middle East is of vital importance not only to you and to Jews, but to humanity in general. For I believe that the free and peace-loving peoples in the world can look upon Israel as a stronghold of democracy in an area where liberal democracy is practically unknown and where the prevailing social and political conditions may be potential dangers to the security and stability of the world. What President Truman is intending to do under his Four Point Program, in assisting under-developed peoples to

School children in Camden, New Jersey celebrate the establishment of the State of Israel, May 16, 1948.
Bettmann/CORBIS

improve their conditions and raise their standards of living, you here to a large extent have been doing right along under most difficult conditions and at great sacrifice.

Important to your future, as you recognize, is the United States of America and American Jewry. Israel, of course, is also important to them.

In this connection, I am pleased that Mr. Elath[1] has been here during our stay. As your Ambassador to the United States, he has rendered invaluable service in bringing our two countries and communities closer together.

I thought I knew it even before I came to this country on this trip, but my visit has made it still more clear to me—and as an American citizen and a Jew I am gratified—that the Israeli people want democracy and, in my opinion, will not accept any dictatorship or totalitarianism from within or from without.

Democracy, like all other human institutions, has its faults and abuses are possible. But the strength of a democratic regime is that these faults and these abuses can be corrected without the destruction of human rights and freedoms which alone make life worth living.

There is no question in my mind that a Jew who wants to remain loyal to the fundamental basis of Judaism and his cultural heritage, will be in the forefront of the struggle for democracy against totalitarianism.

The American Jewish community sees its fortunes tied to the fate of liberal

---

[1] Eliahu Elath became the first Israeli ambassador to the United States shortly after David Ben-Gurion declared Israel an independent Jewish nation in 1948.

democracy in the United States, sustained by its heritage, as Americans and as Jews. We seek to strengthen both of these vital links to the past and to all humanity by enhancing the American democratic and political system, American cultural diversity and American well-being.

As to Israel, the vast majority of American Jewry recognizes the necessity and desirability of helping to make it a strong, viable, self-supporting state. This, for the sake of Israel itself, and the good of the world.

The American Jewish Committee has been active, as have other Jewish organizations in the United States, in rendering, within the framework of their American citizenship, every possible support to Israel; and I am sure that this support will continue and that we shall do all we can to increase further our share in the great historic task of helping Israel to solve its problems and develop as a free, independent and flourishing democracy.

While Israel has naturally placed some burdens on Jews elsewhere, particularly in America, it has, in turn, meant much to Jews throughout the world. For hundreds of thousands in Europe, Africa and the Middle East it has provided a home in which they can attain their full stature of human dignity for the first time. In all Jews, it has inspired pride and admiration, even though in some instances, it has created passing headaches.

Israel's rebirth and progress, coming after the tragedy of European Jewry in the 1930's and in World War II, has done much to raise Jewish morale. Jews in America and everywhere can be more proud than ever of their Jewishness.

But we must, in a true spirit of friendliness, sound a note of caution to Israel and its leaders. Now that the birth pains are over, and even though Israel is undergoing growing pains, it must recognize that the matter of good-will between its citizens and those of other countries is a two-way street: that Israel also has a responsibility in this situation—a responsibility in terms of not affecting adversely the sensibilities of Jews who are citizens of other states by what it says or does.

In this connection, you are realists and want facts and I would be less than frank if I did not point out to you that American Jews vigorously repudiate any suggestion or implication that they are in exile. American Jews—young and old alike, Zionists and non-Zionists alike—are profoundly attached to America. America welcomed their immigrant parents in their need. Under America's free institutions, they and their children have achieved that freedom and sense of security unknown for long centuries of travail. American Jews have truly become Americans; just as have all other oppressed groups that have ever come to America's shores.

To American Jews, America is home. There, exist their thriving roots; there, is the country which they have helped to build; and there, they share its fruits and its destiny. They believe in the future of a democratic society in the United States under which all citizens, irrespective of creed or race, can live on terms of equality. They further believe that, if democracy should fail in America, there would be no future for democracy anywhere in the world, and that the very existence of an independent State of Israel would be problematic. Further, they feel that a world in which it would be possible for Jews to be driven by persecution from America would not be a world safe for Israel either; indeed it is hard to conceive how it would be a world safe for any human being.

The American Jewish community, as you, Mr. Prime Minister, have so eloquently pointed out, has assumed a major part of the responsibility of securing equality of rights and providing generous material help to Jews in other countries. American Jews feel themselves bound to Jews the world over by ties of religion, common historical traditions and in certain respects, by a sense of common destiny. We fully realize that persecution and discrimination against Jews in any country will sooner or later have its impact on the situation of the Jews in other countries, but these problems must be dealt with by each Jewish community itself in accordance with its own wishes, traditions, needs and aspirations.

Jewish communities, particularly American Jewry in view of its influence and its strength, can offer advice, cooperation and help, but should not attempt to speak in the name of other communities or in any way interfere in their internal affairs.

I am happy to note from your statement, Mr. Prime Minister, that the State of Israel takes a similar position. Any other position on the part of the State of Israel would only weaken the American and other Jewish communities of the free, democratic countries and be contrary to the basic interests of Israel itself. The future development of Israel, spiritual, social as well as economic, will largely depend upon a strong and healthy Jewish community in the United States and other free democracies.

We have been greatly distressed that at the very hour when so much has been achieved, harmful and futile discussions and misunderstandings have arisen as to the relations between the people and the State of Israel and the Jews in other countries, particularly in the United States. Harm has been done to the morale and to some extent to the sense of security of the American Jewish community through unwise and unwarranted statements and appeals which ignore the feelings and aspirations of American Jewry.

Even greater harm has been done to the State of Israel itself by weakening the readiness of American Jews to do their full share in the rebuilding of Israel which faces such enormous political, social and economic problems.

Your statement today, Mr. Prime Minister, will, I trust, be followed by unmistakable evidence that the responsible leaders of Israel, and the organizations connected with it, fully understand that future relations between the American Jewish community and the State of Israel must be based on mutual respect for one another's feelings and needs, and on the preservation of the integrity of the two communities and their institutions.

I believe that in your statement today, you have taken a fundamental and historical position which will redound to the best interest not only of Israel, but of the Jews of America and of the world. I am confident that this statement and the spirit in which it has been made, by eliminating the misunderstandings and futile discussions between our two communities, will strengthen them both and will lay the foundation for even closer cooperation.

In closing, permit me to express my deep gratitude for the magnificent reception you and your colleagues have afforded my colleague and me during our stay in this country.

Jacob Blaustein, *American Jewish Year Book* 53 (1952) pp. 565–568. Reprinted by permission of the American Jewish Committee.

A DIFFERENCE OF OPINION ON THE DEATH SENTENCE OF JULIUS AND ETHEL ROSENBERG

IN JULY 1950, the Federal Bureau of Investigation arrested Julius Rosenberg and charged him with helping the Soviet Union steal secrets about the atomic bomb from the United States during World War II. Less than a month later, the government also charged his wife Ethel Rosenberg as an accessory to the crime, largely in an effort to elicit a confession from Julius. In 1951, a jury convicted them of conspiracy to commit espionage and the judge imposed the death sentence. Julius and Ethel Rosenberg were executed in June 1953, concluding one of the most controversial episodes in American history.

For American Jews, the trial brought particular challenges. All five of the defendants involved in the Rosenberg affair were Jewish. (Also arrested were Ethel's brother David Greenglass, Harry Gold, and Morton Sobell.) The federal prosecutor and presiding judge were also Jewish, making the trial very much a Jewish concern, deepened further by the long history of Jewish leftist politics. Jewish opinions about the trial, conviction, and death sentence varied widely. Committed leftists maintained that the Rosenbergs were innocent, while members of the Jewish establishment supported the guilty verdict. Some Jewish leaders endorsed the death sentence, urging Jews to distance themselves from communism, but others insisted that even if the Rosenbergs had committed serious crimes, the death penalty was far too severe a punishment. After the verdict, a committee defending the Rosenbergs, supported largely by communists, argued that anti-Semitism had played a role in the conviction, though most Jewish leaders disagreed. The two selections below, written after the verdict but before the execution, reveal dissenting opinions about the death sentence imposed on the Rosenbergs. Lucy Dawidowicz, a leading Jewish historian and regular columnist, vigorously supported both the verdict and the death penalty, while the editors of *The Reconstructionist*, a liberal Jewish magazine, argued that despite the severity of the crime, the Rosenbergs deserved clemency.

Lucy Dawidowicz, "The Rosenberg Case: 'Hate America' Weapon"

COMMUNIST ORGANIZATIONS ALL over the world are directing protests to President Truman on behalf of Ethel and Julius Rosenberg, convicted on March 30, 1951, and sentenced to death for participating in an espionage ring that passed atomic secrets to Russia. After the failure of several appeals, their execution has been scheduled for the week of January 12, 1953. . . .

The Communists demand the Rosenberg's "liberation." They insist on "equal justice" for their "innocent" clients. They charge that anti-Semitism and race prejudice dominated the court proceedings. The trial is a "judicial outrage," an "uncivilized action" and a "blot on American justice. . . ."

The irrelevance of such slogans to the facts is incredible. The fact that the Rosenbergs received a fair trial was confirmed by the Supreme Court *and* by the American Civil Liberties Union, an organization that has been quite frank on many other occasions in criticizing U.S. courts. The evidence presented at the trial was so cumulative that additional testimony by more prosecution witnesses was rendered superfluous. The defendants were proven guilty beyond the slightest doubt of being spies for Soviet Russia. And, finally, the Rosenbergs' legal counsel has *never* pressed *any* of the fantastic charges of the Rosenberg propaganda apparatus. . . .

And let us remember that the purpose of a death penalty is to serve as a deterrent to the future commission of a serious crime.

Editorial, *The Reconstructionist*

The conviction and sentencing of Ethel and Julius Rosenberg have aroused even greater interest than their dramatic trial and the acts of espionage which led to their conviction. . . .

The argument about the anti-Semitic prejudice is most unusual. It cites the fact that the Judge was a Jew as evidence of bias. Fundamentally no other evidence to support this charge is offered save perhaps the fact that a government prosecutor once indicated reservations about his own Jewish identification. This argument makes it appear as if trial by a Jewish judge of a fellow Jew is *prima facie* evidence of bias. But just imagine that a non-Jew had presided; would the Communists not have charged the judge with a more "classic" form of anti-Semitism? It might also be asked, why, if Judge Kaufman were such a Jewish anti-Semite, did he not sentence to death other Jews involved in the case. Why, for example, was the Jew Greenglass given only thirty years, if, as is alleged, the Judge wanted to kill Jews to absolve himself of identification with other Jews of unsavory reputations? The charge of anti-Semitism is preposterous.

Julius and Ethel Rosenberg, separated by heavy wire as they leave the U.S. Court House after being found guilty by the jury.
Library of Congress, Prints and Photographs Division

*Demonstrators protesting the
Rosenberg death sentence,
June 1953.*
Bettmann/CORBIS

None of the foregoing discussion, however, should be construed as meaning that we are opposed to a commutation of [the] sentence on grounds of clemency. Our purpose was merely to free a plea of clemency of all extraneous and fallacious arguments. On grounds of humanity, the right to impose a death sentence for any crime is questioned by many ethical thinkers. And, admitting the guilt of the Rosenbergs, it is hard to see wherein their moral culpability exceeded that of others involved in the espionage to a degree that would warrant the death sentence. True, they did not cooperate with the Government, but are we prepared to say that such non-cooperation should spell the difference between life and death? Would it not be wiser to permit mercy to temper justice? Might not the execution of the Rosenbergs enable the Communists to make martyrs of them? Might it not keep alive the agitation against the court and give plausibility to the lying charges against the justice of American democracy? The final decision is up to the President. We believe that he would not be making a mistake if he listened to the promptings of humane sentiment not only to the letter of the penal code.

Lucy Dawidowicz, "The Rosenberg Case: 'Hate America' Weapon," *The New Leader*, December 22, 1952, p. 13. Reprinted with permission from *The New Leader* of December 22, 1952. All rights reserved.

Editorial, *The Reconstructionist*, January 9, 1953, pp. 5–6. Reprinted with permission of *The Reconstructionist*.

6

PIONEER OF TELEVISION COMEDY

· SID CAESAR ·

SID CAESAR grew up in Yonkers, New York, where his parents owned a lunch counter. At the restaurant, Caesar was surrounded by a variety of immigrant ethnic dialects that would later become a staple of his comedy. He began his career as a musician, studying saxophone at Juilliard and later playing with many well-known bands. After entertaining the troops while serving in the Coast Guard during World War II, Caesar turned his gift for comedy into a career.

Sid Caesar honed his craft in the Catskills, where he perfected the art of linguistic parody, stringing imitations of foreign words together in his own particular brand of gibberish. The gift of pantomime and the skill for poking fun at everyday situations gave Caesar's comedy its unique flair. Paired with producer Max Liebman, Caesar achieved great success in early television, first in the *Admiral Broadway Review*, which adapted the form of Broadway reviews for the small screen, and later with the immensely popular *Your Show of Shows*, which became a fixture of Saturday night television in the early 1950s. With a group of writers who later became leading figures in American comedy, and often paired with the talented comedienne Imogene Coca, Sid Caesar brought his talent for mime and foreign language double-talk to the revue and sketch comedy showcase. An Emmy award-winning comedian, Caesar continued to perform in films such as *It's a Mad, Mad, Mad, Mad World* and *Silent Movie*, appearing on stage and in film through the 1980s.

In this interview, Caesar discusses his acquisition of ethnic dialects and the comedic style he brought to early television.

M Y FATHER HAD a restaurant. He was in the restaurant business for over 60 years, and I used to come at lunchtime. I used to get out of school, which was just up the block, about two blocks . . . I used to come in, and I used to pick up dishes, to help out, like a bus boy. . . . You go to a certain table, they're all Italian. You go to another table, they're all Polish. You go to another table, they're all French. It was a polyglot but they each had their own table. So as I walked around to pick up dishes, I heard them. And they would teach me words, which were the curse words immediately. They teach you the curse words in their language, and I would say, "Well, sounds like— It sounds dirty." So I picked it up there. I had a good ear. . . .

Each language has a song. Like French: *Pardon, monsieur, avec toi dix cents Allons enfants de la patrie, Le jour de gloire n'est-ce pas lalala.* That's it. It sounds French, but it's not.

German is guttural, more guttural. French is you know very singsong. . . . You can work in Yiddish because what Yiddish is, is lowclass German. That's what Yiddish is. *Is gefallen die. . . .* That's German too. *Ken, kommt, kommt.* That's German. . . .

It's funny. . . . I can look at somebody as Italian, go through the same thing; it's going to be funny. It can be Polish; it can be

Sid Caesar playing the saxophone, ca. 1955.
Library of Congress, Prints and Photographs Division

German; it can be Russian, any language. You know what's happening. You're having an argument, and he said something that he didn't mean. That's all. And they [the audience] understand it.

Comedian Sid Caesar, ca. 1955.
Library of Congress, Prints and Photographs Division

[On *Your Show of Shows*], the writing staff [was] Mel Brooks, Neil Simon, Larry Gelbart, Carl Reiner . . . Mike Stewart. And then we had Woody Allen, and Larry Gelbart. They were all Jewish. There was one guy who wasn't. It was Tony Webster. . . . And that was it.

And [we] did [it] live. Live is a different animal than television today. Live television means you get one chance, one shot. That's it. You've rehearsed and rehearsed. We used to do the show five times before we did the show. I mean, we used to run it through, because [it] was an hour and a half. And you used to have to go through it and go through it and make the changes; then you got to make it with the makeup, then you got to make it with the hairdresser and this and that. Now you got to see if you have time in between to make the changes. And if not, then you got to fix something here or there, make it a little longer, or make yours a little shorter. Because once you got on. . . . I said, "Good evening, ladies and gentlemen. Welcome to *Your Show of Shows*. Your host this evening will be so-and-so." . . . That was the start. We never stopped from there on. . . .

Sid Caesar, interview by David Grubin, June 23, 2006.

7

FIFTY YEARS OF COMEDY

• CARL REINER •

CARL REINER began performing in the Catskills, partici-pated in early television sketch comedy, and moved on to sit-coms and films, crafting a career that spanned several decades and a variety of media. Born in 1922, Reiner grew up in an immigrant Jewish household in the Bronx, surrounded by the rhythms of Jewish culture. After serving in the army during World War II, Reiner worked briefly on Broadway before land-ing a job as a writer on Sid Caesar's *Your Show of Shows* in the 1950s. Joining a talented group of writers, Reiner contributed to the show's enormous popularity during the early years of tel-evision. His experience on *Your Show of Shows* provided the material for the *Dick Van Dyke Show*, which Reiner created, based on his own experiences as a comedy writer. Although he originally imagined himself in the leading role, producers pre-ferred Van Dyke as a less ethnic Rob Petrie, casting Reiner as Alan Brady, the egomaniacal star of the fictional comedy show.

Branching out into a variety of comic mediums, Reiner turned his semi-autobiographical novel, *Enter Laughing*, into a successful play, recorded *The 2,000 Year Old Man* with Mel Brooks, and began directing films. His 1970 film *Where's Poppa* became a cult classic and he went on to direct such blockbuster hits as *Oh God!* as well as several Steve Martin films, including *The Jerk, The Man with Two Brains*, and *Dead Men Don't Wear Plaid*. Carl Reiner always borrowed heavily from patterns of Jewish humor and relied on Yiddish inflections, but crafted comedy that would appeal to a wide audience. In 2000, Reiner received the Mark Twain Prize for American Humor. In this interview, Reiner discusses the creation of the 2,000 Year Old Man routine with Mel Brooks and the role of Jewish humor on *Your Show of Shows*.

THE GENESIS OF the 2,000 Year Old Man is interesting because I had seen a program called "We the People Speak." And it was a news program that was dramatized news. It was Dan Seymour saying, "Last week in Russia, somebody heard Stalin say, a plumber in the toilet . . . overheard, 'Going to blow up the world Thursday.'" And I came into the *Show of Shows* office and I said, "Hey, here's a great thing to do." And they say, "Oh, yeah, it's a funny idea," but they couldn't find a way to work it. But I thought it was so good, I turned to Mel [Brooks], "Here's a man who was actually at the scene of the crucifixion 2000 years ago. Isn't that true, sir?"

And Mel said, "Oh boy."

"You were there, yes."

And from that moment on, I realized I had a live one because for the next twenty minutes I interviewed him about Jesus and about who he was. "A thin lad, right, who always wore sandals? Walked with 12 other guys? Came into the store, never bought anything?" He [Mel Brooks] was so quick. And I kept interviewing for years and years, mainly for years and years at parties, in the office, because we were needing some time to be entertained; we were so . . . tired. I would just start, "You know, Cleopatra," whatever it is. He would come up with something. He never knew what I was going to ask him, and I never knew what he was going to say. And there was born the 2000 Year Old [Man].

FROM 1950 TO 1960, we never did it anyplace but at parties. I remember a couple of big . . . dinner parties, people [would] say, "Get up, get up." I took a tape recorder along so I'd have a record of this brilliance that Mel was doing. And the reason we didn't do it anyplace, records started [be]coming hot in 1958, '59, '60. And everyone [said], "You got to do it. You got to put it on a record." And we said, "No, this is for Jews. This is for old friends. It's Jews and our non-anti-Semitic Christian friends. They'll understand." Because the Jewish accent—remember, [the] war had been only over for five years. 1950—it's five years ago that Hitler was using everything to denigrate Jews. And we were going to denigrate ourselves by making fun of our own accent? Jews will understand the Jewish accent. So we never did it anyplace but for friends.

And then one time in Hollywood . . . there was a party. Joe Fields . . . was a producer. Joe Fields did *On the Town*; he'd written and produced. And he was a big fan of [ours]. He made these royal performances. . . . He [would] invite us to dinner and have everybody in the world there, in Hollywood. (We did it in New York once with every major writer and producer.) And now in Hollywood we did the same thing because Mel came out for a visit and he said, "Oh, we got to get together." [At the party], he had all these . . . A-list people. And after we had finished it, . . . it was two Jews who came up to us. One was George Burns. He says, "Fellows, is that on an album? You got an album of that?" We said no. He says, "Better put it on an album. Going to steal it." Actually said it. . . . Eddie G. Robinson came up and said, "Make a play. Make a play out of that. I want to play the thousand-year-old man." I remember him saying "thousand." I said, "It's two thousand." "Well, whatever. Make a play. I'd like to do him on Broadway." And there was Steve Allen, a *sheygets* [a non-Jew], who came up and said, "Hey fellows, you got to make an album out of this." And we said, "No, no. It's really for friends." And he says, "No, look. I'll tell you what. I'll rent a studio, you make the album . . . and it's yours. If you think it's in bad taste, you just take out what you don't think is right, or throw it away." He didn't want to be our partner. He was one of these guys who liked to get fun out there. He did that on his show. He always had comedians on. He wanted to present and he was so excited. He rented a studio at New World Pacific. . . . We got 200 people together and for two hours and twenty minutes or so, I interviewed Mel—never repeated stuff that we ever did before. Any time I asked him the same question, you get different answers.

Carl Reiner and Mel Brooks performing the 2,000 Year Old Man Sketch at ABC's Hollywood Palace, 1966.
Courtesy of Photofest

There was two hours of stuff [and] we cut it down to 47 minutes. And we listened to it and we said, "Well, you know. I don't know." We put it out and it became a hit.

YOUR SHOW OF SHOWS came about because television needed a variety show. Max Liebman, who had worked in the Poconos, in Tamiment, being the producer-director of musical variety shows, knew how to do it. He would do three in a row, three different ones [shows] in a row. Then audience would change, he can do them again. . . . [T]elevision came and they said, "Want to do [it]?" He was ready. He didn't know he could do thirty-nine [shows]. He knew he [could] do three. But if you get enough writers, and remember, the good writers—he was a very good selector. Max Liebman was the reason that the show worked. He knew how to select writers and he collected them.

Because he collected the greatest talent, every writer of note wanted to write for that bunch. When he got Sid Caesar and Imogene Coca, he started with Mel Tolkin, Lucille Kallen, and later Mel Brooks and Joe Stein and, oh, dozens and dozens of other wonderful writers, and one wonderful *goy*, Tony Webster, who was as brilliant and funny as any of these guys. . . . You weren't asked if you were Jewish. You didn't have to be Jewish, but the Jews are the ones who liked this kind of thing and got experience doing these kind of things in the mountains [the Catskills]. So they were brought in to write the sketches. . . .

[W]e knew we're not working for Jews; we're working for an amalgam of races and religions, so we had to translate something that might have been Jewish and make it universal. I do remember Mel talking, saying one of the funniest things ever. Kidding around in the office, he would be the head writer. . . . One of his jobs was to get everybody back on track. "Gentlemen, gentlemen! Do you realize Jews all over America will be tuned in on Sunday? Hundreds of them." He was joking around that the Jews will be tuned, but we weren't writing for just Jews. But that was his joke. Everything that might have a Jewish tinge to it had to be translated for everybody else. It was interesting. Most of these people were second generation Europeans, and so it wasn't hard for them to think in terms of America rather than Jewish America, because they went to school [here, and] we were a melting pot. Yiddish words, we used. But we were very responsible. If a Yiddish word would get a laugh from people in the audience and somebody said, "What are they laughing at," there would [also] be a joke or a physical action. We're very careful about that, not to just contact our friends and say, "Here, we're making you laugh—nobody [else]." Every time there was a Jewish laugh, there was something covering in that. [All] people would laugh. . . .

Carl Reiner, interview by David Grubin, June 22, 2006.

THEOLOGIAN AND ACTIVIST

• A B R A H A M   J O S H U A   H E S C H E L •

BORN IN Warsaw in 1907, Abraham Joshua Heschel received a thorough education in Jewish texts from the time he was a child. Heschel's parents were both descended from eminent Hasidic rabbinic families. After studying at a Vilna gymnasium, Heschel journeyed to Berlin, where he studied at both a secular university and at one of the leading centers of critical Jewish scholarship. Heschel received a visa to come to the United States just months before the Nazis invaded Poland.

Abraham Heschel arrived in the United States in 1940 and first taught at the Reform movement's Hebrew Union College in Cincinnati before taking a position at the Jewish Theological Seminary in New York. A prolific writer, he published a string of theological works, including *Man Is Not Alone, God in Search of Man, The Sabbath*, and *The Earth is the Lord's*. Heschel's personal religious beliefs translated into deep engagement with the issues of his day. A committed activist in the Civil Rights Movement, Heschel maintained a close friendship with Martin Luther King Jr., and joined in the 1965 march in Selma, Alabama. For Heschel, the crusade for Civil Rights was an expression of religious conviction, and he regarded his participation in that light. In the three selections below—a telegram that Heschel sent to President Kennedy, an excerpt from a letter he wrote to Martin Luther King after the Selma march, and an entry in his personal diary after returning from Selma—Heschel frames the Civil Rights Movement and his own participation in religious terms.

Telegram from Abraham Joshua Heschel to President John F. Kennedy, June 16, 1963

I look forward to privilege of being present at meeting tomorrow four pm. Likelihood exists that Negro problem will be like the weather. Everybody talks about it but nobody does anything about it. Please demand of religious leaders personal involvement not just solemn declaration. We forfeit the right to worship God as long as we continue to humiliate Negroes. Church synagogue have failed. They must repent. Ask of religious leaders to call for national repentance and personal sacrifice. Let religious leaders donate one month's salary toward fund for Negro housing and education. I propose that you Mr. President declare state of moral emergency. A Marshall plan for aid to Negroes is becoming a necessity. The hour calls for moral grandeur and spiritual audacity.

Letter from Abraham Joshua Heschel to Martin Luther King Jr., March 29, 1965, After Returning from the March in Selma

The day we marched together out of Selma was a day of sanctification. That day I hope will never be past to me—that day will continue to be this day. A great

Hasidic sage compares the service of God to a battle being waged in war. An army consists of infantry, artillery, and cavalry. In critical moments cavalry and artillery may step aside from the battle-front. Infantry, however, carries the brunt. I am glad to belong to infantry! May I add that I have rarely in my life been privileged to hear a sermon as glorious as the one you delivered at the service in Selma prior to the march.

Reflections on the Selma March in Heschel's Personal Diary

I thought of my having walked with Hasidic rabbis on various occasions. I felt a sense of the Holy in what I was doing. Dr. King expressed several times to me his appreciation. He said, "I cannot tell you how much your presence means to us. You cannot imagine how often Reverend [C.T.] Vivian and I speak about you." Dr. King said to me that this was the greatest day in his life and the most important civil-rights demonstration. . . . I felt again what I have been thinking about for years—that Jewish religious institutions have again missed a great opportunity, namely, to interpret a civil-rights movement in terms of Judaism. The vast majority of Jews participating actively in it are totally unaware of what the movement means in terms of the prophetic traditions.

Rabbi Abraham Joshua Heschel presenting Dr. Martin Luther King, Jr. with "Judaism and World Peace" Award.

American Jewish Historical Society, Newton Centre, Massachusetts and New York, New York

From the Personal Papers of Abraham Joshua Heschel. Documents provided and permission to print granted by Hannah Susannah Heschel, Executor.

FEMINIST PIONEER

• BETTY FRIEDAN •

WHEN BETTY Friedan published *The Feminine Mystique* in 1963, the book became an instant best-seller and a founding text of the American feminist movement, giving voice to the frustrations and emerging demands of a generation of women. Born in Peoria, Illinois in 1921, Friedan graduated from Smith College in 1942 and later studied psychology at the University of California, Berkeley. After marrying in 1947 and having three children, Friedan began to explore the isolation of suburban housewives who found their ambitions thwarted by a society that insisted they feel fulfilled only as wives and mothers. Friedan argued that in the postwar era, suburban women had been robbed of their independent identities. Although her own Jewish identity was not a central focus of the book, Friedan did (problematically) describe women's suburban existence as a "comfortable concentration camp."

Friedan emerged as a leading figure in the American feminist movement, a founder and the first president of the National Organization for Women. She made a career of writing and teaching about feminism and women's experiences. Later in life, Betty Friedan began to deepen her knowledge of Judaism and Jewish culture. She reflects here on her Jewish background and the evolution of her own Jewish identity.

I DIDN'T HAVE a very Jewish growing up since I was raised in Peoria, Illinois, where there were relatively few Jews. There was one other girl my age who was Jewish, and one boy—his mother told him he had to dance with me at dancing school, so naturally we hated each other. And yet I see it was a very strong factor in my growing up in the sense that it made life a little miserable, because there was covert anti-Semitism. It was the uncomfortable kind of anti-Semitism. It made me an outsider.

I remember very distinctly that it was first oppressive to me when I was in high school. Sororities and fraternities dominated social life in this Midwestern town. All my friends got into sororities and fraternities and I didn't because I was Jewish. So I was isolated then, and I spent much more time reading poetry alone on gravestones in the cemetery than I would have liked to do.

I would have much rather hung out in the hamburger joint, in somebody's jalopy, or with the gang. So being Jewish made me an observer, a marginal person and, I made one of those unconscious vows to myself: "They may not *like* me but they're going to look up to me." Although it was many years before I identified in any way with feminism, I think my passion against injustice came from my experience of being a Jew in Peoria.

I wouldn't be the first of our people to have taken the experience of injustice, the passion against injustice, which, if it's not in our genes, is certainly a product of centuries of experience, and applied it to the largest human category of which one is a part. Jews have been very, very present in centuries of revolutions against one form of injustice or another, one form of oppression or another. . . .

WE DIDN'T HAVE that sense of authenticity from our Jewish experience if we grew up as I did in an assimilated, almost anti-Jewish community. There was the fixing of noses, the changing of names.

I remember becoming very strongly aware of this at Smith. There were four wealthy Jewish girls from Cincinnati in the house where I lived in 1939. There was a petition to the president of the U.S. to open immigration, to relax the quotas that were keeping persecuted people out. The president of Smith College indicated that he would open the doors of the college to women escaping Nazi persecution.

It was my freshman year at Smith, and at the discussion in the house meeting about whether to support the petition a few obviously liberal young women spoke up for this, and the Jewish girls, the upper class, were silent. I was new, but I spoke up for it, of course. It didn't pass. But the petition was left on the hall table, so anyone could sign it individually, and it was on the hall table for four days. I signed it, and these two or three WASP girls signed it. Every day I'd come in from the library or wherever, and I'd look at that petition to see if the girls from Cincinnati had signed it, and they hadn't. . . .

I THINK THAT in a certain sense, my experience as a Jew informed, though unconsciously, a lot of the insights that I applied to women, and the passion that I applied to the situation of women. But then, conversely, the sense of breaking through to your authentic self as a woman prepared me when I began to experience the new form of anti-Semitism in the international women's conferences: the "Zionism as racism"

Betty Friedan, ca. 1960.
Library of Congress, Prints and Photographs Division

form. And I was outraged and appalled. I realized that many of the communist nations, the third-world despotisms, and the neo-fascist nations didn't want their women messing around with women's rights. They had to give lip service to this meeting of the U.N., but they certainly didn't want anything to really happen there. So having a resolution of Zionism as racism did manage to disrupt and preempt the airways and prevent the women of the world from getting together on their own rights; and that kind of red herring outraged me both as a Jew and a feminist.

After the eruption of anti-Semitism at the U.N. I began to speak out as a Jew. Also, within the women's movement I began to make the links with my Jewish experience and my own identity, and I began to get more interested even in theology. For those of us who grew up in an intellectual, secular environment, our intellectual map simply did not include theology. It was a desert when it came to spiritual values. Our spiritual values were political values.

However, my feminism has led me to an unabashed sense of the unity of spirit and political values. Now, four months of the year I'm a visiting distinguished professor at the University of Southern California. And when I'm there, I'm part of a Jewish study group. I have a sense of wanting to know more about the mystery of being Jewish and about a theology that is not pie-in-the-sky and heaven after you're dead.

In my generation of feminists a lot of feminist leadership came from people who happened to be Jewish, though we weren't religious Jews. But the next generation took this taste for authenticity and embraced their Jewish identity. They then immersed themselves—some became rabbis because our new authenticity made us embrace our Judaism rather than deny it or evade it or weaken it. But then, if you are a woman, that brings you right into confrontation with the feminine mystique and the put-down of women in the Jewish world.

I love what the new young women rabbis are imparting to Judaism and bringing into this field—definitions based on female experience, not just male experience.

"Jewish Roots: An Interview with Betty Friedan," *Tikkun: A Monthly Jewish Critique of Politics, Culture and Society* Vol. 3: 1 (Jan/Feb, 1988), pp. 25–29. Reprinted by permission from *Tikkun: A Bimonthly Interfaith Critique of Politics, Culture & Society.*

10

DUAL IDENTITIES

• JULIUS LESTER •

AN AFRICAN American who converted to Judaism, Julius Lester has been a member of both communities, and his diverse career led him to participate in many of the pivotal events of his time. Born in St. Louis in 1939, Lester received his bachelors degree in English from Fisk University in 1960 and began his career as a musician. After moving to New York, Lester hosted radio and television talk shows where he covered the tense days of the Ocean Hill-Brownsville teachers' strike, an event that brought Jews and African Americans into conflict. An active participant in the Civil Rights Movement, Lester worked as a photographer for the Student Nonviolent Coordinating Committee (SNCC), taking photographs in Mississippi and Alabama in the late 1960s.

A writer throughout his life, Lester has published more than thirty books, both fiction and nonfiction, for both children and adults, garnering numerous awards. His works include: *Lovesong: Becoming A Jew* (1988), a chronicle of his spiritual odyssey to Judaism; *Othello: A Novel* (1995), a novelization of the Shakespeare play; and *Day of Tears: A Novel in Dialogue* (2005), that dramatizes a slave auction. Lester has also compiled volumes of African American and Jewish folktales. His *Long Journey Home: Stories from Black History* (1972), was a National Book Award finalist. He served briefly on the faculty of the New School for Social Research and spent many years as a professor at the University of Massachusetts.

In this interview, Julius Lester describes his highly controversial radio broadcast that included the reading of an anti-Semitic poem during the Ocean Hill-Brownsville strike. He also reflects on his conversion to Judaism.

OCEAN HILL-BROWNSVILLE was one of the areas where they had turned control of the schools over to the community in terms of curriculum. 1968 was also the height of Black Power and so there was certainly a lot of emphasis in Ocean Hill-Brownsville on black history, black culture, and teaching from another point of view. So I went to Ocean Hill-Brownsville. I was working for radio station WBAI. I kept reading these things in the paper about anti-Semitism in Ocean Hill-Brownsville. So I went out to see for myself as a reporter for WBAI.

What I found in the school was that there were Jewish teachers still in the school, which certainly had not been clear to me from newspaper reports about it, and the Jewish teachers in the school were certainly supporting community control and what was being taught. I met Les Campbell, and Les Campbell was teaching history in the school. He was a very big man, very, very gentle; very, very soft-spoken. I was really very taken with Les. WBAI was a community radio station . . . and part of what we did at the station was to give access to the media to people who did not have access to the media. . . . I didn't think that Les had been heard from his own point of view. So I invited him on my show. I had a show called, "The Great Proletarian Culture Revolution," and so I invited Les on the show.

Julius Lester, ca. 1987.
Photograph by Stan Sherer

Before we went on the air, Les showed me some poems that a girl in his class had written him, and one of those poems was, "Hey there, Jew boy, you with that yarmulke on your head. Hey there, Jew boy, I wish you were dead." I wanted listeners to know what response was coming from students, in terms of the kind of vitriol that was being spoken about community control. So I asked Les to read the poem on the air. And Les looked at me and he said, "Man, are you crazy?" And I said, I said, "No, I want you, I want people to know that this is one reaction that one black child is having to it." And so Les read the poem on the air and I explained to my listeners that I didn't mean to offend anybody but this is part of the reality of the present situation which you should know about. I took phone calls on the air about the poem and then the next week I played the poem again and took phone calls on the air, because I wanted to give everybody a chance to express their opinion and their views about it. Then the third week I played the poem and nobody called, so I thought it was done with; the incident was done.

The next thing I knew, there was a front page story in the *New York Times* about the playing of an anti-Semitic poem on the air—that the teachers union, the American Federation of Teachers, had filed a complaint with the FCC about the playing of an anti-Semitic poem on the air. The next thing I knew, I was being known as the number one anti-Semite in the country. What was bad about the incident was that the *New York Times* never called me to interview me about why I had done it; no Jewish newspaper called me about why I had done it. I think WCBS in New York was the only station that came and talked to me about it. Teachers union [president] Albert Shanker never said a word to me about anything [or asked], "Why did you do this." So it was clear to me that the teachers union was using this as a weapon in terms of their fight against community control of schools.

I felt playing the poem on the air was important because people don't realize that when children become the object of animosity (and a child identifies with its school, with its teachers) and nobody stops to think about what impact is this having on the children? I felt particularly angry that the AFT, the American Federation of Teachers, the teachers union, that the teachers would not think about what is this doing to the kids. They were protecting their turf which is what unions do, but children are involved in this. There were things being said on picket lines to children going to school, racist things being said and this was being reported in the papers. This was one child's response to this. I just felt it's important for people to know that this is one child's response. This is how one child is expressing her anger and her hurt. You want us to listen to you; you listen to this. They're both ugly, but that's the reality. Certainly I'm a fanatic about the First Amendment and so let every voice be heard.

I was certainly angry at the time, but I was angry in a political context. Airing the poem was one way to express the anger that was also there in the black community. My anger was not a personal antagonism and it certainly was an honest anger and I don't think it was anti-Semitic.

What saved me during that time [was that] the Jews who knew me supported me. The people who knew me personally, the people who had heard the radio shows in question, understood what I was doing. A lot of those people, a lot of my closest friends in New York, were Jews, and those were the people who stood by me.

I wanted people to talk to each other. That was one of things that my radio show was about. I'm going to put on the air black attitudes that you won't read about in the *New York Times* or anyplace else. These are things that are going on in the black community; these are things that black people are thinking that you don't know about. I wanted people to talk to each other. I wanted people to listen to each other.

I BEGAN TO study Judaism [in preparation for a course I was going to teach] and everything I'd been looking for in a religion was there. I'd grown up as the son of a minister, but I had really rejected Christianity. Christianity simply did not meet my spiritual need. In Judaism, I found a religion that was focused on expression of gratitude rather than an emphasis upon sin, a religion where to study was a way of praying, a religion in which people prayed in song. And it was a very sensible religion. It was a religion which you could ask questions. It wasn't a religion where you had to have faith and accept things on the basis of faith. You could question; you could argue; you could disagree. I opened [my course on Blacks and Jews: A comparative Study of Oppression at the University of Massachusetts] with about four or five lectures on the history of Judaism. I began to read what I would call at the time the Old Testament, which I later knew as Torah. I really became very interested in Judaism from preparing that particular course.

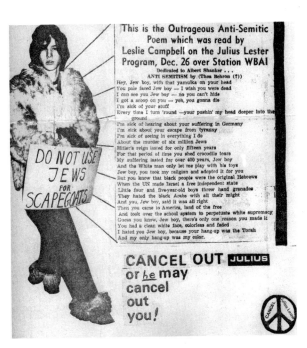

Leaflet protesting the anti-Semitic poem read by Leslie Campbell on Julius Lester's radio program, 1968.
Jewish Defense League, http://www.jdl.org

[When I was about seven years old] my father told [me] the story that my great grandfather was a Jew, Adolph Altschul. Adolph Altschul was the father of my grandmother and my uncle, my great-uncle. And that did something for me, and I wondered, even at age seven, I wondered. . . . That was something that had been there [since childhood] and I remember when I heard on the radio that Sammy Davis Jr., had converted to Judaism, a voice inside me said, "I'm going to do that one day." These things aren't rational and so there's no rational explanation, but because they aren't rational, doesn't mean they aren't real. There was that thread. I was certainly aware of this pull toward Judaism but I really had no meaning to go with it until I began studying in '79.

My father died in August of 1981. About six months after my father died, I had a vision. I have these kind of experiences about once a decade; I hear a voice. [But] this was the first vision I'd had. The vision was that I was a Jew. . . . I decided I would wait on this; I wasn't going to act on this immediately. I waited a couple of weeks and the joy was still there. And so then I called up Yechiel Lander [a rabbi in Amherst, Massachusetts] and told him that I thought I wanted to become a Jew. I studied with him for a year and that was it. The conversion experience was interesting because part of it was terrifying. I did not know what I was doing. I knew I had to do it, but why I was doing it I had no clue. And there were moments when I really wanted to stop and not do it, but I was at a place where I knew I couldn't go back and so I just had to go forward.

The question afterward became, where do I fit in the Jewish world? How do I fit into the Jewish world? I remember the first time I went to services was during that year. It was Yom Kippur and there were moments when I wasn't conscious of myself as a black person, but there were moments when I could be up above myself and see myself as the one black person and [ask myself], "What am I doing here?" It just made no sense at all. But I knew I had to do it and so I had to find my way into the Jewish world.

When I think about identity, when people certainly ask me, "Do you feel more black or do you feel more Jewish? Do you describe yourself as a black Jew or a Jewish black?" My response to that is, I'm me. I'm comprised of many parts. One of those parts is Jewish; one of those parts is being black. They exist in different realms. I refuse to limit myself by any of those ordinary definitions that people use to identify themselves. [Walt] Whitman said it best. "I encompass multitudes." And in my case, that's probably literally true, I encompass multitudes.

Julius Lester, interview by David Grubin, September 14, 2006.

THE JEWISH AMERICANS

11

REFLECTIONS OF AMERICA'S FIRST WOMAN RABBI

• SALLY PRIESAND •

WOMEN HAVE always participated actively in American Jewish religious life, predominating in the pews of synagogues, shouldering primary responsibility for maintaining observance in the home, and gradually asserting themselves in public leadership roles. While Jewish women in America performed valuable behind the scenes work in synagogue sisterhoods and a few exceptional women even preached from the pulpit on occasion, no woman officially served as a rabbi until the Reform movement ordained Sally Priesand in 1972.

By the 1960s, Jewish women had gained access to higher secular education in unprecedented numbers, and in many denominations had been given both significant Jewish education and increased participation in the synagogue. This generation of Jewish women, influenced by the feminist movement and committed to Jewish life, was the first to seek equal rights in all areas of Jewish practice, including the right to become rabbis.

Born in Cleveland, Ohio, Sally Priesand earned both a B.A. in English from the University of Cincinnati and degrees in Hebrew letters from the Hebrew Union College-Jewish Institute of Religion, the Reform movement's seminary. Although previous female applicants had been denied admission to rabbinical school by the institution, the Reform movement decided that the time had come to ordain women as rabbis and admitted Priesand to the entering class in 1968. Overcoming many obstacles, Sally Priesand became America's first woman rabbi in 1972. The Reconstructionist movement, which admitted women immediately when it opened its doors in 1968, ordained its first woman two years later, and the Conservative movement followed in 1985.

Sally Priesand began her rabbinic career at the Stephen Wise Free Synagogue in New York City and currently serves as rabbi emirita of Monmouth Reform Temple in New Jersey. She published the following account of her experience in 1975, just a few years after her ordination.

⌐⌐

ON JUNE 3, 1972 I was ordained rabbi by Hebrew Union College-Jewish Institute of Religion in Cincinnati, Ohio. As I sat in the historic Plum Street Temple, waiting to accept the ancient rite of *s'micha* (ordination), I couldn't help but reflect on the implications of what was about to happen. For thousands of years women in Judaism had been second-class citizens. They were not permitted to own property. They could not serve as witnesses. They did not have the right to initiate divorce proceedings. They were not counted in the *minyan*. Even in Reform Judaism, they were not permitted to participate fully in the life of the synagogue. With my ordination, all that was going to change; one more barrier was about to be broken.

When I entered HUC-JIR, I did not think very much about being a pioneer. I knew only that I wanted to be a rabbi. With the encouragement and support of my parents, I was ready to spend eight years of my life studying for a profession that no woman had yet entered. My decision was an affirmation of my belief in God, in the worth of each individual, and in Judaism as a way of life. It was a tangible action declaring my commitment to the preservation and renewal of our tradition.

As one would expect, there were problems even as I worked toward ordination. Though Reform Judaism had long before declared an official religious equality between men and women, Reform Jews still believed that a woman's place was in the home. They no longer insisted that men and women sit separately during worship services. They allowed women to be counted in the *minyan,* to conduct the service, to serve as witnesses on ritual matters. They demanded that girls receive a religious education equivalent to that provided for boys. They allowed women to become members of the congregation with the privilege of voting and they even permitted them to be elected to offices on synagogue boards. But they were not yet ready for the spiritual leadership of a woman.

Undoubtedly, many believed that I was studying at HUC-JIR to become a *rebbetzin* rather than a rabbi, to marry rather than to officiate. Four years passed (while I

Rabbi Sally Priesand at her ordination as a rabbi, 1972.
The Jacob Rader Marcus Center of the American Jewish Archives

concentrated on my studies at the University of Cincinnati) before people began to realize that I was serious about entering the rabbinate. During that time, I felt that I had to do better than my classmates so that my academic ability would not be questioned. Professors were fair, but occasionally I sensed that some of them would not be overly upset if I failed. And when, in my fifth year, I was ready to serve my first congregation as student rabbi, some congregations refused to accept my services. Still the members of Sinai Temple in Champaign, Illinois, received me warmly.

My sixth year of study brought the beginning of a tremendous amount of publicity. When you are a "first," you are expected to be an expert in everything. Personal appearances, interviews, statements on contemporary issues—all are expected. Surprisingly enough, though I have always considered myself an introvert, I somehow managed to cope with these new pressures. It helped to know that by this time I had the support, or at least the respect, of most of the members of the college community. Dr. Nelson Glueck, the late president of HUC-JIR, was a particular source of strength. His courage in accepting me as a rabbinic student made possible my eventual ordination.

As my eighth and final year drew to a close, I was faced with finding a job. Some congregations refused to interview me. I was disappointed and somewhat discouraged by these refusals. But since I had not expected everyone to welcome me with open arms, I had prepared myself for this possibility. I knew that I needed only one acceptance and I never really doubted that I would find one synagogue ready to accept me.

The offer of a position as assistant rabbi at the Stephen Wise Free Synagogue in New York City was a blessing in the true sense of the word. . . . The only area in which people have shown any real hesitancy has been that of my officiating at funerals.

In addition to my congregational responsibilities, I have lectured extensively throughout the country—an activity which has shown me that congregations and rabbis are ready for change. Ten years ago, women were much more opposed to the idea of a woman rabbi than were men. Since then, however, the feminist movement has made a tremendous contribution in terms of consciousness-raising, and women now demand complete and full participation in synagogue life. This is a significant development because changes will not be made until we change the attitudes of people.

Men and women must learn to overcome their own psychological and emotional objections and regard every human being as a real person with talents and skills and with the option of fulfilling his or her creative potential in any way he or she finds meaningful. Women can aid this process—not by arguing but by doing and becoming, for accomplishments bring respect and respect leads to acceptance. Women must now take the initiative. They should seek and willingly accept new positions of authority in synagogue life.

It is still too soon to assess the impact of my ordination, but I would hope that it would at least mark a transition in our congregations, that sole involvement on the part of women in the synagogue kitchen and the classroom should move toward complete and full participation on the pulpit and in the boardroom as well.

Sally Priesand, *Judaism and the New Woman* (New York: Behrman House, 1975), pp. xiii–xv, xv–xvi. Reprinted with permission of the author.

12

JEWISH FEMINIST PIONEERS

• E Z R A T   N A S H I M •

IN THE early 1970s, as the Reform movement was about to ordain Sally Priesand as the first woman rabbi, Jewish feminism was beginning to come into its own as an organized movement. In the Conservative movement, women had begun participating in an increasing number of ritual practices in many synagogues, but full equality in religious life had yet to be achieved. At the same time, many college-educated Jewish women who had grown up in Conservative synagogues were becoming feminists. These women retained strong Jewish identities and wanted to become full participants in Jewish life.

In 1972, a group of young Jewish women organized to bring feminist concerns to the Conservative movement, calling themselves *Ezrat Nashim*—a phrase that literally means "women's help," but is also the term for the women's section in the ancient Temple and the women's gallery in synagogues. Demanding the elimination of the subordinate treatment of women in Jewish marriage and divorce laws and insisting upon equal access to leadership roles and ritual practices in Conservative Judaism, the women of *Ezrat Nashim* forcefully inserted feminism on the agenda of the Conservative movement. They disseminated their "Call for Change" to the press, which ran with the story, and placed the document in the packets of all those attending the annual convention of the Rabbinical Assembly in 1972. Using the tactics of lobbying and protest learned in the secular feminist movement, Jewish women brought the campaign for women's rights to the Jewish community.

Women and men praying together in an egalitarian minyan *(prayer quorum) at the Jewish Theological Seminary, ca. 1991–1992. Photograph by Alan S. Orling.*

Courtesy of the Ratner Center for the Study of Conservative Judaism, Jewish Theological Seminary.

Jewish Women Call for Change

THE JEWISH TRADITION regarding women, once far ahead of other cultures, has now fallen disgracefully behind in failing to come to terms with developments of the past century.

Accepting the age-old concept of role differentiation on the basis of sex, Judaism saw woman's role as that of wife, mother, and home-maker. Her ritual obligations were domestic and familial: *nerot* [lighting candles], *challah* [performing a required ritual when preparing challah], and *taharat ha-mishpachah* [keeping family purity]. Although the woman was extolled for her domestic achievements, and respected as the foundation of the Jewish family, she was never permitted an active role in the synagogue, court, or house of study. These limitations on the life-patterns open to women, appropriate or even progressive for the rabbinic and medieval periods, are entirely unacceptable to us today.

The social position and self-image of women have changed radically in recent years. It is now universally accepted that women are equal to men in intellectual capacity, leadership ability and spiritual depth. The Conservative movement has tacitly acknowledged this fact by demanding that their female children be educated alongside the males—up to the level of rabbinical school. To educate women and deny them the opportunity to act from this knowledge is an affront to their intelligence, talents, and integrity.

As products of Conservative congregations, religious schools, the Ramah Camps, LTF [Leadership Training Fellowship], USY [United Synagogue Youth], and the Seminary [Jewish Theological Seminary of America], we feel this tension acutely. We are deeply committed to Judaism, but cannot find adequate expression for our total needs and concerns in existing women's social and charitable organizations, such as Sisterhood, Hadassah, etc. Furthermore, the single woman—a new reality in Jewish life—is totally excluded from the organized Jewish community, which views women solely as daughters, wives, and mothers. The educational institutions of the Conservative movement have helped women recognize their intellectual, social and spiritual potential. If the movement then denies women opportunities to demonstrate these capacities as adults, it will force them to turn from the synagogue, and to find fulfillment elsewhere.

It is not enough to say that Judaism views women as separate but equal, nor to point to Judaism's past superiority over other cultures in its treatment of women. We've had enough of apologetics: enough of Bruria, Dvorah, and Esther; enough of *eshet hayil* [Woman of Valor]!

It is time that:

> women be granted membership in synagogues
> women be counted in the minyan [prayer quorum]
> women be allowed full participation in religious observances—*aliyot* [the honor of being called to the Torah] *baalot keriah* [Torah readers], *shelihot zibbur* [leaders of prayer for the congregation]
> women be recognized as witnesses before Jewish law
> women be allowed to initiate divorce
> women be permitted and encouraged to attend Rabbinical and Cantorial schools, and to perform Rabbinical and Cantorial functions in synagogues

women be encouraged to join decision-making bodies, and to assume
professional leadership roles, in synagogues and in the general
    Jewish community
women be considered as bound to fulfill all *mitzvoth* equally with men

For three thousand years, one-half of the Jewish people have been excluded from full participation in Jewish communal life. We call for an end to the second-class status of women in Jewish life.

Ezrat Nashim's "Call for Change" presented to the Rabbinical Assembly of the Conservative movement on March 14, 1972. Reprinted by permission from the personal archive of Paula Hyman.

13

THE FREEDOM SEDER

• ARTHUR WASKOW •

IN APRIL, 1969, approximately 800 people—both Jews and Christians, whites and African Americans—gathered together in the basement of a black church in Washington, D.C., to celebrate the first Freedom Seder. In 1969, Passover fell on the first anniversary of the assassination of Martin Luther King Jr., and Arthur Waskow devised a new Haggadah to mark the occasion. The text blended traditional passages from the Haggadah with the words of Martin Luther King, Gandhi, Nat Turner, and others. One of the most important innovations of the burgeoning Jewish counterculture movement, the Freedom Seder used a traditional Jewish text that celebrated the liberation of the Jewish people and made it relevant to other struggles for liberation occurring in the 1960s. The event received widespread media attention and stirred some controversy, but the Freedom Seder's creative mining of Jewish tradition to address contemporary issues sparked scores of future innovations in Jewish liturgy.

Arthur Waskow, born in Baltimore in 1933 and educated at Johns Hopkins University and the University of Wisconsin, worked as a legislative assistant on Capitol Hill and as a senior fellow at the Peace Research Institute. He was also one of the founders and a longtime fellow of the Institute for Policy Studies. Ordained as a rabbi in the mid-1990s, Waskow has been one of the pioneers of the Jewish renewal movement, founder and director of the Shalom Center, a Jewish institute committed to spirituality, social justice, and environmental issues. Waskow has taught religion at several universities and at the Reconstructionist Rabbinical College. His publications include *Godwrestling, Seasons of Our Joy*, and *Godwrestling Round Two*. In this selection, Rabbi Waskow reflects upon the events that led to the Freedom Seder.

IT BEGAN JUST minutes before Passover in April, 1968. I was 34 years old, had grown up in a Jewish neighborhood in Baltimore with a strong sense that community, neighborhood itself, was warmly Jewish; that freedom and justice were profoundly, hotly Jewish—and that Jewish religion was boring boiler-plate. Except for celebrating the Passover Seder, which brought family, community, freedom, and justice into the same room, I had long ago abandoned the rhythms of Jewish religion.

And then on April 4, 1968, Martin Luther King was murdered.

I was not just a spectator to his passionate life and death. I had spent nine years in Washington working day and night against racial injustice and the Vietnam War—behind a typewriter on Capitol Hill and at the microphone on countless college campuses, sitting in unbearably hot back rooms of Convention Hall in Atlantic City in 1964 when Dr. King came hobbling on a broken leg to beg support for the

First Freedom Seder, April 4, 1969. Left to Right: Rev. Channing Phillips, Arthur Waskow, Colin ("Topper") Carew.
Photograph courtesy of Arthur Waskow.

Mississippi Freedom Democratic Party, marching in 1967 at the Pentagon against the Vietnam War, cruising D.C. streets in a sound truck (with my four-year-old son perched next to me), to turn out votes for Bobby Kennedy in 1968.

On the evening of April 3, Dr. King spoke to a crowd in Memphis: "I am standing on the mountaintop, looking into the Promised Land. I may not reach there, but the people will." Echoes of Moses. By the next night, he was dead.

By noon the next day, Washington, my city, was ablaze. Touch and go it was, whether 18th Street—four houses from my door—would join the flames. Just barely, our neighborhood's interracial ties held fast.

By April 6, there was a curfew. Thousands of Blacks were being herded into jail for breaking it. No whites, of course; the police did not care whether whites were on the streets. My white friends and I tried to turn their blindness to good use: For days we brought food, medicine, doctors from the suburbs into the schools and churches of burnt-out downtown Washington.

And then came the afternoon of April 12. That night, Passover would begin. We would gather—my wife and I, our son, our daughter (just nine months old), with a few friends, for the usual ritual recitation of the Telling of our freedom. Some rollicking songs. Some solemn invocations. Some memories from Seders of the past, in the families where our fathers had chanted—some of them in Hebrew or Yiddish, some in English.

A bubble in time, a bubble isolated from the life, the power, the volcano of the streets. Perhaps, when the rituals were over and the kids had been initiated into the age-old ritual, had taken their first look into this age-old mirror in which Jews saw ourselves as a band of runaway slaves, we might put aside the ancient book and talk about the burning—truly, burning—issues of our lives.

Pharaoh's Army

So I walked home to help prepare to celebrate the Seder. On every block, detachments of the Army. On 18th Street, a Jeep with a machine gun pointing up my block.

Somewhere within me, deeper than my brain or breathing, my blood began to chant; "This is Pharaoh's army, and I am walking home to do the Seder."

> *"This is*
> *Pharaoh's*
> *army,*
> *and I am walking home*
> *to do*
> *the Seder.*
> *This is*
> *Pharaoh's*
> *Army . . . "*

King's speech came back to me. "Standing on the mountaintop, looking into the Promised Land. . . . " The songs we had sung in Atlantic City four years before with Fannie Lou Hamer, who had come from a Mississippi sharecropper's shack to confront the Democratic Party: "Go tell it on the mountain, let my people go!" "Must be the people that Moses led, let my people go!" The sermons I had heard Black preachers speak, half shouting, half chanting: "And on the wings of eagles I will bring you, from slavery, from bondage, yes!—from slavery, to be My people—yes, my beloved people."

Yes, this *is* Pharaoh's army, and I am walking home to do the Seder.

Not again, not ever again, a bubble in time. Not again, not ever again, a ritual recitation before the real life, the real meal, the real conversation.

For on that night, the Haggadah itself, the Telling of our slavery and our freedom, became the real conversation about our real life. The ritual foods, the bitterness of the bitter herb, the pressed-down bread of everyone's oppression, the wine of joy in struggle, became the real meal.

For the first time, we paused in the midst of the Telling itself, to connect the streets with the Seder. For the first time, we noticed the passage that says, "In every generation, one rises up to become an oppressor"; the passage that says, "In every generation, every human being is obligated to say, we ourselves, not our forebears only, go forth from slavery to freedom."

In every generation. Including our own. Always before, we had chanted these passages and gone right on. Tonight we paused. Who and what is our oppressor? How and when shall we go forth to freedom?

To my astonishment, these questions burned like a volcano within me, erupting like the volcano in my city. Why did I care to make this connection? Why was this ancient tale having such an effect on me? How could I respond?

What's a Midrash[1]?

During the next six months, over and over when I faced some crisis in the world, some element of the Jewish story erupted inside me—often in my forebrain only dimly understood, yet with such volcanic power in my heart and belly that I could not turn away. In the fall, I found myself preparing for the next Passover by writing a Haggadah of my own, a script for our own family Seder. I hoped it would deliberately make happen in the future what had already happened, with no deliberation, in the midst of turmoil. I dug out my old Haggadah, the one I had been given when I turned 13, the one with Saul Raskin's luscious drawings of the maidens who saved Moses from the river, the one that stirred my body each spring, those teen-age years. Into its archaic English renderings of Exodus and Psalms, I intertwined passages from King and Thoreau, Ginsberg and Gandhi, the Warsaw Ghetto and a Russian rabbi named Tamaret—wove them all into a new Telling of the tale of freedom. Where the old Haggadah had a silly argument about how many plagues had really afflicted Egypt, I substituted a serious quandary: Were blood and death a necessary part of liberation, or could the nonviolence of King and Gandhi bring a deeper transformation?

---

[1] The term "midrash," based on the Hebrew word "interpretation," refers to a way of reading and interpreting biblical text. The rabbis used this mode of literary exegesis to interpret the Bible and the same sort of technique was used in modern midrash to derive meaning from sacred texts.

Arthur Waskow, *Godwrestling Round 2: Ancient Wisdom, Future Paths* (Woodstock, Vermont: Jewish Lights Publishing, 1996), pp. 9–12. Copyright © 1996 by Arthur Waskow. Reprinted here from *Godwrestling—Round 2: Ancient Wisdom, Future Paths* (Jewish Lights, 1996) by permission of the author. All rights reserved. For further information, write *Awaskow@aol.com*.

This selection from the Freedom Seder *is a "reverse* dayenu.*" The traditional dayenu (which literally means "it would have been enough") is a song of gratitude, comprised of a litany of God's actions on behalf of the Israelites, with the refrain "it would have been enough," after each. In the* Freedom Seder, *participants recite a series of human actions and after each, declare, "it would not be sufficient."*

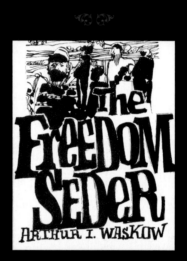

Arthur I. Waskow, The Freedom Seder: A New Haggadah for Passover *Washington, D.C.: The Micah Press, 1969.*

American Jewish Historical Society, Newton Centre, Massachusetts and New York, New York

*For if we were to end a single genocide but not to stop the
   other wars that are killing men and women as we
   sit here, it would not be sufficient;*
*If we were to end those bloody wars but not disarm the
   nations of the weapons that could destroy all Mankind,
   it would not be sufficient;*
*If we were to disarm the nations but not to end the pollution
   and poisoning of our planet, it would not be sufficient;*
*If we were to end the poisoning of our planet but not prevent
   some people from wallowing in luxury while
   others starved, it would not be sufficient;*

If we were to make sure that no one starved but not to end police brutality in many countries, it would not be sufficient;

If we were to end outright police brutality but not to free the daring poets from their jails, it would not be sufficient;

If we were to free the poets from their jails but to cramp the minds of people so that they could not understand the poets, it would not be sufficient;

If we liberated all men and women to understand the free creative poets but forbade them to explore their own inner ecstasies, it would not be sufficient;

If we allowed men and women to explore their inner ecstasies but would not allow them to love one another and share in the human fraternity, it would not be sufficient.

How much then are we in duty bound to struggle, work, share, give, think, plan, feel, organize, sit-in, speak out, dream, hope, and be on behalf of Mankind! For we must end the genocide [in Vietnam],* stop the bloody wars that are killing men and women as we sit here, disarm the nations of the deadly weapons that threaten to destroy us all, end the poisoning of our planet, make sure that no one starves, stop police brutality in many countries, free the poets from their jails, educate us all to understand their poetry, liberate us all to explore our inner ecstasies, and encourage and aid us to love one another and share in the human fraternity. All these!

*Insert any that is current—such as "Biafra," "Black America," "Russia," "Poland," etc.—depending on the situation.

Arthur I. Waskow, *The Freedom Seder: A New Haggadah For Passover* (Washington, D.C.: The Micah Press, 1969), pp. 25–26. Copyright © 1969 by Arthur Waskow. Reprinted here from *The Freedom Seder* (Micah Press, 1969) by permission of the author. All rights reserved. For further information, write Awaskow@aol.com.

ᴂ 14 ᴃ

AN AMERICAN, A JEW,
A WRITER BY TRADE

· SAUL BELLOW ·

ONE OF America's most distinguished authors, Saul Bellow filled his novels with Jewish characters and through them told American stories. Born in Canada in 1915 to immigrant parents from Russia, Bellow moved with his family to Chicago in 1924 where he attended Hebrew school and grew up in a home where Yiddish was regularly spoken. After earning a degree from Northwestern University, Bellow began publishing his first novels in the 1940s. A prolific author, he published *The Adventures of Augie March* in 1954, a book that chronicled the personal journey of the son of immigrant Jewish parents growing up in Chicago. *Herzog*, published in 1964, focuses on the struggles of a middle-aged Jewish professor, looking to find meaning in his life. In *Mr. Sammler's Planet* (1970), Bellow's protagonist Arthur Sammler, a Polish Jew and Holocaust survivor, damaged both physically and psychologically, struggles to find order amid the turbulence of the 1960s. Saul Bellow received the National Book Award for each of these three novels.

In 1967, Bellow traveled to Israel to cover the Six-Day War for *Newsday* and after spending several months in Israel in 1975, published *To Jerusalem and Back: A Personal Account.* The recipient of numerous literary prizes and awards, including the Pulitzer Prize for *Humbolt's Gift* (1975), Bellow was awarded the Nobel Prize for Literature in 1976. That same year, Bellow received the Anti-Defamation League's Democratic Legacy Award and delivered this acceptance speech. Here, Bellow articulates his various identities and locates himself firmly within America's liberal tradition.

⁓

HOW ENVIABLE IT sometimes seems to have a brief and simple history. Ours is neither simple nor brief. You have honored me with an award, and my part in acknowledging this distinction with gratitude, is to make a short speech about America and its Jews, the Jews and their America. The difficulty of this obligation is considerable, for the history we share is full of intricate, cunning and gloomy passages; it is also illuminating and it is noble—it is a large piece of the history of mankind. Many have tried to rid themselves in one way or another of this dreadful historic load by assimilation or other means. I have, myself, never been tempted by the hope of waking from the nightmare of history in a higher state of consciousness and freedom. As much as the next man, I enjoy meditating on such things, but my instincts have attached me to what is actually here, and among the choices that were actually open to me, I have always preferred the liberal and democratic ones—not always in the popular sense of these terms.

When I read last summer in the *American Scholar* an article by Professor Sidney Hook[1] on the great teacher and philosopher Morris R. Cohen,[2] I was stirred by

---

[1] Sidney Hook (1902–1989), prominent philosopher and student of John Dewey's pragmatist school. A Marxist through the 1930s, Hook ultimately renounced Marxism and ended his career as a conservative.

[2] Morris Raphael Cohen (1880–1947), leading philosopher and influential professor at New York's City College and the University of Chicago.

Author Saul Bellow. Photographer: Alfred Eisenstaedt.

Getty Images

Cohen's belief that "the future of liberal civilization" was "bound up with America's survival and its ability to make use of the heritage of human rights formulated by Jefferson and Lincoln." Professor Cohen was no sentimentalist. He was a tough-minded man, not a patriotic rhetorician.

He arrived on the Lower East Side at the age of 12. He knew the slums and the sweatshops. His knowledge of the evils of American life was extensive and unsparing—the history of the Indians and of the Negroes, cruelty, prejudice, mob violence, hysteria, injustice. Acidulous is Hook's word for Cohen's criticism of the U.S.A. Cohen, says Hook, was not a nationalist. He knew that no one chooses the land of his birth. He placed his hopes in the rule of enlightened world law. But Cohen was in some ways piously American. Now piety has become one of our very worst words. It used to be one of the best—think of Wordsworth's desire for "natural piety." Maybe we can do something to rehabilitate the term. Cohen accepted Santayana's definition of piety as "reverence for the sources of one's being." This emotion, says Hook, was naturally acquired by Cohen without ideological indoctrination or blinding.

I understand this without effort. Most of us do. There *are* people for whom it is entirely natural to despise the life that they were born in to. There are others, like myself, who suspect that if we dismiss the life that is waiting for us at birth, we will find ourselves in a void. I was born in Eastern Canada and grew up in Chicago. My parents were Jewish immigrants from Russia. They sent me to a *heder* [Jewish afternoon religious school]. They didn't want me out in the sandlots or playing pool in the poolroom. All these matters were discussed or disputed by us in Yiddish. But when I went to the public library, the books I borrowed were by [American writers] Poe and Melville, Dreiser and Sherwood Anderson. I did not bring home volumes of the Babylonian Talmud to read. I took myself as I was—a kid from the Chicago streets and the child of Jewish parents. I was powerfully stirred by the books brought home from the library, I was moved myself to write something.—These are some of the sources of my being. One could have better sources, undoubtedly. I could make a list of those more desirable sources, but they are not mine, and I cannot revere them. The only life I can love, or hate, is the life that I—that we—have found here, this American life of the Twentieth Century, the life of Americans who are also Jews. Which of these sources, the American or the Jewish, should elicit the greater piety? Are the two exclusive? Must a choice be made? The essence of freedom is that one makes the choice, if choices must be made, for the most profound of personal reasons. It is at this very point that one begins to feel how intensely enviable it is to have a brief and simple history. (But is there any such thing?)

In Israel, I was often and sometimes impatiently asked what sort of Jew I was and how I defined myself and explained my existence. I said that I was an American, a Jew, a writer by trade. I was not insensitive to the Jewish question, I was painfully conscious of the Holocaust, I longed for peace and security in the Jewish State. I added, however, that I had lived in America all my life, that American English was my language, and that (in an oddly universalist way) I was attached to my country and the civilization of which it was a part. But my Israeli questioners or examiners were not satisfied. They were trying to make me justify myself. It was their conviction that the life of a Jew in what they call the Diaspora must inevitably be "inauthentic." Only as a Jew in Israel, some of them told me, could I enter history again and prove the necessity and authenticity of my existence.

I refused to agree with them that my life had been illusion and dust. I do not accept any interpretation of history that declares the deepest experience of any person to be superfluous. To me that smells of totalitarianism. Nor could I accept the suggestion that I repudiate some six decades of life, to dismiss my feelings for some of the sources of my being *because I am a Jew or nothing*. That would wipe out me totally. It would be not only impiety and irreverences, but also self-destruction.

But one need not hold long arguments with views that are so obviously wrong. What underlies the position that I have just rejected is the assumption that America is bound to go the way of other Christian countries and expel or destroy its Jewish population. But *is* it a Christian country like the others? The question almost answers itself as soon as it is asked—this nation is not, in the European sense, a recognizably Christian country. One could write many volumes on what America is *not*. However, there is no need, in a brief talk on an occasion such as this to make grandiose statements about liberal democracy. It is sufficient to say in the most matter of fact way what is or should be obvious to everyone. In spite of the vastness and oppressiveness of corporate and governmental powers the principle of the moral equality of all human beings has not been rejected in the United States. Not yet, at any rate. Sigmund Freud, I remember reading, once observed that America was an interesting experiment, but that he did not believe that it would succeed. Well, maybe not. But it would be base to abandon it. To do so would destroy our reverence for the sources of our being. We would inflict on ourselves a mutilation from which we might never recover. And if Cohen is right, and the future of liberal civilization is bound up with America's survival, the damage would be universal and irreparable.

Saul Bellow, "I Said That I Was an American, a Jew, a Writer by Trade," Reprinted from Jacob Rader Marcus, *The Jew in the American World: A Source Book* (Detroit: Wayne State University Press, 1996), pp. 520–522. Copyright © 1996, with the permission of Wayne State University Press.

ᨏ 15 ᨒ

POLITICAL PLAYWRIGHT

• TONY KUSHNER •

WHEN TONY Kushner's *Angels in America* burst on the scene in the early 1990s, the two-part, seven-hour drama instantly garnered critical acclaim, winning a Pulitzer Prize and two Tony Awards. The play weaves together personal relationships and broad political themes as it chronicles life in the age of AIDS. Its author has emerged as one of America's leading playwrights, not only bringing political and social issues to the stage but also becoming an outspoken critic, wrestling with the pressing issues of contemporary society.

Born in 1956 and raised in a Jewish family in Lake Charles, Louisiana, Kushner came to New York in the 1970s to attend college at Columbia University and later graduate school at New York University. A gay man and a socialist who is deeply engaged with Jewish culture, Tony Kushner brings multiple identities to his work, and his plays reflect his social and political concerns. Kushner's play *Slavs!* (1994) explores the dissolution of the Soviet Union and the legacy of communism for its people. *Homebody/Kabul* (2001), a play written before September 11, focuses on a British housewife who becomes obsessed with the exotic and tragic history of Afghanistan. His *Caroline, or Change* (2004), set in Louisiana in 1963, is a semi-autobiographical musical set in Civil Rights-era Louisiana that tackles issues of race and class; the title character is an African American maid who works for a Southern Jewish family. In addition to his plays, Kushner is also a prolific writer of essays and commentary. He provided the text for *The Art of Maurice Sendak: 1980 to the Present* (2003), and also co-edited *Wrestling with Zion: Progressive Jewish-American Responses to the Israeli-Palestinian Conflict*.

In this interview, Kushner reflects on his own Jewish identity and political beliefs, expressing pride in being an American and a "Diaspora Jew."

⁓

I GREW UP in a town of about 60,000 people. There were about 140 Jews, maybe 200 Jews. There was a shul; it's still there. It's called Temple Sinai. It was built, I think, at the end of the nineteenth century. Lake Charles itself only was founded after the Civil War, so there were Jews there almost immediately. And they did well and built this little, beautiful Victorian shul, and the community that I grew up in was, at the time (I was born in 1956) . . . a sixty-year-old community. . . . Several generations had come and there was a sense of permanence. But there was also definitely a sense of being a very, very tiny group of people who were not like the majority culture. . . .

The bayou country is much more Catholic than Baptist. It's Cajun and Creole. It's sort of a Mediterranean kind of mix of people anyway, and they're . . . fairly isolated. It's not very urban. So people were sort of left alone. I didn't experience a great deal of . . . anti-Semitism, but mostly just a certain degree of like alienness. . . . I grew up feeling very acutely aware of being different, and also very proud of it; it made me special. I liked my difference. I've said this a lot, but I think that it was also, even

*Playwright Tony Kushner, ca.
2005. Photographer: Evan
Agostini.*
Getty Images

before I was in any way prepared to admit it, as a gay kid, it was a way
of feeling different without having to admit all the ways in which I was
feeling different. And there was a way that I felt different from all the
other kids I was at school with, that was endorsed by my parents,
namely that I was a Jewish kid. And I could be proud of that. Even if
they didn't get it, my parents got it, and my parents made sure that I
never felt in any way apologetic for it. And that gave me a model of
being different that you don't have to apologize for. . . .

I DON'T THINK that America is necessarily Jerusalem, but I believe the
Fourteenth Amendment to the U.S. Constitution is Jerusalem. I believe
that pluralist, secular democracy is as close as we're likely to come to
Jerusalem on this earth, in the sense that the hopes and aspirations of
the millennia are most likely to be realized in such a legal and political
and juridical context. I'm moved by that. I think that there was a way
that the Jews who created the Maxwell House Haggadah—and who
were part of my family and part of my community in Lake Charles—
read American history as being another chapter in Jewish history, as
expressing certain themes in Jewish history that were coming to a kind of a satisfac-
tory conclusion. [T]here was a certain degree of pride in that—that we had contributed to this history. We had created Louis Dembitz Brandeis. We had contributed
quite specifically, [through] Felix Frankfurter. We were the people that created
some of the laws and some of the understanding that led to ideas in the U.S. Constitution of protecting minorities from majoritarian tyranny. I'm moved by that now
and I feel very powerfully identified with it. . . .

I THINK FOR a lot of queer Jews, Yiddish became a kind of a way to make friends
with Judaism after feeling a certain degree of distance created by Jewish homo-
phobia. Like most major religions, Judaism isn't particularly good [and] Orthodox
Judaism is not good about gay people. There's a powerful way in which we feel alien-
ated from our Jewishness. I think that Yiddish, Yiddish language, Yiddish music (for
me it was quite specifically hearing a Klezmatics CD for the first time, and hearing
Lorin Sklamberg [accordionist and vocalist with the Klezmatics] sing), it was
another take on Jewish masculinity, on Jewish gender. That was a part of it, at least
for me. It was a notion of power that wasn't . . . macho, sabra [a Jew born in Israel],
Zionist power. It was something else. It had to do with the Diaspora. It had to do
with a complicated, tortured relationship between our lived experience and, in the

case of Yiddish, German culture. And it was the tongue of our grandmothers. It was the tongue of a lost world. I was very moved by it when I heard it. It's somewhere in my head, and my grandmother sang me Yiddish songs when I was a little kid. So Yiddish became a doorway back to certain aspects of Judaism . . . when I was coming out as a gay man . . . .

I started out writing a play, my second play, *Angels in America*, and I wrote a gay play. But I didn't expect to write a Jewish play. And I wrote a Jewish play. It has one scene in it that's almost never done, but there's a scene in it that's in Yiddish, in "Perestroika," between the grandmother and a rabbi, a long stretch of dialogue in untranslated Yiddish. So I found myself sort of a Yiddish playwright and a Jewish playwright, which didn't surprise me, but a Jewish playwright who had written a Jewish play, with the rabbi at the beginning and Ethel Rosenberg and the *kaddish* and the whole thing. That moved me. . . .

I NEED TO identify myself as a gay man because I live in a homophobic culture. I need to identify myself as a Jew for positive reasons, because I love Jewish culture and being Jewish. . . .

I'm a diasporan gay Jewish American socialist, or a gay American socialist diasporan Jew. You take your pick. I'm perfectly happy with that. I want to be thought of as all of those things. If I'm writing a play about Afghanistan, I want everybody to know that the play is written by a gay Jewish American socialist.

Tony Kushner, interview by David Grubin, June 1, 2006.

16

SUPREME COURT JUSTICE

• RUTH BADER GINSBURG •

IN RUTH Bader Ginsburg's Supreme Court chambers hangs a poster with the biblical verse from Deuteronomy: *Justice, justice shall thou pursue.* The sign in her office reflects the connection that she has always made between Jewish tradition and the practice of law. Born in 1933 in Brooklyn, New York, Ginsburg attended college at Cornell University, where she graduated first woman in her class. She began her law school career at Harvard and completed it at Columbia University (relocating to New York when her husband Martin found a job there), and was elected to Law Review at both institutions. In 1972, Ginsburg became a tenured member of the Columbia Law School faculty and also served as counsel to the Women's Rights Project of the American Civil Liberties Union, arguing several cases about women's rights before the Supreme Court. President Jimmy Carter appointed her to the U.S. Court of Appeals for the District of Columbia Circuit in 1980. In 1993, President Clinton nominated her to the Supreme Court.

Ruth Bader Ginsburg has always strongly asserted her Jewish identity. She attended Hebrew school and recalls her disappointment at not having the opportunity to become a Bat Mitzvah as a young girl. At the age of seventeen, she remembers feeling dismayed when, as a woman, she was not permitted to be part of the *minyan* gathered to say *Kaddish* after her mother died. Throughout her life, Ginsburg has maintained a positive connection to Jewish identity and considers Judaism's focus on texts and laws a foundation for her own commitment to justice and the legal system. In this interview, Ginsburg reflects on her background and Jewish identity.

⁓

VISITORS TO MY chambers will see visible signs of my Jewishness. Those signs include at least three *zedek* [justice] posters. The English translation is "Justice, justice shalt thou pursue," the famous line from *Deuteronomy*. A fine etching showing men negotiating the marriage contract of Ruth and Boaz is displayed on the door leading directly into my own room. In the corridor just outside my chambers, I have placed a primitive style print of a true gem, the Synagogue in the Sand in St. Thomas, second oldest synagogue in the Western Hemisphere. On the doorpost of my personal entrance, you will find a very large, beautifully crafted silver mezuzah, a gift to me from eleventh and twelfth graders at the Shulamith School for Girls in Brooklyn. The year the Shulamith students visited, I had a law clerk who had herself attended the Shulamith School.

Jews are known as "people of the book." Reasoning is prized by Jews. After all, the highest calling was to be a Talmudic scholar. Jews thrive on arguing. When the professions opened up to Jews, law was a natural for them. Many Jews became lawyers, and some of those lawyers later became judges. The obligation to reason why is indeed part of the Jewish tradition.

My personal heroine from the Bible is Deborah, who was a prophet, a judge, and a military leader at the same time. . . .

Justice Ruth Bader Ginsburg, 1994. Photograph by Richard Strauss.

I took Hebrew school rather seriously; most of the boys and girls in the class didn't. But there was no question of preparing for a bat-mitzvah, because that ceremony didn't exist in the United States in my growing up years.[1] I attended my male cousins' bar-mitzvahs, and felt left out of that recognition of one's membership in the Jewish community. I suppose the hardest for me were the days following my mother's death. I was then just 17. During the week of mourning, our home was filled with women. And yet when time came to say the *Kaddish*, only men counted, only men could compose the *minyan* gathered to recite the prayer. I never understood why that should be so.

I no longer observe the customs and ceremonies. But my Jewish heritage is surely part of what I am. It has stood me in good stead throughout my career as a lawyer, a law teacher, and a judge. What is the difference between a bookkeeper in New York's garment district and a U.S. Supreme Court Justice? One generation, my life bears witness. My mother was a bookkeeper in New York's garment district. I'm sure she never even dreamed that I would one day be seated on the U.S. Supreme Court. [T]he love of learning . . . was instilled in me at an early age, particularly by my mother. . . .

Jews know what it's like to be outsiders. So when we have issues that concern fundamental fairness, equality, and respect for human dignity, Jews can understand the situation of a racial, ethnic, or religious minority very well, because after all, that's what we have been ever since the Diaspora.

---

[1] Rabbi Mordecai Kaplan initiated the first American Bat Mitzvah celebration in a very brief ceremony for his daughter Judith in 1922, but decades would pass before it became a widespread practice.

Justice Ruth Bader Ginsburg, interview by David Grubin, August 3, 2006. Revised and printed with permission of Justice Ruth Bader Ginsburg.

17

HUMORIST AND COLUMNIST

• ART BUCHWALD •

A PULITZER Prize-winner for outstanding commentary, Art Buchwald is best known for his long-running column in the *Washington Post*. Born in 1925 to immigrant parents who ran a curtain and drapery business, Buchwald ran away at the age of seventeen to join the marines during World War II. He returned home for brief stay in college at the University of Southern California, but never earned his degree after the university discovered that he had not received a high school diploma. At the age of only twenty-two, Buchwald left for Paris, where he began working as a correspondent. Hired by the *Herald Tribune* to write a syndicated column, Buchwald became widely popular for his wry humor and gift for political satire. Returning to the United States in the early 1960s, Buchwald became a syndicated columnist, bringing his satiric perspective and political wit to newspapers across the country. After a long illness which he wrote about in his last book, *Too Soon to Say Goodbye*, Buchwald died in January 2007 at the age of 81.

As America celebrated its bicentennial in July 1976, Art Buchwald wrote this piece, titled "A Letter to Pop," addressed to his father who had died four years earlier. The letter pays homage not only to Buchwald's own father but also to all the immigrants who came to America in search of a better life.

July Fourth

Dear Pop:

It's been four years since you passed away at the age of seventy-nine. On this Bicentennial holiday, with all the hoopla and overkill, I am not taking the 200th anniversary of the country lightly, mainly because I know you wouldn't.

First, I would like to thank you for leaving your home in Galicia which you once explained was part of [Austrian] Poland, in 1910, when you were seventeen years old. I know it wasn't an easy trip for you. You had to cross Europe all by yourself, and then you had to find a ship in Rotterdam that would take you to New York City.

I've tried to imagine what it was like for a seventeen-year-old boy to arrive at Ellis Island without being able to speak a word of English. There were thousands like you, and fortunately there were people who came before you to help you through the maze of paper work and bewildering ways of New York.

You wound up on the Lower East Side with so many of your fellow-immigrants.

They offered you a chance to go to night school, but you said you would learn English by reading every New York City newspaper every day. You kept reading them for sixty-two years and you seemed to know more about the country and the world than any of your children who had been "educated" in American schools.

I know you started out working in a raincoat factory fourteen or fifteen hours a day, and when World War I came you worked even longer. They wouldn't let you serve in the Army because [as an immigrant from Hapsburg territory] you were considered an "enemy alien."

Then you went into the curtain and drapery business—The Aetna Curtain Co. The business consisted of you, a man named Sammy who helped you hang the drapes, and a seamstress. "Gimbel's we're not," you used to tell me, much to my chagrin. But you did save enough money to bring your two sisters and a brother to America. And you did manage to get out of the Lower East Side.

"Making it in America in those days," you once told me, "was moving to the Bronx."

*Columnist Art Buchwald.
Photographer: Theo
Westenberger.*
Getty Images

You even got as far as Mt. Vernon, when business was good, before the depression. Then during the depression it was back to the Bronx.

The thing I shall always remember is how you felt about the United States. You kept telling me there was no better place to live than America. And I could never appreciate this unless I was a Jew who had lived in Europe.

You were like so many foreign-born Americans—Jewish, Russian, Italian, Irish, German, Scandinavian and Greek—who considered this country the only land where your children would have a chance to become what they wanted to be.

You told me, "Everyone has dreams for their children, but here it's possible to make them come true."

Well, Pop, I just wanted you to know, as far as your children are concerned, you made the right decision when you left Poland. There are four of us, [who are like] all first-generation Americans whose mothers and fathers arrived here in more or less the same way.

I don't know if all those great men in 1776 had you immigrants in mind when they signed the Declaration of Independence and formed a new country, but even if they didn't they made it possible for you and millions like you to come to a free land.

So let the tall ships sail and the fireworks explode. We're probably over-doing it, but if you were here I'm sure you would say, "It's probably a good thing people remember what a great place this country is, even if it's going to cost the city a lot of money."

Art Buchwald, "A Letter to Pop, July 4, 1976," *Jewish Digest* (September, 1976), pp. 75–76. Reprinted with permission of the Art Buchwald estate.

INDEX

of Ford, Henry, 201–2, 235–37
Frank lynching as, 108, 194–96
at Grand Union Hotel, 84–86
immigration quotas, 111, 215
and Jewish economic success, 200–202, 295–96
in late 1800s, 20, 91–92, 115
as motivation for Jews, 339–41
New Deal as "Jew Deal," 213
in Ocean Hill-Brownsville strike, 344
in post-revolutionary America, 39–43
post-World War II, 286–88, 313
public office oath requirement, 24–27
Rosenberg trial and, 326–27
in state laws, 11–12
university quotas, 200, 229–33
in U.S. during World War II, 215, 277–79
Ararat community (New York), 45
Arizona, 75–76, 79–80
Ashkenazic Jews, 3, 15
atomic bomb, 312

B

Bakst, William, 124–26
Balfour Declaration, 106, 235
Bar Mitzvah ceremony, 285
Bartholdi Pedestal Fund, 89
Baruch, Bernard, 213
baseball, 155–58, 260–64
Bat Mitzvah ceremony, 297, 371, 372
Becker, Meyer, 83
Bellow, Saul, 362–65
Benesch, Alfred A., 229–33
Ben-Gurion, David, 289, 318
Benjamin, Judah P., 17
Benny, Jack, 301
Berg, Gertrude, 206–7, 246–49
Bergson, Peter, 217
Berle, Milton (Berlinger, Milton), 301
Berlin, Irving, 203, 204–5
Billboard (magazine), 247
Bill of Rights, 25
Bintel Brief, 98, 136–41
Blacks. *See* African Americans and Jewish Americans
"Black vs. Jew" (*Time* magazine), 295
Blaustein, Jacob, 289, 318–23
B'nai B'rith (Sons of the Covenant), 18, 214
Board of Delegates of American Israelites, 19
Braeme, Charlotte, 148
Brandeis, Louis D., 104, 106, 181–84
Brice, Fanny, 203, 204, 302
Bridget Loves Bernie (television series), 302–3
British Prince (vessel), 117
Bronx, N.Y., 198, 199, 221–24, 375

Brooklyn, N.Y., 3, 198–99, 295–96
Brooklyn Jewish Center, 210
Brooks, Mel, 332–34
Bruce, Lenny, 300
Buchwald, Art, 373–76
Bunche, Ralph, 293
Bund (General Jewish Workers Union of Poland and Russia), 134
Burns, George, 333

C

Caesar, Sid, 301–2, 328–30
Cahan, Abraham, 90, 98, 131–35, 136–41
Cairo Genizah, 178
"Call for Change" (*Ezrat Nashim),* 352–54
Calof, Abraham, 119
Calof, Rachel, 119–22
Campbell, Les, 343–44
Cardozo, Isaac N., 52
Carew, Colin "Topper," 357
Caroline, or Change (Kushner), 367
Carter, Jimmy, 291
Carvalho, D. N., 52
Castle Garden, N.Y., 90, 118
"Catechism for Jewish Children" (Leeser), 60–61
The Cat in the Hat (Dr. Seuss), 304
Catskills, 206–7, 328, 331
Challenging Years (Wise), 273–75
Champaign, Ill., 349
Chaney, James, 294–95
Chapters From My Life (Harkavy), 115–18
Charleston, S.C., 15, 36–38, 49, 50–52
Chicago, Ill., 67, 93, 152
Chicago Daily Tribune, 85–86
Christianity, 345, 365
Cincinnati, Ohio
Congregation Bene Jeshurun (Plum Street Temple), 16, 18, 62, 348
Hebrew Union College, 110
circumcision set, 5
City College (New York City, N.Y.), 199
"A City of Refuge for the Jews" (Noah), 45–48
Civil Rights Movement, 293–95, 335–37, 342, 355–57
Civil War, 17–18, 65–71, 84
cloakmakers strike, 104, 181
clothing industry
Jewish entrepreneurs, 19–20, 100–101, 104
Lemlich organizing workers, 159–61
sweatshops, 100–101, 105–6, 142–43, 144–49
Triangle Shirtwaist Factory fire, 162–63
See also labor movement
Cohen, Andy, 157
Cohen, E. P., 52
Cohen, Elliot, 311–14

Cohen, Morris Raphael, 363–64
Cohn, Al, 255–56
Commentary (magazine), 311–14
commune farms, 117, 118, 134
communism, U.S. campaign against, 292–93
Communist Party, 223–24, 226–28, 325–26
Congregation Bene Jeshurun (Cincinnati, Ohio), 16, 62
Congregation Beth Elohim (Charleston, S.C.), 49, 50
Congregation Beth Shalom (Philadelphia, Pa.), 285
Congregation Jeshuat Israel (Newport, R.I.), 6
Congregation Mikveh Israel (Philadelphia, Pa.), 11, 58, 72
Congregation Rodeph Shalom (Philadelphia, Pa.), 15
Congregation Shearith Israel (New York City, N.Y.), 6–7
Conservative Judaism
    in America, 110–11
    among East European immigrants, 108–10, 210–11
    and Jewish feminism, 297, 351–54
    Kaplan's influence on, 239
    Schechter and, 178–80
    Women's League for Conservative Judaism, 210–12
Constitution of the United States, 11, 12, 24–27, 74, 368
Coolidge, Calvin, 236–37
Coughlin, Father Charles, 213, 282
Crossfire (film), 286–87
cultural pluralism, 182

D

The Daily Worker (newspaper), 227
Dawidowicz, Lucy, 325–26
Dearborn Independent (newspaper), 201, 236
Die Deborah (weekly newspaper), 62
DeHaas, Jacob, 182–84
DeLancey, Oliver, 32, 34
Delancey, Phila Franks, 10, 33–35
democracy
    in America, 321–22
    Goldman's view of, 172–74
    in Israel, 320–21
    as Jerusalem, 368
    republics as, 41–42
    in Zionist movement, 182
Democratic Party, 212–13
demonstration against Hitler, 216, 217
Detroit Tigers, 207, 260–63, 299
Devils Lake, N.D., 119–22
Diaries of Mordecai M. Kaplan, 240–41

The Diary of Anne Frank (book, play, film), 290–91
Dick Van Dyke Show (television program), 302, 331
divorce procedures, 297, 348, 351–54
Dr. Seuss, 304
dumbbell tenements, 94
Dutch West India Company, 2
Dworkin, Susan, 316–17

E

East European immigrants
    activism of, 105–10
    and labor movement 104–106, 159–163
    arrival in U.S., 21, 87–88, 90–93
    colonization in Russia, 266–68
    and Conservative Judaism, 108–10, 210–11
    hometown societies of, 123–26
    and NCJW, 151, 153
    and Reform movement, 109, 110
    from Russia, 115–16, 133–34, 292
    and Zionist movement, 106–7, 181–84, 235
    See also European Jews
Edelstadt, David, 116
education
    effect on Jewish women, 347, 351, 353
    importance to Jewish immigrants, 95–96, 248, 372
    religious schools, 285, 303
    of second generation Americans, 199–200, 208–12
    secular Yiddish schools, 222
    university quotas, 200, 229–33
    wages of children vs., 96, 101, 140–41
    women's role in, 57–59
    youth's desire for, 137–38
    See also specific schools and universities
Educational Alliance (New York City, N.Y.), 95
The Education of Abraham Cahan (Cahan), 132–35
Eichmann, Adolf, 291
Eilberg, Amy, 297
Einhorn, David, 16, 17
Einstein, Albert, 269–71
Elath, Eliahu, 320
Ellis Island, N.Y., 90
Emma Lazarus Federation of Jewish Women's Club, 160
employment, 99–101, 200, 228. *See also* clothing industry; peddlers and peddling
Enter Laughing (Reiner), 332
entertainment industry
    and Catskills resorts, 206–7, 328, 331
    radio programs, 206–7, 246–49, 301, 342–46
    vaudeville, 257–59
    See also movie industry; television programs; Yiddish theater; *specific entertainers*
Etz Chaim Yeshiva, 242–43